I0010909

Administration Guide

SUSE Linux Enterprise Desktop 12 SP3

Administration Guide

SUSE Linux Enterprise Desktop 12 SP3

Covers system administration tasks like maintaining, monitoring and customizing an initially installed system.

Publication Date: September 01, 2017

SUSE LLC
10 Canal Park Drive
Suite 200
Cambridge MA 02141
USA
https://www.suse.com/documentation

Changes to original document: page numbers added to top right corner of book.

Contents

About This Guide

This guide is intended for use by professional network and system administrators during the operation of SUSE® Linux Enterprise. As such, it is solely concerned with ensuring that SUSE Linux Enterprise is properly configured and that the required services on the network are available to allow it to function properly as initially installed. This guide does not cover the process of ensuring that SUSE Linux Enterprise offers proper compatibility with your enterprise's application software or that its core functionality meets those requirements. It assumes that a full requirements audit has been done and the installation has been requested, or that a test installation for such an audit has been requested.

This guide contains the following:

Support and Common Tasks

SUSE Linux Enterprise offers a wide range of tools to customize various aspects of the system. This part introduces a few of them.

System

Learn more about the underlying operating system by studying this part. SUSE Linux Enterprise supports several hardware architectures and you can use this to adapt your own applications to run on SUSE Linux Enterprise. The boot loader and boot procedure information assists you in understanding how your Linux system works and how your own custom scripts and applications may blend in with it.

Services

SUSE Linux Enterprise is designed to be a network operating system. SUSE® Linux Enterprise Desktop includes client support for many network services. It integrates well into heterogeneous environments including MS Windows clients and servers.

Mobile Computers

Laptops, and the communication between mobile devices like PDAs, or cellular phones and SUSE Linux Enterprise need some special attention. Take care for power conservation and for the integration of different devices into a changing network environment. Also get in touch with the background technologies that provide the needed functionality.

Troubleshooting

Provides an overview of finding help and additional documentation when you need more information or want to perform specific tasks. There is also a list of the most frequent problems with explanations how to fix them.

1 Available Documentation

Note: Online Documentation and Latest Updates

Documentation for our products is available at http://www.suse.com/documentation/ ↗, where you can also find the latest updates, and browse or download the documentation in various formats.

In addition, the product documentation is usually available in your installed system under `/usr/share/doc/manual`.

The following documentation is available for this product:

Article "Installation Quick Start"
: Lists the system requirements and guides you step-by-step through the installation of SUSE Linux Enterprise Desktop from DVD, or from an ISO image.

Book "Deployment Guide"
: Shows how to install single or multiple systems and how to exploit the product inherent capabilities for a deployment infrastructure. Choose from various approaches, ranging from a local installation or a network installation server to a mass deployment using a remote-controlled, highly-customized, and automated installation technique.

Administration Guide
: Covers system administration tasks like maintaining, monitoring and customizing an initially installed system.

Book "Security Guide"
: Introduces basic concepts of system security, covering both local and network security aspects. Shows how to use the product inherent security software like AppArmor or the auditing system that reliably collects information about any security-relevant events.

Book "System Analysis and Tuning Guide"
: An administrator's guide for problem detection, resolution and optimization. Find how to inspect and optimize your system by means of monitoring tools and how to efficiently manage resources. Also contains an overview of common problems and solutions and of additional help and documentation resources.

Book "GNOME User Guide"

Introduces the GNOME desktop of SUSE Linux Enterprise Desktop. It guides you through using and configuring the desktop and helps you perform key tasks. It is intended mainly for end users who want to make efficient use of GNOME as their default desktop.

2 Feedback

Several feedback channels are available:

Bugs and Enhancement Requests

For services and support options available for your product, refer to http://www.suse.com/support/ ↗.

Help for openSUSE is provided by the community. Refer to https://en.opensuse.org/Portal:Support ↗ for more information.

To report bugs for a product component, go to https://scc.suse.com/support/requests ↗, log in, and click *Create New*.

User Comments

We want to hear your comments about and suggestions for this manual and the other documentation included with this product. Use the User Comments feature at the bottom of each page in the online documentation or go to http://www.suse.com/documentation/feedback.html ↗ and enter your comments there.

Mail

For feedback on the documentation of this product, you can also send a mail to `doc-team@suse.com`. Make sure to include the document title, the product version and the publication date of the documentation. To report errors or suggest enhancements, provide a concise description of the problem and refer to the respective section number and page (or URL).

3 Documentation Conventions

The following notices and typographical conventions are used in this documentation:

- `/etc/passwd`: directory names and file names
- *`PLACEHOLDER`*: replace *`PLACEHOLDER`* with the actual value

- `PATH`: the environment variable PATH
- **`ls`**, `--help`: commands, options, and parameters
- `user`: users or groups
- `package name` : name of a package
- `Alt`, `Alt`–`F1`: a key to press or a key combination; keys are shown in uppercase as on a keyboard
- *File*, *File* › *Save As*: menu items, buttons
- *Dancing Penguins* (Chapter *Penguins*, ↑Another Manual): This is a reference to a chapter in another manual.
- Commands that must be run with `root` privileges. Often you can also prefix these commands with the **`sudo`** command to run them as non-privileged user.

```
root # command
tux > sudo command
```

- Commands that can be run by non-privileged users.

```
tux > command
```

- Notices

Warning: Warning Notice

Vital information you must be aware of before proceeding. Warns you about security issues, potential loss of data, damage to hardware, or physical hazards.

Important: Important Notice

Important information you should be aware of before proceeding.

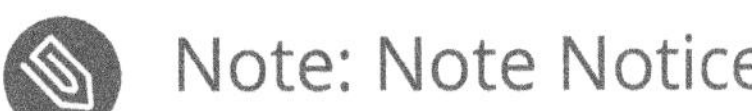

Note: Note Notice

Additional information, for example about differences in software versions.

Helpful information, like a guideline or a piece of practical advice.

4 About the Making of This Documentation

This documentation is written in SUSEDoc, a subset of DocBook 5 (http://www.docbook.org) ↗. The XML source files were validated by **jing** (see https://code.google.com/p/jing-trang/ ↗), processed by **xsltproc**, and converted into XSL-FO using a customized version of Norman Walsh's stylesheets. The final PDF is formatted through FOP from Apache Software Foundation (https://xmlgraphics.apache.org/fop) ↗. The open source tools and the environment used to build this documentation are provided by the DocBook Authoring and Publishing Suite (DAPS). The project's home page can be found at https://github.com/openSUSE/daps ↗.

The XML source code of this documentation can be found at https://github.com/SUSE/doc-sle ↗.

I Common Tasks

1 Bash and Bash Scripts

Today, many people use computers with a graphical user interface (GUI) like GNOME. Although they offer lots of features, their use is limited when it comes to the execution of automated tasks. Shells are a good addition to GUIs and this chapter gives you an overview of some aspects of shells, in this case Bash.

1.1 What is "The Shell"?

Traditionally, *the* shell is Bash (Bourne again Shell). When this chapter speaks about "the shell" it means Bash. There are actually more available shells than Bash (ash, csh, ksh, zsh, ...), each employing different features and characteristics. If you need further information about other shells, search for *shell* in YaST.

1.1.1 Knowing the Bash Configuration Files

A shell can be invoked as an:

1. **Interactive login shell.** This is used when logging in to a machine, invoking Bash with the `--login` option or when logging in to a remote machine with SSH.
2. **"Ordinary" interactive shell.** This is normally the case when starting xterm, konsole, gnome-terminal or similar tools.
3. **Non-interactive shell.** This is used when invoking a shell script at the command line.

Depending on which type of shell you use, different configuration files are being read. The following tables show the login and non-login shell configuration files.

TABLE 1.1: BASH CONFIGURATION FILES FOR LOGIN SHELLS

File	Description
`/etc/profile`	Do not modify this file, otherwise your modifications can be destroyed during your next update!

File	Description
`/etc/profile.local`	Use this file if you extend `/etc/profile`
`/etc/profile.d/`	Contains system-wide configuration files for specific programs
`~/.profile`	Insert user specific configuration for login shells here

Note that the login shell also sources the configuration files listed under *Table 1.2, "Bash Configuration Files for Non-Login Shells"*.

TABLE 1.2: BASH CONFIGURATION FILES FOR NON-LOGIN SHELLS

`/etc/bash.bashrc`	Do not modify this file, otherwise your modifications can be destroyed during your next update!
`/etc/bash.bashrc.local`	Use this file to insert your system-wide modifications for Bash only
`~/.bashrc`	Insert user specific configuration here

Additionally, Bash uses some more files:

TABLE 1.3: SPECIAL FILES FOR BASH

File	Description
`~/.bash_history`	Contains a list of all commands you have been typing
`~/.bash_logout`	Executed when logging out

1.1.2 The Directory Structure

The following table provides a short overview of the most important higher-level directories that you find on a Linux system. Find more detailed information about the directories and important subdirectories in the following list.

TABLE 1.4: OVERVIEW OF A STANDARD DIRECTORY TREE

Directory	Contents
`/`	Root directory—the starting point of the directory tree.
`/bin`	Essential binary files, such as commands that are needed by both the system administrator and normal users. Usually also contains the shells, such as Bash.
`/boot`	Static files of the boot loader.
`/dev`	Files needed to access host-specific devices.
`/etc`	Host-specific system configuration files.
`/home`	Holds the home directories of all users who have accounts on the system. However, `root` 's home directory is not located in `/home` but in `/root`.
`/lib`	Essential shared libraries and kernel modules.
`/media`	Mount points for removable media.
`/mnt`	Mount point for temporarily mounting a file system.
`/opt`	Add-on application software packages.
`/root`	Home directory for the superuser `root`.
`/sbin`	Essential system binaries.
`/srv`	Data for services provided by the system.
`/tmp`	Temporary files.
`/usr`	Secondary hierarchy with read-only data.
`/var`	Variable data such as log files.
`/windows`	Only available if you have both Microsoft Windows* and Linux installed on your system. Contains the Windows data.

The following list provides more detailed information and gives some examples of which files and subdirectories can be found in the directories:

`/bin`

Contains the basic shell commands that may be used both by `root` and by other users. These commands include **`ls`**, **`mkdir`**, **`cp`**, **`mv`**, **`rm`** and **`rmdir`**. `/bin` also contains Bash, the default shell in SUSE Linux Enterprise Desktop.

`/boot`

Contains data required for booting, such as the boot loader, the kernel, and other data that is used before the kernel begins executing user-mode programs.

`/dev`

Holds device files that represent hardware components.

`/etc`

Contains local configuration files that control the operation of programs like the X Window System. The `/etc/init.d` subdirectory contains LSB init scripts that can be executed during the boot process.

`/home/`*`USERNAME`*

Holds the private data of every user who has an account on the system. The files located here can only be modified by their owner or by the system administrator. By default, your e-mail directory and personal desktop configuration are located here in the form of hidden files and directories, such as `.gconf/` and `.config`.

Note: Home Directory in a Network Environment

If you are working in a network environment, your home directory may be mapped to a directory in the file system other than `/home`.

`/lib`

Contains the essential shared libraries needed to boot the system and to run the commands in the root file system. The Windows equivalent for shared libraries are DLL files.

`/media`

Contains mount points for removable media, such as CD-ROMs, flash disks, and digital cameras (if they use USB). `/media` generally holds any type of drive except the hard disk of your system. When your removable medium has been inserted or connected to the system and has been mounted, you can access it from here.

`/mnt`
: This directory provides a mount point for a temporarily mounted file system. `root` may mount file systems here.

`/opt`
: Reserved for the installation of third-party software. Optional software and larger add-on program packages can be found here.

`/root`
: Home directory for the `root` user. The personal data of `root` is located here.

`/run`
: A tmpfs directory used by `systemd` and various components. `/var/run` is a symbolic link to `/run`.

`/sbin`
: As the `s` indicates, this directory holds utilities for the superuser. `/sbin` contains the binaries essential for booting, restoring and recovering the system in addition to the binaries in `/bin`.

`/srv`
: Holds data for services provided by the system, such as FTP and HTTP.

`/tmp`
: This directory is used by programs that require temporary storage of files.

> **Important: Cleaning up /tmp at Boot Time**
>
> Data stored in `/tmp` is not guaranteed to survive a system reboot. It depends, for example, on settings made in `/etc/tmpfiles.d/tmp.conf`.

`/usr`
: `/usr` has nothing to do with users, but is the acronym for Unix system resources. The data in `/usr` is static, read-only data that can be shared among various hosts compliant with the `Filesystem Hierarchy Standard` (FHS). This directory contains all application programs including the graphical desktops such as GNOME and establishes a secondary hierarchy in the file system. `/usr` holds several subdirectories, such as `/usr/bin`, `/usr/sbin`, `/usr/local`, and `/usr/share/doc`.

`/usr/bin`
: Contains generally accessible programs.

`/usr/sbin`

Contains programs reserved for the system administrator, such as repair functions.

`/usr/local`

In this directory the system administrator can install local, distribution-independent extensions.

`/usr/share/doc`

Holds various documentation files and the release notes for your system. In the `manual` subdirectory find an online version of this manual. If more than one language is installed, this directory may contain versions of the manuals for different languages.

Under `packages` find the documentation included in the software packages installed on your system. For every package, a subdirectory `/usr/share/doc/packages/PACKAGE-NAME` is created that often holds README files for the package and sometimes examples, configuration files or additional scripts.

If HOWTOs are installed on your system `/usr/share/doc` also holds the `howto` subdirectory in which to find additional documentation on many tasks related to the setup and operation of Linux software.

`/var`

Whereas `/usr` holds static, read-only data, `/var` is for data which is written during system operation and thus is variable data, such as log files or spooling data. For an overview of the most important log files you can find under `/var/log/`, refer to *Table 34.1, "Log Files"*.

`/windows`

Only available if you have both Microsoft Windows and Linux installed on your system. Contains the Windows data available on the Windows partition of your system. Whether you can edit the data in this directory depends on the file system your Windows partition uses. If it is FAT32, you can open and edit the files in this directory. For NTFS, SUSE Linux Enterprise Desktop also includes write access support. However, the driver for the NTFS-3g file system has limited functionality.

1.2 Writing Shell Scripts

Shell scripts provide a convenient way to perform a wide range of tasks: collecting data, searching for a word or phrase in a text and other useful things. The following example shows a small shell script that prints a text:

EXAMPLE 1.1: A SHELL SCRIPT PRINTING A TEXT

```
#!/bin/sh ❶
# Output the following line: ❷
echo "Hello World" ❸
```

❶ The first line begins with the *Shebang* characters (`#!`) which is an indicator that this file is a script. The script is executed with the specified interpreter after the Shebang, in this case **`/bin/sh`**.

❷ The second line is a comment beginning with the hash sign. It is recommended to comment difficult lines to remember what they do.

❸ The third line uses the built-in command **`echo`** to print the corresponding text.

Before you can run this script you need some prerequisites:

1. Every script should contain a Shebang line (as in the example above.) If the line is missing, you need to call the interpreter manually.
2. You can save the script wherever you want. However, it is a good idea to save it in a directory where the shell can find it. The search path in a shell is determined by the environment variable `PATH`. Usually a normal user does not have write access to `/usr/bin`. Therefore it is recommended to save your scripts in the users' directory `~/bin/`. The above example gets the name `hello.sh`.
3. The script needs executable permissions. Set the permissions with the following command:

   ```
   chmod +x ~/bin/hello.sh
   ```

If you have fulfilled all of the above prerequisites, you can execute the script in the following ways:

1. **As Absolute Path.** The script can be executed with an absolute path. In our case, it is **`~/bin/hello.sh`**.
2. **Everywhere.** If the `PATH` environment variable contains the directory where the script is located, you can execute the script with **`hello.sh`**.

1.3 Redirecting Command Events

Each command can use three channels, either for input or output:

- **Standard Output.** This is the default output channel. Whenever a command prints something, it uses the standard output channel.
- **Standard Input.** If a command needs input from users or other commands, it uses this channel.
- **Standard Error.** Commands use this channel for error reporting.

To redirect these channels, there are the following possibilities:

`Command > File`

Saves the output of the command into a file, an existing file will be deleted. For example, the **`ls`** command writes its output into the file `listing.txt`:

```
ls > listing.txt
```

`Command >> File`

Appends the output of the command to a file. For example, the **`ls`** command appends its output to the file `listing.txt`:

```
ls >> listing.txt
```

`Command < File`

Reads the file as input for the given command. For example, the **`read`** command reads in the content of the file into the variable:

```
read a < foo
```

`Command1 | Command2`

Redirects the output of the left command as input for the right command. For example, the **`cat`** command outputs the content of the `/proc/cpuinfo` file. This output is used by **`grep`** to filter only those lines which contain `cpu`:

```
cat /proc/cpuinfo | grep cpu
```

Every channel has a *file descriptor*: 0 (zero) for standard input, 1 for standard output and 2 for standard error. It is allowed to insert this file descriptor before a `<` or `>` character. For example, the following line searches for a file starting with `foo`, but suppresses its errors by redirecting it to `/dev/null`:

```
find / -name "foo*" 2>/dev/null
```

1.4 Using Aliases

An alias is a shortcut definition of one or more commands. The syntax for an alias is:

```
alias NAME=DEFINITION
```

For example, the following line defines an alias **`lt`** that outputs a long listing (option `-l`), sorts it by modification time (`-t`), and prints it in reverse sorted order (`-r`):

```
alias lt='ls -ltr'
```

To view all alias definitions, use **`alias`**. Remove your alias with **`unalias`** and the corresponding alias name.

1.5 Using Variables in Bash

A shell variable can be global or local. Global variables, or environment variables, can be accessed in all shells. In contrast, local variables are visible in the current shell only.

To view all environment variables, use the **`printenv`** command. If you need to know the value of a variable, insert the name of your variable as an argument:

```
printenv PATH
```

A variable, be it global or local, can also be viewed with **`echo`**:

```
echo $PATH
```

To set a local variable, use a variable name followed by the equal sign, followed by the value:

```
PROJECT="SLED"
```

Do not insert spaces around the equal sign, otherwise you get an error. To set an environment variable, use **export**:

```
export NAME="tux"
```

To remove a variable, use **unset**:

```
unset NAME
```

The following table contains some common environment variables which can be used in you shell scripts:

TABLE 1.5: USEFUL ENVIRONMENT VARIABLES

HOME	the home directory of the current user
HOST	the current host name
LANG	when a tool is localized, it uses the language from this environment variable. English can also be set to C
PATH	the search path of the shell, a list of directories separated by colon
PS1	specifies the normal prompt printed before each command
PS2	specifies the secondary prompt printed when you execute a multi-line command
PWD	current working directory
USER	the current user

1.5.1 Using Argument Variables

For example, if you have the script **foo.sh** you can execute it like this:

```
foo.sh "Tux Penguin" 2000
```

To access all the arguments which are passed to your script, you need positional parameters. These are `$1` for the first argument, `$2` for the second, and so on. You can have up to nine parameters. To get the script name, use `$0`.

The following script **`foo.sh`** prints all arguments from 1 to 4:

```
#!/bin/sh
echo \"$1\" \"$2\" \"$3\" \"$4\"
```

If you execute this script with the above arguments, you get:

```
"Tux Penguin" "2000" "" ""
```

1.5.2 Using Variable Substitution

Variable substitutions apply a pattern to the content of a variable either from the left or right side. The following list contains the possible syntax forms:

`${VAR#pattern}`

removes the shortest possible match from the left:

```
file=/home/tux/book/book.tar.bz2
echo ${file#*/}
home/tux/book/book.tar.bz2
```

`${VAR##pattern}`

removes the longest possible match from the left:

```
file=/home/tux/book/book.tar.bz2
echo ${file##*/}
book.tar.bz2
```

`${VAR%pattern}`

removes the shortest possible match from the right:

```
file=/home/tux/book/book.tar.bz2
echo ${file%.*}
/home/tux/book/book.tar
```

`${VAR%%pattern}`

removes the longest possible match from the right:

```
file=/home/tux/book/book.tar.bz2
```

```
echo ${file%%.*}
/home/tux/book/book
```

`${VAR/pattern_1/pattern_2}`
: substitutes the content of *VAR* from the *PATTERN_1* with *PATTERN_2*:

```
file=/home/tux/book/book.tar.bz2
echo ${file/tux/wilber}
/home/wilber/book/book.tar.bz2
```

1.6 Grouping and Combining Commands

Shells allow you to concatenate and group commands for conditional execution. Each command returns an exit code which determines the success or failure of its operation. If it is 0 (zero) the command was successful, everything else marks an error which is specific to the command.

The following list shows, how commands can be grouped:

`Command1 ; Command2`
: executes the commands in sequential order. The exit code is not checked. The following line displays the content of the file with **cat** and then prints its file properties with **ls** regardless of their exit codes:

```
cat filelist.txt ; ls -l filelist.txt
```

`Command1 && Command2`
: runs the right command, if the left command was successful (logical AND). The following line displays the content of the file and prints its file properties only, when the previous command was successful (compare it with the previous entry in this list):

```
cat filelist.txt && ls -l filelist.txt
```

`Command1 || Command2`
: runs the right command, when the left command has failed (logical OR). The following line creates only a directory in `/home/wilber/bar` when the creation of the directory in `/home/tux/foo` has failed:

```
mkdir /home/tux/foo || mkdir /home/wilber/bar
```

`funcname(){ ... }`

creates a shell function. You can use the positional parameters to access its arguments. The following line defines the function `hello` to print a short message:

```
hello() { echo "Hello $1"; }
```

You can call this function like this:

```
hello Tux
```

which prints:

```
Hello Tux
```

1.7 Working with Common Flow Constructs

To control the flow of your script, a shell has **`while`**, **`if`**, **`for`** and **`case`** constructs.

1.7.1 The if Control Command

The **`if`** command is used to check expressions. For example, the following code tests whether the current user is Tux:

```
if test $USER = "tux"; then
  echo "Hello Tux."
else
  echo "You are not Tux."
fi
```

The test expression can be as complex or simple as possible. The following expression checks if the file `foo.txt` exists:

```
if test -e /tmp/foo.txt ; then
  echo "Found foo.txt"
fi
```

The test expression can also be abbreviated in angled brackets:

```
if [ -e /tmp/foo.txt ] ; then
  echo "Found foo.txt"
```

```
fi
```

Find more useful expressions at http://www.cyberciti.biz/nixcraft/linux/docs/uniqlinuxfeatures/lsst/ch03sec02.html ↗.

1.7.2 Creating Loops with the **for** Command

The **for** loop allows you to execute commands to a list of entries. For example, the following code prints some information about PNG files in the current directory:

```
for i in *.png; do
 ls -l $i
done
```

1.8 For More Information

Important information about Bash is provided in the man pages **man bash**. More about this topic can be found in the following list:

- http://tldp.org/LDP/Bash-Beginners-Guide/html/index.html ↗—Bash Guide for Beginners
- http://tldp.org/HOWTO/Bash-Prog-Intro-HOWTO.html ↗—BASH Programming - Introduction HOW-TO
- http://tldp.org/LDP/abs/html/index.html ↗—Advanced Bash-Scripting Guide
- http://www.grymoire.com/Unix/Sh.html ↗—Sh - the Bourne Shell

2 sudo

Many commands and system utilities need to be run as `root` to modify files and/or perform tasks that only the super user is allowed to. For security reasons and to avoid accidentally running dangerous commands, it is generally advisable not to log in directly as `root`. Instead, it is recommended to work as a normal, unprivileged user and use the **sudo** command to run commands with elevated privileges.

On SUSE Linux Enterprise Desktop, **sudo** is configured by default to work similarly to su. However, **sudo** offers the possibility to allow users to run commands with privileges of any other user in a highly configurable manner. This can be used to assign roles with specific privileges to certain users and groups. It is for example possible to allow members of the group `users` to run a command with the privileges of `wilber`. Access to the command can be further restricted by, for example, forbidding to specify any command options. While su always requires the `root` password for authentication with PAM, **sudo** can be configured to authenticate with your own credentials. This increases security by not having to share the `root` password. For example, you can allow members of the group `users` to run a command **frobnicate** as `wilber`, with the restriction that no arguments are specified. This can be used to assign roles with specific abilities to certain users and groups.

2.1 Basic **sudo** Usage

sudo is simple to use, yet very powerful.

2.1.1 Running a Single Command

Logged in as normal user, you can run any command as `root` by adding **sudo** before it. It will prompt for the root password and, if authenticated successfully, run the command as `root`:

```
tux > id -un❶
tux
tux > sudo id -un
root's password:❷
root
tux > id -un
tux❸
tux > sudo id -un
❹
```

```
root
```

1. The **id -un** command prints the login name of the current user.
2. The password is not shown during input, neither as clear text nor as bullets.
3. Only commands started with **sudo** are run with elevated privileges. If you run the same command without the **sudo** prefix, it is run with the privileges of the current user again.
4. For a limited amount of time, you do not need to enter the `root` password again.

Tip: I/O Redirection

I/O redirection does not work as you would probably expect:

```
tux >  sudo echo s > /proc/sysrq-trigger
bash: /proc/sysrq-trigger: Permission denied
tux >  sudo cat < /proc/1/maps
bash: /proc/1/maps: Permission denied
```

Only the **echo** / **cat** binary is run with elevated privileges, while the redirection is performed by the user's shell with user privileges. You can either start a shell like in *Section 2.1.2, "Starting a Shell"* or use the **dd** utility instead:

```
echo s | sudo dd of=/proc/sysrq-trigger
sudo dd if=/proc/1/maps | cat
```

2.1.2 Starting a Shell

Having to add **sudo** before every command can be cumbersome. While you could specify a shell as a command **sudo bash**, it is recommended to rather use one of the built-in mechanisms to start a shell:

`sudo -s (<command>)`

Starts a shell specified by the `SHELL` environment variable or the target user's default shell. If a command is given, it is passed to the shell (with the `-c` option), else the shell is run in interactive mode.

```
tux:~ > sudo -i
root's password:
root:/home/tux # exit
```

```
tux:~ >
```

`sudo -i (<command>)`

Like `-s`, but starts the shell as login shell. This means that the shell's start-up files (`.profile` etc.) are processed and the current working directory is set to the target user's home directory.

```
tux:~ > sudo -i
root's password:
root:~ # exit
tux:~ >
```

2.1.3 Environment Variables

By default, **sudo** does not propagate environment variables:

```
tux > ENVVAR=test env | grep ENVVAR
ENVVAR=test
tux > ENVVAR=test sudo env | grep ENVVAR
root's password:
❶
tux >
```

 The empty output shows that the environment variable `ENVVAR` did not exist in the context of the command run with **sudo**.

This behavior can be changed by the `env_reset` option, see *Table 2.1, "Useful Flags and Options"*.

2.2 Configuring sudo

sudo is a very flexible tool with extensive configuration.

> **Note: Locked yourself out of sudo**
>
> If you accidentally locked yourself out of **sudo**, use **su -** and the `root` password to get a root shell. To fix the error, run **visudo**.

2.2.1 Editing the Configuration Files

The main policy configuration file for **sudo** is `/etc/sudoers`. As it is possible to lock yourself out of the system due to errors in this file, it is strongly recommended to use **visudo** for editing. It will prevent simultaneous changes to the opened file and check for syntax errors before saving the modifications.

Despite its name, you can also use editors other than vi by setting the `EDITOR` environment variable, for example:

```
sudo EDITOR=/usr/bin/nano visudo
```

However, the `/etc/sudoers` file itself is supplied by the system packages and modifications may break on updates. Therefore, it is recommended to put custom configuration into files in the `/etc/sudoers.d/` directory. Any file in there is automatically included. To create or edit a file in that subdirectory, run:

```
sudo visudo -f /etc/sudoers.d/NAME
```

Alternatively with a different editor (for example **nano**):

```
sudo EDITOR=/usr/bin/nano visudo -f /etc/sudoers.d/NAME
```

Note: Ignored Files in /etc/sudoers.d

The `#includedir` command in `/etc/sudoers`, used for `/etc/sudoers.d`, ignores files that end in `~` (tilde) or contain a `.` (dot).

For more information on the **visudo** command, run **man 8 visudo**.

2.2.2 Basic sudoers Configuration Syntax

In the sudoers configuration files, there are two types of options: strings and flags. While strings can contain any value, flags can be turned either ON or OFF. The most important syntax constructs for sudoers configuration files are:

```
# Everything on a line after a # gets ignored ❶
Defaults !insults # Disable the insults flag ❷
Defaults env_keep += "DISPLAY HOME" # Add DISPLAY and HOME to env_keep
tux ALL = NOPASSWD: /usr/bin/frobnicate, PASSWD: /usr/bin/journalctl ❸
```

1. There are two exceptions: `#include` and `#includedir` are normal commands. Followed by digits, it specifies a UID.
2. Remove the `!` to set the specified flag to ON.
3. See *Section 2.2.3, "Rules in sudoers"*.

TABLE 2.1: USEFUL FLAGS AND OPTIONS

Option name	Description	Example
`targetpw`	This flag controls whether the invoking user is required to enter the password of the target user (ON) (for example `root`) or the invoking user (OFF).	`Defaults targetpw # Turn targetpw flag ON`
`rootpw`	If set, **`sudo`** will prompt for the `root` password instead of the target user's or the invoker's. The default is OFF.	`Defaults !rootpw # Turn rootpw flag OFF`
`env_reset`	If set, **`sudo`** constructs a minimal environment with only `TERM`, `PATH`, `HOME`, `MAIL`, `SHELL`, `LOGNAME`, `USER`, `USERNAME`, and `SUDO_*` set. Additionally, variables listed in `env_keep` get imported from the calling environment. The default is ON.	`Defaults env_reset # Turn env_reset flag ON`

`env_keep`	List of environment variables to keep when the `env_reset` flag is ON.	`# Set env_keep to contain EDITOR and PROMPT`
		`Defaults env_keep = "EDITOR PROMPT"`
		`Defaults env_keep += "JRE_HOME" # Add JRE_HOME`
		`Defaults env_keep -= "JRE_HOME" # Remove JRE_HOME`

Option name	Description	Example

`env_delete`	List of environment variables to remove when the `env_reset` flag is OFF.	`# Set env_delete to contain EDITOR and PROMPT`
		`Defaults env_delete = "EDITOR PROMPT"`
		`Defaults env_delete += "JRE_HOME" # Add JRE_HOME`
		`Defaults env_delete -= "JRE_HOME" # Remove JRE_HOME`

The `Defaults` token can also be used to create aliases for a collection of users, hosts, and commands. Furthermore, it is possible to apply an option only to a specific set of users.

For detailed information about the `/etc/sudoers` configuration file, consult **`man 5 sudoers`**.

2.2.3 Rules in sudoers

Rules in the sudoers configuration can be very complex, so this section will only cover the basics. Each rule follows the basic scheme (`[]` marks optional parts):

```
#Who      Where          As whom      Tag                   What
User_List Host_List = [(User_List)] [NOPASSWD:|PASSWD:] Cmnd_List
```

SYNTAX FOR SUDOERS RULES

`User_List`

One or more (separated by `,`) identifiers: Either a user name, a group in the format `%GROUPNAME` or a user ID in the format `#UID`. Negation can be performed with a `!` prefix.

`Host_List`

One or more (separated by `,`) identifiers: Either a (fully qualified) host name or an IP address. Negation can be performed with a `!` prefix. `ALL` is the usual choice for `Host_List`.

`NOPASSWD:|PASSWD:`

The user will not be prompted for a password when running commands matching `CMDSPEC` after `NOPASSWD:`.

`PASSWD` is the default, it only needs to be specified when both are on the same line:

```
tux ALL = PASSWD: /usr/bin/foo, NOPASSWD: /usr/bin/bar
```

`Cmnd_List`

One or more (separated by `,`) specifiers: A path to an executable, followed by allowed arguments or nothing.

```
/usr/bin/foo     # Anything allowed
/usr/bin/foo bar # Only "/usr/bin/foo bar" allowed
/usr/bin/foo ""  # No arguments allowed
```

`ALL` can be used as `User_List`, `Host_List`, and `Cmnd_List`.

A rule that allows `tux` to run all commands as root without entering a password:

```
tux ALL = NOPASSWD: ALL
```

A rule that allows `tux` to run **`systemctl restart apache2`**:

```
tux ALL = /usr/bin/systemctl restart apache2
```

A rule that allows `tux` to run **`wall`** as `admin` with no arguments:

```
tux ALL = (admin) /usr/bin/wall ""
```

Warning: Dangerous constructs

Constructs of the kind

```
ALL ALL = ALL
```

must not be used without `Defaults targetpw`, otherwise anyone can run commands as `root`.

2.3 Common Use Cases

Although the default configuration is often sufficient for simple setups and desktop environments, custom configurations can be very useful.

2.3.1 Using **sudo** without root Password

In cases with special restrictions ("user X can only run command Y as `root`") it is not possible. In other cases, it is still favorable to have some kind of separation. By convention, members of the group `wheel` can run all commands with **`sudo`** as root.

1. Add yourself to the `wheel` group

   If your user account is not already member of the `wheel` group, add it by running **`sudo usermod -a -G wheel`** *`USERNAME`* and logging out and in again. Verify that the change was successful by running **`groups`** *`USERNAME`*.

2. Make authentication with the invoking user's password the default.

   Create the file `/etc/sudoers.d/userpw` with **`visudo`** (see *Section 2.2.1, "Editing the Configuration Files"*) and add:

   ```
   Defaults !targetpw
   ```

3. Select a new default rule.

   Depending on whether you want users to re-enter their passwords, uncomment the specific line in `/etc/sudoers` and comment out the default rule.

   ```
   ## Uncomment to allow members of group wheel to execute any command
   # %wheel ALL=(ALL) ALL

   ## Same thing without a password
   # %wheel ALL=(ALL) NOPASSWD: ALL
   ```

4. Make the default rule more restrictive

   Comment out or remove the allow-everything rule in `/etc/sudoers`:

   ```
   ALL     ALL=(ALL) ALL   # WARNING! Only use this together with 'Defaults targetpw'!
   ```

   #### Warning: Dangerous rule in sudoers

   Do not forget this step, otherwise *any* user can execute *any* command as `root`!

5. Test the configuration

   Try to run **`sudo`** as member and non-member of `wheel`.

   ```
   tux:~ > groups
   users wheel
   ```

```
tux:~ > sudo id -un
tux's password:
root
wilber:~ > groups
users
wilber:~ > sudo id -un
wilber is not in the sudoers file.  This incident will be reported.
```

2.3.2 Using **sudo** with X.Org Applications

When starting graphical applications with **sudo**, you will encounter the following error:

```
tux > sudo xterm
xterm: Xt error: Can't open display: %s
xterm: DISPLAY is not set
```

YaST will pick the ncurses interface instead of the graphical one.

To use X.Org in applications started with **sudo**, the environment variables `DISPLAY` and `XAUTHORITY` need to be propagated. To configure this, create the file `/etc/sudoers.d/xorg`, (see *Section 2.2.1, "Editing the Configuration Files"*) and add the following line:

```
Defaults env_keep += "DISPLAY XAUTHORITY"
```

If not set already, set the `XAUTHORITY` variable as follows:

```
export XAUTHORITY=~/.Xauthority
```

Now X.Org applications can be run as usual:

```
sudo yast2
```

2.4 More Information

A quick overview about the available command line switches can be retrieved by **sudo --help**. An explanation and other important information can be found in the man page: **man 8 sudo**, while the configuration is documented in **man 5 sudoers**.

3 YaST Online Update

SUSE offers a continuous stream of software security updates for your product. By default, the update applet is used to keep your system up-to-date. Refer to *Book "Deployment Guide", Chapter 9 "Installing or Removing Software", Section 9.4 "Keeping the System Up-to-date"* for further information on the update applet. This chapter covers the alternative tool for updating software packages: YaST Online Update.

The current patches for SUSE® Linux Enterprise Desktop are available from an update software repository. If you have registered your product during the installation, an update repository is already configured. If you have not registered SUSE Linux Enterprise Desktop, you can do so by starting the *Product Registration* in YaST. Alternatively, you can manually add an update repository from a source you trust. To add or remove repositories, start the Repository Manager with *Software › Software Repositories* in YaST. Learn more about the Repository Manager in *Book "Deployment Guide", Chapter 9 "Installing or Removing Software", Section 9.3 "Managing Software Repositories and Services"*.

Note: Error on Accessing the Update Catalog

If you are not able to access the update catalog, this might be because of an expired subscription. Normally, SUSE Linux Enterprise Desktop comes with a one-year or three-year subscription, during which you have access to the update catalog. This access will be denied after the subscription ends.

If an access to the update catalog is denied, you will see a warning message prompting you to visit the SUSE Customer Center and check your subscription. The SUSE Customer Center is available at https://scc.suse.com// ↗.

SUSE provides updates with different relevance levels:

Security Updates

Fix severe security hazards and should always be installed.

Recommended Updates

Fix issues that could compromise your computer.

Optional Updates

Fix non-security relevant issues or provide enhancements.

3.1 The Online Update Dialog

To open the YaST *Online Update* dialog, start YaST and select *Software* › *Online Update*. Alternatively, start it from the command line with `yast2 online_update`.

The *Online Update* window consists of four sections.

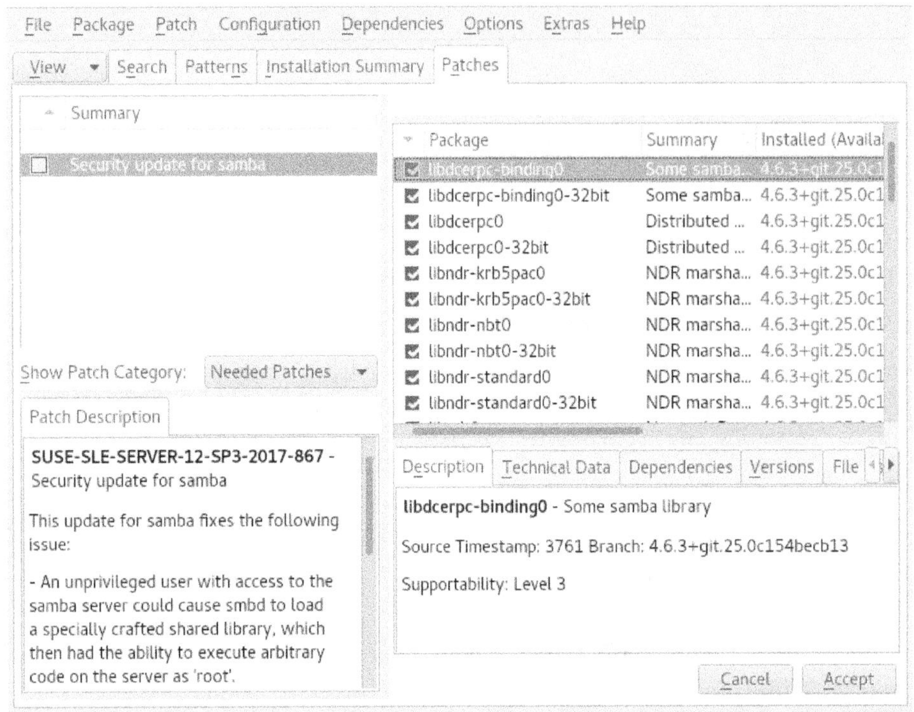

FIGURE 3.1: YAST ONLINE UPDATE

The *Summary* section on the left lists the available patches for SUSE Linux Enterprise Desktop. The patches are sorted by security relevance: `security`, `recommended`, and `optional`. You can change the view of the *Summary* section by selecting one of the following options from *Show Patch Category*:

***Needed Patches* (default view)**

Non-installed patches that apply to packages installed on your system.

Unneeded Patches

Patches that either apply to packages not installed on your system, or patches that have requirements which have already have been fulfilled (because the relevant packages have already been updated from another source).

All Patches

All patches available for SUSE Linux Enterprise Desktop.

Each list entry in the *Summary* section consists of a symbol and the patch name. For an overview of the possible symbols and their meaning, press `Shift`–`F1`. Actions required by `Security` and `Recommended` patches are automatically preset. These actions are *Autoinstall, Autoupdate* and *Autodelete.*

If you install an up-to-date package from a repository other than the update repository, the requirements of a patch for this package may be fulfilled with this installation. In this case a check mark is displayed in front of the patch summary. The patch will be visible in the list until you mark it for installation. This will in fact not install the patch (because the package already is up-to-date), but mark the patch as having been installed.

Select an entry in the *Summary* section to view a short *Patch Description* at the bottom left corner of the dialog. The upper right section lists the packages included in the selected patch (a patch can consist of several packages). Click an entry in the upper right section to view details about the respective package that is included in the patch.

3.2 Installing Patches

The YaST Online Update dialog allows you to either install all available patches at once or manually select the desired patches. You may also revert patches that have been applied to the system.

By default, all new patches (except `optional` ones) that are currently available for your system are already marked for installation. They will be applied automatically once you click *Accept* or *Apply*. If one or multiple patches require a system reboot, you will be notified about this before the patch installation starts. You can then either decide to continue with the installation of the selected patches, skip the installation of all patches that need rebooting and install the rest, or go back to the manual patch selection.

PROCEDURE 3.1: APPLYING PATCHES WITH YAST ONLINE UPDATE

1. Start YaST and select *Software* › *Online Update*.
2. To automatically apply all new patches (except `optional` ones) that are currently available for your system, press *Apply* or *Accept*.
3. First modify the selection of patches that you want to apply:
   a. Use the respective filters and views that the interface provides. For details, refer to *Section 3.1, "The Online Update Dialog"*.

b. Select or deselect patches according to your needs and wishes by right-clicking the patch and choosing the respective action from the context menu.

Important: Always Apply Security Updates

Do not deselect any `security`-related patches without a very good reason. These patches fix severe security hazards and prevent your system from being exploited.

c. Most patches include updates for several packages. If you want to change actions for single packages, right-click a package in the package view and choose an action.

d. To confirm your selection and apply the selected patches, proceed with *Apply* or *Accept*.

4. After the installation is complete, click *Finish* to leave the YaST *Online Update*. Your system is now up-to-date.

3.3 Automatic Online Update

YaST also offers the possibility to set up an automatic update with daily, weekly or monthly schedule. To use the respective module, you need to install the `yast2-online-update-configuration` package first.

By default, updates are downloaded as delta RPMs. Since rebuilding RPM packages from delta RPMs is a memory- and processor-intensive task, certain setups or hardware configurations might require you to disable the use of delta RPMs for the sake of performance.

Some patches, such as kernel updates or packages requiring license agreements, require user interaction, which would cause the automatic update procedure to stop. You can configure to skip patches that require user interaction.

PROCEDURE 3.2: CONFIGURING THE AUTOMATIC ONLINE UPDATE

1. After installation, start YaST and select *Software* › *Online Update Configuration*. Alternatively, start the module with **`yast2 online_update_configuration`** from the command line.

2. Activate *Automatic Online Update*.

3. Choose the update interval: *Daily*, *Weekly*, or *Monthly*.
4. To automatically accept any license agreements, activate *Agree with Licenses*.
5. Select if you want to *Skip Interactive Patches* in case you want the update procedure to proceed fully automatically.

Important: Skipping Patches

If you select to skip any packages that require interaction, run a manual *Online Update* occasionally to install those patches, too. Otherwise you might miss important patches.

6. To automatically install all packages recommended by updated packages, activate *Include Recommended Packages*.
7. To disable the use of delta RPMs (for performance reasons), deactivate *Use Delta RPMs*.
8. To filter the patches by category (such as security or recommended), activate *Filter by Category* and add the appropriate patch categories from the list. Only patches of the selected categories will be installed. Others will be skipped.
9. Confirm your configuration with *OK*.

The automatic online update does not automatically restart the system afterward. If there are package updates that require a system reboot, you need to do this manually.

4 YaST

YaST is the installation and configuration tool for SUSE Linux Enterprise Desktop. It has a graphical interface and the capability to customize your system quickly during and after the installation. It can be used to set up hardware, configure the network, system services, and tune your security settings.

4.1 Advanced Key Combinations

YaST has a set of advanced key combinations.

`Print Screen`
: Take and save a screenshot. May not be available when YaST is running under some desktop environments.

`Shift`–`F4`
: Enable/disable the color palette optimized for vision impaired users.

`Shift`–`F7`
: Enable/disable logging of debug messages.

`Shift`–`F8`
: Open a file dialog to save log files to a non-standard location.

`Ctrl`–`Shift`–`Alt`–`D`
: Send a DebugEvent. YaST modules can react to this by executing special debugging actions. The result depends on the specific YaST module.

`Ctrl`–`Shift`–`Alt`–`M`
: Start/stop macro recorder.

`Ctrl`–`Shift`–`Alt`–`P`
: Replay macro.

`Ctrl`–`Shift`–`Alt`–`S`
: Show style sheet editor.

`Ctrl`–`Shift`–`Alt`–`T`
: Dump widget tree to the log file.

Ctrl – Shift – Alt – X

Open a terminal window (xterm). Useful for installation process via VNC.

Ctrl – Shift – Alt – Y

Show widget tree browser.

5 YaST in Text Mode

This section is intended for system administrators and experts who do not run an X server on their systems and depend on the text-based installation tool. It provides basic information about starting and operating YaST in text mode.

YaST in text mode uses the ncurses library to provide an easy pseudo-graphical user interface. The ncurses library is installed by default. The minimum supported size of the terminal emulator in which to run YaST is 80x25 characters.

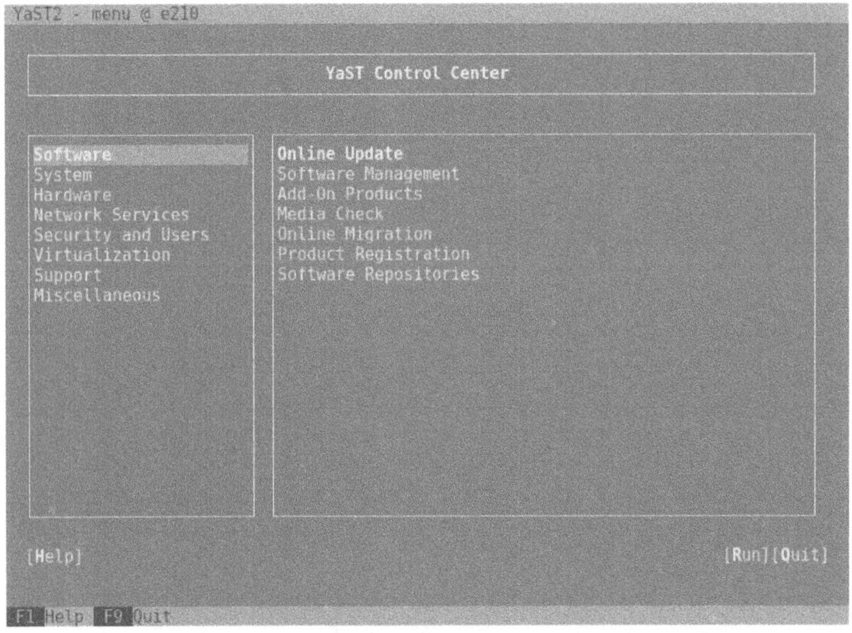

FIGURE 5.1: MAIN WINDOW OF YAST IN TEXT MODE

When you start YaST in text mode, the YaST control center appears (see Figure 5.1). The main window consists of three areas. The left frame features the categories to which the various modules belong. This frame is active when YaST is started and therefore it is marked by a bold white border. The active category is selected. The right frame provides an overview of the modules available in the active category. The bottom frame contains the buttons for *Help* and *Quit*.

When you start the YaST control center, the category *Software* is selected automatically. Use ↓ and ↑ to change the category. To select a module from the category, activate the right frame with → and then use ↓ and ↑ to select the module. Keep the arrow keys pressed to scroll through the list of available modules. The selected module is selected. Press Enter to start the active module.

Various buttons or selection fields in the module contain a highlighted letter (yellow by default). Use Alt–highlighted_letter to select a button directly instead of navigating there with →|. Exit the YaST control center by pressing Alt–Q or by selecting *Quit* and pressing Enter.

Tip: Refreshing YaST Dialogs

If a YaST dialog gets corrupted or distorted (for example, while resizing the window), press Ctrl–L to refresh and restore its contents.

5.1 Navigation in Modules

The following description of the control elements in the YaST modules assumes that all function keys and Alt key combinations work and are not assigned to different global functions. Read *Section 5.3, "Restriction of Key Combinations"* for information about possible exceptions.

Navigation among Buttons and Selection Lists

Use →| to navigate among the buttons and frames containing selection lists. To navigate in reverse order, use Alt–→| or Shift–→| combinations.

Navigation in Selection Lists

Use the arrow keys (↑ and ↓) to navigate among the individual elements in an active frame containing a selection list. If individual entries within a frame exceed its width, use Shift–→ or Shift–← to scroll horizontally to the right and left. Alternatively, use Ctrl–E or Ctrl–A. This combination can also be used if using → or ← results in changing the active frame or the current selection list, as in the control center.

Buttons, Radio Buttons, and Check Boxes

To select buttons with empty square brackets (check boxes) or empty parentheses (radio buttons), press Space or Enter. Alternatively, radio buttons and check boxes can be selected directly with Alt–highlighted_letter. In this case, you do not need to confirm with Enter. If you navigate to an item with →|, press Enter to execute the selected action or activate the respective menu item.

Function Keys

The function keys (F1 ... F12) enable quick access to the various buttons. Available function key combinations (FX) are shown in the bottom line of the YaST screen. Which function keys are actually mapped to which buttons depend on the active YaST module, because the different modules offer different buttons (*Details*, *Info*, *Add*, *Delete*, etc.). Use F10 for *Accept*, *OK*, *Next*, and *Finish*. Press F1 to access the YaST help.

Using Navigation Tree in ncurses Mode

Some YaST modules use a navigation tree in the left part of the window to select configuration dialogs. Use the arrow keys (↑ and ↓) to navigate in the tree. Use Space to open or close tree items. In ncurses mode, Enter must be pressed after a selection in the navigation tree to show the selected dialog. This is an intentional behavior to save time consuming redraws when browsing through the navigation tree.

Selecting Software in the Software Installation Module

Use the filters on the left side to limit the amount of displayed packages. Installed packages are marked with the letter `i`. To change the status of a package, press Space or Enter . Alternatively, use the *Actions* menu to select the needed status change (install, delete, update, taboo or lock).

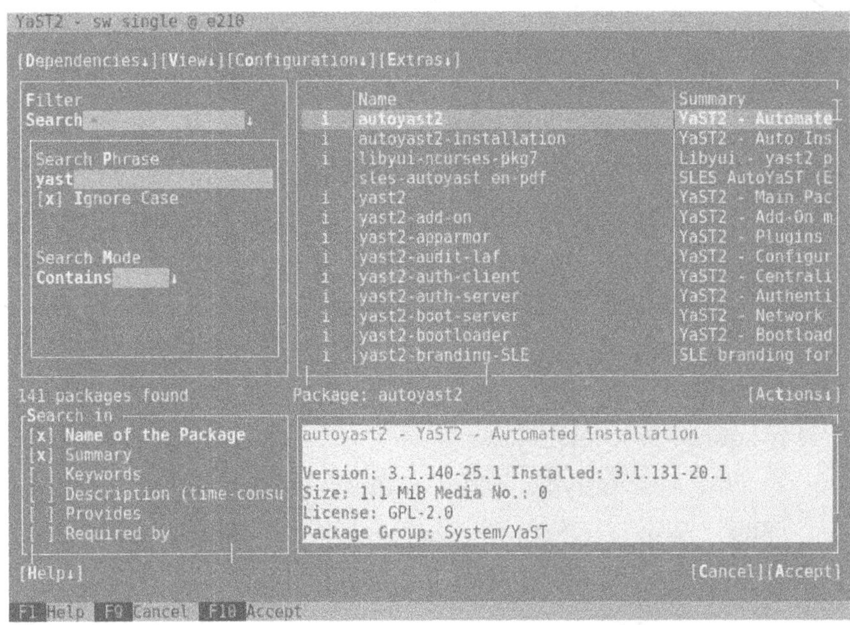

FIGURE 5.2: THE SOFTWARE INSTALLATION MODULE

5.2 Advanced Key Combinations

YaST in text mode has a set of advanced key combinations.

Shift–F1

Show a list of advanced hotkeys.

Shift–F4

Change color schema.

Ctrl–\

Quit the application.

Ctrl–L

Refresh screen.

Ctrl–D F1

Show a list of advanced hotkeys.

Ctrl–D Shift–D

Dump dialog to the log file as a screenshot.

Ctrl–D Shift–Y

Open YDialogSpy to see the widget hierarchy.

5.3 Restriction of Key Combinations

If your window manager uses global Alt combinations, the Alt combinations in YaST might not work. Keys like Alt or Shift can also be occupied by the settings of the terminal.

Replacing Alt with Esc

Alt shortcuts can be executed with Esc instead of Alt. For example, Esc–H replaces Alt–H. (First press Esc, *then* press H.)

Backward and Forward Navigation with Ctrl–F and Ctrl–B

If the Alt and Shift combinations are occupied by the window manager or the terminal, use the combinations Ctrl–F (forward) and Ctrl–B (backward) instead.

Restriction of Function Keys

The function keys (F1 ... F12) are also used for functions. Certain function keys might be occupied by the terminal and may not be available for YaST. However, the Alt key combinations and function keys should always be fully available on a pure text console.

5.4 YaST Command Line Options

Besides the text mode interface, YaST provides a pure command line interface. To get a list of YaST command line options, enter:

```
yast -h
```

5.4.1 Starting the Individual Modules

To save time, the individual YaST modules can be started directly. To start a module, enter:

```
yast <module_name>
```

View a list of all module names available on your system with **`yast -l`** or **`yast --list`**. Start the network module, for example, with **`yast lan`**.

5.4.2 Installing Packages from the Command Line

If you know a package name and the package is provided by any of your active installation repositories, you can use the command line option `-i` to install the package:

```
yast -i <package_name>
```

or

```
yast --install <package_name>
```

PACKAGE_NAME can be a single short package name (for example `gvim`) installed with dependency checking, or the full path to an RPM package which is installed without dependency checking.

If you need a command line based software management utility with functionality beyond what YaST provides, consider using Zypper. This utility uses the same software management library that is also the foundation for the YaST package manager. The basic usage of Zypper is covered in *Section 6.1, "Using Zypper"*.

5.4.3 Command Line Parameters of the YaST Modules

To use YaST functionality in scripts, YaST provides command line support for individual modules. Not all modules have command line support. To display the available options of a module, enter:

```
yast <module_name> help
```

If a module does not provide command line support, the module is started in text mode and the following message appears:

```
This YaST module does not support the command line interface.
```

6 Managing Software with Command Line Tools

This chapter describes Zypper and RPM, two command line tools for managing software. For a definition of the terminology used in this context (for example, `repository`, `patch`, or `update`) refer to *Book* "Deployment Guide", *Chapter 9 "Installing or Removing Software", Section 9.1 "Definition of Terms"*.

6.1 Using Zypper

Zypper is a command line package manager for installing, updating and removing packages a well as for managing repositories. It is especially useful for accomplishing remote software management tasks or managing software from shell scripts.

6.1.1 General Usage

The general syntax of Zypper is:

```
zypper [--global-options] COMMAND  [--command-options] [arguments]
```

The components enclosed in brackets are not required. See **`zypper help`** for a list of general options and all commands. To get help for a specific command, type **`zypper help`** *`COMMAND`*.

Zypper Commands

The simplest way to execute Zypper is to type its name, followed by a command. For example, to apply all needed patches to the system, use:

```
tux > sudo zypper patch
```

Global Options

Additionally, you can choose from one or more global options by typing them immediately before the command:

```
tux > sudo zypper --non-interactive patch
```

In the above example, the option `--non-interactive` means that the command is run without asking anything (automatically applying the default answers).

Command-Specific Options

To use options that are specific to a particular command, type them immediately after the command:

```
tux > sudo zypper patch --auto-agree-with-licenses
```

In the above example, `--auto-agree-with-licenses` is used to apply all needed patches to a system without you being asked to confirm any licenses. Instead, license will be accepted automatically.

Arguments

Some commands require one or more arguments. For example, when using the command **`install`**, you need to specify which package or which packages you want to *install*:

```
tux > sudo zypper install mplayer
```

Some options also require a single argument. The following command will list all known patterns:

```
tux > zypper search -t pattern
```

You can combine all of the above. For example, the following command will install the `aspell-de` and `aspell-fr` packages from the `factory` repository while being verbose:

```
tux > sudo zypper -v install --from factory aspell-de aspell-fr
```

The `--from` option makes sure to keep all repositories enabled (for solving any dependencies) while requesting the package from the specified repository.

Most Zypper commands have a `dry-run` option that does a simulation of the given command. It can be used for test purposes.

```
tux > sudo zypper remove --dry-run MozillaFirefox
```

Zypper supports the global `--userdata STRING` option. You can specify a string with this option, which gets written to Zypper's log files and plug-ins (such as the Btrfs plug-in). It can be used to mark and identify transactions in log files.

```
tux > sudo zypper --userdata STRING patch
```

6.1.2 Installing and Removing Software with Zypper

To install or remove packages, use the following commands:

```
tux > sudo zypper install PACKAGE_NAME
sudo zypper remove PACKAGE_NAME
```

Warning: Do Not Remove Mandatory System Packages

Do not remove mandatory system packages like `glibc` , `zypper` , `kernel` . If they are removed, the system can become unstable or stop working altogether.

6.1.2.1 Selecting Which Packages to Install or Remove

There are various ways to address packages with the commands **`zypper install`** and **`zypper remove`**.

By Exact Package Name

```
tux > sudo zypper install MozillaFirefox
```

By Exact Package Name and Version Number

```
tux > sudo zypper install MozillaFirefox-52.2
```

By Repository Alias and Package Name

```
tux > sudo zypper install mozilla:MozillaFirefox
```

Where `mozilla` is the alias of the repository from which to install.

By Package Name Using Wild Cards

You can select all packages that have names starting or ending with a certain string. Use wild cards with care, especially when removing packages. The following command will install all packages starting with “Moz”:

```
tux > sudo zypper install 'Moz*'
```

Tip: Removing all -debuginfo Packages

When debugging a problem, you sometimes need to temporarily install a lot of `-debuginfo` packages which give you more information about running processes. After your debugging session finishes and you need to clean the environment, run the following:

```
tux > sudo zypper remove '*-debuginfo'
```

By Capability

For example, if you want to install a Perl module without knowing the name of the package, capabilities come in handy:

```
tux > sudo zypper install firefox
```

By Capability, Hardware Architecture, or Version

Together with a capability, you can specify a hardware architecture and a version:

- The name of the desired hardware architecture is appended to the capability after a full stop. For example, to specify the AMD64/Intel 64 architectures (which in Zypper is named `x86_64`), use:

```
tux > sudo zypper install 'firefox.x86_64'
```

- Versions must be appended to the end of the string and must be preceded by an operator: `<` (lesser than), `<=` (lesser than or equal), `=` (equal), `>=` (greater than or equal), `>` (greater than).

```
tux > sudo zypper install 'firefox>=52.2'
```

- You can also combine a hardware architecture and version requirement:

```
tux > sudo zypper install 'firefox.x86_64>=52.2'
```

By Path to the RPM file

You can also specify a local or remote path to a package:

```
tux > sudo zypper install /tmp/install/MozillaFirefox.rpm
tux > sudo zypper install http://download.example.com/MozillaFirefox.rpm
```

6.1.2.2 Combining Installation and Removal of Packages

To install and remove packages simultaneously, use the `+/-` modifiers. To install `emacs` and simultaneously remove `vim` , use:

```
tux > sudo zypper install emacs -vim
```

To remove `emacs` and simultaneously install `vim` , use:

```
tux > sudo zypper remove emacs +vim
```

To prevent the package name starting with the `-` being interpreted as a command option, always use it as the second argument. If this is not possible, precede it with `--`:

```
tux > sudo zypper install -emacs +vim       # Wrong
tux > sudo zypper install vim -emacs        # Correct
tux > sudo zypper install -- -emacs +vim    # Correct
tux > sudo zypper remove emacs +vim         # Correct
```

6.1.2.3 Cleaning Up Dependencies of Removed Packages

If (together with a certain package), you automatically want to remove any packages that become unneeded after removing the specified package, use the `--clean-deps` option:

```
tux > sudo zypper rm PACKAGE_NAME --clean-deps
```

6.1.2.4 Using Zypper in Scripts

By default, Zypper asks for a confirmation before installing or removing a selected package, or when a problem occurs. You can override this behavior using the `--non-interactive` option. This option must be given before the actual command (**`install`**, **`remove`**, and **`patch`**), as can be seen in the following:

```
tux > sudo zypper --non-interactive install PACKAGE_NAME
```

This option allows the use of Zypper in scripts and cron jobs.

6.1.2.5 Installing or Downloading Source Packages

To install the corresponding source package of a package, use:

```
tux > zypper source-install PACKAGE_NAME
```

When executed as `root`, the default location to install source packages is `/usr/src/packages/` and `~/rpmbuild` when run as user. These values can be changed in your local **`rpm`** configuration.

This command will also install the build dependencies of the specified package. If you do not want this, add the switch `-D`:

```
tux > sudo zypper source-install -D PACKAGE_NAME
```

To install only the build dependencies use `-d`.

```
tux > sudo zypper source-install -d PACKAGE_NAME
```

Of course, this will only work if you have the repository with the source packages enabled in your repository list (it is added by default, but not enabled). See *Section 6.1.5, "Managing Repositories with Zypper"* for details on repository management.

A list of all source packages available in your repositories can be obtained with:

```
tux > zypper search -t srcpackage
```

You can also download source packages for all installed packages to a local directory. To download source packages, use:

```
tux > zypper source-download
```

The default download directory is `/var/cache/zypper/source-download`. You can change it using the `--directory` option. To only show missing or extraneous packages without downloading or deleting anything, use the `--status` option. To delete extraneous source packages, use the `--delete` option. To disable deleting, use the `--no-delete` option.

6.1.2.6 Installing Packages from Disabled Repositories

Normally you can only install or refresh packages from enabled repositories. The `--plus-content` *`TAG`* option helps you specify repositories to be refreshed, temporarily enabled during the current Zypper session, and disabled after it completes.

For example, to enable repositories that may provide additional `-debuginfo` or `-debugsource` packages, use `--plus-content debug`. You can specify this option multiple times.

To temporarily enable such 'debug' repositories to install a specific `-debuginfo` package, use the option as follows:

```
tux > sudo zypper --plus-content debug \
   install "debuginfo(build-id)=eb844a5c20c70a59fc693cd1061f851fb7d046f4"
```

The `build-id` string is reported by **`gdb`** for missing debuginfo packages.

6.1.2.7 Utilities

To verify whether all dependencies are still fulfilled and to repair missing dependencies, use:

```
tux > zypper verify
```

In addition to dependencies that must be fulfilled, some packages “recommend” other packages. These recommended packages are only installed if actually available and installable. In case recommended packages were made available after the recommending package has been installed (by adding additional packages or hardware), use the following command:

```
tux > sudo zypper install-new-recommends
```

This command is very useful after plugging in a Web cam or Wi-Fi device. It will install drivers for the device and related software, if available. Drivers and related software are only installable if certain hardware dependencies are fulfilled.

6.1.3 Updating Software with Zypper

There are three different ways to update software using Zypper: by installing patches, by installing a new version of a package or by updating the entire distribution. The latter is achieved with **`zypper dist-upgrade`**. Upgrading SUSE Linux Enterprise Desktop is discussed in *Book "Deployment Guide", Chapter 15 "Upgrading SUSE Linux Enterprise"*.

6.1.3.1 Installing All Needed Patches

To install all officially released patches that apply to your system, run:

```
tux > sudo zypper patch
```

All patches available from repositories configured on your computer are checked for their relevance to your installation. If they are relevant (and not classified as `optional` or `feature`), they are installed immediately. Note that the official update repository is only available after registering your SUSE Linux Enterprise Desktop installation.

If a patch that is about to be installed includes changes that require a system reboot, you will be warned before.

The plain **`zypper patch`** command does not apply patches from third party repositories. To update also the third party repositories, use the `with-update` command option as follows:

```
tux > sudo zypper patch --with update
```

To install also optional patches, use:

```
tux > sudo zypper patch --with-optional
```

To install all patches relating to a specific Bugzilla issue, use:

```
tux > sudo zypper patch --bugzilla=NUMBER
```

To install all patches relating to a specific CVE database entry, use:

```
tux > sudo zypper patch --cve=NUMBER
```

For example, to install a security patch with the CVE number `CVE-2010-2713`, execute:

```
tux > sudo zypper patch --cve=CVE-2010-2713
```

To install only patches which affect Zypper and the package management itself, use:

```
tux > sudo zypper patch --updatestack-only
```

Bear in mind that other command options that would also update other repositories will be dropped if you use the `updatestack-only` command option.

6.1.3.2 Listing Patches

To find out whether patches are available, Zypper allows viewing the following information:

Number of Needed Patches

To list the number of needed patches (patches that apply to your system but are not yet installed), use `patch-check`:

```
tux > zypper patch-check
Loading repository data...
Reading installed packages...
5 patches needed (1 security patch)
```

This command can be combined with the `--updatestack-only` option to list only the patches which affect Zypper and the package management itself.

List of Needed Patches

To list all needed patches (patches that apply to your system but are not yet installed), use `list-patches`:

```
tux > zypper list-patches
Loading repository data...
Reading installed packages...

Repository     | Name        | Version | Category | Status  | Summary
---------------+-------------+---------+----------+---------+---------
SLES12-Updates | SUSE-2014-8 | 1       | security | needed  | openssl: Update for OpenSSL
```

List of All Patches

To list all patches available for SUSE Linux Enterprise Desktop, regardless of whether they are already installed or apply to your installation, use `zypper patches`.

It is also possible to list and install patches relevant to specific issues. To list specific patches, use the `zypper list-patches` command with the following options:

By Bugzilla Issues

To list all needed patches that relate to Bugzilla issues, use the option `--bugzilla`.
To list patches for a specific bug, you can also specify a bug number: `--bugzilla=NUMBER`.
To search for patches relating to multiple Bugzilla issues, add commas between the bug numbers, for example:

```
tux > zypper list-patches --bugzilla=972197,956917
```

By CVE Number

To list all needed patches that relate to an entry in the CVE database (Common Vulnerabilities and Exposures), use the option `--cve`.

To list patches for a specific CVE database entry, you can also specify a CVE number: `--cve=NUMBER`. To search for patches relating to multiple CVE database entries, add commas between the CVE numbers, for example:

```
tux > zypper list-patches --bugzilla=CVE-2016-2315,CVE-2016-2324
```

To list all patches regardless of whether they are needed, use the option `--all` additionally. For example, to list all patches with a CVE number assigned, use:

```
tux > zypper list-patches --all --cve
Issue | No.            | Patch              | Category    | Severity  | Status
------+----------------+--------------------+-------------+-----------+----------
cve   | CVE-2015-0287 | SUSE-SLE-Module.. | recommended | moderate  | needed
cve   | CVE-2014-3566 | SUSE-SLE-SERVER.. | recommended | moderate  | not needed
[...]
```

6.1.3.3 Installing New Package Versions

If a repository contains only new packages, but does not provide patches, **`zypper patch`** does not show any effect. To update all installed packages with newer available versions (while maintaining system integrity), use:

```
tux > sudo zypper update
```

To update individual packages, specify the package with either the update or install command:

```
tux > sudo zypper update PACKAGE_NAME
sudo zypper install PACKAGE_NAME
```

A list of all new installable packages can be obtained with the command:

```
tux > zypper list-updates
```

Note that this command only lists packages that match the following criteria:

- has the same vendor like the already installed package,
- is provided by repositories with at least the same priority than the already installed package,
- is installable (all dependencies are satisfied).

A list of *all* new available packages (regardless whether installable or not) can be obtained with:

```
tux > sudo zypper list-updates --all
```

To find out why a new package cannot be installed, use the **zypper install** or **zypper update** command as described above.

6.1.3.4 Identifying Orphaned Packages

Whenever you remove a repository from Zypper or upgrade your system, some packages can get in an "orphaned" state. These *orphaned* packages belong to no active repository anymore. The following command gives you a list of these:

```
tux > sudo zypper packages --orphaned
```

With this list, you can decide if a package is still needed or can be removed safely.

6.1.4 Identifying Processes and Services Using Deleted Files

When patching, updating or removing packages, there may be running processes on the system which continue to use files having been deleted by the update or removal. Use **zypper ps** to list processes using deleted files. In case the process belongs to a known service, the service name is listed, making it easy to restart the service. By default **zypper ps** shows a table:

```
tux > zypper ps
PID   | PPID | UID | User  | Command      | Service      | Files
------+------+-----+-------+--------------+--------------+-------------------
814   | 1    | 481 | avahi | avahi-daemon | avahi-daemon | /lib64/ld-2.19.s->
      |      |     |       |              |              | /lib64/libdl-2.1->
      |      |     |       |              |              | /lib64/libpthrea->
      |      |     |       |              |              | /lib64/libc-2.19->
```

```
[...]
```

PID: ID of the process

PPID: ID of the parent process

UID: ID of the user running the process

Login: Login name of the user running the process

Command: Command used to execute the process

Service: Service name (only if command is associated with a system service)

Files: The list of the deleted files

The output format of `zypper ps` can be controlled as follows:

`zypper ps -s`

Create a short table not showing the deleted files.

```
tux > zypper ps -s
PID   | PPID | UID  | User    | Command      | Service
------+------+------+---------+--------------+--------------
814   | 1    | 481  | avahi   | avahi-daemon | avahi-daemon
817   | 1    | 0    | root    | irqbalance   | irqbalance
1567  | 1    | 0    | root    | sshd         | sshd
1761  | 1    | 0    | root    | master       | postfix
1764  | 1761 | 51   | postfix | pickup       | postfix
1765  | 1761 | 51   | postfix | qmgr         | postfix
2031  | 2027 | 1000 | tux     | bash         |
```

`zypper ps -ss`

Show only processes associated with a system service.

```
PID   | PPID | UID  | User    | Command      | Service
------+------+------+---------+--------------+--------------
814   | 1    | 481  | avahi   | avahi-daemon | avahi-daemon
817   | 1    | 0    | root    | irqbalance   | irqbalance
1567  | 1    | 0    | root    | sshd         | sshd
1761  | 1    | 0    | root    | master       | postfix
1764  | 1761 | 51   | postfix | pickup       | postfix
1765  | 1761 | 51   | postfix | qmgr         | postfix
```

`zypper ps -sss`

Only show system services using deleted files.

```
avahi-daemon
irqbalance
postfix
sshd
```

zypper ps --print "systemctl status %s"

Show the commands to retrieve status information for services which might need a restart.

```
systemctl status avahi-daemon
systemctl status irqbalance
systemctl status postfix
systemctl status sshd
```

For more information about service handling refer to *Chapter 14, The systemd Daemon*.

6.1.5 Managing Repositories with Zypper

All installation or patch commands of Zypper rely on a list of known repositories. To list all repositories known to the system, use the command:

```
tux > zypper repos
```

The result will look similar to the following output:

EXAMPLE 6.1: ZYPPER—LIST OF KNOWN REPOSITORIES

```
tux > zypper repos
# | Alias         | Name          | Enabled | Refresh
--+---------------+---------------+---------+--------
1 | SLEHA-12-GEO  | SLEHA-12-GEO  | Yes     | No
2 | SLEHA-12      | SLEHA-12      | Yes     | No
3 | SLES12        | SLES12        | Yes     | No
```

When specifying repositories in various commands, an alias, URI or repository number from the **zypper repos** command output can be used. A repository alias is a short version of the repository name for use in repository handling commands. Note that the repository numbers can change after modifying the list of repositories. The alias will never change by itself.

By default, details such as the URI or the priority of the repository are not displayed. Use the following command to list all details:

```
tux > zypper repos -d
```

6.1.5.1 Adding Repositories

To add a repository, run

```
tux > sudo zypper addrepo URI ALIAS
```

URI can either be an Internet repository, a network resource, a directory or a CD or DVD (see http://en.opensuse.org/openSUSE:Libzypp_URIs for details). The *ALIAS* is a shorthand and unique identifier of the repository. You can freely choose it, with the only exception that it needs to be unique. Zypper will issue a warning if you specify an alias that is already in use.

6.1.5.2 Refreshing Repositories

zypper enables you to fetch changes in packages from configured repositories. To fetch the changes, run:

```
tux > sudo zypper refresh
```

Note: Default Behavior of **zypper**

By default, some commands perform **refresh** automatically, so you do not need to run the command explicitly.

The **refresh** command enables you to view changes also in disabled repositories, by using the `--plus-content` option:

```
tux > sudo zypper --plus-content refresh
```

This option fetches changes in repositories, but keeps the disabled repositories in the same state —disabled.

6.1.5.3 Removing Repositories

To remove a repository from the list, use the command **zypper removerepo** together with the alias or number of the repository you want to delete. For example, to remove the repository `SLEHA-12-GEO` from *Example 6.1, "Zypper—List of Known Repositories"*, use one of the following commands:

```
tux > sudo zypper removerepo 1
tux > sudo zypper removerepo "SLEHA-12-GEO"
```

6.1.5.4 Modifying Repositories

Enable or disable repositories with **`zypper modifyrepo`**. You can also alter the repository's properties (such as refreshing behavior, name or priority) with this command. The following command will enable the repository named `updates`, turn on auto-refresh and set its priority to 20:

```
tux > sudo zypper modifyrepo -er -p 20 'updates'
```

Modifying repositories is not limited to a single repository—you can also operate on groups:

`-a`: all repositories
`-l`: local repositories
`-t`: remote repositories
`-m` *`TYPE`*: repositories of a certain type (where *`TYPE`* can be one of the following: `http`, `https`, `ftp`, `cd`, `dvd`, `dir`, `file`, `cifs`, `smb`, `nfs`, `hd`, `iso`)

To rename a repository alias, use the `renamerepo` command. The following example changes the alias from `Mozilla Firefox` to `firefox`:

```
tux > sudo zypper renamerepo 'Mozilla Firefox' firefox
```

6.1.6 Querying Repositories and Packages with Zypper

Zypper offers various methods to query repositories or packages. To get lists of all products, patterns, packages or patches available, use the following commands:

```
tux > zypper products
tux > zypper patterns
tux > zypper packages
tux > zypper patches
```

To query all repositories for certain packages, use `search`. To get information regarding particular packages, use the `info` command.

6.1.6.1 `zypper search` Usage

The **`zypper search`** command works on package names, or, optionally, on package summaries and descriptions. String wrapped in `/` are interpreted as regular expressions. By default, the search is not case-sensitive.

Simple search for a package name containing `fire`

```
tux > zypper search "fire"
```

Simple search for the exact package `MozillaFirefox`

```
tux > zypper search --match-exact "MozillaFirefox"
```

Also search in package descriptions and summaries

```
tux > zypper search -d fire
```

Only display packages not already installed

```
tux > zypper search -u fire
```

Display packages containing the string `fir` not followed be `e`

```
tux > zypper se "/fir[^e]/"
```

6.1.6.2 `zypper what-provides` Usage

To search for packages which provide a special capability, use the command `what-provides`. For example, if you want to know which package provides the Perl module `SVN::Core`, use the following command:

```
tux > zypper what-provides 'perl(SVN::Core)'
```

The `what-provides` *`PACKAGE_NAME`* is similar to **`rpm -q --whatprovides`** *`PACKAGE_NAME`*, but RPM is only able to query the RPM database (that is the database of all installed packages). Zypper, on the other hand, will tell you about providers of the capability from any repository, not only those that are installed.

6.1.6.3 `zypper info` Usage

To query single packages, use **`info`** with an exact package name as an argument. This displays detailed information about a package. In case the package name does not match any package name from repositories, the command outputs detailed information for non-package matches. If you request a specific type (by using the `-t` option) and the type does not exist, the command outputs other available matches but without detailed information.

If you specify a source package, the command displays binary packages built from the source package. If you specify a binary package, the command outputs the source packages used to build the binary package.

To also show what is required/recommended by the package, use the options `--requires` and `--recommends`:

```
tux > zypper info --requires MozillaFirefox
```

6.1.7 Configuring Zypper

Zypper now comes with a configuration file, allowing you to permanently change Zypper's behavior (either system-wide or user-specific). For system-wide changes, edit `/etc/zypp/zypper.conf`. For user-specific changes, edit `~/.zypper.conf`. If `~/.zypper.conf` does not yet exist, you can use `/etc/zypp/zypper.conf` as a template: copy it to `~/.zypper.conf` and adjust it to your liking. Refer to the comments in the file for help about the available options.

6.1.8 Troubleshooting

If you have trouble accessing packages from configured repositories (for example, Zypper cannot find a certain package even though you know it exists in one the repositories), refreshing the repositories may help:

```
tux > sudo zypper refresh
```

If that does not help, try

```
tux > sudo zypper refresh -fdb
```

This forces a complete refresh and rebuild of the database, including a forced download of raw metadata.

6.1.9 Zypper Rollback Feature on Btrfs File System

If the Btrfs file system is used on the root partition and **snapper** is installed, Zypper automatically calls **snapper** when committing changes to the file system to create appropriate file system snapshots. These snapshots can be used to revert any changes made by Zypper. See *Chapter 7, System Recovery and Snapshot Management with Snapper* for more information.

6.1.10 For More Information

For more information on managing software from the command line, enter **zypper help**, **zypper help** *COMMAND* or refer to the **zypper(8)** man page. For a complete and detailed command reference, cheat sheets with the most important commands, and information on how to use Zypper in scripts and applications, refer to http://en.opensuse.org/SDB:Zypper_usage ↗. A list of software changes for the latest SUSE Linux Enterprise Desktop version can be found at http://en.opensuse.org/openSUSE:Zypper versions ↗.

6.2 RPM—the Package Manager

RPM (RPM Package Manager) is used for managing software packages. Its main commands are **rpm** and **rpmbuild**. The powerful RPM database can be queried by the users, system administrators and package builders for detailed information about the installed software.

Essentially, **rpm** has five modes: installing, uninstalling (or updating) software packages, rebuilding the RPM database, querying RPM bases or individual RPM archives, integrity checking of packages and signing packages. **rpmbuild** can be used to build installable packages from pristine sources.

Installable RPM archives are packed in a special binary format. These archives consist of the program files to install and certain meta information used during the installation by **rpm** to configure the software package or stored in the RPM database for documentation purposes. RPM archives normally have the extension `.rpm`.

Tip: Software Development Packages

For several packages, the components needed for software development (libraries, headers, include files, etc.) have been put into separate packages. These development packages are only needed if you want to compile software yourself (for example, the most recent GNOME packages). They can be identified by the name extension `-devel`, such as the packages `alsa-devel` and `gimp-devel`.

6.2.1 Verifying Package Authenticity

RPM packages have a GPG signature. To verify the signature of an RPM package, use the command **rpm --checksig** *PACKAGE*-1.2.3.rpm to determine whether the package originates from SUSE or from another trustworthy facility. This is especially recommended for update packages from the Internet.

While fixing issues in the operating system, you might need to install a Problem Temporary Fix (PTF) into a production system. The packages provided by SUSE are signed against a special PTF key. However, in contrast to SUSE Linux Enterprise 11, this key is not imported by default on SUSE Linux Enterprise 12 systems. To manually import the key, use the following command:

```
tux > sudo rpm --import \
/usr/share/doc/packages/suse-build-key/suse_ptf_key.asc
```

After importing the key, you can install PTF packages on your system.

6.2.2 Managing Packages: Install, Update, and Uninstall

Normally, the installation of an RPM archive is quite simple: **rpm -i** *PACKAGE*.rpm. With this command the package is installed, but only if its dependencies are fulfilled and if there are no conflicts with other packages. With an error message, **rpm** requests those packages that need to be installed to meet dependency requirements. In the background, the RPM database ensures that no conflicts arise—a specific file can only belong to one package. By choosing different options, you can force **rpm** to ignore these defaults, but this is only for experts. Otherwise, you risk compromising the integrity of the system and possibly jeopardize the ability to update the system.

The options `-U` or `--upgrade` and `-F` or `--freshen` can be used to update a package (for example, **rpm -F** *PACKAGE*.rpm). This command removes the files of the old version and immediately installs the new files. The difference between the two versions is that `-U` installs packages that previously did not exist in the system, while `-F` merely updates previously installed packages. When updating, **rpm** updates configuration files carefully using the following strategy:

- If a configuration file was not changed by the system administrator, **rpm** installs the new version of the appropriate file. No action by the system administrator is required.
- If a configuration file was changed by the system administrator before the update, **rpm** saves the changed file with the extension `.rpmorig` or `.rpmsave` (backup file) and installs the version from the new package. This is done only if the originally installed file and

the newer version are different. If this is the case, compare the backup file (`.rpmorig` or `.rpmsave`) with the newly installed file and make your changes again in the new file. Afterward, delete all `.rpmorig` and `.rpmsave` files to avoid problems with future updates.

- `.rpmnew` files appear if the configuration file already exists *and* if the `noreplace` label was specified in the `.spec` file.

Following an update, `.rpmsave` and `.rpmnew` files should be removed after comparing them, so they do not obstruct future updates. The `.rpmorig` extension is assigned if the file has not previously been recognized by the RPM database.

Otherwise, `.rpmsave` is used. In other words, `.rpmorig` results from updating from a foreign format to RPM. `.rpmsave` results from updating from an older RPM to a newer RPM. `.rpmnew` does not disclose any information to whether the system administrator has made any changes to the configuration file. A list of these files is available in `/var/adm/rpmconfigcheck`. Some configuration files (like `/etc/httpd/httpd.conf`) are not overwritten to allow continued operation.

The `-U` switch is *not* just an equivalent to uninstalling with the `-e` option and installing with the `-i` option. Use `-U` whenever possible.

To remove a package, enter **`rpm -e`** *`PACKAGE`*. This command only deletes the package if there are no unresolved dependencies. It is theoretically impossible to delete Tcl/Tk, for example, as long as another application requires it. Even in this case, RPM calls for assistance from the database. If such a deletion is, for whatever reason, impossible (even if *no* additional dependencies exist), it may be helpful to rebuild the RPM database using the option `--rebuilddb`.

6.2.3 Delta RPM Packages

Delta RPM packages contain the difference between an old and a new version of an RPM package. Applying a delta RPM onto an old RPM results in a completely new RPM. It is not necessary to have a copy of the old RPM because a delta RPM can also work with an installed RPM. The delta RPM packages are even smaller in size than patch RPMs, which is an advantage when transferring update packages over the Internet. The drawback is that update operations with delta RPMs involved consume considerably more CPU cycles than plain or patch RPMs.

The **makedeltarpm** and **applydelta** binaries are part of the delta RPM suite (package `deltarpm`) and help you create and apply delta RPM packages. With the following commands, you can create a delta RPM called `new.delta.rpm`. The following command assumes that `old.rpm` and `new.rpm` are present:

```
tux > sudo makedeltarpm old.rpm new.rpm new.delta.rpm
```

Using **applydeltarpm**, you can reconstruct the new RPM from the file system if the old package is already installed:

```
tux > sudo applydeltarpm new.delta.rpm new.rpm
```

To derive it from the old RPM without accessing the file system, use the `-r` option:

```
tux > sudo applydeltarpm -r old.rpm new.delta.rpm new.rpm
```

See `/usr/share/doc/packages/deltarpm/README` for technical details.

6.2.4 RPM Queries

With the `-q` option **rpm** initiates queries, making it possible to inspect an RPM archive (by adding the option `-p`) and to query the RPM database of installed packages. Several switches are available to specify the type of information required. See *Table 6.1, "The Most Important RPM Query Options"*.

TABLE 6.1: THE MOST IMPORTANT RPM QUERY OPTIONS

`-i`	Package information
`-l`	File list
`-f FILE`	Query the package that contains the file *`FILE`* (the full path must be specified with *`FILE`*)
`-s`	File list with status information (implies `-l`)
`-d`	List only documentation files (implies `-l`)
`-c`	List only configuration files (implies `-l`)

`--dump`	File list with complete details (to be used with `-l`, `-c`, or `-d`)
`--provides`	List features of the package that another package can request with `--requires`
`--requires`, `-R`	Capabilities the package requires
`--scripts`	Installation scripts (preinstall, postinstall, uninstall)

For example, the command **`rpm -q -i wget`** displays the information shown in *Example 6.2, "rpm -q -i wget"*.

EXAMPLE 6.2: rpm -q -i wget

```
Name        : wget
Version     : 1.14
Release     : 17.1
Architecture: x86_64
Install Date: Mon 30 Jan 2017 14:01:29 CET
Group       : Productivity/Networking/Web/Utilities
Size        : 2046483
License     : GPL-3.0+
Signature   : RSA/SHA256, Thu 08 Dec 2016 07:48:44 CET, Key ID 70af9e8139db7c82
Source RPM  : wget-1.14-17.1.src.rpm
Build Date  : Thu 08 Dec 2016 07:48:34 CET
Build Host  : sheep09
Relocations : (not relocatable)
Packager    : https://www.suse.com/
Vendor      : SUSE LLC <https://www.suse.com/>
URL         : http://www.gnu.org/software/wget/
Summary     : A Tool for Mirroring FTP and HTTP Servers
Description :
Wget enables you to retrieve WWW documents or FTP files from a server.
This can be done in script files or via the command line.
Distribution: SUSE Linux Enterprise 12
```

The option `-f` only works if you specify the complete file name with its full path. Provide as many file names as desired. For example:

```
tux > rpm -q -f /bin/rpm /usr/bin/wget
rpm-4.11.2-15.1.x86_64
wget-1.14-17.1.x86_64
```

If only part of the file name is known, use a shell script as shown in *Example 6.3, "Script to Search for Packages"*. Pass the partial file name to the script shown as a parameter when running it.

EXAMPLE 6.3: SCRIPT TO SEARCH FOR PACKAGES

```
#! /bin/sh
for i in $(rpm -q -a -l | grep $1); do
    echo "\"$i\" is in package:"
    rpm -q -f $i
    echo ""
done
```

The command **`rpm -q --changelog`** *`PACKAGE`* displays a detailed list of change information about a specific package, sorted by date.

With the installed RPM database, verification checks can be made. Initiate these with `-V`, or `--verify`. With this option, **`rpm`** shows all files in a package that have been changed since installation. **`rpm`** uses eight character symbols to give some hints about the following changes:

TABLE 6.2: RPM VERIFY OPTIONS

`5`	MD5 check sum
`S`	File size
`L`	Symbolic link
`T`	Modification time
`D`	Major and minor device numbers
`U`	Owner
`G`	Group
`M`	Mode (permissions and file type)

In the case of configuration files, the letter `c` is printed. For example, for changes to `/etc/wgetrc` (`wget` package):

```
tux > rpm -V wget
S.5....T c /etc/wgetrc
```

The files of the RPM database are placed in `/var/lib/rpm`. If the partition `/usr` has a size of 1 GB, this database can occupy nearly 30 MB, especially after a complete update. If the database is much larger than expected, it is useful to rebuild the database with the option `--rebuilddb`. Before doing this, make a backup of the old database. The **`cron`** script **`cron.daily`** makes daily copies of the database (packed with gzip) and stores them in `/var/adm/backup/rpmdb`. The number of copies is controlled by the variable `MAX_RPMDB_BACKUPS` (default: `5`) in `/etc/sysconfig/backup`. The size of a single backup is approximately 1 MB for 1 GB in `/usr`.

6.2.5 Installing and Compiling Source Packages

All source packages carry a `.src.rpm` extension (source RPM).

Note: Installed Source Packages

Source packages can be copied from the installation medium to the hard disk and unpacked with YaST. They are not, however, marked as installed (`[i]`) in the package manager. This is because the source packages are not entered in the RPM database. Only *installed* operating system software is listed in the RPM database. When you “install” a source package, only the source code is added to the system.

The following directories must be available for **`rpm`** and **`rpmbuild`** in `/usr/src/packages` (unless you specified custom settings in a file like `/etc/rpmrc`):

`SOURCES`
: for the original sources (`.tar.bz2` or `.tar.gz` files, etc.) and for distribution-specific adjustments (mostly `.diff` or `.patch` files)

`SPECS`
: for the `.spec` files, similar to a meta Makefile, which control the *build* process

`BUILD`
: all the sources are unpacked, patched and compiled in this directory

`RPMS`
: where the completed binary packages are stored

`SRPMS`
: here are the source RPMs

When you install a source package with YaST, all the necessary components are installed in `/usr/src/packages`: the sources and the adjustments in `SOURCES` and the relevant `.spec` file in `SPECS`.

Warning: System Integrity

Do not experiment with system components (`glibc`, `rpm`, etc.), because this endangers the stability of your system.

The following example uses the `wget.src.rpm` package. After installing the source package, you should have files similar to those in the following list:

```
/usr/src/packages/SOURCES/wget-1.11.4.tar.bz2
/usr/src/packages/SOURCES/wgetrc.patch
/usr/src/packages/SPECS/wget.spec
```

`rpmbuild` `-bX` `/usr/src/packages/SPECS/wget.spec` starts the compilation. *X* is a wild card for various stages of the build process (see the output of `--help` or the RPM documentation for details). The following is merely a brief explanation:

`-bp`

Prepare sources in `/usr/src/packages/BUILD`: unpack and patch.

`-bc`

Do the same as `-bp`, but with additional compilation.

`-bi`

Do the same as `-bp`, but with additional installation of the built software. Caution: if the package does not support the BuildRoot feature, you might overwrite configuration files.

`-bb`

Do the same as `-bi`, but with the additional creation of the binary package. If the compile was successful, the binary should be in `/usr/src/packages/RPMS`.

`-ba`

Do the same as `-bb`, but with the additional creation of the source RPM. If the compilation was successful, the binary should be in `/usr/src/packages/SRPMS`.

`--short-circuit`

Skip some steps.

The binary RPM created can now be installed with `rpm -i` or, preferably, with `rpm -U`. Installation with `rpm` makes it appear in the RPM database.

Keep in mind, the `BuildRoot` directive in the spec file is deprecated since SUSE Linux Enterprise Desktop 12. If you still need this feature, use the `--buildroot` option as a workaround.For a more detailed background, see the support database at https://www.suse.com/support/kb/doc?id=7017104.

6.2.6 Compiling RPM Packages with build

The danger with many packages is that unwanted files are added to the running system during the build process. To prevent this use `build`, which creates a defined environment in which the package is built. To establish this chroot environment, the **`build`** script must be provided with a complete package tree. This tree can be made available on the hard disk, via NFS, or from DVD. Set the position with **`build --rpms`** *`DIRECTORY`*. Unlike **`rpm`**, the **`build`** command looks for the `.spec` file in the source directory. To build `wget` (like in the above example) with the DVD mounted in the system under `/media/dvd`, use the following commands as `root`:

```
root # cd /usr/src/packages/SOURCES/
root # mv ../SPECS/wget.spec .
root # build --rpms /media/dvd/suse/ wget.spec
```

Subsequently, a minimum environment is established at `/var/tmp/build-root`. The package is built in this environment. Upon completion, the resulting packages are located in `/var/tmp/build-root/usr/src/packages/RPMS`.

The **`build`** script offers several additional options. For example, cause the script to prefer your own RPMs, omit the initialization of the build environment or limit the **`rpm`** command to one of the above-mentioned stages. Access additional information with **`build`** `--help` and by reading the **`build`** man page.

6.2.7 Tools for RPM Archives and the RPM Database

Midnight Commander (**`mc`**) can display the contents of RPM archives and copy parts of them. It represents archives as virtual file systems, offering all usual menu options of Midnight Commander. Display the `HEADER` with F3. View the archive structure with the cursor keys and Enter. Copy archive components with F5.

A full-featured package manager is available as a YaST module. For details, see *Book* "Deployment Guide", *Chapter 9 "Installing or Removing Software"*.

7 System Recovery and Snapshot Management with Snapper

Being able to do file system snapshots providing the ability to do rollbacks on Linux is a feature that was often requested in the past. Snapper, with the `Btrfs` file system or thin-provisioned LVM volumes now fills that gap.

`Btrfs`, a new copy-on-write file system for Linux, supports file system snapshots (a copy of the state of a subvolume at a certain point of time) of subvolumes (one or more separately mountable file systems within each physical partition). Snapshots are also supported on thin-provisioned LVM volumes formatted with XFS, Ext4 or Ext3. Snapper lets you create and manage these snapshots. It comes with a command line and a YaST interface. Starting with SUSE Linux Enterprise Server 12 it is also possible to boot from `Btrfs` snapshots—see *Section 7.3, "System Rollback by Booting from Snapshots"* for more information.

Using Snapper you can perform the following tasks:

- Undo system changes made by **`zypper`** and YaST. See *Section 7.2, "Using Snapper to Undo Changes"* for details.
- Restore files from previous snapshots. See *Section 7.2.2, "Using Snapper to Restore Files"* for details.
- Do a system rollback by booting from a snapshot. See *Section 7.3, "System Rollback by Booting from Snapshots"* for details.
- Manually create snapshots on the fly and manage existing snapshots. See *Section 7.5, "Manually Creating and Managing Snapshots"* for details.

7.1 Default Setup

Snapper on SUSE Linux Enterprise Desktop is set up to serve as an "undo and recovery tool" for system changes. By default, the root partition (`/`) of SUSE Linux Enterprise Desktop is formatted with `Btrfs`. Taking snapshots is automatically enabled if the root partition (`/`) is big enough (approximately more than 16 GB). Taking snapshots on partitions other than `/` is not enabled by default.

Tip: Enabling Snapper in the Installed System

If you disabled Snapper during the installation, you can enable it at any time later. To do so, create a default Snapper configuration for the root file system by running

```
tux > sudo snapper -c root create-config /
```

Afterward enable the different snapshot types as described in *Section 7.1.3.1, "Disabling/Enabling Snapshots"*.

Keep in mind that snapshots require a Btrfs root file system with subvolumes set up as proposed by the installer and a partition size of at least 16 GB.

When a snapshot is created, both the snapshot and the original point to the same blocks in the file system. So, initially a snapshot does not occupy additional disk space. If data in the original file system is modified, changed data blocks are copied while the old data blocks are kept for the snapshot. Therefore, a snapshot occupies the same amount of space as the data modified. So, over time, the amount of space a snapshot allocates, constantly grows. As a consequence, deleting files from a `Btrfs` file system containing snapshots may *not* free disk space!

Note: Snapshot Location

Snapshots always reside on the same partition or subvolume on which the snapshot has been taken. It is not possible to store snapshots on a different partition or subvolume.

As a result, partitions containing snapshots need to be larger than "normal" partitions. The exact amount strongly depends on the number of snapshots you keep and the amount of data modifications. As a rule of thumb you should consider using twice the size than you normally would. To prevent disks from running out of space, old snapshots are automatically cleaned up. Refer to *Section 7.1.3.4, "Controlling Snapshot Archiving"* for details.

7.1.1 Types of Snapshots

Although snapshots themselves do not differ in a technical sense, we distinguish between three types of snapshots, based on the events that trigger them:

Timeline Snapshots

A single snapshot is created every hour. Old snapshots are automatically deleted. By default, the first snapshot of the last ten days, months, and years are kept. Timeline snapshots are disabled by default.

Installation Snapshots

Whenever one or more packages are installed with YaST or Zypper, a pair of snapshots is created: one before the installation starts ("Pre") and another one after the installation has finished ("Post"). In case an important system component such as the kernel has been installed, the snapshot pair is marked as important (`important=yes`). Old snapshots are automatically deleted. By default the last ten important snapshots and the last ten "regular" (including administration snapshots) snapshots are kept. Installation snapshots are enabled by default.

Administration Snapshots

Whenever you administrate the system with YaST, a pair of snapshots is created: one when a YaST module is started ("Pre") and another when the module is closed ("Post"). Old snapshots are automatically deleted. By default the last ten important snapshots and the last ten "regular" snapshots (including installation snapshots) are kept. Administration snapshots are enabled by default.

7.1.2 Directories That Are Excluded from Snapshots

Some directories need to be excluded from snapshots for different reasons. The following list shows all directories that are excluded:

`/boot/grub2/i386-pc`, `/boot/grub2/x86_64-efi`, `/boot/grub2/powerpc-ieee1275`, `/boot/grub2/s390x-emu`

A rollback of the boot loader configuration is not supported. The directories listed above are architecture-specific. The first two directories are present on AMD64/Intel 64 machines, the latter two on IBM POWER and on IBM z Systems, respectively.

`/home`

If `/home` does not reside on a separate partition, it is excluded to avoid data loss on rollbacks.

`/opt`, `/var/opt`

Third-party products usually get installed to `/opt`. It is excluded to avoid uninstalling these applications on rollbacks.

`/srv`

Contains data for Web and FTP servers. It is excluded to avoid data loss on rollbacks.

`/tmp`, `/var/tmp`, `/var/cache`, `/var/crash`

All directories containing temporary files and caches are excluded from snapshots.

`/usr/local`

This directory is used when manually installing software. It is excluded to avoid uninstalling these installations on rollbacks.

`/var/lib/libvirt/images`

The default location for virtual machine images managed with libvirt. Excluded to ensure virtual machine images are not replaced with older versions during a rollback. By default, this subvolume is created with the option `no copy on write`.

`/var/lib/mailman`, `/var/spool`

Directories containing mails or mail queues are excluded to avoid a loss of mails after a rollback.

`/var/lib/named`

Contains zone data for the DNS server. Excluded from snapshots to ensure a name server can operate after a rollback.

`/var/lib/mariadb`, `/var/lib/mysql`, `/var/lib/pgqsl`

These directories contain database data. By default, these subvolumes are created with the option `no copy on write`.

`/var/log`

Log file location. Excluded from snapshots to allow log file analysis after the rollback of a broken system.

7.1.3 Customizing the Setup

SUSE Linux Enterprise Desktop comes with a reasonable default setup, which should be sufficient for most use cases. However, all aspects of taking automatic snapshots and snapshot keeping can be configured according to your needs.

7.1.3.1 Disabling/Enabling Snapshots

Each of the three snapshot types (timeline, installation, administration) can be enabled or disabled independently.

Disabling/Enabling Timeline Snapshots

Enabling. `snapper-c root set-config "TIMELINE_CREATE=yes"`

Disabling. `snapper -c root set-config "TIMELINE_CREATE=no"`
Timeline snapshots are enabled by default, except for the root partition.

Disabling/Enabling Installation Snapshots

Enabling: Install the package `snapper-zypp-plugin`

Disabling: Uninstall the package `snapper-zypp-plugin`
Installation snapshots are enabled by default.

Disabling/Enabling Administration Snapshots

Enabling: Set `USE_SNAPPER` to `yes` in `/etc/sysconfig/yast2`.

Disabling: Set `USE_SNAPPER` to `no` in `/etc/sysconfig/yast2`.
Administration snapshots are enabled by default.

7.1.3.2 Controlling Installation Snapshots

Taking snapshot pairs upon installing packages with YaST or Zypper is handled by the `snapper-zypp-plugin`. An XML configuration file, `/etc/snapper/zypp-plugin.conf` defines, when to make snapshots. By default the file looks like the following:

```
<?xml version="1.0" encoding="utf-8"?>
<snapper-zypp-plugin-conf>
 <solvables>
  <solvable match="w" ❶ important="true" ❷ >kernel-* ❸ </solvable>
  <solvable match="w" important="true">dracut</solvable>
```

```
 6   <solvable match="w" important="true">glibc</solvable>
 7   <solvable match="w" important="true">systemd*</solvable>
 8   <solvable match="w" important="true">udev</solvable>
 9   <solvable match="w">*</solvable> ❹
10  </solvables>
11 </snapper-zypp-plugin-conf>
```

❶ The match attribute defines whether the pattern is a Unix shell-style wild card (`w`) or a Python regular expression (`re`).

❷ If the given pattern matches and the corresponding package is marked as important (for example kernel packages), the snapshot will also be marked as important.

❸ Pattern to match a package name. Based on the setting of the `match` attribute, special characters are either interpreted as shell wild cards or regular expressions. This pattern matches all package names starting with `kernel-`.

❹ This line unconditionally matches all packages.

With this configuration snapshot, pairs are made whenever a package is installed (line 9). When the kernel, dracut, glibc, systemd, or udev packages marked as important are installed, the snapshot pair will also be marked as important (lines 4 to 8). All rules are evaluated.

To disable a rule, either delete it or deactivate it using XML comments. To prevent the system from making snapshot pairs for every package installation for example, comment line 9:

```
 1 <?xml version="1.0" encoding="utf-8"?>
 2 <snapper-zypp-plugin-conf>
 3  <solvables>
 4   <solvable match="w" important="true">kernel-*</solvable>
 5   <solvable match="w" important="true">dracut</solvable>
 6   <solvable match="w" important="true">glibc</solvable>
 7   <solvable match="w" important="true">systemd*</solvable>
 8   <solvable match="w" important="true">udev</solvable>
 9   <!-- <solvable match="w">*</solvable> -->
10  </solvables>
11 </snapper-zypp-plugin-conf>
```

7.1.3.3 Creating and Mounting New Subvolumes

Creating a new subvolume underneath the `/` hierarchy and permanently mounting it is supported. Such a subvolume will be excluded from snapshots. You need to make sure not to create it inside an existing snapshot, since you would not be able to delete snapshots anymore after a rollback.

SUSE Linux Enterprise Desktop is configured with the `/@/` subvolume which serves as an independent root for permanent subvolumes such as `/opt`, `/srv`, `/home` and others. Any new subvolumes you create and permanently mount need to be created in this initial root file system.

To do so, run the following commands. In this example, a new subvolume `/usr/important` is created from `/dev/sda2`.

```
tux > sudo mount /dev/sda2 -o subvol=@ /mnt
tux > sudo btrfs subvolume create /mnt/usr/important
tux > sudo umount /mnt
```

The corresponding entry in `/etc/fstab` needs to look like the following:

```
/dev/sda2 /usr/important btrfs subvol=@/usr/important 0 0
```

Tip: Disable Copy-On-Write (cow)

A subvolume may contain files that constantly change, such as virtualized disk images, database files, or log files. If so, consider disabling the copy-on-write feature for this volume, to avoid duplication of disk blocks. Use the `nodatacow` mount option in `/etc/fstab` to do so:

```
/dev/sda2 /usr/important btrfs nodatacow,subvol=@/usr/important 0 0
```

To alternatively disable copy-on-write for single files or directories, use the command **`chattr +C`** *`PATH`*.

7.1.3.4 Controlling Snapshot Archiving

Snapshots occupy disk space. To prevent disks from running out of space and thus causing system outages, old snapshots are automatically deleted. By default, up to ten important installation and administration snapshots and up to ten regular installation and administration snapshots are kept. If these snapshots occupy more than 50% of the root file system size, additional snapshots will be deleted. A minimum of four important and two regular snapshots are always kept.

Refer to *Section 7.4.1, "Managing Existing Configurations"* for instructions on how to change these values.

7.1.3.5 Using Snapper on Thin-Provisioned LVM Volumes

Apart from snapshots on `Btrfs` file systems, Snapper also supports taking snapshots on thin-provisioned LVM volumes (snapshots on regular LVM volumes are *not* supported) formatted with XFS, Ext4 or Ext3. For more information and setup instructions on LVM volumes, refer to *Book* "Deployment Guide", *Chapter 8 "Advanced Disk Setup", Section 8.2 "LVM Configuration"*.

To use Snapper on a thin-provisioned LVM volume you need to create a Snapper configuration for it. On LVM it is required to specify the file system with `--fstype=lvm(FILESYSTEM)`. `ext3`, `etx4` or `xfs` are valid values for `FILESYSTEM`. Example:

```
tux > sudo snapper -c lvm create-config --fstype="lvm(xfs)" /thin_lvm
```

You can adjust this configuration according to your needs as described in *Section 7.4.1, "Managing Existing Configurations"*.

7.2 Using Snapper to Undo Changes

Snapper on SUSE Linux Enterprise Desktop is preconfigured to serve as a tool that lets you undo changes made by **`zypper`** and YaST. For this purpose, Snapper is configured to create a pair of snapshots before and after each run of **`zypper`** and YaST. Snapper also lets you restore system files that have been accidentally deleted or modified. Timeline snapshots for the root partition need to be enabled for this purpose—see *Section 7.1.3.1, "Disabling/Enabling Snapshots"* for details.

By default, automatic snapshots as described above are configured for the root partition and its subvolumes. To make snapshots available for other partitions such as `/home` for example, you can create custom configurations.

Important: Undoing Changes Compared to Rollback

When working with snapshots to restore data, it is important to know that there are two fundamentally different scenarios Snapper can handle:

Undoing Changes

When undoing changes as described in the following, two snapshots are being compared and the changes between these two snapshots are made undone. Using this method also allows to explicitly select the files that should be restored.

Rollback

When doing rollbacks as described in *Section 7.3, "System Rollback by Booting from Snapshots"*, the system is reset to the state at which the snapshot was taken.

When undoing changes, it is also possible to compare a snapshot against the current system. When restoring *all* files from such a comparison, this will have the same result as doing a rollback. However, using the method described in *Section 7.3, "System Rollback by Booting from Snapshots"* for rollbacks should be preferred, since it is faster and allows you to review the system before doing the rollback.

Warning: Data Consistency

There is no mechanism to ensure data consistency when creating a snapshot. Whenever a file (for example, a database) is written at the same time as the snapshot is being created, it will result in a corrupted or partly written file. Restoring such a file will cause problems. Furthermore, some system files such as `/etc/mtab` must never be restored. Therefore it is strongly recommended to *always* closely review the list of changed files and their diffs. Only restore files that really belong to the action you want to revert.

7.2.1 Undoing YaST and Zypper Changes

If you set up the root partition with `Btrfs` during the installation, Snapper—preconfigured for doing rollbacks of YaST or Zypper changes—will automatically be installed. Every time you start a YaST module or a Zypper transaction, two snapshots are created: a "pre-snapshot" capturing the state of the file system before the start of the module and a "post-snapshot" after the module has been finished.

Using the YaST Snapper module or the **`snapper`** command line tool, you can undo the changes made by YaST/Zypper by restoring files from the "pre-snapshot". Comparing two snapshots the tools also allow you to see which files have been changed. You can also display the differences between two versions of a file (diff).

PROCEDURE 7.1: UNDOING CHANGES USING THE YAST *SNAPPER* MODULE

1. Start the *Snapper* module from the *Miscellaneous* section in YaST or by entering **`yast2 snapper`**.

2. Make sure *Current Configuration* is set to *root*. This is always the case unless you have manually added own Snapper configurations.

3. Choose a pair of pre- and post-snapshots from the list. Both, YaST and Zypper snapshot pairs are of the type *Pre & Post*. YaST snapshots are labeled as `zypp(y2base)` in the *Description column*; Zypper snapshots are labeled `zypp(zypper)`.

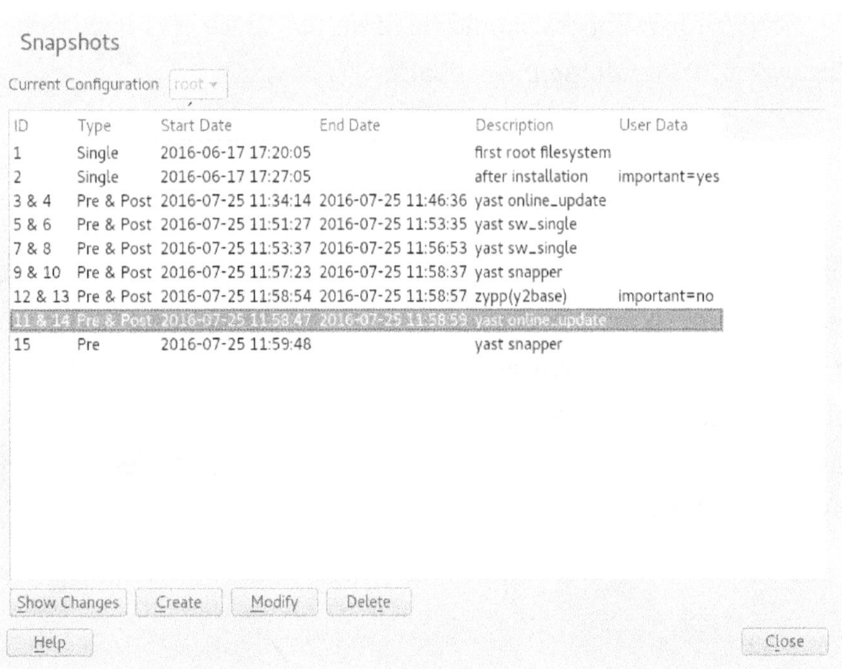

4. Click *Show Changes* to open the list of files that differ between the two snapshots.

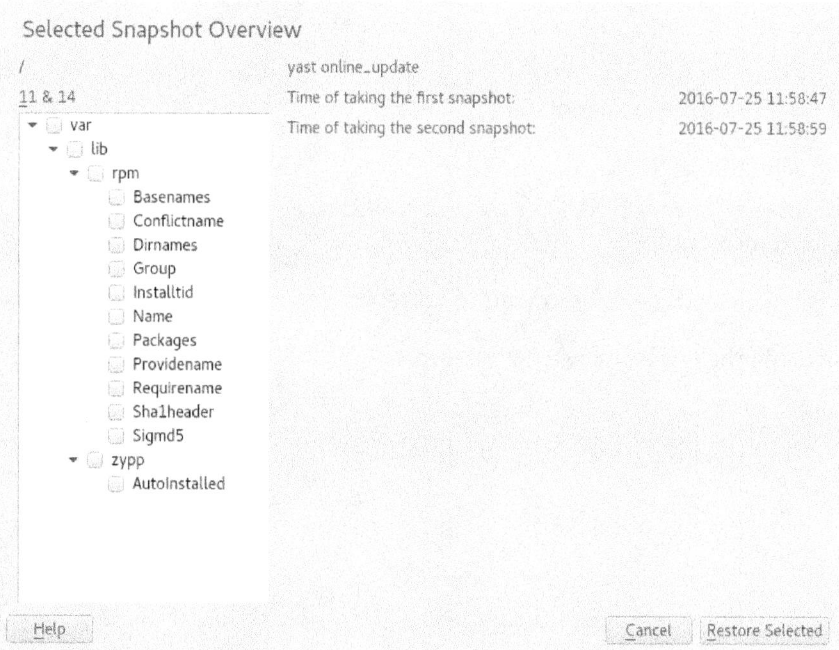

5. Review the list of files. To display a "diff" between the pre- and post-version of a file, select it from the list.

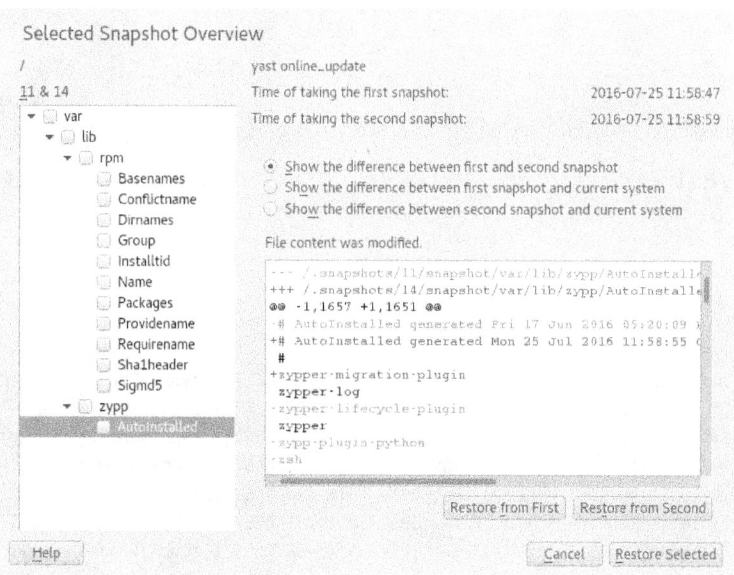

6. To restore one or more files, select the relevant files or directories by activating the respective check box. Click *Restore Selected* and confirm the action by clicking *Yes*.

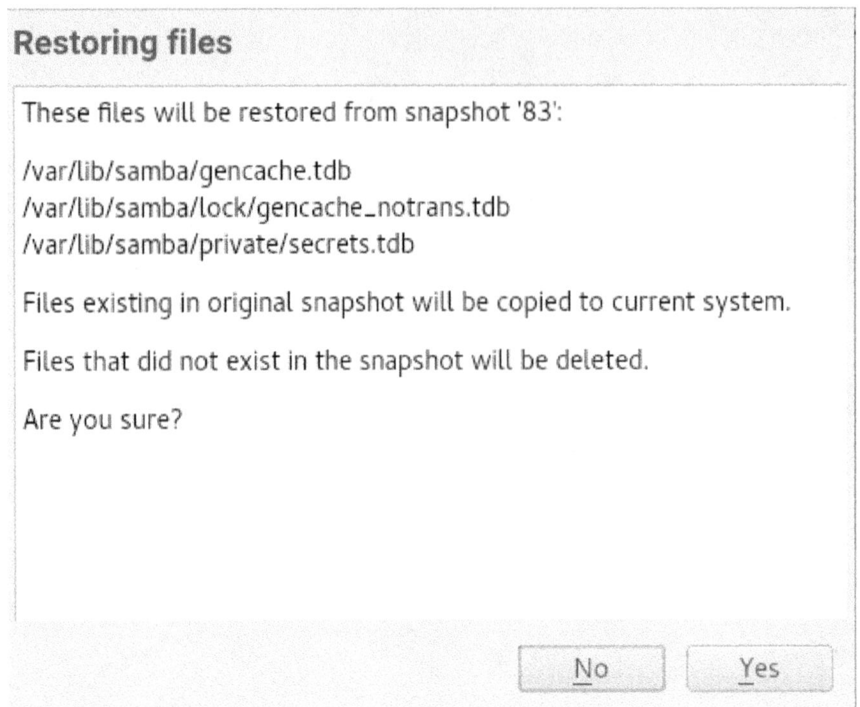
Restoring files

These files will be restored from snapshot '83':

/var/lib/samba/gencache.tdb
/var/lib/samba/lock/gencache_notrans.tdb
/var/lib/samba/private/secrets.tdb

Files existing in original snapshot will be copied to current system.

Files that did not exist in the snapshot will be deleted.

Are you sure?

No Yes

To restore a single file, activate its diff view by clicking its name. Click *Restore From First* and confirm your choice with *Yes*.

PROCEDURE 7.2: UNDOING CHANGES USING THE snapper COMMAND

1. Get a list of YaST and Zypper snapshots by running **`snapper list -t pre-post`**. YaST snapshots are labeled as `yast MODULE_NAME` in the *Description column*; Zypper snapshots are labeled `zypp(zypper)`.

```
tux > sudo snapper list -t pre-post
Pre # | Post # | Pre Date                      | Post Date                     | Description
------+--------+-------------------------------+-------------------------------+--------------
311   | 312    | Tue 06 May 2014 14:05:46 CEST | Tue 06 May 2014 14:05:52 CEST | zypp(y2base)
340   | 341    | Wed 07 May 2014 16:15:10 CEST | Wed 07 May 2014 16:15:16 CEST | zypp(zypper)
342   | 343    | Wed 07 May 2014 16:20:38 CEST | Wed 07 May 2014 16:20:42 CEST | zypp(y2base)
344   | 345    | Wed 07 May 2014 16:21:23 CEST | Wed 07 May 2014 16:21:24 CEST | zypp(zypper)
346   | 347    | Wed 07 May 2014 16:41:06 CEST | Wed 07 May 2014 16:41:10 CEST | zypp(y2base)
348   | 349    | Wed 07 May 2014 16:44:50 CEST | Wed 07 May 2014 16:44:53 CEST | zypp(y2base)
350   | 351    | Wed 07 May 2014 16:46:27 CEST | Wed 07 May 2014 16:46:38 CEST | zypp(y2base)
```

2. Get a list of changed files for a snapshot pair with **`snapper status`** *`PRE..POST`*. Files with content changes are marked with c, files that have been added are marked with + and deleted files are marked with -.

```
tux > sudo snapper status 350..351
+..... /usr/share/doc/packages/mikachan-fonts
```

```
+..... /usr/share/doc/packages/mikachan-fonts/COPYING
+..... /usr/share/doc/packages/mikachan-fonts/dl.html
c..... /usr/share/fonts/truetype/fonts.dir
c..... /usr/share/fonts/truetype/fonts.scale
+..... /usr/share/fonts/truetype/#####-p.ttf
+..... /usr/share/fonts/truetype/#####-pb.ttf
+..... /usr/share/fonts/truetype/#####-ps.ttf
+..... /usr/share/fonts/truetype/#####.ttf
c..... /var/cache/fontconfig/7ef2298fde41cc6eeb7af42e48b7d293-x86_64.cache-4
c..... /var/lib/rpm/Basenames
c..... /var/lib/rpm/Dirnames
c..... /var/lib/rpm/Group
c..... /var/lib/rpm/Installtid
c..... /var/lib/rpm/Name
c..... /var/lib/rpm/Packages
c..... /var/lib/rpm/Providename
c..... /var/lib/rpm/Requirename
c..... /var/lib/rpm/Sha1header
c..... /var/lib/rpm/Sigmd5
```

3. To display the diff for a certain file, run **`snapper diff`** *`PRE`*..*`POST`* *`FILENAME`*. If you do not specify *`FILENAME`*, a diff for all files will be displayed.

```
tux > sudo snapper diff 350..351 /usr/share/fonts/truetype/fonts.scale
--- /.snapshots/350/snapshot/usr/share/fonts/truetype/fonts.scale       2014-04-23
 15:58:57.000000000 +0200
+++ /.snapshots/351/snapshot/usr/share/fonts/truetype/fonts.scale       2014-05-07
 16:46:31.000000000 +0200
@@ -1,4 +1,4 @@
-1174
+1486
 ds=y:ai=0.2:luximr.ttf -b&h-luxi mono-bold-i-normal--0-0-0-0-c-0-iso10646-1
 ds=y:ai=0.2:luximr.ttf -b&h-luxi mono-bold-i-normal--0-0-0-0-c-0-iso8859-1
[...]
```

4. To restore one or more files run **`snapper -v undochange`** *`PRE`*..*`POST`* *`FILENAMES`*. If you do not specify a *`FILENAMES`*, all changed files will be restored.

```
tux > sudo snapper -v undochange 350..351
     create:0 modify:13 delete:7
     undoing change...
     deleting /usr/share/doc/packages/mikachan-fonts
     deleting /usr/share/doc/packages/mikachan-fonts/COPYING
     deleting /usr/share/doc/packages/mikachan-fonts/dl.html
     deleting /usr/share/fonts/truetype/#####-p.ttf
     deleting /usr/share/fonts/truetype/#####-pb.ttf
```

```
deleting /usr/share/fonts/truetype/#####-ps.ttf
deleting /usr/share/fonts/truetype/#####.ttf
modifying /usr/share/fonts/truetype/fonts.dir
modifying /usr/share/fonts/truetype/fonts.scale
modifying /var/cache/fontconfig/7ef2298fde41cc6eeb7af42e48b7d293-x86_64.cache-4
modifying /var/lib/rpm/Basenames
modifying /var/lib/rpm/Dirnames
modifying /var/lib/rpm/Group
modifying /var/lib/rpm/Installtid
modifying /var/lib/rpm/Name
modifying /var/lib/rpm/Packages
modifying /var/lib/rpm/Providename
modifying /var/lib/rpm/Requirename
modifying /var/lib/rpm/Sha1header
modifying /var/lib/rpm/Sigmd5
undoing change done
```

Warning: Reverting User Additions

Reverting user additions via undoing changes with Snapper is not recommended. Since certain directories are excluded from snapshots, files belonging to these users will remain in the file system. If a user with the same user ID as a deleted user is created, this user will inherit the files. Therefore it is strongly recommended to use the YaST *User and Group Management* tool to remove users.

7.2.2 Using Snapper to Restore Files

Apart from the installation and administration snapshots, Snapper creates timeline snapshots. You can use these backup snapshots to restore files that have accidentally been deleted or to restore a previous version of a file. By using Snapper's diff feature you can also find out which modifications have been made at a certain point of time.

Being able to restore files is especially interesting for data, which may reside on subvolumes or partitions for which snapshots are not taken by default. To be able to restore files from home directories, for example, create a separate Snapper configuration for `/home` doing automatic timeline snapshots. See *Section 7.4, "Creating and Modifying Snapper Configurations"* for instructions.

Warning: Restoring Files Compared to Rollback

Snapshots taken from the root file system (defined by Snapper's root configuration), can be used to do a system rollback. The recommended way to do such a rollback is to boot from the snapshot and then perform the rollback. See *Section 7.3, "System Rollback by Booting from Snapshots"* for details.

Performing a rollback would also be possible by restoring all files from a root file system snapshot as described below. However, this is not recommended. You may restore single files, for example a configuration file from the `/etc` directory, but not the complete list of files from the snapshot.

This restriction only affects snapshots taken from the root file system!

PROCEDURE 7.3: RESTORING FILES USING THE YAST *SNAPPER* MODULE

1. Start the *Snapper* module from the *Miscellaneous* section in YaST or by entering **`yast2 snapper`**.
2. Choose the *Current Configuration* from which to choose a snapshot.
3. Select a timeline snapshot from which to restore a file and choose *Show Changes*. Timeline snapshots are of the type *Single* with a description value of *timeline*.
4. Select a file from the text box by clicking the file name. The difference between the snapshot version and the current system is shown. Activate the check box to select the file for restore. Do so for all files you want to restore.
5. Click *Restore Selected* and confirm the action by clicking *Yes*.

PROCEDURE 7.4: RESTORING FILES USING THE `snapper` COMMAND

1. Get a list of timeline snapshots for a specific configuration by running the following command:

```
tux > sudo snapper -c CONFIG list -t single | grep timeline
```

   `CONFIG` needs to be replaced by an existing Snapper configuration. Use **`snapper list-configs`** to display a list.

2. Get a list of changed files for a given snapshot by running the following command:

```
tux > sudo snapper -c CONFIG status SNAPSHOT_ID..0
```

Replace *SNAPSHOT_ID* by the ID for the snapshot from which you want to restore the file(s).

3. Optionally list the differences between the current file version and the one from the snapshot by running

```
tux > sudo snapper -c CONFIG diff SNAPSHOT_ID..0 FILE NAME
```

If you do not specify *<FILE NAME>*, the difference for all files are shown.

4. To restore one or more files, run

```
tux > sudo snapper -c CONFIG -v undochange SNAPSHOT_ID..0 FILENAME1 FILENAME2
```

If you do not specify file names, all changed files will be restored.

7.3 System Rollback by Booting from Snapshots

The GRUB 2 version included on SUSE Linux Enterprise Desktop can boot from Btrfs snapshots. Together with Snapper's rollback feature, this allows to recover a misconfigured system. Only snapshots created for the default Snapper configuration (`root`) are bootable.

Important: Supported Configuration

As of SUSE Linux Enterprise Desktop 12 SP3 system rollbacks are only supported if the default subvolume configuration of the root partition has not been changed.

When booting a snapshot, the parts of the file system included in the snapshot are mounted read-only; all other file systems and parts that are excluded from snapshots are mounted read-write and can be modified.

Important: Undoing Changes Compared to Rollback

When working with snapshots to restore data, it is important to know that there are two fundamentally different scenarios Snapper can handle:

Undoing Changes

When undoing changes as described in *Section 7.2, "Using Snapper to Undo Changes"*, two snapshots are compared and the changes between these two snapshots are reverted. Using this method also allows to explicitly exclude selected files from being restored.

Rollback

When doing rollbacks as described in the following, the system is reset to the state at which the snapshot was taken.

To do a rollback from a bootable snapshot, the following requirements must be met. When doing a default installation, the system is set up accordingly.

REQUIREMENTS FOR A ROLLBACK FROM A BOOTABLE SNAPSHOT

- The root file system needs to be Btrfs. Booting from LVM volume snapshots is not supported.
- The root file system needs to be on a single device, a single partition and a single subvolume. Directories that are excluded from snapshots, such as `/srv` (see *Section 7.1.2, "Directories That Are Excluded from Snapshots"* for a full list) may reside on separate partitions.
- The system needs to be bootable via the installed boot loader.

To perform a rollback from a bootable snapshot, do as follows:

1. Boot the system. In the boot menu choose *Bootable snapshots* and select the snapshot you want to boot. The list of snapshots is listed by date—the most recent snapshot is listed first.
2. Log in to the system. Carefully check whether everything works as expected. Note that you cannot write to any directory that is part of the snapshot. Data you write to other directories will *not* get lost, regardless of what you do next.

3. Depending on whether you want to perform the rollback or not, choose your next step:

   a. If the system is in a state where you do not want to do a rollback, reboot to boot into the current system state. You can then choose a different snapshot, or start the rescue system.

   b. To perform the rollback, run

   ```
   tux > sudo snapper rollback
   ```

   and reboot afterward. On the boot screen, choose the default boot entry to reboot into the reinstated system. A snapshot of the file system status before the rollback is created. The default subvolume for root will be replaced with a fresh read-write snapshot. For details, see *Section 7.3.1, "Snapshots after Rollback"*.
   It is useful to add a description for the snapshot with the `-d` option. For example:

   ```
   New file system root since rollback on DATE TIME
   ```

Tip: Rolling Back to a Specific Installation State

If snapshots are not disabled during installation, an initial bootable snapshot is created at the end of the initial system installation. You can go back to that state at any time by booting this snapshot. The snapshot can be identified by the description `after installation`.

A bootable snapshot is also created when starting a system upgrade to a service pack or a new major release (provided snapshots are not disabled).

7.3.1 Snapshots after Rollback

Before a rollback is performed, a snapshot of the running file system is created. The description references the ID of the snapshot that was restored in the rollback.

Snapshots created by rollbacks receive the value `number` for the `Cleanup` attribute. The rollback snapshots are therefore automatically deleted when the set number of snapshots is reached. Refer to *Section 7.6, "Automatic Snapshot Clean-Up"* for details. If the snapshot contains important data, extract the data from the snapshot before it is removed.

7.3.1.1 Example of Rollback Snapshot

For example, after a fresh installation the following snapshots are available on the system:

```
root # snapper --iso list
Type   | # |     | Cleanup | Description           | Userdata
-------+---+ ... +---------+-----------------------+-------------
single | 0 |     |         | current               |
single | 1 |     |         | first root filesystem |
single | 2 |     | number  | after installation    | important=yes
```

After running **`sudo snapper rollback`** snapshot `3` is created and contains the state of the system before the rollback was executed. Snapshot `4` is the new default Btrfs subvolume and thus the system after a reboot.

```
root # snapper --iso list
Type   | # |     | Cleanup | Description           | Userdata
-------+---+ ... +---------+-----------------------+-------------
single | 0 |     |         | current               |
single | 1 |     | number  | first root filesystem |
single | 2 |     | number  | after installation    | important=yes
single | 3 |     | number  | rollback backup of #1 | important=yes
single | 4 |     |         |                       |
```

7.3.2 Accessing and Identifying Snapshot Boot Entries

To boot from a snapshot, reboot your machine and choose *Start Bootloader from a read-only snapshot*. A screen listing all bootable snapshots opens. The most recent snapshot is listed first, the oldest last. Use the keys ↓ and ↑ to navigate and press Enter to activate the selected snapshot. Activating a snapshot from the boot menu does not reboot the machine immediately, but rather opens the boot loader of the selected snapshot.

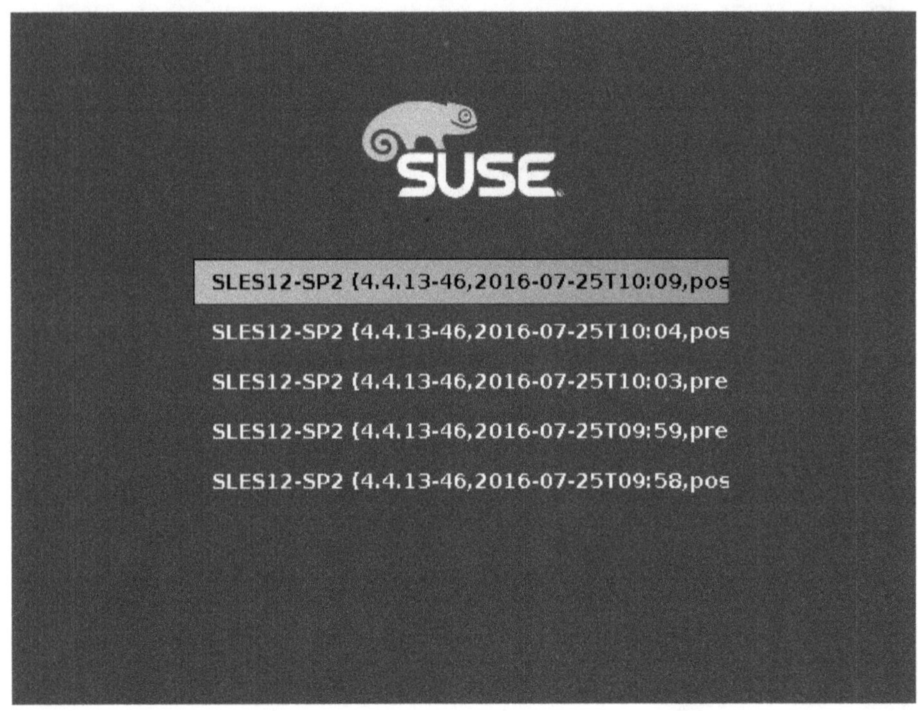

FIGURE 7.1: BOOT LOADER: SNAPSHOTS

Each snapshot entry in the boot loader follows a naming scheme which makes it possible to identify it easily:

```
[*] ❶ OS ❷ (KERNEL ❸ ,DATE ❹ TTIME ❺ ,DESCRIPTION ❻ )
```

❶ If the snapshot was marked `important`, the entry is marked with a `*`.

❷ Operating system label.

❹ Date in the format `YYYY-MM-DD`.

❺ Time in the format `HH:MM`.

❻ This field contains a description of the snapshot. In case of a manually created snapshot this is the string created with the option `--description` or a custom string (see *Tip: Setting a Custom Description for Boot Loader Snapshot Entries*). In case of an automatically created snapshot, it is the tool that was called, for example `zypp(zypper)` or `yast_sw_single`. Long descriptions may be truncated, depending on the size of the boot screen.

Tip: Setting a Custom Description for Boot Loader Snapshot Entries

It is possible to replace the default string in the description field of a snapshot with a custom string. This is for example useful if an automatically created description is not sufficient, or a user-provided description is too long. To set a custom string *STRING* for snapshot *NUMBER*, use the following command:

```
tux > sudo snapper modify --userdata "bootloader=STRING" NUMBER
```

The description should be no longer than 25 characters—everything that exceeds this size will not be readable on the boot screen.

7.3.3 Limitations

A *complete* system rollback, restoring the complete system to the identical state as it was in when a snapshot was taken, is not possible.

7.3.3.1 Directories Excluded from Snapshots

Root file system snapshots do not contain all directories. See *Section 7.1.2, "Directories That Are Excluded from Snapshots"* for details and reasons. As a general consequence, data from these directories is not restored, resulting in the following limitations.

Add-ons and Third Party Software may be Unusable after a Rollback

Applications and add-ons installing data in subvolumes excluded from the snapshot, such as `/opt`, may not work after a rollback, if others parts of the application data are also installed on subvolumes included in the snapshot. Re-install the application or the add-on to solve this problem.

File Access Problems

If an application had changed file permissions and/or ownership in between snapshot and current system, the application may not be able to access these files. Reset permissions and/or ownership for the affected files after the rollback.

Incompatible Data Formats

If a service or an application has established a new data format in between snapshot and current system, the application may not be able to read the affected data files after a rollback.

Subvolumes with a Mixture of Code and Data

Subvolumes like `/srv` may contain a mixture of code and data. A rollback may result in non-functional code. A downgrade of the PHP version, for example, may result in broken PHP scripts for the Web server.

User Data

If a rollback removes users from the system, data that is owned by these users in directories excluded from the snapshot, is not removed. If a user with the same user ID is created, this user will inherit the files. Use a tool like **`find`** to locate and remove orphaned files.

7.3.3.2 No Rollback of Boot Loader Data

A rollback of the boot loader is not possible, since all “stages” of the boot loader must fit together. This cannot be guaranteed when doing rollbacks of `/boot`.

7.4 Creating and Modifying Snapper Configurations

The way Snapper behaves is defined in a configuration file that is specific for each partition or `Btrfs` subvolume. These configuration files reside under `/etc/snapper/configs/`.

In case the root file system is big enough (approximately 12 GB), snapshots are automatically enabled for the root file system `/` upon installation. The corresponding default configuration is named `root`. It creates and manages the YaST and Zypper snapshot. See *Section 7.4.1.1, “Configuration Data”* for a list of the default values.

Note: Minimum Root File System Size for Enabling Snapshots

As explained in *Section 7.1, “Default Setup”*, enabling snapshots requires additional free space in the root file system. The amount depends on the amount of packages installed and the amount of changes made to the volume that is included in snapshots. The snapshot frequency and the number of snapshots that get archived also matter.

There is a minimum root file system size that is required in order to automatically enable snapshots during the installation. As of SUSE Linux Enterprise Desktop 12 SP3 this size is approximately 12 GB. This value may change in the future, depending on architecture and the size of the base system. It depends on the values for the following tags in the file `/control.xml` from the installation media:

```
<root_base_size>
<btrfs_increase_percentage>
```

It is calculated with the following formula: *ROOT_BASE_SIZE* * (1 + *BTRFS_INCREASE_PERCENTAGE*/100)

Keep in mind that this value is a minimum size. Consider using more space for the root file system. As a rule of thumb, double the size you would use when not having enabled snapshots.

You may create your own configurations for other partitions formatted with `Btrfs` or existing subvolumes on a `Btrfs` partition. In the following example we will set up a Snapper configuration for backing up the Web server data residing on a separate, `Btrfs`-formatted partition mounted at `/srv/www`.

After a configuration has been created, you can either use **`snapper`** itself or the YaST *Snapper* module to restore files from these snapshots. In YaST you need to select your *Current Configuration*, while you need to specify your configuration for **`snapper`** with the global switch `-c` (for example, **`snapper -c myconfig list`**).

To create a new Snapper configuration, run **`snapper create-config`**:

```
tux > sudo snapper -c www-data 1 create-config /srv/www 2
```

1. Name of configuration file.
2. Mount point of the partition or `Btrfs` subvolume on which to take snapshots.

This command will create a new configuration file `/etc/snapper/configs/www-data` with reasonable default values (taken from `/etc/snapper/config-templates/default`). Refer to Section 7.4.1, "Managing Existing Configurations" for instructions on how to adjust these defaults.

Tip: Configuration Defaults

Default values for a new configuration are taken from `/etc/snapper/config-templates/default`. To use your own set of defaults, create a copy of this file in the same directory and adjust it to your needs. To use it, specify the `-t` option with the create-config command:

```
tux > sudo snapper -c www-data create-config -t MY_DEFAULTS /srv/www
```

7.4.1 Managing Existing Configurations

The **`snapper`** offers several subcommands for managing existing configurations. You can list, show, delete and modify them:

List Configurations

Use the command **`snapper list-configs`** to get all existing configurations:

```
tux > sudo snapper list-configs
Config | Subvolume
-------+----------
root   | /
usr    | /usr
local  | /local
```

Show a Configuration

Use the subcommand **`snapper -c`** *`CONFIG`* **`get-config`** to display the specified configuration. *`Config`* needs to be replaced by a configuration name shown by **`snapper list-configs`**. See *Section 7.4.1.1, "Configuration Data"* for more information on the configuration options.

To display the default configuration run

```
tux > sudo snapper -c root get-config
```

Modify a Configuration

Use the subcommand **`snapper -c`** *`CONFIG`* **`set-config`** *`OPTION=VALUE`* to modify an option in the specified configuration. *`Config`* needs to be replaced by a configuration name shown by **`snapper list-configs`**. Possible values for *`OPTION`* and *`VALUE`* are listed in *Section 7.4.1.1, "Configuration Data"*.

Delete a Configuration

Use the subcommand **snapper -c** ***CONFIG*** **delete-config** to delete a configuration. *Config* needs to be replaced by a configuration name shown by **snapper list-configs**.

7.4.1.1 Configuration Data

Each configuration contains a list of options that can be modified from the command line. The following list provides details for each option. To change a value, run **snapper -c** ***CONFIG*** **set-config** "*KEY=VALUE*".

ALLOW_GROUPS, ALLOW_USERS

Granting permissions to use snapshots to regular users. See *Section 7.4.1.2, "Using Snapper as Regular User"* for more information.

The default value is "".

BACKGROUND_COMPARISON

Defines whether pre and post snapshots should be compared in the background after creation.

The default value is "yes".

EMPTY_*

Defines the clean-up algorithm for snapshots pairs with identical pre and post snapshots. See *Section 7.6.3, "Cleaning Up Snapshot Pairs That Do Not Differ"* for details.

FSTYPE

File system type of the partition. Do not change.

The default value is "btrfs".

NUMBER_*

Defines the clean-up algorithm for installation and admin snapshots. See *Section 7.6.1, "Cleaning Up Numbered Snapshots"* for details.

QGROUP / SPACE_LIMIT

Adds quota support to the clean-up algorithms. See *Section 7.6.5, "Adding Disk Quota Support"* for details.

SUBVOLUME

Mount point of the partition or subvolume to snapshot. Do not change.

The default value is "/".

`SYNC_ACL`

If Snapper is used by regular users (see Section 7.4.1.2, "Using Snapper as Regular User"), the users must be able to access the `.snapshot` directories and to read files within them. If SYNC_ACL is set to `yes`, Snapper automatically makes them accessible using ACLs for users and groups from the ALLOW_USERS or ALLOW_GROUPS entries.

The default value is `"no"`.

`TIMELINE_CREATE`

If set to `yes`, hourly snapshots are created. Valid values: `yes`, `no`.

The default value is `"no"`.

`TIMELINE_CLEANUP` / `TIMELINE_LIMIT_*`

Defines the clean-up algorithm for timeline snapshots. See Section 7.6.2, "Cleaning Up Timeline Snapshots" for details.

7.4.1.2 Using Snapper as Regular User

By default Snapper can only be used by `root`. However, there are cases in which certain groups or users need to be able to create snapshots or undo changes by reverting to a snapshot:

- Web site administrators who want to take snapshots of `/srv/www`
- Users who want to take a snapshot of their home directory

For these purposes Snapper configurations that grant permissions to users or/and groups can be created. The corresponding `.snapshots` directory needs to be readable and accessible by the specified users. The easiest way to achieve this is to set the SYNC_ACL option to `yes`.

PROCEDURE 7.5: ENABLING REGULAR USERS TO USE SNAPPER

Note that all steps in this procedure need to be run by `root`.

1. If not existing, create a Snapper configuration for the partition or subvolume on which the user should be able to use Snapper. Refer to Section 7.4, "Creating and Modifying Snapper Configurations" for instructions. Example:

```
tux > sudo snapper --config web_data create /srv/www
```

2. The configuration file is created under `/etc/snapper/configs/CONFIG`, where CONFIG is the value you specified with `-c/--config` in the previous step (for example `/etc/snapper/configs/web_data`). Adjust it according to your needs; see Section 7.4.1, "Managing Existing Configurations" for details.

3. Set values for `ALLOW_USERS` and/or `ALLOW_GROUPS` to grant permissions to users and/or groups, respectively. Multiple entries need to be separated by Space. To grant permissions to the user `www_admin` for example, run:

```
tux > sudo snapper -c web_data set-config "ALLOW_USERS=www_admin" SYNC_ACL="yes"
```

4. The given Snapper configuration can now be used by the specified user(s) and/or group(s). You can test it with the `list` command, for example:

```
www_admin:~ > snapper -c web_data list
```

7.5 Manually Creating and Managing Snapshots

Snapper is not restricted to creating and managing snapshots automatically by configuration; you can also create snapshot pairs ("before and after") or single snapshots manually using either the command-line tool or the YaST module.

All Snapper operations are carried out for an existing configuration (see *Section 7.4, "Creating and Modifying Snapper Configurations"* for details). You can only take snapshots of partitions or volumes for which a configuration exists. By default the system configuration (`root`) is used. If you want to create or manage snapshots for your own configuration you need to explicitly choose it. Use the *Current Configuration* drop-down box in YaST or specify the `-c` on the command line (**`snapper -c`** *`MYCONFIG COMMAND`*).

7.5.1 Snapshot Metadata

Each snapshot consists of the snapshot itself and some metadata. When creating a snapshot you also need to specify the metadata. Modifying a snapshot means changing its metadata—you cannot modify its content. Use **`snapper list`** to show existing snapshots and their metadata:

`snapper --config home list`

Lists snapshots for the configuration `home`. To list snapshots for the default configuration (root), use **`snapper -c root list`** or **`snapper list`**.

`snapper list -a`

Lists snapshots for all existing configurations.

`snapper list -t pre-post`

Lists all pre and post snapshot pairs for the default (`root`) configuration.

`snapper list -t single`

Lists all snapshots of the type `single` for the default (`root`) configuration.

The following metadata is available for each snapshot:

- **Type**: Snapshot type, see *Section 7.5.1.1, "Snapshot Types"* for details. This data cannot be changed.
- **Number**: Unique number of the snapshot. This data cannot be changed.
- **Pre Number**: Specifies the number of the corresponding pre snapshot. For snapshots of type post only. This data cannot be changed.
- **Description**: A description of the snapshot.
- **Userdata**: An extended description where you can specify custom data in the form of a comma-separated key=value list: `reason=testing, project=foo`. This field is also used to mark a snapshot as important (`important=yes`) and to list the user that created the snapshot (user=tux).
- **Cleanup-Algorithm**: Cleanup-algorithm for the snapshot, see *Section 7.6, "Automatic Snapshot Clean-Up"* for details.

7.5.1.1 Snapshot Types

Snapper knows three different types of snapshots: pre, post, and single. Physically they do not differ, but Snapper handles them differently.

`pre`

Snapshot of a file system *before* a modification. Each `pre` snapshot has got a corresponding `post` snapshot. Used for the automatic YaST/Zypper snapshots, for example.

`post`

Snapshot of a file system *after* a modification. Each `post` snapshot has got a corresponding `pre` snapshot. Used for the automatic YaST/Zypper snapshots, for example.

`single`

Stand-alone snapshot. Used for the automatic hourly snapshots, for example. This is the default type when creating snapshots.

7.5.1.2 Cleanup-algorithms

Snapper provides three algorithms to clean up old snapshots. The algorithms are executed in a daily cron job. It is possible to define the number of different types of snapshots to keep in the Snapper configuration (see *Section 7.4.1, "Managing Existing Configurations"* for details).

number

Deletes old snapshots when a certain snapshot count is reached.

timeline

Deletes old snapshots having passed a certain age, but keeps several hourly, daily, monthly, and yearly snapshots.

empty-pre-post

Deletes pre/post snapshot pairs with empty diffs.

7.5.2 Creating Snapshots

Creating a snapshot is done by running **`snapper create`** or by clicking *Create* in the YaST module *Snapper*. The following examples explain how to create snapshots from the command line. It should be easy to adopt them when using the YaST interface.

Tip: Snapshot Description

You should always specify a meaningful description to later be able to identify its purpose. Even more information can be specified via the user data option.

`snapper create --description "Snapshot for week 2 2014"`

Creates a stand-alone snapshot (type single) for the default (`root`) configuration with a description. Because no cleanup-algorithm is specified, the snapshot will never be deleted automatically.

`snapper --config home create --description "Cleanup in ~tux"`

Creates a stand-alone snapshot (type single) for a custom configuration named `home` with a description. Because no cleanup-algorithm is specified, the snapshot will never be deleted automatically.

`snapper --config home create --description "Daily data backup" --cleanup-algorithm timeline` >

Creates a stand-alone snapshot (type single) for a custom configuration named `home` with a description. The file will automatically be deleted when it meets the criteria specified for the timeline cleanup-algorithm in the configuration.

`snapper create --type pre --print-number --description "Before the Apache config cleanup" --userdata "important=yes"`

Creates a snapshot of the type `pre` and prints the snapshot number. First command needed to create a pair of snapshots used to save a "before" and "after" state. The snapshot is marked as important.

`snapper create --type post --pre-number 30 --description "After the Apache config cleanup" --userdata "important=yes"`

Creates a snapshot of the type `post` paired with the `pre` snapshot number `30`. Second command needed to create a pair of snapshots used to save a "before" and "after" state. The snapshot is marked as important.

`snapper create --command` *`COMMAND`* `--description "Before and after COMMAND"`

Automatically creates a snapshot pair before and after running *`COMMAND`*. This option is only available when using snapper on the command line.

7.5.3 Modifying Snapshot Metadata

Snapper allows you to modify the description, the cleanup algorithm, and the user data of a snapshot. All other metadata cannot be changed. The following examples explain how to modify snapshots from the command line. It should be easy to adopt them when using the YaST interface.

To modify a snapshot on the command line, you need to know its number. Use **`snapper list`** to display all snapshots and their numbers.

The YaST *Snapper* module already lists all snapshots. Choose one from the list and click *Modify*.

`snapper modify --cleanup-algorithm "timeline"` 10

Modifies the metadata of snapshot 10 for the default (`root`) configuration. The cleanup algorithm is set to `timeline`.

`snapper --config home modify --description "daily backup" -cleanup-algorithm "timeline" 120`

Modifies the metadata of snapshot 120 for a custom configuration named `home`. A new description is set and the cleanup algorithm is unset.

7.5.4 Deleting Snapshots

To delete a snapshot with the YaST *Snapper* module, choose a snapshot from the list and click *Delete*.

To delete a snapshot with the command line tool, you need to know its number. Get it by running **`snapper list`**. To delete a snapshot, run **`snapper delete`** *`NUMBER`*.

Deleting the current default subvolume snapshot is not allowed.

When deleting snapshots with Snapper, the freed space will be claimed by a Btrfs process running in the background. Thus the visibility and the availability of free space is delayed. In case you need space freed by deleting a snapshot to be available immediately, use the option `--sync` with the delete command.

Tip: Deleting Snapshot Pairs

When deleting a `pre` snapshot, you should always delete its corresponding `post` snapshot (and vice versa).

`snapper delete 65`

Deletes snapshot 65 for the default (`root`) configuration.

`snapper -c home delete 89 90`

Deletes snapshots 89 and 90 for a custom configuration named `home`.

`snapper delete --sync 23`

Deletes snapshot 23 for the default (`root`) configuration and makes the freed space available immediately.

Tip: Delete Unreferenced Snapshots

Sometimes the Btrfs snapshot is present but the XML file containing the metadata for Snapper is missing. In this case the snapshot is not visible for Snapper and needs to be deleted manually:

```
btrfs subvolume delete /.snapshots/SNAPSHOTNUMBER/snapshot
rm -rf /.snapshots/SNAPSHOTNUMBER
```

Tip: Old Snapshots Occupy More Disk Space

If you delete snapshots to free space on your hard disk, make sure to delete old snapshots first. The older a snapshot is, the more disk space it occupies.

Snapshots are also automatically deleted by a daily cron job. Refer to *Section 7.5.1.2, "Cleanup-algorithms"* for details.

7.6 Automatic Snapshot Clean-Up

Snapshots occupy disk space and over time the amount of disk space occupied by the snapshots may become large. To prevent disks from running out of space, Snapper offers algorithms to automatically delete old snapshots. These algorithms differentiate between timeline snapshots and numbered snapshots (administration plus installation snapshot pairs). You can specify the number of snapshots to keep for each type.

In addition to that, you can optionally specify a disk space quota, defining the maximum amount of disk space the snapshots may occupy. It is also possible to automatically delete pre and post snapshots pairs that do not differ.

A clean-up algorithm is always bound to a single Snapper configuration, so you need to configure algorithms for each configuration. To prevent certain snapshots from being automatically deleted, refer to *Q:*.

The default setup (`root`) is configured to do clean-up for numbered snapshots and empty pre and post snapshot pairs. Quota support is enabled—snapshots may not occupy more than 50% of the available disk space of the root partition. Timeline snapshots are disabled by default, therefore the timeline clean-up algorithm is also disabled.

7.6.1 Cleaning Up Numbered Snapshots

Cleaning up numbered snapshots—administration plus installation snapshot pairs—is controlled by the following parameters of a Snapper configuration.

`NUMBER_CLEANUP`

Enables or disables clean-up of installation and admin snapshot pairs. If enabled, snapshot pairs are deleted when the total snapshot count exceeds a number specified with `NUMBER_LIMIT` and/or `NUMBER_LIMIT_IMPORTANT` *and* an age specified with `NUMBER_MIN_AGE`. Valid values: `yes` (enable), `no` (disable).
The default value is `"yes"`.
Example command to change or set:

```
tux > sudo snapper -c CONFIG set-config "NUMBER_CLEANUP=no"
```

`NUMBER_LIMIT` / `NUMBER_LIMIT_IMPORTANT`

Defines how many regular and/or important installation and administration snapshot pairs to keep. Only the youngest snapshots will be kept. Ignored if `NUMBER_CLEANUP` is set to `"no"`.
The default value is `"2-10"` for `NUMBER_LIMIT` and `"4-10"` for `NUMBER_LIMIT_IMPORTANT`.
Example command to change or set:

```
tux > sudo snapper -c CONFIG set-config "NUMBER_LIMIT=10"
```

Important: Ranged Compared to Constant Values

In case quota support is enabled (see *Section 7.6.5, "Adding Disk Quota Support"*) the limit needs to be specified as a minimum-maximum range, for example `2-10`. If quota support is disabled, a constant value, for example `10`, needs to be provided, otherwise cleaning-up will fail with an error.

`NUMBER_MIN_AGE`

Defines the minimum age in seconds a snapshot must have before it can automatically be deleted. Snapshots younger than the value specified here will not be deleted, regardless of how many exist.
The default value is `"1800"`.

Example command to change or set:

```
tux > sudo snapper -c CONFIG set-config "NUMBER_MIN_AGE=864000"
```

Note: Limit and Age

NUMBER_LIMIT, NUMBER_LIMIT_IMPORTANT and NUMBER_MIN_AGE are always evaluated. Snapshots are only deleted when *all* conditions are met.

If you always want to keep the number of snapshots defined with NUMBER_LIMIT* regardless of their age, set NUMBER_MIN_AGE to 0.

The following example shows a configuration to keep the last 10 important and regular snapshots regardless of age:

```
NUMBER_CLEANUP=yes
NUMBER_LIMIT_IMPORTANT=10
NUMBER_LIMIT=10
NUMBER_MIN_AGE=0
```

On the other hand, if you do not want to keep snapshots beyond a certain age, set NUMBER_LIMIT* to 0 and provide the age with NUMBER_MIN_AGE.

The following example shows a configuration to only keep snapshots younger than ten days:

```
NUMBER_CLEANUP=yes
NUMBER_LIMIT_IMPORTANT=0
NUMBER_LIMIT=0
NUMBER_MIN_AGE=864000
```

7.6.2 Cleaning Up Timeline Snapshots

Cleaning up timeline snapshots is controlled by the following parameters of a Snapper configuration.

TIMELINE_CLEANUP

Enables or disables clean-up of timeline snapshots. If enabled, snapshots are deleted when the total snapshot count exceeds a number specified with TIMELINE_LIMIT_* *and* an age specified with TIMELINE_MIN_AGE. Valid values: yes, no.
The default value is "yes".

Example command to change or set:

```
tux > sudo snapper -c CONFIG set-config "TIMELINE_CLEANUP=yes"
```

TIMELINE_LIMIT_DAILY, TIMELINE_LIMIT_HOURLY, TIMELINE_LIMIT_MONTHLY, TIMELINE_LIMIT_WEEKLY, TIMELINE_LIMIT_YEARLY

Number of snapshots to keep for hour, day, month, week, and year.

The default value for each entry is "10", except for TIMELINE_LIMIT_WEEKLY, which is set to "0" by default.

TIMELINE_MIN_AGE

Defines the minimum age in seconds a snapshot must have before it can automatically be deleted.

The default value is "1800".

EXAMPLE 7.1: EXAMPLE TIMELINE CONFIGURATION

```
TIMELINE_CLEANUP="yes"
TIMELINE_CREATE="yes"
TIMELINE_LIMIT_DAILY="7"
TIMELINE_LIMIT_HOURLY="24"
TIMELINE_LIMIT_MONTHLY="12"
TIMELINE_LIMIT_WEEKLY="4"
TIMELINE_LIMIT_YEARLY="2"
TIMELINE_MIN_AGE="1800"
```

This example configuration enables hourly snapshots which are automatically cleaned up. TIMELINE_MIN_AGE and TIMELINE_LIMIT_* are always both evaluated. In this example, the minimum age of a snapshot before it can be deleted is set to 30 minutes (1800 seconds). Since we create hourly snapshots, this ensures that only the latest snapshots are kept. If TIMELINE_LIMIT_DAILY is set to not zero, this means that the first snapshot of the day is kept, too.

SNAPSHOTS TO BE KEPT

- Hourly: The last 24 snapshots that have been made.
- Daily: The first daily snapshot that has been made is kept from the last seven days.
- Monthly: The first snapshot made on the last day of the month is kept for the last twelve months.

- Weekly: The first snapshot made on the last day of the week is kept from the last four weeks.
- Yearly: The first snapshot made on the last day of the year is kept for the last two years.

7.6.3 Cleaning Up Snapshot Pairs That Do Not Differ

As explained in *Section 7.1.1, "Types of Snapshots"*, whenever you run a YaST module or execute Zypper, a pre snapshot is created on start-up and a post snapshot is created when exiting. In case you have not made any changes there will be no difference between the pre and post snapshots. Such "empty" snapshot pairs can be automatically be deleted by setting the following parameters in a Snapper configuration:

`EMPTY_PRE_POST_CLEANUP`
: If set to `yes`, pre and post snapshot pairs that do not differ will be deleted.
The default value is `"yes"`.

`EMPTY_PRE_POST_MIN_AGE`
: Defines the minimum age in seconds a pre and post snapshot pair that does not differ must have before it can automatically be deleted.
The default value is `"1800"`.

7.6.4 Cleaning Up Manually Created Snapshots

Snapper does not offer custom clean-up algorithms for manually created snapshots. However, you can assign the number or timeline clean-up algorithm to a manually created snapshot. If you do so, the snapshot will join the "clean-up queue" for the algorithm you specified. You can specify a clean-up algorithm when creating a snapshot, or by modifying an existing snapshot:

`snapper create --description "Test" --cleanup-algorithm number`
: Creates a stand-alone snapshot (type single) for the default (root) configuration and assigns the `number` clean-up algorithm.

`snapper modify --cleanup-algorithm "timeline" 25`
: Modifies the snapshot with the number 25 and assigns the clean-up algorithm `timeline`.

7.6.5 Adding Disk Quota Support

In addition to the number and/or timeline clean-up algorithms described above, Snapper supports quotas. You can define what percentage of the available space snapshots are allowed to occupy. This percentage value always applies to the Btrfs subvolume defined in the respective Snapper configuration.

If Snapper was enabled during the installation, quota support is automatically enabled. In case you manually enable Snapper at a later point in time, you can enable quota support by running **`snapper setup-quota`**. This requires a valid configuration (see *Section 7.4, "Creating and Modifying Snapper Configurations"* for more information).

Quota support is controlled by the following parameters of a Snapper configuration.

`QGROUP`

The Btrfs quota group used by Snapper. If not set, run **`snapper setup-quota`**. If already set, only change if you are familiar with **`man 8 btrfs-qgroup`**. This value is set with **`snapper setup-quota`** and should not be changed.

`SPACE_LIMIT`

Limit of space snapshots are allowed to use in fractions of 1 (100%). Valid values range from 0 to 1 (0.1 = 10%, 0.2 = 20%, ...).

The following limitations and guidelines apply:

- Quotas are only activated in *addition* to an existing number and/or timeline clean-up algorithm. If no clean-up algorithm is active, quota restrictions are not applied.
- With quota support enabled, Snapper will perform two clean-up runs if required. The first run will apply the rules specified for number and timeline snapshots. Only if the quota is exceeded after this run, the quota-specific rules will be applied in a second run.
- Even if quota support is enabled, Snapper will always keep the number of snapshots specified with the `NUMBER_LIMIT*` and `TIMELINE_LIMIT*` values, even if the quota will be exceeded. It is therefore recommended to specify ranged values (`MIN-MAX`) for `NUMBER_LIMIT*` and `TIMELINE_LIMIT*` to ensure the quota can be applied.
  If, for example, `NUMBER_LIMIT=5-20` is set, Snapper will perform a first clean-up run and reduce the number of regular numbered snapshots to 20. In case these 20 snapshots exceed the quota, Snapper will delete the oldest ones in a second run until the quota is met. A minimum of five snapshots will always be kept, regardless of the amount of space they occupy.

7.7 Frequently Asked Questions

Q: *Why does Snapper Never Show Changes in `/var/log`, `/tmp` and Other Directories?*

A: For some directories we decided to exclude them from snapshots. See *Section 7.1.2, "Directories That Are Excluded from Snapshots"* for a list and reasons. To exclude a path from snapshots we create a subvolume for that path.

Q: *How much disk space is used by snapshots? How to free disk space?*

A: Displaying the amount of disk space a snapshot allocates is currently not supported by the `Btrfs` tools. However, if you have quota enabled, it is possible to determine how much space would be freed if *all* snapshots would be deleted:

1. Get the quota group ID (`1/0` in the following example):

```
tux > sudo snapper -c root get-config | grep QGROUP
QGROUP                    | 1/0
```

2. Rescan the subvolume quotas:

```
tux > sudo btrfs quota rescan -w /
```

3. Show the data of the quota group (`1/0` in the following example):

```
tux > sudo btrfs qgroup show / | grep "1/0"
1/0            4.80GiB     108.82MiB
```

   The third column shows the amount of space that would be freed when deleting all snapshots (`108.82MiB`).

To free space on a `Btrfs` partition containing snapshots you need to delete unneeded snapshots rather than files. Older snapshots occupy more space than recent ones. See *Section 7.1.3.4, "Controlling Snapshot Archiving"* for details.

Doing an upgrade from one service pack to another results in snapshots occupying a lot of disk space on the system subvolumes, because a lot of data gets changed (package updates). Manually deleting these snapshots after they are no longer needed is recommended. See *Section 7.5.4, "Deleting Snapshots"* for details.

Q: *Can I Boot a Snapshot from the Boot Loader?*

A: Yes—refer to *Section 7.3, "System Rollback by Booting from Snapshots"* for details.

Q: *How to make a snapshot permanent?*

A: Currently Snapper does not offer means to prevent a snapshot from being deleted manually. However, you can prevent snapshots from being automatically deleted by clean-up algorithms. Manually created snapshots (see *Section 7.5.2, "Creating Snapshots"*) have no clean-up algorithm assigned unless you specify one with `--cleanup-algorithm`. Automatically created snapshots always either have the `number` or `timeline` algorithm assigned. To remove such an assignment from one or more snapshots, proceed as follows:

1. List all available snapshots:

```
tux > sudo snapper list -a
```

2. Memorize the number of the snapshot(s) you want to prevent from being deleted.

3. Run the following command and replace the number placeholders with the number(s) you memorized:

```
tux > sudo snapper modify --cleanup-algorithm "" #1 #2 #n
```

4. Check the result by running **`snapper list -a`** again. The entry in the column `Cleanup` should now be empty for the snapshots you modified.

Q: *Where can I get more information on Snapper?*

A: See the Snapper home page at http://snapper.io/.

8 Remote Access with VNC

Virtual Network Computing (VNC) enables you to control a remote computer via a graphical desktop (as opposed to a remote shell access). VNC is platform-independent and lets you access the remote machine from any operating system.

SUSE Linux Enterprise Desktop supports two different kinds of VNC sessions: One-time sessions that "live" as long as the VNC connection from the client is kept up, and persistent sessions that "live" until they are explicitly terminated.

Note: Session Types

A machine can offer both kinds of sessions simultaneously on different ports, but an open session cannot be converted from one type to the other.

8.1 The **vncviewer** Client

To connect to a VNC service provided by a server, a client is needed. The default in SUSE Linux Enterprise Desktop is **vncviewer**, provided by the `tigervnc` package.

8.1.1 Connecting Using the vncviewer CLI

To start your VNC viewer and initiate a session with the server, use the command:

```
vncviewer jupiter.example.com:1
```

Instead of the VNC display number you can also specify the port number with two colons:

```
vncviewer jupiter.example.com::5901
```

Note: Display and Port Number

The actual display or port number you specify in the VNC client must be the same as the display or port number picked by the **vncserver** command on the target machine. See *Section 8.3, "Persistent VNC Sessions"* for further info.

8.1.2 Connecting Using the vncviewer GUI

By running `vncviewer` without specifying `--listen` or a host to connect to, it will show a window to ask for connection details. Enter the host into the *VNC server* field like in *Section 8.1.1, "Connecting Using the vncviewer CLI"* and click *Connect*.

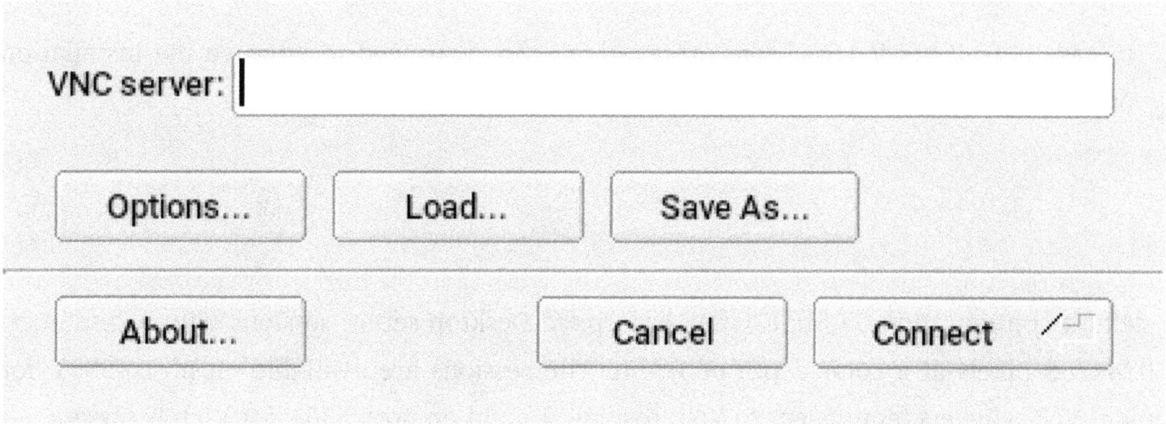

VNC server:

Options... Load... Save As...

About... Cancel Connect

FIGURE 8.1: VNCVIEWER

8.1.3 Notification of Unencrypted Connections

The VNC protocol supports different kinds of encrypted connections, not to be confused with password authentication. If a connection does not use TLS, the text "(Connection not encrypted!)" can be seen in the window title of the VNC viewer.

8.2 One-time VNC Sessions

A one-time session is initiated by the remote client. It starts a graphical login screen on the server. This way you can choose the user which starts the session and, if supported by the login manager, the desktop environment. When you terminate the client connection to such a VNC session, all applications started within that session will be terminated, too. One-time VNC sessions cannot be shared, but it is possible to have multiple sessions on a single host at the same time.

PROCEDURE 8.1: ENABLING ONE-TIME VNC SESSIONS

1. Start *YaST* › *Network Services* › *Remote Administration (VNC)*.

2. Check *Allow Remote Administration.*
3. If necessary, also check *Open Port in Firewall* (for example, when your network interface is configured to be in the External Zone). If you have more than one network interface, restrict opening the firewall ports to a specific interface via *Firewall Details*.
4. Confirm your settings with *Finish.*
5. In case not all needed packages are available yet, you need to approve the installation of missing packages.

8.2.1 Available Configurations

The default configuration on SUSE Linux Enterprise Desktop serves sessions with a resolution of 1024x768 pixels at a color depth of 16-bit. The sessions are available on ports `5901` for "regular" VNC viewers (equivalent to VNC display `1`) and on port `5801` for Web browsers.

Other configurations can be made available on different ports. Ask your system administrator for details if you need to modify the configuration.

VNC display numbers and X display numbers are independent in one-time sessions. A VNC display number is manually assigned to every configuration that the server supports (:1 in the example above). Whenever a VNC session is initiated with one of the configurations, it automatically gets a free X display number.

By default, both the VNC client and server try to communicate securely via a self-signed SSL certificate, which is generated after installation. You can either use the default one, or replace it with your own. When using the self-signed certificate, you need to confirm its signature before the first connection.

8.2.2 Initiating a One-time VNC Session

To connect to a persistent VNC session, a VNC viewer must be installed, see also *Section 8.1, "The `vncviewer` Client"*.

8.2.3 Configuring One-time VNC Sessions

You can skip this section, if you do not need or want to modify the default configuration.

One-time VNC sessions are started via the `xinetd` daemon. A configuration file is located at `/etc/xinetd.d/vnc`. By default it offers six configuration blocks: three for VNC viewers (`vnc1` to `vnc3`), and three serving a Java applet (`vnchttpd1` to `vnchttpd3`). By default only `vnc1` and `vnchttpd1` are active.

To activate a configuration, comment the line `disable = yes` with a `#` character in the first column, or remove that line completely. To deactivate a configuration uncomment or add that line.

The **`Xvnc`** server can be configured via the `server_args` option—see **`Xnvc --help`** for a list of options.

When adding custom configurations, make sure they are not using ports that are already in use by other configurations, other services, or existing persistent VNC sessions on the same host.

Activate configuration changes by entering the following command:

```
sudo systemctl reload xinetd
```

Important: Firewall and VNC Ports

When activating Remote Administration as described in *Procedure 8.1, "Enabling One-time VNC Sessions"*, the ports `5801` and `5901` are opened in the firewall. If the network interface serving the VNC sessions is protected by a firewall, you need to manually open the respective ports when activating additional ports for VNC sessions. See *Book "Security Guide", Chapter 15 "Masquerading and Firewalls"* for instructions.

8.3 Persistent VNC Sessions

A persistent VNC session is initiated on the server. The session and all applications started in this session run regardless of client connections until the session is terminated.

A persistent session can be accessed from multiple clients simultaneously. This is ideal for demonstration purposes where one client has full access and all other clients have view-only access. Another use case are trainings where the trainer might need access to the trainee's desktop. However, most of the times you probably do not want to share your VNC session.

In contrast to one-time sessions that start a display manager, a persistent session starts a ready-to-operate desktop that runs as the user that started the VNC session. Access to persistent sessions is protected by a password.

Access to persistent sessions is protected by two possible types of passwords:

- a regular password that grants full access or
- an optional view-only password that grants a non-interactive (view-only) access.

A session can have multiple client connections of both kinds at once.

PROCEDURE 8.2: STARTING A PERSISTENT VNC SESSION

1. Open a shell and make sure you are logged in as the user that should own the VNC session.
2. If the network interface serving the VNC sessions is protected by a firewall, you need to manually open the port used by your session in the firewall. If starting multiple sessions you may alternatively open a range of ports. See *Book "Security Guide", Chapter 15 "Masquerading and Firewalls"* for details on how to configure the firewall.
   vncserver uses the ports `5901` for display `:1`, `5902` for display `:2`, and so on. For persistent sessions, the VNC display and the X display usually have the same number.
3. To start a session with a resolution of 1024x769 pixel and with a color depth of 16-bit, enter the following command:

   ```
   vncserver -geometry 1024x768 -depth 16
   ```

   The **vncserver** command picks an unused display number when none is given and prints its choice. See **man 1 vncserver** for more options.

When running **vncserver** for the first time, it asks for a password for full access to the session. If needed, you can also provide a password for view-only access to the session.

The password(s) you are providing here are also used for future sessions started by the same user. They can be changed with the **vncpasswd** command.

Important: Security Considerations

Make sure to use strong passwords of significant length (eight or more characters). Do not share these passwords.

To terminate the session shut down the desktop environment that runs inside the VNC session from the VNC viewer as you would shut it down if it was a regular local X session.

If you prefer to manually terminate a session, open a shell on the VNC server and make sure you are logged in as the user that owns the VNC session you want to terminate. Run the following command to terminate the session that runs on display `:1`: **`vncserver -kill :1`**

8.3.1 Connecting to a Persistent VNC Session

To connect to a persistent VNC session, a VNC viewer must be installed, see also *Section 8.1, "The `vncviewer` Client"*.

8.3.2 Configuring Persistent VNC Sessions

Persistent VNC sessions can be configured by editing `$HOME/.vnc/xstartup`. By default this shell script starts the same GUI/window manager it was started from. In SUSE Linux Enterprise Desktop this will either be GNOME or IceWM. If you want to start your session with a window manager of your choice, set the variable `WINDOWMANAGER`:

```
WINDOWMANAGER=gnome vncserver -geometry 1024x768
WINDOWMANAGER=icewm vncserver -geometry 1024x768
```

Note: One Configuration for Each User

Persistent VNC sessions are configured in a single per-user configuration. Multiple sessions started by the same user will all use the same start-up and password files.

8.4 Encrypted VNC Communication

If the VNC server is set up properly, all communication between the VNC server and the client is encrypted. The authentication happens at the beginning of the session, the actual data transfer only begins afterward.

Whether for a one-time or a persistent VNC session, security options are configured via the `-securitytypes` parameter of the **`/usr/bin/Xvnc`** command located on the `server_args` line. The `-securitytypes` parameter selects both authentication method and encryption. It has the following options:

AUTHENTICATIONS

None, TLSNone, X509None

No authentication.

VncAuth, TLSVnc, X509Vnc

Authentication using custom password.

Plain, TLSPlain, X509Plain

Authentication using PAM to verify user's password.

ENCRYPTIONS

None, VncAuth, Plain

No encryption.

TLSNone, TLSVnc, TLSPlain

Anonymous TLS encryption. Everything is encrypted, but there is no verification of the remote host. So you are protected against passive attackers, but not against man-in-the-middle attackers.

X509None, X509Vnc, X509Plain

TLS encryption with certificate. If you use a self-signed certificate, you will be asked to verify it on the first connection. On subsequent connections you will be warned only if the certificate changed. So you are protected against everything except man-in-the-middle on the first connection (similar to typical SSH usage). If you use a certificate signed by a certificate authority matching the machine name, then you get full security (similar to typical HTTPS usage).

Tip: Path to Certificate and Key

With X509 based encryption, you need to specify the path to the X509 certificate and the key with `-X509Cert` and `-X509Key` options.

If you select multiple security types separated by comma, the first one supported and allowed by both client and server will be used. That way you can configure opportunistic encryption on the server. This is useful if you need to support VNC clients that do not support encryption.

On the client, you can also specify the allowed security types to prevent a downgrade attack if you are connecting to a server which you know has encryption enabled (although our vncviewer will warn you with the "Connection not encrypted!" message in that case).

9 File Copying with RSync

Today, a typical user has several computers: home and workplace machines, a laptop, a smartphone or a tablet. This makes the task of keeping files and documents in sync across multiple devices all more important.

Warning: Risk of Data Loss

Before you start using a synchronization tool, you should familiarize yourself with its features and functionality. Make sure to back up your important files.

9.1 Conceptual Overview

For synchronizing a large amount of data over a slow network connection, Rsync offers a reliable method of transmitting only changes within files. This applies not only to text files but also binary files. To detect the differences between files, Rsync subdivides the files into blocks and computes check sums over them.

Detecting changes requires some computing power. So make sure that machines on both ends have enough resources, including RAM.

Rsync can be particularly useful when large amounts of data containing only minor changes need to be transmitted regularly. This is often the case when working with backups. Rsync can also be useful for mirroring staging servers that store complete directory trees of Web servers to a Web server in a DMZ.

Despite its name, Rsync is not a synchronization tool. Rsync is a tool that copies data only in one direction at a time. It does not and cannot do the reverse. If you need a bidirectional tool which is able to synchronize both source and destination, use Csync.

9.2 Basic Syntax

Rsync is a command-line tool that has the following basic syntax:

```
rsync [OPTION] SOURCE [SOURCE]... DEST
```

You can use Rsync on any local or remote machine, provided you have access and write permissions. It is possible to have multiple *SOURCE* entries. The *SOURCE* and *DEST* placeholders can be paths, URLs, or both.

Below are the most common Rsync options:

`-v`
: Outputs more verbose text

`-a`
: Archive mode; copies files recursively and preserves timestamps, user/group ownership, file permissions, and symbolic links

`-z`
: Compresses the transmitted data

Note: Trailing Slashes Count

When working with Rsync, you should pay particular attention to trailing slashes. A trailing slash after the directory denotes the *content* of the directory. No trailing slash denotes the *directory itself*.

9.3 Copying Files and Directories Locally

The following description assumes that the current user has write permissions to the directory `/var/backup`. To copy a single file from one directory on your machine to another path, use the following command:

```
tux > rsync -avz backup.tar.xz /var/backup/
```

The file `backup.tar.xz` is copied to `/var/backup/`; the absolute path will be `/var/backup/backup.tar.xz`.

Do not forget to add the *trailing slash* after the `/var/backup/` directory! If you do not insert the slash, the file `backup.tar.xz` is copied to `/var/backup` (file) *not* inside the directory `/var/backup/`!

Copying a directory is similar to copying a single file. The following example copies the directory `tux/` and its content into the directory `/var/backup/`:

```
tux > rsync -avz tux /var/backup/
```

Find the copy in the absolute path `/var/backup/tux/`.

9.4 Copying Files and Directories Remotely

The Rsync tool is required on both machines. To copy files from or to remote directories requires an IP address or a domain name. A user name is optional if your current user names on the local and remote machine are the same.

To copy the file `file.tar.xz` from your local host to the remote host `192.168.1.1` with same users (being local and remote), use the following command:

```
tux > rsync -avz file.tar.xz  tux@192.168.1.1:
```

Depending on what you prefer, these commands are also possible and equivalent:

```
tux > rsync -avz file.tar.xz 192.168.1.1:~
tux > rsync -avz file.tar.xz 192.168.1.1:/home/tux
```

In all cases with standard configuration, you will be prompted to enter your passphrase of the remote user. This command will copy `file.tar.xz` to the home directory of user `tux` (usually `/home/tux`).

Copying a directory remotely is similar to copying a directory locally. The following example copies the directory `tux/` and its content into the remote directory `/var/backup/` on the `192.168.1.1` host:

```
tux > rsync -avz tux 192.168.1.1:/var/backup/
```

Assuming you have write permissions on the host `192.168.1.1`, you will find the copy in the absolute path `/var/backup/tux`.

9.5 Configuring and Using an Rsync Server

Rsync can run as a daemon (`rsyncd`) listing on default port 873 for incoming connections. This daemon can receive “copying targets”.

The following description explains how to create an Rsync server on `jupiter` with a *backup* target. This target can be used to store your backups. To create an Rsync server, do the following:

PROCEDURE 9.1: SETTING UP AN RSYNC SERVER

1. On jupiter, create a directory to store all your backup files. In this example, we use `/var/backup`:

   ```
   root # mkdir /var/backup
   ```

2. Specify ownership. In this case, the directory is owned by user `tux` in group `users`:

   ```
   root # chown tux.users /var/backup
   ```

3. Configure the rsyncd daemon.
   We will separate the configuration file into a main file and some "modules" which hold your backup target. This makes it easier to add additional targets later. Global values can be stored in `/etc/rsyncd.d/*.inc` files, whereas your modules are placed in `/etc/rsyncd.d/*.conf` files:

   a. Create a directory `/etc/rsyncd.d/`:

      ```
      root # mkdir /etc/rsyncd.d/
      ```

   b. In the main configuration file `/etc/rsyncd.conf`, add the following lines:

      ```
      # rsyncd.conf main configuration file
      log file = /var/log/rsync.log
      pid file = /var/lock/rsync.lock

      &merge /etc/rsyncd.d ❶
      &include /etc/rsyncd.d ❷
      ```

      ❶ Merges global values from `/etc/rsyncd.d/*.inc` files into the main configuration file.

      ❷ Loads any modules (or targets) from `/etc/rsyncd.d/*.conf` files. These files should not contain any references to global values.

   c. Create your module (your backup target) in the file `/etc/rsyncd.d/backup.conf` with the following lines:

      ```
      # backup.conf: backup module
      [backup] ❶
      ```

```
uid = tux ❷
gid = users ❷
path = /var/backup ❸
auth users = tux ❹
secrets file = /etc/rsyncd.secrets ❺
comment = Our backup target
```

❶ The *backup* target. You can use any name you like. However, it is a good idea to name a target according to its purpose and use the same name in your `*.conf` file.

❷ Specifies the user name or group name that is used when the file transfer takes place.

❸ Defines the path to store your backups (from Step 1).

❹ Specifies a comma-separated list of allowed users. In its simplest form, it contains the user names that are allowed to connect to this module. In our case, only user `tux` is allowed.

❺ Specifies the path of a file that contains lines with user names and plain passwords.

d. Create the `/etc/rsyncd.secrets` file with the following content and replace *PASSPHRASE*:

```
# user:passwd
tux:PASSPHRASE
```

e. Make sure the file is only readable by `root`:

```
root # chmod 0600 /etc/rsyncd.secrets
```

4. Start and enable the rsyncd daemon with:

```
root # systemctl enable rsyncd
root # systemctl start rsyncd
```

5. Test the access to your Rsync server:

```
tux > rsync jupiter::
```

You should see a response that looks like this:

```
backup          Our backup target
```

Otherwise, check your configuration file, firewall and network settings.

The above steps create an Rsync server that can now be used to store backups. The example also creates a log file listing all connections. This file is stored in /var/log/rsyncd.log. This is useful if you want to debug your transfers.

To list the content of your backup target, use the following command:

```
rsync -avz jupiter::backup
```

This command lists all files present in the directory /var/backup on the server. This request is also logged in the log file /var/log/rsyncd.log. To start an actual transfer, provide a source directory. Use . for the current directory. For example, the following command copies the current directory to your Rsync backup server:

```
rsync -avz . jupiter::backup
```

By default, Rsync does not delete files and directories when it runs. To enable deletion, the additional option --delete must be stated. To ensure that no newer files are deleted, the option --update can be used instead. Any conflicts that arise must be resolved manually.

9.6 For More Information

CSync

Bidirectional file synchronizer, see https://www.csync.org/.

RSnapshot

Creates incremental backups, see http://rsnapshot.org.

Unison

A file synchronizer similar to CSync but with a graphical interface, see http://www.seas.upenn.edu/~bcpierce/unison/.

Rear

A disaster recovery framework, see the *Administration Guide* of the SUSE Linux Enterprise High Availability Extension https://www.suse.com/documentation/sle-ha-12/.

10 GNOME Configuration for Administrators

This chapter introduces GNOME configuration options which administrators can use to adjust system-wide settings, such as customizing menus, installing themes, configuring fonts, changing preferred applications, and locking down capabilities.

These configuration options are stored in the GConf system. Access the GConf system with tools such as the **`gconftool-2`** command line interface or the **`gconf-editor`** GUI tool.

10.1 Starting Applications Automatically

To automatically start applications in GNOME, use one of the following methods:

- **To run applications for each user:** Put `.desktop` files in `/usr/share/gnome/autostart`.
- **To run applications for an individual user:** Put `.desktop` files in `~/.config/autostart`.

To disable an application that starts automatically, add `X-Autostart-enabled=false` to the `.desktop` file.

10.2 Automounting and Managing Media Devices

GNOME Files (**`nautilus`**) monitors volume-related events and responds with a user-specified policy. You can use GNOME Files to automatically mount hotplugged drives and inserted removable media, automatically run programs, and play audio CDs or video DVDs. GNOME Files can also automatically import photos from a digital camera.

System administrators can set system-wide defaults. For more information, see *Section 10.3, "Changing Preferred Applications"*.

10.3 Changing Preferred Applications

To change users' preferred applications, edit `/etc/gnome_defaults.conf`. Find further hints within this file.

For more information about MIME types, see http://www.freedesktop.org/Standards/shared-mime-info-spec ↗.

10.4 Adding Document Templates

To add document templates for users, fill in the `Templates` directory in a user's home directory. You can do this manually for each user by copying the files into `~/Templates`, or system-wide by adding a `Templates` directory with documents to `/etc/skel` before the user is created.

A user creates a new document from a template by right-clicking the desktop and selecting *Create Document*.

10.5 For More Information

For more information, see http://help.gnome.org/admin/ ↗.

II Booting a Linux System

11 Introduction to the Booting Process

Booting a Linux system involves different components and tasks. The hardware itself is initialized by the BIOS or the UEFI, which starts the kernel by means of a boot loader. After this point, the boot process is completely controlled by the operating system and handled by `systemd`. `systemd` provides a set of "targets" that boot setups for everyday usage, maintenance or emergencies.

11.1 The Linux Boot Process

The Linux boot process consists of several stages, each represented by a different component. The following list briefly summarizes the boot process and features all the major components involved:

1. **BIOS/UEFI.** After turning on the computer, the BIOS or the UEFI initializes the screen and keyboard, and tests the main memory. Up to this stage, the machine does not access any mass storage media. Subsequently, the information about the current date, time, and the most important peripherals are loaded from the CMOS values. When the first hard disk and its geometry are recognized, the system control passes from the BIOS to the boot loader. If the BIOS supports network booting, it is also possible to configure a boot server that provides the boot loader. On AMD64/Intel 64 systems, PXE boot is needed. Other architectures commonly use the BOOTP protocol to get the boot loader. For more information on UEFI, refer to *Chapter 12, UEFI (Unified Extensible Firmware Interface)*.

2. **Boot Loader.** The first physical 512-byte data sector of the first hard disk is loaded into the main memory and the *boot loader* that resides at the beginning of this sector takes over. The commands executed by the boot loader determine the remaining part of the boot process. Therefore, the first 512 bytes on the first hard disk are called the *Master Boot Record* (MBR). The boot loader then passes control to the actual operating system, in this case, the Linux kernel. More information about GRUB 2, the Linux boot loader, can be found in *Chapter 13, The Boot Loader GRUB 2*. For a network boot, the BIOS acts as the boot loader. It gets the boot image from the boot server and starts the system. This is completely independent of local hard disks.
   If the root file system fails to mount from within the boot environment, it must be checked and repaired before the boot can continue. The file system checker will be automatically started for Ext3 and Ext4 file systems. The repair process is not automated for XFS and

Btrfs file systems, and the user is be presented with information describing the options available to repair the file system. When the file system has been successfully repaired, exiting the boot environment will cause the system to retry mounting the root file system. If successful, the boot will continue normally.

3. **Kernel and `initramfs`.** To pass system control, the boot loader loads both the kernel and an initial RAM-based file system (`initramfs`) into memory. The contents of the `initramfs` can be used by the kernel directly. `initramfs` contains a small executable called `init` that handles the mounting of the real root file system. If special hardware drivers are needed before the mass storage can be accessed, they must be in `initramfs`. For more information about `initramfs`, refer to *Section 11.2, "initramfs"*. If the system does not have a local hard disk, the `initramfs` must provide the root file system for the kernel. This can be done using a network block device like iSCSI or SAN, but it is also possible to use NFS as the root device.

Note: The init Process Naming

Two different programs are commonly named "init":

a. the `initramfs` process mounting the root file system

b. the operating system process setting up the system

In this chapter we will therefore refer to them as "`init` on `initramfs`" and "`systemd`", respectively.

4. **`init` on `initramfs`.** This program performs all actions needed to mount the proper root file system. It provides kernel functionality for the needed file system and device drivers for mass storage controllers with `udev`. After the root file system has been found, it is checked for errors and mounted. If this is successful, the `initramfs` is cleaned and the `systemd` daemon on the root file system is executed. For more information about `init` on `initramfs`, refer to *Section 11.3, "Init on initramfs"*. Find more information about `udev` in *Chapter 22, Dynamic Kernel Device Management with udev*.

5. **`systemd`.** By starting services and mounting file systems, `systemd` handles the actual booting of the system. `systemd` is described in *Chapter 14, The systemd Daemon*.

11.2 initramfs

`initramfs` is a small cpio archive that the kernel can load into a RAM disk. It provides a minimal Linux environment that enables the execution of programs before the actual root file system is mounted. This minimal Linux environment is loaded into memory by BIOS or UEFI routines and does not have specific hardware requirements other than sufficient memory. The `initramfs` archive must always provide an executable named `init` that executes the `systemd` daemon on the root file system for the boot process to proceed.

Before the root file system can be mounted and the operating system can be started, the kernel needs the corresponding drivers to access the device on which the root file system is located. These drivers may include special drivers for certain kinds of hard disks or even network drivers to access a network file system. The needed modules for the root file system may be loaded by `init` on `initramfs`. After the modules are loaded, `udev` provides the `initramfs` with the needed devices. Later in the boot process, after changing the root file system, it is necessary to regenerate the devices. This is done by the `systemd` unit `udev.service` with the command **`udevtrigger`**.

If you need to change hardware (for example, hard disks), and this hardware requires different drivers to be in the kernel at boot time, you must update the `initramfs` file. This is done by calling **`dracut`** `-f` (the option `-f` overwrites the existing initramfs file). To add a driver for the new hardware, edit `/etc/dracut.conf.d/01-dist.conf` and add the following line.

```
force_drivers+="DRIVER1"
```

Replace *`DRIVER1`* with the module name of the driver. If you need to add more than one driver, list them space-separated (*`DRIVER1 DRIVER2`*).

Important: Updating initramfs or init

The boot loader loads `initramfs` or `init` in the same way as the kernel. It is not necessary to re-install GRUB 2 after updating `initramfs` or `init`, because GRUB 2 searches the directory for the right file when booting.

Tip: Changing Kernel Variables

If you change the values of kernel variables via the **sysctl** interface by editing related files (/etc/sysctl.conf or /etc/sysctl.d/*.conf), the change will be lost on the next system reboot. Even if you load the values with **sysctl --system** at runtime, the changes are not saved into the initramfs file. You need to update it by calling **dracut -f** (the option -f overwrites the existing initramfs file).

11.3 Init on initramfs

The main purpose of init on initramfs is to prepare the mounting of and access to the real root file system. Depending on your system configuration, init on initramfs is responsible for the following tasks.

Loading Kernel Modules

Depending on your hardware configuration, special drivers may be needed to access the hardware components of your computer (the most important component being your hard disk). To access the final root file system, the kernel needs to load the proper file system drivers.

Providing Block Special Files

For each loaded module, the kernel generates device events. udev handles these events and generates the required special block files on a RAM file system in /dev. Without those special files, the file system and other devices would not be accessible.

Managing RAID and LVM Setups

If you configured your system to hold the root file system under RAID or LVM, init on initramfs sets up LVM or RAID to enable access to the root file system later.

To change your /usr or swap partitions directly without the help of YaST, further actions are needed. If you forget these steps, your system will start in emergency mode. To avoid starting in emergency mode, perform the following steps:

PROCEDURE 11.1: UPDATING INIT RAM DISK WHEN SWITCHING TO LOGICAL VOLUMES

1. Edit the corresponding entry in /etc/fstab and replace your previous partitions with the logical volume.

2. Execute the following commands:

```
root # mount -a
root # swapon -a
```

3. Regenerate your initial RAM disk (initramfs) with **`mkinitrd`** or **`dracut`**.

4. For z Systems, additionally run **`grub2-install`**.

Find more information about RAID and LVM in *Book "Deployment Guide", Chapter 8 "Advanced Disk Setup"*.

Managing Network Configuration

If you configured your system to use a network-mounted root file system (mounted via NFS), `init` on `initramfs` must make sure that the proper network drivers are loaded and that they are set up to allow access to the root file system.

If the file system resides on a network block device like iSCSI or SAN, the connection to the storage server is also set up by `init` on `initramfs`. SUSE Linux Enterprise Desktop supports booting from a secondary iSCSI target if the primary target is not available. .

When `init` on `initramfs` is called during the initial boot as part of the installation process, its tasks differ from those mentioned above:

Finding the Installation Medium

When starting the installation process, your machine loads an installation kernel and a special `init` containing the YaST installer. The YaST installer is running in a RAM file system and needs to have information about the location of the installation medium to access it for installing the operating system.

Initiating Hardware Recognition and Loading Appropriate Kernel Modules

As mentioned in *Section 11.2, "initramfs"*, the boot process starts with a minimum set of drivers that can be used with most hardware configurations. `init` starts an initial hardware scanning process that determines the set of drivers suitable for your hardware configuration. These drivers are used to generate a custom `initramfs` that is needed to boot the system. If the modules are not needed for boot but for coldplug, the modules can be loaded with `systemd`; for more information, see *Section 14.6.4, "Loading Kernel Modules"*.

Loading the Installation System

When the hardware is properly recognized, the appropriate drivers are loaded. The `udev` program creates the special device files and `init` starts the installation system with the YaST installer.

Starting YaST

Finally, `init` starts YaST, which starts package installation and system configuration.

12 UEFI (Unified Extensible Firmware Interface)

UEFI (Unified Extensible Firmware Interface) is the interface between the firmware that comes with the system hardware, all the hardware components of the system, and the operating system.

UEFI is becoming more and more available on PC systems and thus is replacing the traditional PC-BIOS. UEFI, for example, properly supports 64-bit systems and offers secure booting ("Secure Boot", firmware version 2.3.1c or better required), which is one of its most important features. Lastly, with UEFI a standard firmware will become available on all x86 platforms.

UEFI additionally offers the following advantages:

- Booting from large disks (over 2 TiB) with a GUID Partition Table (GPT).
- CPU-independent architecture and drivers.
- Flexible pre-OS environment with network capabilities.
- CSM (Compatibility Support Module) to support booting legacy operating systems via a PC-BIOS-like emulation.

For more information, see http://en.wikipedia.org/wiki/Unified_Extensible_Firmware_Interface ↗. The following sections are not meant as a general UEFI overview; these are only hints about how some features are implemented in SUSE Linux Enterprise Desktop.

12.1 Secure Boot

In the world of UEFI, securing the bootstrapping process means establishing a chain of trust. The "platform" is the root of this chain of trust; in the context of SUSE Linux Enterprise Desktop, the mainboard and the on-board firmware could be considered the "platform". In other words, it is the hardware vendor, and the chain of trust flows from that hardware vendor to the component manufacturers, the OS vendors, etc.

The trust is expressed via public key cryptography. The hardware vendor puts a so-called Platform Key (PK) into the firmware, representing the root of trust. The trust relationship with operating system vendors and others is documented by signing their keys with the Platform Key.

Finally, security is established by requiring that no code will be executed by the firmware unless it has been signed by one of these "trusted" keys—be it an OS boot loader, some driver located in the flash memory of some PCI Express card or on disk, or be it an update of the firmware itself.

To use Secure Boot, you need to have your OS loader signed with a key trusted by the firmware, and you need the OS loader to verify that the kernel it loads can be trusted.

Key Exchange Keys (KEK) can be added to the UEFI key database. This way, you can use other certificates, as long as they are signed with the private part of the PK.

12.1.1 Implementation on SUSE Linux Enterprise Desktop

Microsoft's Key Exchange Key (KEK) is installed by default.

Note: GUID Partitioning Table (GPT) Required

The Secure Boot feature is enabled by default on UEFI/x86_64 installations. You can find the *Enable Secure Boot Support* option in the *Boot Code Options* tab of the *Boot Loader Settings* dialog. It supports booting when the secure boot is activated in the firmware, while making it possible to boot when it is deactivated.

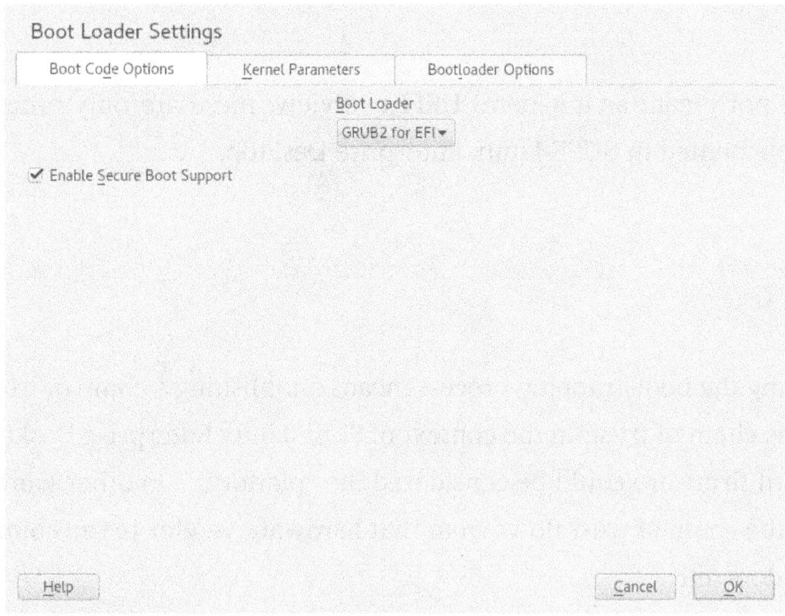

FIGURE 12.1: SECURE BOOT SUPPORT

The Secure Boot feature requires that a GUID Partitioning Table (GPT) replaces the old partitioning with a Master Boot Record (MBR). If YaST detects EFI mode during the installation, it will try to create a GPT partition. UEFI expects to find the EFI programs on a FAT-formatted EFI System Partition (ESP).

Supporting UEFI Secure Boot essentially requires having a boot loader with a digital signature that the firmware recognizes as a trusted key. That key is trusted by the firmware a priori, without requiring any manual intervention.

There are two ways of getting there. One is to work with hardware vendors to have them endorse a SUSE key, which SUSE then signs the boot loader with. The other way is to go through Microsoft's Windows Logo Certification program to have the boot loader certified and have Microsoft recognize the SUSE signing key (that is, have it signed with their KEK). By now, SUSE got the loader signed by UEFI Signing Service (that is Microsoft in this case).

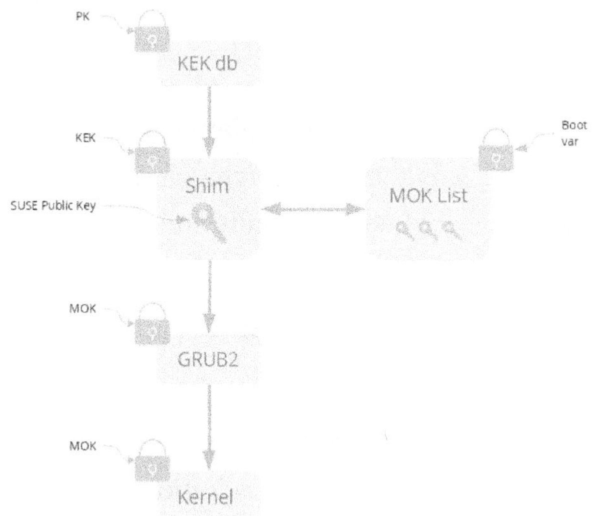

FIGURE 12.2: UEFI: SECURE BOOT PROCESS

At the implementation layer, SUSE uses the `shim` loader which is installed by default. It is a smart solution that avoids legal issues, and simplifies the certification and signing step considerably. The `shim` loader's job is to load a boot loader such as GRUB 2 and verify it; this boot loader in turn will load kernels signed by a SUSE key only. SUSE provides this functionality since SLE11 SP3 on fresh installations with UEFI Secure Boot enabled.

There are two types of trusted users:

- First, those who hold the keys. The Platform Key (PK) allows almost everything. The Key Exchange Key (KEK) allows all a PK can except changing the PK.
- Second, anyone with physical access to the machine. A user with physical access can reboot the machine, and configure UEFI.

UEFI offers two types of variables to fulfill the needs of those users:

- The first is the so-called "Authenticated Variables", which can be updated from both within the boot process (the so-called Boot Services Environment) and the running OS. This can be done only when the new value of the variable is signed with the same key that the old value of the variable was signed with. And they can only be appended to or changed to a value with a higher serial number.
- The second is the so-called "Boot Services Only Variables". These variables are accessible to any code that runs during the boot process. After the boot process ends and before the OS starts, the boot loader must call the `ExitBootServices` call. After that, these variables are no longer accessible, and the OS cannot touch them.

The various UEFI key lists are of the first type, as this allows online updating, adding, and blacklisting of keys, drivers, and firmware fingerprints. It is the second type of variable, the "Boot Services Only Variable", that helps to implement Secure Boot in a secure and open source-friendly manner, and thus compatible with GPLv3.

SUSE starts with `shim`—a small and simple EFI boot loader signed by SUSE and Microsoft.

This allows `shim` to load and execute.

`shim` then goes on to verify that the boot loader it wants to load is trusted. In a default situation `shim` will use an independent SUSE certificate embedded in its body. In addition, `shim` will allow to "enroll" additional keys, overriding the default SUSE key. In the following, we call them "Machine Owner Keys" or MOKs for short.

Next the boot loader will verify and then boot the kernel, and the kernel will do the same on the modules.

12.1.2 MOK (Machine Owner Key)

If the user ("machine owner") wants to replace any components of the boot process, Machine Owner Keys (MOKs) are to be used. The `mokutils` tool will help with signing components and managing MOKs.

The enrollment process begins with rebooting the machine and interrupting the boot process (for example, pressing a key) when `shim` loads. `shim` will then go into enrollment mode, allowing the user to replace the default SUSE key with keys from a file on the boot partition. If the user chooses to do so, `shim` will then calculate a hash of that file and put the result in a "Boot Services Only" variable. This allows `shim` to detect any change of the file made outside of Boot Services and thus avoid tampering with the list of user-approved MOKs.

All of this happens during boot time—only verified code is executing now. Therefore, only a user present at the console can use the machine owner's set of keys. It cannot be malware or a hacker with remote access to the OS because hackers or malware can only change the file, but not the hash stored in the "Boot Services Only" variable.

The boot loader, after having been loaded and verified by `shim`, will call back to `shim` when it wants to verify the kernel—to avoid duplication of the verification code. `Shim` will use the same list of MOKs for this and tell the boot loader whether it can load the kernel.

This way, you can install your own kernel or boot loader. It is only necessary to install a new set of keys and authorize them by being physically present during the first reboot. Because MOKs are a list and not not a single MOK, you can make `shim` trust keys from several vendors, allowing dual- and multi-boot from the boot loader.

12.1.3 Booting a Custom Kernel

The following is based on http://en.opensuse.org/openSUSE:UEFI#Booting_a_custom_kernel ↗.

Secure Boot does not prevent you from using a self-compiled kernel. You must sign it with your own certificate and make that certificate known to the firmware or MOK.

1. Create a custom X.509 key and certificate used for signing:

   ```
   openssl req -new -x509 -newkey rsa:2048 -keyout key.asc \
     -out cert.pem -nodes -days 666 -subj "/CN=$USER/"
   ```

   For more information about creating certificates, see http://en.opensuse.org/openSUSE:UEFI_Image_File_Sign_Tools#Create_Your_Own_Certificate ↗.

2. Package the key and the certificate as a PKCS#12 structure:

   ```
   openssl pkcs12 -export -inkey key.asc -in cert.pem \
     -name kernel_cert -out cert.p12
   ```

3. Generate an NSS database for use with **`pesign`**:

   ```
   certutil -d . -N
   ```

4. Import the key and the certificate contained in PKCS#12 into the NSS database:

```
pk12util -d . -i cert.p12
```

5. “Bless” the kernel with the new signature using **pesign**:

```
pesign -n . -c kernel_cert -i arch/x86/boot/bzImage \
  -o vmlinuz.signed -s
```

6. List the signatures on the kernel image:

```
pesign -n . -S -i vmlinuz.signed
```

   At that point, you can install the kernel in `/boot` as usual. Because the kernel now has a custom signature the certificate used for signing needs to be imported into the UEFI firmware or MOK.

7. Convert the certificate to the DER format for import into the firmware or MOK:

```
openssl x509 -in cert.pem -outform der -out cert.der
```

8. Copy the certificate to the ESP for easier access:

```
sudo cp cert.der /boot/efi/
```

9. Use **mokutil** to launch the MOK list automatically.

   - a. Import the certificate to MOK:

```
mokutil --root-pw --import cert.der
```

     The `--root-pw` option enables usage of the `root` user directly.

     b. Check the list of certificates that are prepared to be enrolled:

```
mokutil --list-new
```

     c. Reboot the system; `shim` should launch MokManager. You need to enter the `root` password to confirm the import of the certificate to the MOK list.

     d. Check if the newly imported key was enrolled:

```
mokutil --list-enrolled
```

- a. Alternatively, this is the procedure if you want to launch MOK manually: Reboot

  b. In the GRUB 2 menu press the 'c' key.

  c. Type:

```
chainloader $efibootdir/MokManager.efi
boot
```

  d. Select *Enroll key from disk.*

  e. Navigate to the `cert.der` file and press Enter.

  f. Follow the instructions to enroll the key. Normally this should be pressing '0' and then 'y' to confirm.
  Alternatively, the firmware menu may provide ways to add a new key to the Signature Database.

12.1.4 Using Non-Inbox Drivers

There is no support for adding non-inbox drivers (that is, drivers that do not come with SUSE Linux Enterprise Desktop) during installation with Secure Boot enabled. The signing key used for SolidDriver/PLDP is not trusted by default.

It is possible to install third party drivers during installation with Secure Boot enabled in two different ways. In both cases:

- Add the needed keys to the firmware database via firmware/system management tools before the installation. This option depends on the specific hardware you are using. Consult your hardware vendor for more information.

- Use a bootable driver ISO from https://drivers.suse.com/ or your hardware vendor to enroll the needed keys in the MOK list at first boot.

To use the bootable driver ISO to enroll the driver keys to the MOK list, follow these steps:

1. Burn the ISO image above to an empty CD/DVD medium.

2. Start the installation using the new CD/DVD medium, having the standard installation media at hand or a URL to a network installation server.

If doing a network installation, enter the URL of the network installation source on the boot command line using the `install=` option.
If doing installation from optical media, the installer will first boot from the driver kit and then ask to insert the first installation disk of the product.

3. An initrd containing updated drivers will be used for installation.

For more information, see https://drivers.suse.com/doc/Usage/Secure_Boot_Certificate.html.

12.1.5 Features and Limitations

When booting in Secure Boot mode, the following features apply:

- Installation to UEFI default boot loader location, a mechanism to keep or restore the EFI boot entry.
- Reboot via UEFI.
- Xen hypervisor will boot with UEFI when there is no legacy BIOS to fall back to.
- UEFI IPv6 PXE boot support.
- UEFI videomode support, the kernel can retrieve video mode from UEFI to configure KMS mode with the same parameters.
- UEFI booting from USB devices is supported.

When booting in Secure Boot mode, the following limitations apply:

- To ensure that Secure Boot cannot be easily circumvented, some kernel features are disabled when running under Secure Boot.
- Boot loader, kernel, and kernel modules must be signed.
- Kexec and Kdump are disabled.
- Hibernation (suspend on disk) is disabled.
- Access to `/dev/kmem` and `/dev/mem` is not possible, not even as root user.
- Access to the I/O port is not possible, not even as root user. All X11 graphical drivers must use a kernel driver.
- PCI BAR access through sysfs is not possible.

- `custom_method` in ACPI is not available.
- debugfs for asus-wmi module is not available.
- the `acpi_rsdp` parameter does not have any effect on the kernel.

12.2 For More Information

- http://www.uefi.org ↗ —UEFI home page where you can find the current UEFI specifications.
- Blog posts by Olaf Kirch and Vojtěch Pavlík (the chapter above is heavily based on these posts):
  - http://www.suse.com/blogs/uefi-secure-boot-plan/ ↗
  - http://www.suse.com/blogs/uefi-secure-boot-overview/ ↗
  - http://www.suse.com/blogs/uefi-secure-boot-details/ ↗
- http://en.opensuse.org/openSUSE:UEFI ↗ —UEFI with openSUSE.

13 The Boot Loader GRUB 2

This chapter describes how to configure GRUB 2, the boot loader used in SUSE® Linux Enterprise Desktop. It is the successor to the traditional GRUB boot loader—now called "GRUB Legacy". GRUB 2 has been the default boot loader in SUSE® Linux Enterprise Desktop since version 12. A YaST module is available for configuring the most important settings. The boot procedure as a whole is outlined in *Chapter 11, Introduction to the Booting Process*. For details on Secure Boot support for UEFI machines, see *Chapter 12, UEFI (Unified Extensible Firmware Interface)*.

13.1 Main Differences between GRUB Legacy and GRUB 2

- The configuration is stored in different files.
- More file systems are supported (for example, Btrfs).
- Can directly read files stored on LVM or RAID devices.
- The user interface can be translated and altered with themes.
- Includes a mechanism for loading modules to support additional features, such as file systems, etc.
- Automatically searches for and generates boot entries for other kernels and operating systems, such as Windows.
- Includes a minimal Bash-like console.

13.2 Configuration File Structure

The configuration of GRUB 2 is based on the following files:

`/boot/grub2/grub.cfg`

This file contains the configuration of the GRUB 2 menu items. It replaces `menu.lst` used in GRUB Legacy. `grub.cfg` is automatically generated by the `grub2-mkconfig` command, and should not be edited.

`/boot/grub2/custom.cfg`
: This optional file is directly sourced by `grub.cfg` at boot time and can be used to add custom items to the boot menu. Starting with SUSE Linux Enterprise Desktop these entries will also be parsed when using **`grub-once`**.

`/etc/default/grub`
: This file controls the user settings of GRUB 2 and usually includes additional environmental settings such as backgrounds and themes.

Scripts under `/etc/grub.d/`
: The scripts in this directory are read during execution of the `grub2-mkconfig` command. Their instructions are integrated into the main configuration file `/boot/grub/grub.cfg`.

`/etc/sysconfig/bootloader`
: This configuration file is used when configuring the boot loader with YaST and every time a new kernel is installed. It is evaluated by the perl-bootloader which modifies the boot loader configuration file (for example `/boot/grub2/grub.cfg` for GRUB 2) accordingly. `/etc/sysconfig/bootloader` is not a GRUB 2-specific configuration file—the values are applied to any boot loader installed on SUSE Linux Enterprise Desktop.

`/boot/grub2/x86_64-efi`, `/boot/grub2/power-ieee1275`, `/boot/grub2/s390x`
: These configuration files contain architecture-specific options.

GRUB 2 can be controlled in various ways. Boot entries from an existing configuration can be selected from the graphical menu (splash screen). The configuration is loaded from the file `/boot/grub2/grub.cfg` which is compiled from other configuration files (see below). All GRUB 2 configuration files are considered system files, and you need `root` privileges to edit them.

Note: Activating Configuration Changes

After having manually edited GRUB 2 configuration files, you need to run `grub2-mkconfig` to activate the changes. However, this is not necessary when changing the configuration with YaST, since it will automatically run `grub2-mkconfig`.

13.2.1 The File /boot/grub2/grub.cfg

The graphical splash screen with the boot menu is based on the GRUB 2 configuration file /boot/grub2/grub.cfg, which contains information about all partitions or operating systems that can be booted by the menu.

Every time the system is booted, GRUB 2 loads the menu file directly from the file system. For this reason, GRUB 2 does not need to be re-installed after changes to the configuration file. grub.cfg is automatically rebuilt with kernel installations or removals.

grub.cfg is compiled by the grub2-mkconfig from the file /etc/default/grub and scripts found in the /etc/grub.d/ directory. Therefore you should never edit the file manually. Instead, edit the related source files or use the YaST *Boot Loader* module to modify the configuration as described in Section 13.3, "Configuring the Boot Loader with YaST".

13.2.2 The File /etc/default/grub

More general options of GRUB 2 belong here, such as the time the menu is displayed, or the default OS to boot. To list all available options, see the output of the following command:

```
grep "export GRUB_DEFAULT" -A50 /usr/sbin/grub2-mkconfig | grep GRUB_
```

In addition to already defined variables, the user may introduce their own variables, and use them later in the scripts found in the /etc/grub.d directory.

After having edited /etc/default/grub, run grub2-mkconfig to update the main configuration file.

Note: Scope

All options set in this file are general options that affect all boot entries. Specific options for Xen kernels or the Xen hypervisor can be set via the GRUB_*_XEN_* configuration options. See below for details.

GRUB_DEFAULT

Sets the boot menu entry that is booted by default. Its value can be a numeric value, the complete name of a menu entry, or "saved".

GRUB_DEFAULT=2 boots the third (counted from zero) boot menu entry.

GRUB_DEFAULT="2>0" boots the first submenu entry of the third top-level menu entry.

`GRUB_DEFAULT="Example boot menu entry"` boots the menu entry with the title "Example boot menu entry".

`GRUB_DEFAULT=saved` boots the entry specified by the **grub2-reboot** or **grub2-set-default** commands. While **grub2-reboot** sets the default boot entry for the next reboot only, **grub2-set-default** sets the default boot entry until changed.

`GRUB_HIDDEN_TIMEOUT`

Waits the specified number of seconds for the user to press a key. During the period no menu is shown unless the user presses a key. If no key is pressed during the time specified, the control is passed to `GRUB_TIMEOUT`. `GRUB_HIDDEN_TIMEOUT=0` first checks whether Shift is pressed and shows the boot menu if yes, otherwise immediately boots the default menu entry. This is the default when only one bootable OS is identified by GRUB 2.

`GRUB_HIDDEN_TIMEOUT_QUIET`

If `false` is specified, a countdown timer is displayed on a blank screen when the `GRUB_HIDDEN_TIMEOUT` feature is active.

`GRUB_TIMEOUT`

Time period in seconds the boot menu is displayed before automatically booting the default boot entry. If you press a key, the timeout is cancelled and GRUB 2 waits for you to make the selection manually. `GRUB_TIMEOUT=-1` will cause the menu to be displayed until you select the boot entry manually.

`GRUB_CMDLINE_LINUX`

Entries on this line are added at the end of the boot entries for normal and recovery mode. Use it to add kernel parameters to the boot entry.

`GRUB_CMDLINE_LINUX_DEFAULT`

Same as `GRUB_CMDLINE_LINUX` but the entries are appended in the normal mode only.

`GRUB_CMDLINE_LINUX_RECOVERY`

Same as `GRUB_CMDLINE_LINUX` but the entries are appended in the recovery mode only.

`GRUB_CMDLINE_LINUX_XEN_REPLACE`

This entry will completely replace the `GRUB_CMDLINE_LINUX` parameters for all Xen boot entries.

`GRUB_CMDLINE_LINUX_XEN_REPLACE_DEFAULT`

Same as `GRUB_CMDLINE_LINUX_XEN_REPLACE` but it will only replace parameters of `GRUB_CMDLINE_LINUX_DEFAULT`.

`GRUB_CMDLINE_XEN`

This entry specifies the kernel parameters for the Xen guest kernel only—the operation principle is the same as for `GRUB_CMDLINE_LINUX`.

`GRUB_CMDLINE_XEN_DEFAULT`

Same as `GRUB_CMDLINE_XEN`—the operation principle is the same as for `GRUB_CMDLINE_LINUX_DEFAULT`.

`GRUB_TERMINAL`

Enables and specifies an input/output terminal device. Can be `console` (PC BIOS and EFI consoles), `serial` (serial terminal), `ofconsole` (Open Firmware console), or the default `gfxterm` (graphics-mode output). It is also possible to enable more than one device by quoting the required options, for example `GRUB_TERMINAL="console serial"`.

`GRUB_GFXMODE`

The resolution used for the `gfxterm` graphical terminal. Note that you can only use modes supported by your graphics card (VBE). The default is 'auto', which tries to select a preferred resolution. You can display the screen resolutions available to GRUB 2 by typing **`vbeinfo`** in the GRUB 2 command line. The command line is accessed by typing C when the GRUB 2 boot menu screen is displayed.

You can also specify a color depth by appending it to the resolution setting, for example `GRUB_GFXMODE=1280x1024x24`.

`GRUB_BACKGROUND`

Set a background image for the `gfxterm` graphical terminal. The image must be a file readable by GRUB 2 at boot time, and it must end with the `.png`, `.tga`, `.jpg`, or `.jpeg` suffix. If necessary, the image will be scaled to fit the screen.

`GRUB_DISABLE_OS_PROBER`

If this option is set to `true`, automatic searching for other operating systems is disabled. Only the kernel images in `/boot/` and the options from your own scripts in `/etc/grub.d/` are detected.

`SUSE_BTRFS_SNAPSHOT_BOOTING`

If this option is set to `true`, GRUB 2 can boot directly into Snapper snapshots. For more information, see *Section 7.3, "System Rollback by Booting from Snapshots"*.

Note: Parameter Handling

All `*_DEFAULT` parameters can be configured manually or with YaST.

For a complete list of options, see the GNU GRUB manual (http://www.gnu.org/software/grub/manual/grub.html#Simple-configuration). For a complete list of possible parameters, see http://en.opensuse.org/Linuxrc.

13.2.3 Scripts in /etc/grub.d

The scripts in this directory are read during execution of the `grub2-mkconfig` command, and their instructions are incorporated into `/boot/grub2/grub.cfg`. The order of menu items in `grub.cfg` is determined by the order in which the files in this directory are run. Files with a leading numeral are executed first, beginning with the lowest number. `00_header` is run before `10_linux`, which would run before `40_custom`. If files with alphabetic names are present, they are executed after the numerically-named files. Only executable files generate output to `grub.cfg` during execution of **`grub2-mkconfig`**. By default all files in the `/etc/grub.d` directory are executable. The most important scripts are:

`00_header`
: Sets environmental variables such as system file locations, display settings, themes, and previously saved entries. It also imports preferences stored in the `/etc/default/grub`. Normally you do not need to make changes to this file.

`10_linux`
: Identifies Linux kernels on the root device and creates relevant menu entries. This includes the associated recovery mode option if enabled. Only the latest kernel is displayed on the main menu page, with additional kernels included in a submenu.

`30_os-prober`
: This script uses **`OS-prober`** to search for Linux and other operating systems and places the results in the GRUB 2 menu. There are sections to identify specific other operating systems, such as Windows or macOS.

`40_custom`
: This file provides a simple way to include custom boot entries into `grub.cfg`. Make sure that you do not change the `exec tail -n +3 $0` part at the beginning.

`90_persistent`
: This is a special script that copies a corresponding part of the `grub.cfg` file and outputs it back unchanged. This way you can modify that part of `grub.cfg` directly and the change survives the execution of `grub2-mkconfig`.

The processing sequence is set by the preceding numbers with the lowest number being executed first. If scripts are preceded by the same number the alphabetical order of the complete name decides the order.

13.2.4 Mapping between BIOS Drives and Linux Devices

In GRUB Legacy, the `device.map` configuration file was used to derive Linux device names from BIOS drive numbers. The mapping between BIOS drives and Linux devices cannot always be guessed correctly. For example, GRUB Legacy would get a wrong order if the boot sequence of IDE and SCSI drives is exchanged in the BIOS configuration.

GRUB 2 avoids this problem by using device ID strings (UUIDs) or file system labels when generating `grub.cfg`. GRUB 2 utilities create a temporary device map on the fly, which is usually sufficient, particularly in the case of single-disk systems.

However, if you need to override the GRUB 2's automatic device mapping mechanism, create your custom mapping file `/boot/grub2/device.map`. The following example changes the mapping to make `DISK 3` the boot disk. Note that GRUB 2 partition numbers start with `1` and not with `0` as in GRUB Legacy.

```
(hd1)  /dev/disk-by-id/DISK3 ID
(hd2)  /dev/disk-by-id/DISK1 ID
(hd3)  /dev/disk-by-id/DISK2 ID
```

13.2.5 Editing Menu Entries during the Boot Procedure

Being able to directly edit menu entries is useful when the system does not boot anymore because of a faulty configuration. It can also be used to test new settings without altering the system configuration.

1. In the graphical boot menu, select the entry you want to edit with the arrow keys.
2. Press E to open the text-based editor.
3. Use the arrow keys to move to the line you want to edit.

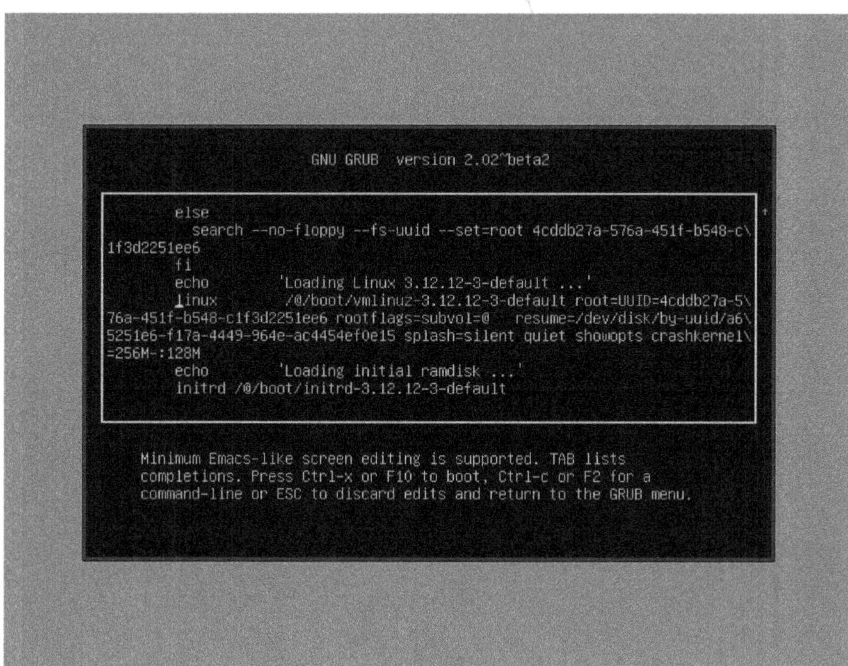

FIGURE 13.1: GRUB 2 BOOT EDITOR

Now you have two options:

a. Add space-separated parameters to the end of the line starting with `linux` or `linuxefi` to edit the kernel parameters. A complete list of parameters is available at http://en.opensuse.org/Linuxrc.

b. Or edit the general options to change for example the kernel version. The →| key suggests all possible completions.

4. Press F10 to boot the system with the changes you made or press Esc to discard your edits and return to the GRUB 2 menu.

Changes made this way only apply to the current boot process and are not saved permanently.

Important: Keyboard Layout During the Boot Procedure

The US keyboard layout is the only one available when booting. See *Figure 34.2, "US Keyboard Layout"*.

Note: Boot Loader on the Installation Media

The Boot Loader of the installation media on systems with a traditional BIOS is still GRUB Legacy. To add boot options, select an entry and start typing. Additions you make to the installation boot entry will be permanently saved in the installed system.

Note: Editing GRUB 2 Menu Entries on z Systems

Cursor movement and editing commands on IBM z Systems differ—see *Section 13.4, "Differences in Terminal Usage on z Systems"* for details.

13.2.6 Setting a Boot Password

Even before the operating system is booted, GRUB 2 enables access to file systems. Users without root permissions can access files in your Linux system to which they have no access after the system is booted. To block this kind of access or to prevent users from booting certain menu entries, set a boot password.

Important: Booting Requires Password

If set, the boot password is required on every boot, which means the system does not boot automatically.

Proceed as follows to set a boot password. Alternatively use YaST (*Protect Boot Loader with Password*).

1. Encrypt the password using **grub2-mkpasswd-pbkdf2:**

```
tux >  sudo grub2-mkpasswd-pbkdf2
Password: ****
Reenter password: ****
PBKDF2 hash of your password is grub.pbkdf2.sha512.10000.9CA4611006FE96BC77A...
```

2. Paste the resulting string into the file `/etc/grub.d/40_custom` together with the **set superusers** command.

```
set superusers="root"
```

```
password_pbkdf2 root grub.pbkdf2.sha512.10000.9CA4611006FE96BC77A...
```

3. Run `grub2-mkconfig` to import the changes into the main configuration file.

After you reboot, you will be prompted for a user name and a password when trying to boot a menu entry. Enter `root` and the password you typed during the **`grub2-mkpasswd-pbkdf2`** command. If the credentials are correct, the system will boot the selected boot entry.

For more information, see https://www.gnu.org/software/grub/manual/grub.html#Security ↗.

13.3 Configuring the Boot Loader with YaST

The easiest way to configure general options of the boot loader in your SUSE Linux Enterprise Desktop system is to use the YaST module. In the *YaST Control Center*, select *System* › *Boot Loader*. The module shows the current boot loader configuration of your system and allows you to make changes.

Use the *Boot Code Options* tab to view and change settings related to type, location and advanced loader settings. You can choose whether to use GRUB 2 in standard or EFI mode.

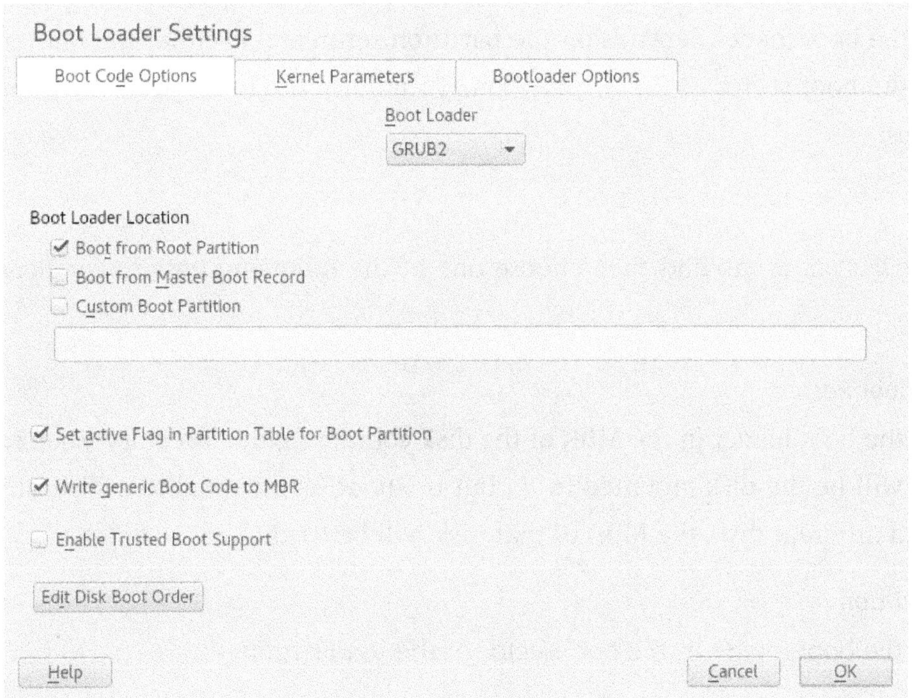

FIGURE 13.2: BOOT CODE OPTIONS

Important: EFI Systems require GRUB2-EFI

If you have an EFI system you can only install GRUB2-EFI, otherwise your system is no longer bootable.

Important: Reinstalling the Boot Loader

To reinstall the boot loader, make sure to change a setting in YaST and then change it back. For example, to reinstall GRUB2-EFI, select *GRUB2* first and then immediately switch back to *GRUB2-EFI*.

Otherwise, the boot loader may only be partially reinstalled.

Note: Custom Boot Loader

To use a boot loader other than the ones listed, select *Do Not Install Any Boot Loader*. Read the documentation of your boot loader carefully before choosing this option.

13.3.1 Modifying the Boot Loader Location

The default location of the boot loader depends on the partition setup and is either the Master Boot Record (MBR) or the boot sector of the `/` partition. To modify the location of the boot loader, follow these steps:

PROCEDURE 13.1: CHANGING THE BOOT LOADER LOCATION

1. Select the *Boot Code Options* tab and then choose one of the following options for *Boot Loader Location*:

   Boot from Master Boot Record

   This installs the boot loader in the MBR of the disk containing the directory `/boot`. Usually this will be the disk mounted to `/`, but if `/boot` is mounted to a separate partition on a different disk, the MBR of that disk will be used.

   Boot from Root Partition

   This installs the boot loader in the boot sector of the `/` partition.

   Custom Boot Partition

   Use this option to specify the location of the boot loader manually.

2. Click *OK* to apply your changes.

13.3.2 Adjusting the Disk Order

If your computer has more than one hard disk, you can specify the boot sequence of the disks. For more information, see *Section 13.2.4, "Mapping between BIOS Drives and Linux Devices"*.

PROCEDURE 13.2: SETTING THE DISK ORDER

1. Open the *Boot Code Options* tab.
2. Click *Boot Loader Installation Details*.
3. If more than one disk is listed, select a disk and click *Up* or *Down* to reorder the displayed disks.
4. Click *OK* two times to save the changes.

13.3.3 Configuring Advanced Options

Advanced boot options can be configured via the *Boot Loader Options* tab.

13.3.3.1 *Boot Loader Options* Tab

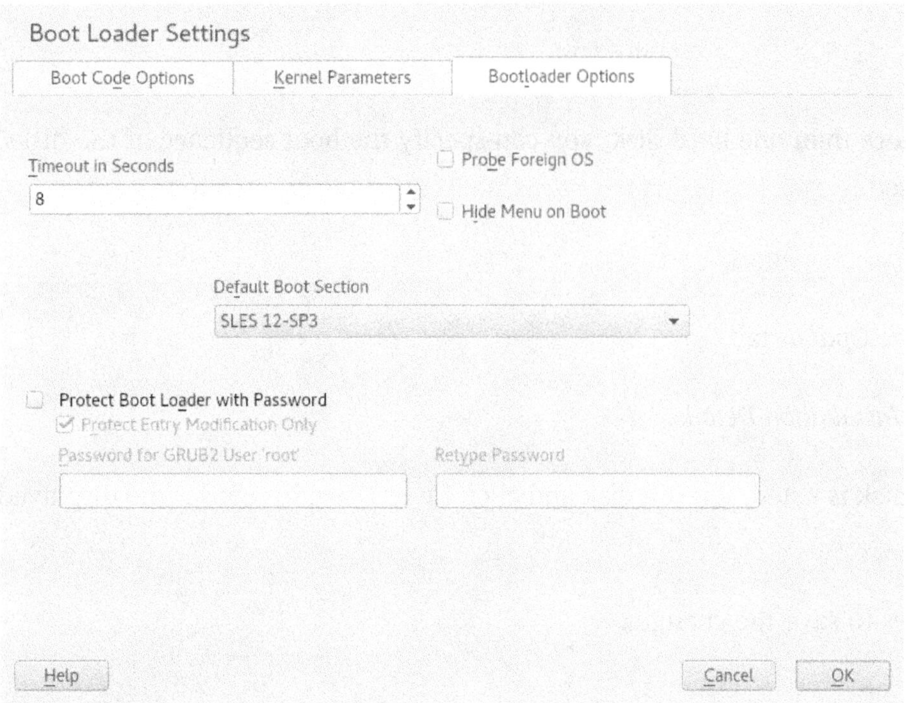

FIGURE 13.3: BOOT LOADER OPTIONS

Boot Loader Time-Out

Change the value of *Time-Out in Seconds* by typing in a new value and clicking the appropriate arrow key with your mouse.

Probe Foreign OS

When selected, the boot loader searches for other systems like Windows or other Linux installations.

Hide Menu on Boot

Hides the boot menu and boots the default entry.

Adjusting the Default Boot Entry

Select the desired entry from the "Default Boot Section" list. Note that the " > " sign in the boot entry name delimits the boot section and its subsection.

Protect Boot Loader with Password

Protects the boot loader and the system with an additional password. For more information, see *Section 13.2.6, "Setting a Boot Password"*.

13.3.3.2 *Kernel Parameters* Tab

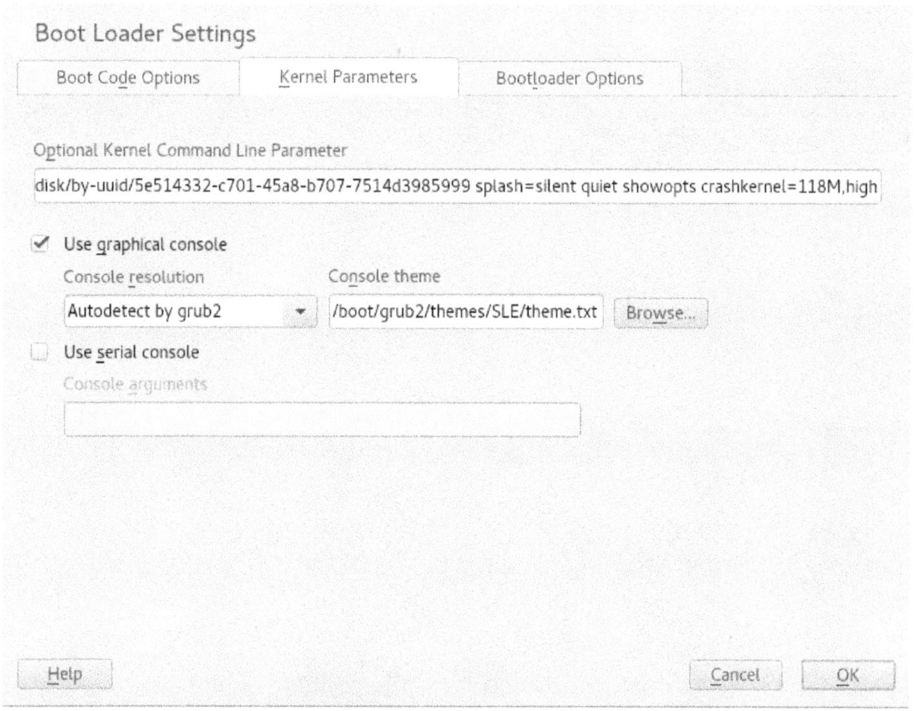

FIGURE 13.4: KERNEL PARAMETERS

VGA Mode

The VGA Mode option specifies the default screen resolution during the boot process.

Kernel Command Line Parameter

The optional kernel parameters are added at the end of the default parameters. For a list of all possible parameters, see http://en.opensuse.org/Linuxrc.

Use graphical console

When checked, the boot menu appears on a graphical splash screen rather than in a text mode. The resolution of the boot screen can be then set from the *Console resolution* list, and graphical theme definition file can be specified with the *Console theme* file-chooser.

Use Serial Console

If your machine is controlled via a serial console, activate this option and specify which COM port to use at which speed. See **`info grub`** or http://www.gnu.org/software/grub/manual/grub.html#Serial-terminal

13.3.3.3 *Boot Code Options* Tab

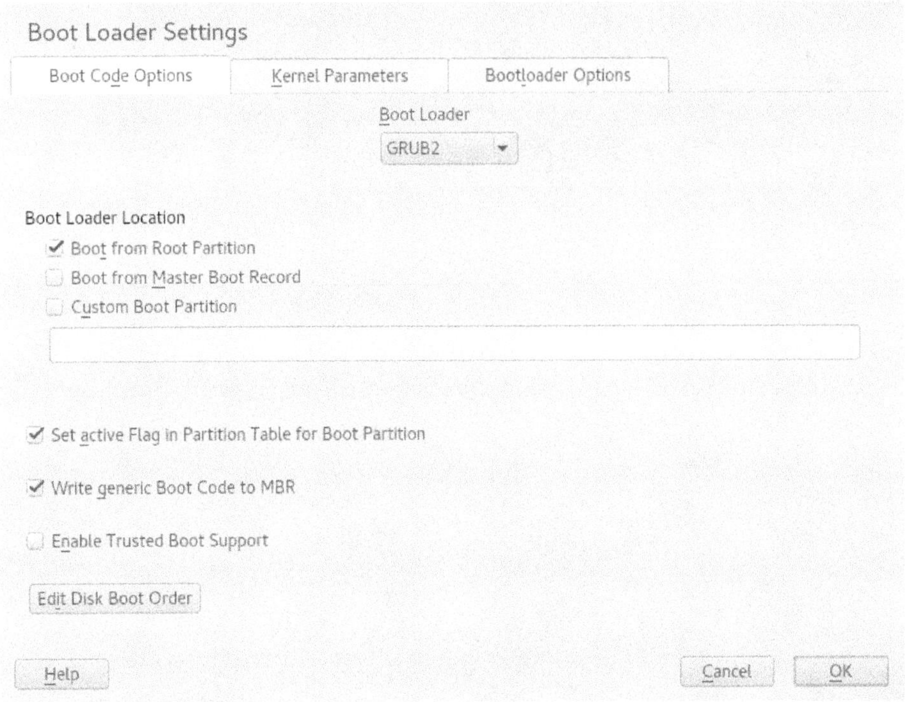

FIGURE 13.5: CODE OPTIONS

Set Active Flag in Partition Table for Boot Partition

Activates the partition that contains the boot loader. Some legacy operating systems (such as Windows) can only boot from an active partition.

Write Generic Boot Code to MBR

Replaces the current MBR with generic, operating system independent code.

Enable Trusted Boot Support

Starts TrustedGRUB2 which supports trusted computing functionality (Trusted Platform Module (TPM)). For more information refer to https://github.com/Sirrix-AG/TrustedGRUB2 ↗.

13.4 Differences in Terminal Usage on z Systems

On 3215 and 3270 terminals there are some differences and limitations on how to move the cursor and how to issue editing commands within GRUB 2.

13.4.1 Limitations

Interactivity

Interactivity is strongly limited. Typing often does not result in visual feedback. To see where the cursor is, type an underscore (_).

Note: 3270 Compared to 3215

The 3270 terminal is much better at displaying and refreshing screens than the 3215 terminal.

Cursor Movement

"Traditional" cursor movement is not possible. Alt, Meta, Ctrl and the cursor keys do not work. To move the cursor, use the key combinations listed in *Section 13.4.2, "Key Combinations"*.

Caret

The caret (^) is used as a control character. To type a literal ^ followed by a letter, type ^, ^, *LETTER*.

Enter

The Enter key does not work, use ^–J instead.

13.4.2 Key Combinations

Common Substitutes:	^–J	engage ("Enter")
	^–L	abort, return to previous "state"
	^–I	tab completion (in edit and shell mode)
Keys Available in Menu Mode:	^–A	first entry
	^–E	last entry
	^–P	previous entry

	^-N	next entry
	^-G	previous page
	^-C	next page
	^-F	boot selected entry or enter submenu (same as ^-J)
	E	edit selected entry
	C	enter GRUB-Shell
Keys Available in Edit Mode:	^-P	previous line
	^-N	next line
	^-B	backward char
	^-F	forward char
	^-A	beginning of line
	^-E	end of line
	^-H	backspace
	^-D	delete
	^-K	kill line
	^-Y	yank
	^-O	open line
	^-L	refresh screen
	^-X	boot entry
	^-C	enter GRUB-Shell

Keys Available in Command Line Mode:	^–P	previous command
	^–N	next command from history
	^–A	beginning of line
	^–E	end of line
	^–B	backward char
	^–F	forward char
	^–H	backspace
	^–D	delete
	^–K	kill line
	^–U	discard line
	^–Y	yank

13.5 Helpful GRUB 2 Commands

grub2-mkconfig

Generates a new /boot/grub2/grub.cfg based on /etc/default/grub and the scripts from /etc/grub.d/.

EXAMPLE 13.1: USAGE OF GRUB2-MKCONFIG

```
grub2-mkconfig -o /boot/grub2/grub.cfg
```

Tip: Syntax Check

Running **grub2-mkconfig** without any parameters prints the configuration to STDOUT where it can be reviewed. Use grub2-script-check after /boot/grub2/grub.cfg has been written to check its syntax.

Important: `grub2-mkconfig` Cannot Repair UEFI Secure Boot Tables

If you are using UEFI Secure Boot and your system is not reaching GRUB 2 correctly anymore, you may need to additionally reinstall Shim and regenerate the UEFI boot table. To do so, use:

```
root # shim-install --config-file=/boot/grub2/grub.cfg
```

`grub2-mkrescue`

Creates a bootable rescue image of your installed GRUB 2 configuration.

EXAMPLE 13.2: USAGE OF GRUB2-MKRESCUE

```
grub2-mkrescue -o save_path/name.iso iso
```

`grub2-script-check`

Checks the given file for syntax errors.

EXAMPLE 13.3: USAGE OF GRUB2-SCRIPT-CHECK

```
grub2-script-check /boot/grub2/grub.cfg
```

`grub2-once`

Set the default boot entry for the next boot only. To get the list of available boot entries use the `--list` option.

EXAMPLE 13.4: USAGE OF GRUB2-ONCE

```
grub2-once number_of_the_boot_entry
```

Tip: `grub2-once` Help

Call the program without any option to get a full list of all possible options.

13.6 More Information

Extensive information about GRUB 2 is available at http://www.gnu.org/software/grub/ ↗. Also refer to the **`grub`** info page. You can also search for the keyword "GRUB 2" in the Technical Information Search at http://www.suse.com/support ↗ to get information about special issues.

14 The systemd Daemon

The program `systemd` is the process with process ID 1. It is responsible for initializing the system in the required way. `systemd` is started directly by the kernel and resists signal 9, which normally terminates processes. All other programs are either started directly by systemd or by one of its child processes.

Starting with SUSE Linux Enterprise Desktop 12 systemd is a replacement for the popular System V init daemon. `systemd` is fully compatible with System V init (by supporting init scripts). One of the main advantages of systemd is that it considerably speeds up boot time by aggressively paralleling service starts. Furthermore, systemd only starts a service when it is really needed. Daemons are not started unconditionally at boot time, but rather when being required for the first time. systemd also supports Kernel Control Groups (cgroups), snapshotting and restoring the system state and more. See http://www.freedesktop.org/wiki/Software/systemd/ ↗ for details.

14.1 The systemd Concept

This section will go into detail about the concept behind systemd.

14.1.1 What Is systemd

systemd is a system and session manager for Linux, compatible with System V and LSB init scripts. The main features are:

- provides aggressive parallelization capabilities
- uses socket and D-Bus activation for starting services
- offers on-demand starting of daemons
- keeps track of processes using Linux cgroups
- supports snapshotting and restoring of the system state
- maintains mount and automount points
- implements an elaborate transactional dependency-based service control logic

14.1.2 Unit File

A unit configuration file contains information about a service, a socket, a device, a mount point, an automount point, a swap file or partition, a start-up target, a watched file system path, a timer controlled and supervised by systemd, a temporary system state snapshot, a resource management slice or a group of externally created processes. "Unit file" is a generic term used by systemd for the following:

- **Service.** Information about a process (for example running a daemon); file ends with .service
- **Targets.** Used for grouping units and as synchronization points during start-up; file ends with .target
- **Sockets.** Information about an IPC or network socket or a file system FIFO, for socket-based activation (like `inetd`); file ends with .socket
- **Path.** Used to trigger other units (for example running a service when files change); file ends with .path
- **Timer.** Information about a timer controlled, for timer-based activation; file ends with .timer
- **Mount point.** Usually auto-generated by the fstab generator; file ends with .mount
- **Automount point.** Information about a file system automount point; file ends with .automount
- **Swap.** Information about a swap device or file for memory paging; file ends with .swap
- **Device.** Information about a device unit as exposed in the sysfs/udev(7) device tree; file ends with .device
- **Scope / Slice.** A concept for hierarchically managing resources of a group of processes; file ends with .scope/.slice

For more information about systemd.unit see http://www.freedesktop.org/software/systemd/man/systemd.unit.html

14.2 Basic Usage

The System V init system uses several commands to handle services—the init scripts, **insserv**, **telinit** and others. systemd makes it easier to manage services, since there is only one command to memorize for the majority of service-handling tasks: **systemctl**. It uses the "command plus subcommand" notation like **git** or **zypper**:

```
systemctl GENERAL OPTIONS SUBCOMMAND SUBCOMMAND OPTIONS
```

See **man 1 systemctl** for a complete manual.

Tip: Terminal Output and Bash Completion

If the output goes to a terminal (and not to a pipe or a file, for example) systemd commands send long output to a pager by default. Use the `--no-pager` option to turn off paging mode.

systemd also supports bash-completion, allowing you to enter the first letters of a subcommand and then press →| to automatically complete it. This feature is only available in the `bash` shell and requires the installation of the package `bash-completion`.

14.2.1 Managing Services in a Running System

Subcommands for managing services are the same as for managing a service with System V init (**start**, **stop**, ...). The general syntax for service management commands is as follows:

systemd

```
systemctl reload|restart|start|status|stop|... MY_SERVICE(S)
```

System V init

```
rcMY_SERVICE(S) reload|restart|start|status|stop|...
```

systemd allows you to manage several services in one go. Instead of executing init scripts one after the other as with System V init, execute a command like the following:

```
systemctl start MY_1ST_SERVICE MY_2ND_SERVICE
```

To list all services available on the system:

```
systemctl list-unit-files --type=service
```

The following table lists the most important service management commands for systemd and System V init:

TABLE 14.1: SERVICE MANAGEMENT COMMANDS

Task	systemd Command	System V init Command
Starting.	`start`	`start`
Stopping.	`stop`	`stop`
Restarting. Shuts down services and starts them afterward. If a service is not yet running it will be started.	`restart`	`restart`
Restarting conditionally. Restarts services if they are currently running. Does nothing for services that are not running.	`try-restart`	`try-restart`
Reloading. Tells services to reload their configuration files without interrupting operation. Use case: Tell Apache to reload a modified `httpd.conf` configuration file. Note that not all services support reloading.	`reload`	`reload`
Reloading or restarting. Reloads services if reloading is supported, otherwise restarts them. If a service is not yet running it will be started.	`reload-or-restart`	`n/a`
Reloading or restarting conditionally. Reloads services if reloading is supported, otherwise restarts them if currently running. Does nothing for services that are not running.	`reload-or-try-restart`	`n/a`

Task	systemd Command	System V init Command
Getting detailed status information. Lists information about the status of services. The `systemd` command shows details such as description, executable, status, cgroup, and messages last issued by a service (see *Section 14.6.8, "Debugging Services"*). The level of details displayed with the System V init differs from service to service.	`status`	`status`
Getting short status information. Shows whether services are active or not.	`is-active`	`status`

14.2.2 Permanently Enabling/Disabling Services

The service management commands mentioned in the previous section let you manipulate services for the current session. systemd also lets you permanently enable or disable services, so they are automatically started when requested or are always unavailable. You can either do this by using YaST, or on the command line.

14.2.2.1 Enabling/Disabling Services on the Command Line

The following table lists enabling and disabling commands for systemd and System V init:

> **Important: Service Start**
>
> When enabling a service on the command line, it is not started automatically. It is scheduled to be started with the next system start-up or runlevel/target change. To immediately start a service after having enabled it, explicitly run **`systemctl start`** *`MY_SERVICE`* or **`rc`** *`MY_SERVICE`* **`start`**.

TABLE 14.2: COMMANDS FOR ENABLING AND DISABLING SERVICES

Task	`systemd` Command	System V init Command
Enabling.	**`systemctl enable`** *`MY_SERVICE(S)`*	**`insserv`** *`MY_SERVICE(S)`*, **`chkconfig -a`** *`MY_SERVICE(S)`*
Disabling.	**`systemctl disable`** *`MY_SERVICE(S)`*`.service`	**`insserv -r`** *`MY_SERVICE(S)`*, **`chkconfig -d`** *`MY_SERVICE(S)`*
Checking. Shows whether a service is enabled or not.	**`systemctl is-enabled`** *`MY_SERVICE`*	**`chkconfig`** *`MY_SERVICE`*
Re-enabling. Similar to restarting a service, this command first disables and then enables a service. Useful to re-enable a service with its defaults.	**`systemctl reenable`** *`MY_SERVICE`*	n/a
Masking. After "disabling" a service, it can still be started manually. To completely disable a service, you need to mask it. Use with care.	**`systemctl mask`** *`MY_SERVICE`*	n/a
Unmasking. A service that has been masked can only be used again after it has been unmasked.	**`systemctl unmask`** *`MY_SERVICE`*	n/a

14.3 System Start and Target Management

The entire process of starting the system and shutting it down is maintained by systemd. From this point of view, the kernel can be considered a background process to maintain all other processes and adjust CPU time and hardware access according to requests from other programs.

14.3.1 Targets Compared to Runlevels

With System V init the system was booted into a so-called "Runlevel". A runlevel defines how the system is started and what services are available in the running system. Runlevels are numbered; the most commonly known ones are `0` (shutting down the system), `3` (multiuser with network) and `5` (multiuser with network and display manager).

systemd introduces a new concept by using so-called "target units". However, it remains fully compatible with the runlevel concept. Target units are named rather than numbered and serve specific purposes. For example, the targets `local-fs.target` and `swap.target` mount local file systems and swap spaces.

The target `graphical.target` provides a multiuser system with network and display manager capabilities and is equivalent to runlevel 5. Complex targets, such as `graphical.target` act as "meta" targets by combining a subset of other targets. Since systemd makes it easy to create custom targets by combining existing targets, it offers great flexibility.

The following list shows the most important systemd target units. For a full list refer to **`man 7 systemd.special`**.

SELECTED SYSTEMD TARGET UNITS

`default.target`

The target that is booted by default. Not a "real" target, but rather a symbolic link to another target like `graphic.target`. Can be permanently changed via YaST (see *Section 14.4, "Managing Services with YaST"*). To change it for a session, use the kernel parameter `systemd.unit=`*`MY_TARGET.target`* at the boot prompt.

`emergency.target`

Starts an emergency shell on the console. Only use it at the boot prompt as `systemd.unit=emergency.target`.

`graphical.target`

Starts a system with network, multiuser support and a display manager.

`halt.target`
: Shuts down the system.

`mail-transfer-agent.target`
: Starts all services necessary for sending and receiving mails.

`multi-user.target`
: Starts a multiuser system with network.

`reboot.target`
: Reboots the system.

`rescue.target`
: Starts a single-user system without network.

To remain compatible with the System V init runlevel system, systemd provides special targets named `runlevelX.target` mapping the corresponding runlevels numbered `X`.

If you want to know the current target, use the command: **`systemctl get-default`**

TABLE 14.3: SYSTEM V RUNLEVELS AND `systemd` TARGET UNITS

System V runlevel	`systemd` target	Purpose
0	`runlevel0.target`, `halt.target`, `poweroff.target`	System shutdown
1, S	`runlevel1.target`, `rescue.target`,	Single-user mode
2	`runlevel2.target`, `multi-user.target`,	Local multiuser without remote network
3	`runlevel3.target`, `multi-user.target`,	Full multiuser with network
4	`runlevel4.target`	Unused/User-defined
5	`runlevel5.target`, `graphical.target`,	Full multiuser with network and display manager

System V runlevel	`systemd` target	Purpose
6	`runlevel6.target`, `reboot.target`,	System reboot

Important: systemd Ignores `/etc/inittab`

The runlevels in a System V init system are configured in `/etc/inittab`. systemd does *not* use this configuration. Refer to *Section 14.5.3, "Creating Custom Targets"* for instructions on how to create your own bootable target.

14.3.1.1 Commands to Change Targets

Use the following commands to operate with target units:

Task	systemd Command	System V init Command
Change the current target/runlevel	**`systemctl isolate`** *`MY_TARGET`*.target	**`telinit`** *`X`*
Change to the default target/runlevel	**`systemctl default`**	n/a
Get the current target/runlevel	**`systemctl list-units --type=target`** With systemd there is usually more than one active target. The command lists all currently active targets.	**`who -r`** or **`runlevel`**
persistently change the default runlevel	Use the Services Manager or run the following command: **`ln -sf /usr/lib/systemd/system/`** *`MY_TARGET`*.target /etc/systemd/system/default.target	Use the Services Manager or change the line **`id:`** *`X`*:initdefault: in `/etc/inittab`

Task	systemd Command	System V init Command
Change the default runlevel for the current boot process	Enter the following option at the boot prompt **systemd.unit=** *MY_TARGET*.target	Enter the desired runlevel number at the boot prompt.
Show a target's/runlevel's dependencies	**systemctl show -p "Requires"** *MY_TARGET*.target **systemctl show -p "Wants"** *MY_TARGET*.target “Requires” lists the hard dependencies (the ones that must be resolved), whereas “Wants” lists the soft dependencies (the ones that get resolved if possible).	n/a

14.3.2 Debugging System Start-Up

systemd offers the means to analyze the system start-up process. You can review the list of all services and their status (rather than having to parse `/varlog/`). systemd also allows you to scan the start-up procedure to find out how much time each service start-up consumes.

14.3.2.1 Review Start-Up of Services

To review the complete list of services that have been started since booting the system, enter the command **systemctl**. It lists all active services like shown below (shortened). To get more information on a specific service, use **systemctl status** *MY_SERVICE*.

EXAMPLE 14.1: LIST ACTIVE SERVICES

```
root # systemctl
UNIT                        LOAD   ACTIVE SUB       JOB DESCRIPTION
[...]
iscsi.service               loaded active exited    Login and scanning of iSC+
kmod-static-nodes.service   loaded active exited    Create list of required s+
libvirtd.service            loaded active running   Virtualization daemon
nscd.service                loaded active running   Name Service Cache Daemon
```

```
ntpd.service                loaded active running   NTP Server Daemon
polkit.service              loaded active running   Authorization Manager
postfix.service             loaded active running   Postfix Mail Transport Ag+
rc-local.service            loaded active exited    /etc/init.d/boot.local Co+
rsyslog.service             loaded active running   System Logging Service
[...]
LOAD   = Reflects whether the unit definition was properly loaded.
ACTIVE = The high-level unit activation state, i.e. generalization of SUB.
SUB    = The low-level unit activation state, values depend on unit type.

161 loaded units listed. Pass --all to see loaded but inactive units, too.
To show all installed unit files use 'systemctl list-unit-files'.
```

To restrict the output to services that failed to start, use the `--failed` option:

EXAMPLE 14.2: LIST FAILED SERVICES

```
root # systemctl --failed
UNIT                   LOAD   ACTIVE SUB    JOB DESCRIPTION
apache2.service        loaded failed failed     apache
NetworkManager.service loaded failed failed     Network Manager
plymouth-start.service loaded failed failed     Show Plymouth Boot Screen

[...]
```

14.3.2.2 Debug Start-Up Time

To debug system start-up time, systemd offers the **`systemd-analyze`** command. It shows the total start-up time, a list of services ordered by start-up time and can also generate an SVG graphic showing the time services took to start in relation to the other services.

Listing the System Start-Up Time

```
root # systemd-analyze
Startup finished in 2666ms (kernel) + 21961ms (userspace) = 24628ms
```

Listing the Services Start-Up Time

```
root # systemd-analyze blame
  6472ms systemd-modules-load.service
  5833ms remount-rootfs.service
  4597ms network.service
```

```
  4254ms systemd-vconsole-setup.service
  4096ms postfix.service
  2998ms xdm.service
  2483ms localnet.service
  2470ms SuSEfirewall2_init.service
  2189ms avahi-daemon.service
  2120ms systemd-logind.service
  1210ms xinetd.service
  1080ms ntp.service
[...]
    75ms fbset.service
    72ms purge-kernels.service
    47ms dev-vda1.swap
    38ms bluez-coldplug.service
    35ms splash_early.service
```

Services Start-Up Time Graphics

```
root # systemd-analyze plot > jupiter.example.com-startup.svg
```

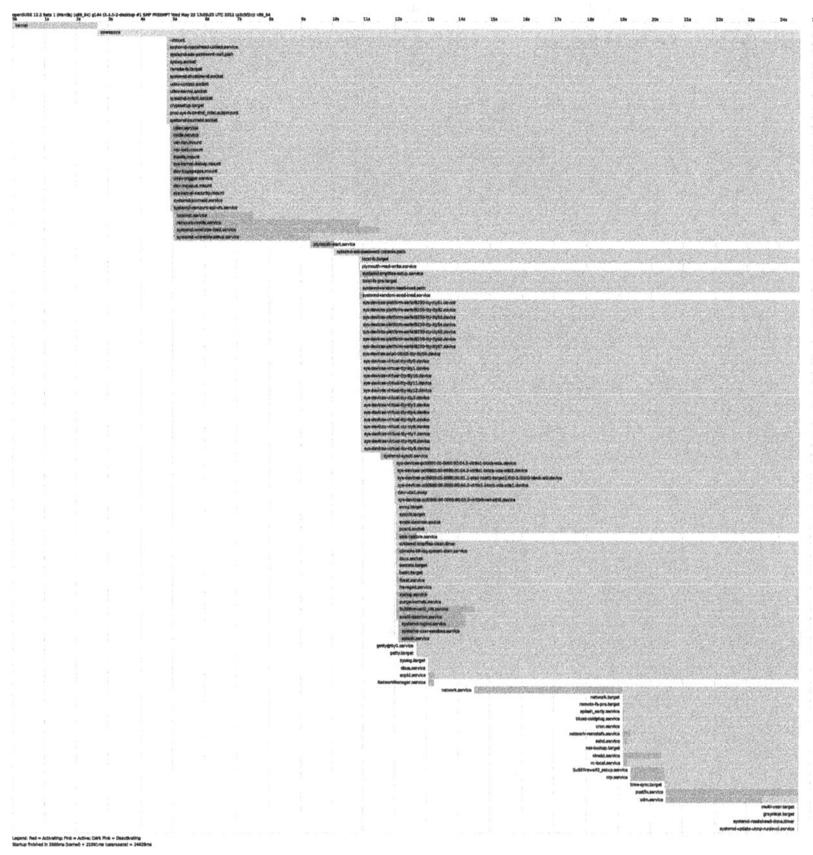

14.3.2.3 Review the Complete Start-Up Process

The above-mentioned commands let you review the services that started and the time it took to start them. If you need to know more details, you can tell `systemd` to verbosely log the complete start-up procedure by entering the following parameters at the boot prompt:

```
systemd.log_level=debug systemd.log_target=kmsg
```

Now `systemd` writes its log messages into the kernel ring buffer. View that buffer with **`dmesg`**:

```
dmesg -T | less
```

14.3.3 System V Compatibility

systemd is compatible with System V, allowing you to still use existing System V init scripts. However, there is at least one known issue where a System V init script does not work with systemd out of the box: starting a service as a different user via **`su`** or **`sudo`** in init scripts will result in a failure of the script, producing an "Access denied" error.

When changing the user with **`su`** or **`sudo`**, a PAM session is started. This session will be terminated after the init script is finished. As a consequence, the service that has been started by the init script will also be terminated. To work around this error, proceed as follows:

1. Create a service file wrapper with the same name as the init script plus the file name extension `.service`:

   ```
   [Unit]
   Description=DESCRIPTION
   After=network.target

   [Service]
   User=USER
   Type=forking ①
   PIDFile=PATH TO PID FILE ①
   ExecStart=PATH TO INIT SCRIPT start
   ExecStop=PATH TO INIT SCRIPT stop
   ExecStopPost=/usr/bin/rm -f PATH TO PID FILE ①

   [Install]
   WantedBy=multi-user.target ②
   ```

   Replace all values written in *`UPPERCASE LETTERS`* with appropriate values.

1. Optional—only use if the init script starts a daemon.
2. `multi-user.target` also starts the init script when booting into `graphical.target`. If it should only be started when booting into the display manager, user `graphical.target` here.

2. Start the daemon with **`systemctl start`** *`APPLICATION`*.

14.4 Managing Services with YaST

Basic service management can also be done with the YaST Services Manager module. It supports starting, stopping, enabling and disabling services. It also lets you show a service's status and change the default target. Start the YaST module with *YaST* › *System* › *Services Manager*.

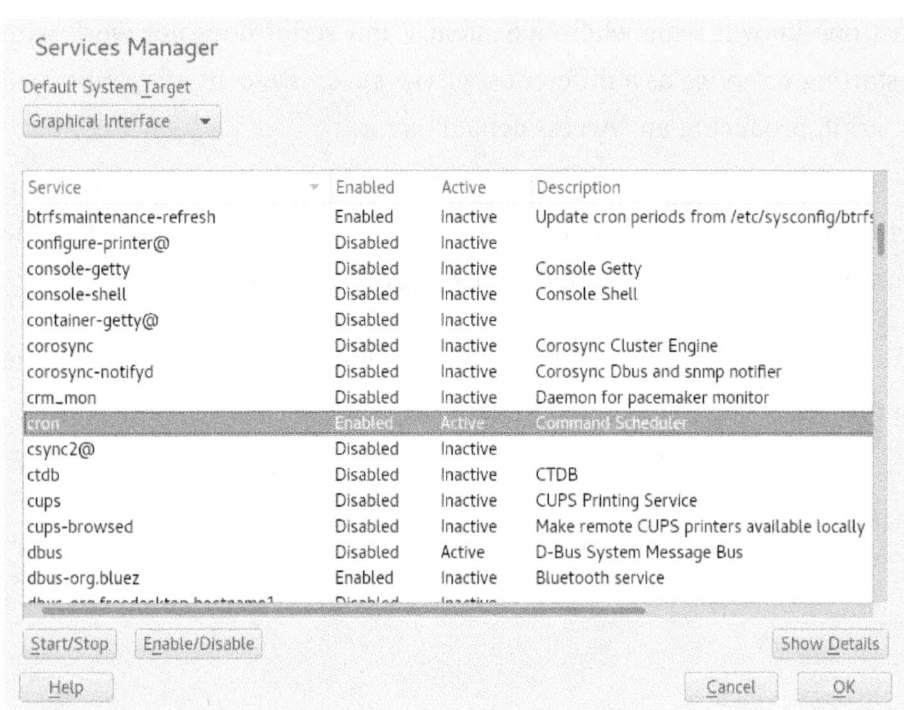

FIGURE 14.1: SERVICES MANAGER

Changing the *Default System Target*

To change the target the system boots into, choose a target from the *Default System Target* drop-down box. The most often used targets are *Graphical Interface* (starting a graphical login screen) and *Multi-User* (starting the system in command line mode).

Starting or Stopping a Service

Select a service from the table. The *Active* column shows whether it is currently running (*Active*) or not (*Inactive*). Toggle its status by choosing *Start/Stop*.

Starting or stopping a service changes its status for the currently running session. To change its status throughout a reboot, you need to enable or disable it.

Enabling or Disabling a Service

Select a service from the table. The *Enabled* column shows whether it is currently *Enabled* or *Disabled*. Toggle its status by choosing *Enable/Disable*.

By enabling or disabling a service you configure whether it is started during booting (*Enabled*) or not (*Disabled*). This setting will not affect the current session. To change its status in the current session, you need to start or stop it.

View a Status Messages

To view the status message of a service, select it from the list and choose *Show Details*. The output you will see is identical to the one generated by the command `systemctl -l status MY_SERVICE`.

Warning: Faulty Runlevel Settings May Damage Your System

Faulty runlevel settings may make your system unusable. Before applying your changes, make absolutely sure that you know their consequences.

14.5 Customization of systemd

The following sections contain some examples for `systemd` customization.

Warning: Avoiding Overwritten Customization

Always do systemd customization in `/etc/systemd/`, *never* in `/usr/lib/systemd/`. Otherwise your changes will be overwritten by the next update of systemd.

14.5.1 Customizing Service Files

The systemd service files are located in `/usr/lib/systemd/system`. If you want to customize them, proceed as follows:

1. Copy the files you want to modify from `/usr/lib/systemd/system` to `/etc/systemd/system`. Keep the file names identical to the original ones.
2. Modify the copies in `/etc/systemd/system` according to your needs.
3. For an overview of your configuration changes, use the **`systemd-delta`** command. It can compare and identify configuration files that override other configuration files. For details, refer to the **`systemd-delta`** man page.

The modified files in `/etc/systemd` will take precedence over the original files in `/usr/lib/systemd/system`, provided that their file name is the same.

14.5.2 Creating "Drop-in" Files

If you only want to add a few lines to a configuration file or modify a small part of it, you can use so-called "drop-in" files. Drop-in files let you extend the configuration of unit files without having to edit or override the unit files themselves.

For example, to change one value for the *FOOBAR* service located in `/usr/lib/systemd/system/FOOBAR.SERVICE`, proceed as follows:

1. Create a directory called `/etc/systemd/system/MY_SERVICE.service.d/`.
   Note the `.d` suffix. The directory must otherwise be named like the service that you want to patch with the drop-in file.
2. In that directory, create a file `WHATEVERMODIFICATION.conf`.
   Make sure it only contains the line with the value that you want to modify.
3. Save your changes to the file. It will be used as an extension of the original file.

14.5.3 Creating Custom Targets

On System V init SUSE systems, runlevel 4 is unused to allow administrators to create their own runlevel configuration. systemd allows you to create any number of custom targets. It is suggested to start by adapting an existing target such as `graphical.target`.

1. Copy the configuration file `/usr/lib/systemd/system/graphical.target` to `/etc/systemd/system/MY_TARGET.target` and adjust it according to your needs.

2. The configuration file copied in the previous step already covers the required ("hard") dependencies for the target. To also cover the wanted ("soft") dependencies, create a directory `/etc/systemd/system/MY_TARGET.target.wants`.

3. For each wanted service, create a symbolic link from `/usr/lib/systemd/system` into `/etc/systemd/system/MY_TARGET.target.wants`.

4. Once you have finished setting up the target, reload the systemd configuration to make the new target available:

```
systemctl daemon-reload
```

14.6 Advanced Usage

The following sections cover advanced topics for system administrators. For even more advanced systemd documentation, refer to Lennart Pöttering's series about systemd for administrators at http://0pointer.de/blog/projects ↗.

14.6.1 Cleaning Temporary Directories

`systemd` supports cleaning temporary directories regularly. The configuration from the previous system version is automatically migrated and active. `tmpfiles.d`—which is responsible for managing temporary files—reads its configuration from `/etc/tmpfiles.d/*.conf` , `/run/tmpfiles.d/*.conf`, and `/usr/lib/tmpfiles.d/*.conf` files. Configuration placed in `/etc/tmpfiles.d/*.conf` overrides related configurations from the other two directories (`/usr/lib/tmpfiles.d/*.conf` is where packages store their configuration files).

The configuration format is one line per path containing action and path, and optionally mode, ownership, age and argument fields, depending on the action. The following example unlinks the X11 lock files:

```
Type Path               Mode UID  GID  Age Argument
r    /tmp/.X[0-9]*-lock
```

To get the status the tmpfile timer:

```
systemctl status systemd-tmpfiles-clean.timer
```

```
systemd-tmpfiles-clean.timer - Daily Cleanup of Temporary Directories
 Loaded: loaded (/usr/lib/systemd/system/systemd-tmpfiles-clean.timer; static)
 Active: active (waiting) since Tue 2014-09-09 15:30:36 CEST; 1 weeks 6 days ago
   Docs: man:tmpfiles.d(5)
         man:systemd-tmpfiles(8)

Sep 09 15:30:36 jupiter systemd[1]: Starting Daily Cleanup of Temporary Directories.
Sep 09 15:30:36 jupiter systemd[1]: Started Daily Cleanup of Temporary Directories.
```

For more information on temporary files handling, see **`man 5 tmpfiles.d`**.

14.6.2 System Log

Section 14.6.8, "Debugging Services" explains how to view log messages for a given service. However, displaying log messages is not restricted to service logs. You can also access and query the complete log messages written by `systemd`—the so-called "Journal". Use the command **`systemd-journalctl`** to display the complete log messages starting with the oldest entries. Refer to **`man 1 systemd-journalctl`** for options such as applying filters or changing the output format.

14.6.3 Snapshots

You can save the current state of `systemd` to a named snapshot and later revert to it with the **`isolate`** subcommand. This is useful when testing services or custom targets, because it allows you to return to a defined state at any time. A snapshot is only available in the current session and will automatically be deleted on reboot. A snapshot name must end in `.snapshot`.

Create a Snapshot

```
systemctl snapshot MY_SNAPSHOT.snapshot
```

Delete a Snapshot

```
systemctl delete MY_SNAPSHOT.snapshot
```

View a Snapshot

```
systemctl show MY_SNAPSHOT.snapshot
```

Activate a Snapshot

```
systemctl isolate MY_SNAPSHOT.snapshot
```

14.6.4 Loading Kernel Modules

With systemd, kernel modules can automatically be loaded at boot time via a configuration file in /etc/modules-load.d. The file should be named *MODULE*.conf and have the following content:

```
# load module MODULE at boot time
MODULE
```

In case a package installs a configuration file for loading a kernel module, the file gets installed to /usr/lib/modules-load.d. If two configuration files with the same name exist, the one in /etc/modules-load.d tales precedence.

For more information, see the modules-load.d(5) man page.

14.6.5 Performing Actions before Loading a Service

With System V init actions that need to be performed before loading a service, needed to be specified in /etc/init.d/before.local . This procedure is no longer supported with systemd. If you need to do actions before starting services, do the following:

Loading Kernel Modules

Create a drop-in file in /etc/modules-load.d directory (see **man modules-load.d** for the syntax)

Creating Files or Directories, Cleaning-up Directories, Changing Ownership

Create a drop-in file in /etc/tmpfiles.d (see **man tmpfiles.d** for the syntax)

Other Tasks

Create a system service file, for example /etc/systemd/system/before.service, from the following template:

```
[Unit]
Before=NAME OF THE SERVICE YOU WANT THIS SERVICE TO BE STARTED BEFORE
[Service]
Type=oneshot
RemainAfterExit=true
ExecStart=YOUR_COMMAND
# beware, executable is run directly, not through a shell, check the man pages
# systemd.service and systemd.unit for full syntax
[Install]
# target in which to start the service
```

```
WantedBy=multi-user.target
#WantedBy=graphical.target
```

When the service file is created, you should run the following commands (as `root`):

```
systemctl daemon-reload
systemctl enable before
```

Every time you modify the service file, you need to run:

```
systemctl daemon-reload
```

14.6.6 Kernel Control Groups (cgroups)

On a traditional System V init system it is not always possible to clearly assign a process to the service that spawned it. Some services, such as Apache, spawn a lot of third-party processes (for example CGI or Java processes), which themselves spawn more processes. This makes a clear assignment difficult or even impossible. Additionally, a service may not terminate correctly, leaving some children alive.

systemd solves this problem by placing each service into its own cgroup. cgroups are a kernel feature that allows aggregating processes and all their children into hierarchical organized groups. systemd names each cgroup after its service. Since a non-privileged process is not allowed to “leave” its cgroup, this provides an effective way to label all processes spawned by a service with the name of the service.

To list all processes belonging to a service, use the command **`systemd-cgls`**. The result will look like the following (shortened) example:

EXAMPLE 14.3: LIST ALL PROCESSES BELONGING TO A SERVICE

```
root # systemd-cgls --no-pager
├─1 /usr/lib/systemd/systemd --switched-root --system --deserialize 20
├─user.slice
│ └─user-1000.slice
│   ├─session-102.scope
│   │ ├─12426 gdm-session-worker [pam/gdm-password]
│   │ ├─15831 gdm-session-worker [pam/gdm-password]
│   │ ├─15839 gdm-session-worker [pam/gdm-password]
│   │ ├─15858 /usr/lib/gnome-terminal-server

[...]
```

```
└─system.slice
  ├─systemd-hostnamed.service
  │ └─17616 /usr/lib/systemd/systemd-hostnamed
  ├─cron.service
  │ └─1689 /usr/sbin/cron -n
  ├─ntpd.service
  │ └─1328 /usr/sbin/ntpd -p /var/run/ntp/ntpd.pid -g -u ntp:ntp -c /etc/ntp.conf
  ├─postfix.service
  │ ├─ 1676 /usr/lib/postfix/master -w
  │ ├─ 1679 qmgr -l -t fifo -u
  │ └─15590 pickup -l -t fifo -u
  ├─sshd.service
  │ └─1436 /usr/sbin/sshd -D

[...]
```

See *Book "System Analysis and Tuning Guide", Chapter 9 "Kernel Control Groups"* for more information about cgroups.

14.6.7 Terminating Services (Sending Signals)

As explained in *Section 14.6.6, "Kernel Control Groups (cgroups)"*, it is not always possible to assign a process to its parent service process in a System V init system. This makes it difficult to terminate a service and all of its children. Child processes that have not been terminated will remain as zombie processes.

systemd's concept of confining each service into a cgroup makes it possible to clearly identify all child processes of a service and therefore allows you to send a signal to each of these processes. Use **`systemctl kill`** to send signals to services. For a list of available signals refer to **`man 7 signals`**.

Sending `SIGTERM` to a Service

`SIGTERM` is the default signal that is sent.

```
systemctl kill MY_SERVICE
```

Sending *`SIGNAL`* to a Service

Use the `-s` option to specify the signal that should be sent.

```
systemctl kill -s SIGNAL MY_SERVICE
```

Selecting Processes

By default the **kill** command sends the signal to `all` processes of the specified cgroup. You can restrict it to the `control` or the `main` process. The latter is for example useful to force a service to reload its configuration by sending `SIGHUP`:

```
systemctl kill -s SIGHUP --kill-who=main MY_SERVICE
```

Warning: Terminating or Restarting the D-Bus Service is Not Supported

The D-Bus service is the message bus for communication between systemd clients and the systemd manager that is running as pid 1. Even though `dbus` is a stand-alone daemon, it is an integral part of the init infrastructure.

Terminating `dbus` or restarting it in the running system is similar to an attempt to terminate or restart pid 1. It will break systemd client/server communication and make most systemd functions unusable.

Therefore, terminating or restarting `dbus` is neither recommended nor supported.

14.6.8 Debugging Services

By default, systemd is not overly verbose. If a service was started successfully, no output will be produced. In case of a failure, a short error message will be displayed. However, **systemctl status** provides means to debug start-up and operation of a service.

systemd comes with its own logging mechanism ("The Journal") that logs system messages. This allows you to display the service messages together with status messages. The **status** command works similar to **tail** and can also display the log messages in different formats, making it a powerful debugging tool.

Show Service Start-Up Failure

Whenever a service fails to start, use **systemctl status** *MY_SERVICE* to get a detailed error message:

```
root # systemctl start apache2
Job failed. See system journal and 'systemctl status' for details.
root # systemctl status apache2
   Loaded: loaded (/usr/lib/systemd/system/apache2.service; disabled)
   Active: failed (Result: exit-code) since Mon, 04 Jun 2012 16:52:26 +0200; 29s ago
```

```
   Process: 3088 ExecStart=/usr/sbin/start_apache2 -D SYSTEMD -k start (code=exited,
 status=1/FAILURE)
   CGroup: name=systemd:/system/apache2.service

Jun 04 16:52:26 g144 start_apache2[3088]: httpd2-prefork: Syntax error on line
205 of /etc/apache2/httpd.conf: Syntax error on li...alHost>
```

Show Last *N* Service Messages

The default behavior of the **`status`** subcommand is to display the last ten messages a service issued. To change the number of messages to show, use the `--lines=N` parameter:

```
systemctl status ntp
systemctl --lines=20 status ntp
```

Show Service Messages in Append Mode

To display a "live stream" of service messages, use the `--follow` option, which works like **`tail`** `-f`:

```
systemctl --follow status ntp
```

Messages Output Format

The `--output=MODE` parameter allows you to change the output format of service messages. The most important modes available are:

`short`

The default format. Shows the log messages with a human readable time stamp.

`verbose`

Full output with all fields.

`cat`

Terse output without time stamps.

14.7 More Information

For more information on systemd refer to the following online resources:

Homepage

http://www.freedesktop.org/wiki/Software/systemd

systemd for Administrators

Lennart Pöttering, one of the systemd authors, has written a series of blog entries (13 at the time of writing this chapter). Find them at http://0pointer.de/blog/projects ↗.

III System

15 32-Bit and 64-Bit Applications in a 64-Bit System Environment

SUSE® Linux Enterprise Desktop is available for 64-bit platforms. This does not necessarily mean that all the applications included have already been ported to 64-bit platforms. SUSE Linux Enterprise Desktop supports the use of 32-bit applications in a 64-bit system environment. This chapter offers a brief overview of how this support is implemented on 64-bit SUSE Linux Enterprise Desktop platforms. It explains how 32-bit applications are executed and how 32-bit applications should be compiled to enable them to run both in 32-bit and 64-bit system environments. Additionally, find information about the kernel API and an explanation of how 32-bit applications can run under a 64-bit kernel.

SUSE Linux Enterprise Desktop for the 64-bit platforms amd64 and Intel 64 is designed so that existing 32-bit applications run in the 64-bit environment "out-of-the-box." This support means that you can continue to use your preferred 32-bit applications without waiting for a corresponding 64-bit port to become available.

15.1 Runtime Support

Important: Conflicts Between Application Versions

If an application is available both for 32-bit and 64-bit environments, parallel installation of both versions is bound to lead to problems. In such cases, decide on one of the two versions and install and use this.

An exception to this rule is PAM (pluggable authentication modules). SUSE Linux Enterprise Desktop uses PAM in the authentication process as a layer that mediates between user and application. On a 64-bit operating system that also runs 32-bit applications it is necessary to always install both versions of a PAM module.

To be executed correctly, every application requires a range of libraries. Unfortunately, the names for the 32-bit and 64-bit versions of these libraries are identical. They must be differentiated from each other in another way.

To retain compatibility with the 32-bit version, the libraries are stored at the same place in the system as in the 32-bit environment. The 32-bit version of `libc.so.6` is located under `/lib/libc.so.6` in both the 32-bit and 64-bit environments.

All 64-bit libraries and object files are located in directories called `lib64`. The 64-bit object files that you would normally expect to find under `/lib` and `/usr/lib` are now found under `/lib64` and `/usr/lib64`. This means that there is space for the 32-bit libraries under `/lib` and `/usr/lib`, so the file name for both versions can remain unchanged.

Subdirectories of 32-bit `/lib` directories which contain data content that does not depend on the word size are not moved. This scheme conforms to LSB (Linux Standards Base) and FHS (File System Hierarchy Standard).

15.2 Software Development

Both 32-bit and 64-bit objects can be generated with a biarch development toolchain. A biarch development toolchain allows generation of 32-bit and 64-bit objects. The compilation of 64-bit objects is the default on almost all platforms. 32-bit objects can be generated if special flags are used. This special flag is `-m32` for GCC. The flags for the binutils are architecture-dependent, but GCC transfers the correct flags to linkers and assemblers. A biarch development toolchain currently exists for amd64 (supports development for x86 and amd64 instructions), for z Systems and for POWER. 32-bit objects are normally created on the POWER platform. The `-m64` flag must be used to generate 64-bit objects.

A biarch development toolchain allows generation of 32-bit and 64-bit objects. The default is to compile 64-bit objects. It is possible to generate 32-bit objects by using special flags. For GCC, this special flag is `-m32`.

All header files must be written in an architecture-independent form. The installed 32-bit and 64-bit libraries must have an API (application programming interface) that matches the installed header files. The normal SUSE Linux Enterprise Desktop environment is designed according to this principle. In the case of manually updated libraries, resolve these issues yourself.

15.3 Software Compilation on Biarch Platforms

To develop binaries for the other architecture on a biarch architecture, the respective libraries for the second architecture must additionally be installed. These packages are called `rpmname-32bit`. You also need the respective headers and libraries from the `rpmname-devel` packages and the development libraries for the second architecture from `rpmname-devel-32bit`.

Most open source programs use an **`autoconf`**-based program configuration. To use **`autoconf`** for configuring a program for the second architecture, overwrite the normal compiler and linker settings of **`autoconf`** by running the **`configure`** script with additional environment variables.

The following example refers to an x86_64 system with x86 as the second architecture.

1. Use the 32-bit compiler:

```
CC="gcc -m32"
```

2. Instruct the linker to process 32-bit objects (always use **`gcc`** as the linker front-end):

```
LD="gcc -m32"
```

3. Set the assembler to generate 32-bit objects:

```
AS="gcc -c -m32"
```

4. Specify linker flags, such as the location of 32-bit libraries, for example:

```
LDFLAGS="-L/usr/lib"
```

5. Specify the location for the 32-bit object code libraries:

```
--libdir=/usr/lib
```

6. Specify the location for the 32-bit X libraries:

```
--x-libraries=/usr/lib
```

Not all of these variables are needed for every program. Adapt them to the respective program.

An example **`configure`** call to compile a native 32-bit application on x86_64 could appear as follows:

```
CC="gcc -m32"
LDFLAGS="-L/usr/lib;"
```

```
./configure --prefix=/usr --libdir=/usr/lib --x-libraries=/usr/lib
make
make install
```

15.4 Kernel Specifications

The 64-bit kernels for AMD64/Intel 64 offer both a 64-bit and a 32-bit kernel ABI (application binary interface). The latter is identical with the ABI for the corresponding 32-bit kernel. This means that the 32-bit application can communicate with the 64-bit kernel in the same way as with the 32-bit kernel.

The 32-bit emulation of system calls for a 64-bit kernel does not support all the APIs used by system programs. This depends on the platform. For this reason, few applications, like **lspci**, must be compiled.

A 64-bit kernel can only load 64-bit kernel modules that have been specially compiled for this kernel. It is not possible to use 32-bit kernel modules.

Tip: Kernel-loadable Modules

Some applications require separate kernel-loadable modules. If you intend to use such a 32-bit application in a 64-bit system environment, contact the provider of this application and SUSE to make sure that the 64-bit version of the kernel-loadable module and the 32-bit compiled version of the kernel API are available for this module.

16 `journalctl`: Query the systemd Journal

When `systemd` replaced traditional init scripts in SUSE Linux Enterprise 12 (see *Chapter 14, The systemd Daemon*), it introduced its own logging system called *journal*. There is no need to run a `syslog` based service anymore, as all system events are written in the journal.

The journal itself is a system service managed by `systemd`. Its full name is `systemd-journald.service`. It collects and stores logging data by maintaining structured indexed journals based on logging information received from the kernel, user processes, standard input, and system service errors. The `systemd-journald` service is on by default:

```
# systemctl status systemd-journald
systemd-journald.service - Journal Service
   Loaded: loaded (/usr/lib/systemd/system/systemd-journald.service; static)
   Active: active (running) since Mon 2014-05-26 08:36:59 EDT; 3 days ago
     Docs: man:systemd-journald.service(8)
           man:journald.conf(5)
 Main PID: 413 (systemd-journal)
   Status: "Processing requests..."
   CGroup: /system.slice/systemd-journald.service
           └─413 /usr/lib/systemd/systemd-journald
[...]
```

16.1 Making the Journal Persistent

The journal stores log data in `/run/log/journal/` by default. Because the `/run/` directory is volatile by nature, log data is lost at reboot. To make the log data persistent, the directory `/var/log/journal/` with correct ownership and permissions must exist, where the systemd-journald service can store its data. `systemd` will create the directory for you—and switch to persistent logging—if you do the following:

1. As `root`, open `/etc/systemd/journald.conf` for editing.

```
# vi /etc/systemd/journald.conf
```

2. Uncomment the line containing `Storage=` and change it to

```
[...]
[Journal]
Storage=persistent
#Compress=yes
```

```
[...]
```

3. Save the file and restart systemd-journald:

```
systemctl restart systemd-journald
```

16.2 journalctl Useful Switches

This section introduces several common useful options to enhance the default **journalctl** behavior. All switches are described in the **journalctl** manual page, **man 1 journalctl**.

Tip: Messages Related to a Specific Executable

To show all journal messages related to a specific executable, specify the full path to the executable:

```
journalctl /usr/lib/systemd/systemd
```

-f

Shows only the most recent journal messages, and prints new log entries as they are added to the journal.

-e

Prints the messages and jumps to the end of the journal, so that the latest entries are visible within the pager.

-r

Prints the messages of the journal in reverse order, so that the latest entries are listed first.

-k

Shows only kernel messages. This is equivalent to the field match `_TRANSPORT=kernel` (see *Section 16.3.3, "Filtering Based on Fields"*).

-u

Shows only messages for the specified `systemd` unit. This is equivalent to the field match `_SYSTEMD_UNIT=UNIT` (see *Section 16.3.3, "Filtering Based on Fields"*).

```
# journalctl -u apache2
[...]
Jun 03 10:07:11 pinkiepie systemd[1]: Starting The Apache Webserver...
```

```
Jun 03 10:07:12 pinkiepie systemd[1]: Started The Apache Webserver.
```

16.3 Filtering the Journal Output

When called without switches, **journalctl** shows the full content of the journal, the oldest entries listed first. The output can be filtered by specific switches and fields.

16.3.1 Filtering Based on a Boot Number

journalctl can filter messages based on a specific system boot. To list all available boots, run

```
# journalctl --list-boots
-1 097ed2cd99124a2391d2cffab1b566f0 Mon 2014-05-26 08:36:56 EDT—Fri 2014-05-30 05:33:44
 EDT
 0 156019a44a774a0bb0148a92df4af81b Fri 2014-05-30 05:34:09 EDT—Fri 2014-05-30 06:15:01
 EDT
```

The first column lists the boot offset: `0` for the current boot, `-1` for the previous one, `-2` for the one prior to that, etc. The second column contains the boot ID followed by the limiting time stamps of the specific boot.

Show all messages from the current boot:

```
# journalctl -b
```

If you need to see journal messages from the previous boot, add an offset parameter. The following example outputs the previous boot messages:

```
# journalctl -b -1
```

Another way is to list boot messages based on the boot ID. For this purpose, use the _BOOT_ID field:

```
# journalctl _BOOT_ID=156019a44a774a0bb0148a92df4af81b
```

16.3.2 Filtering Based on Time Interval

You can filter the output of **journalctl** by specifying the starting and/or ending date. The date specification should be of the format "2014-06-30 9:17:16". If the time part is omitted, midnight is assumed. If seconds are omitted, ":00" is assumed. If the date part is omitted, the current day is assumed. Instead of numeric expression, you can specify the keywords "yesterday", "today", or "tomorrow". They refer to midnight of the day before the current day, of the current day, or of the day after the current day. If you specify "now", it refers to the current time. You can also specify relative times prefixed with `-` or `+`, referring to times before or after the current time.

Show only new messages since now, and update the output continuously:

```
# journalctl --since "now" -f
```

Show all messages since last midnight till 3:20am:

```
# journalctl --since "today" --until "3:20"
```

16.3.3 Filtering Based on Fields

You can filter the output of the journal by specific fields. The syntax of a field to be matched is `FIELD_NAME=MATCHED_VALUE`, such as `_SYSTEMD_UNIT=httpd.service`. You can specify multiple matches in a single query to filter the output messages even more. See **`man 7 systemd.journal-fields`** for a list of default fields.

Show messages produced by a specific process ID:

```
# journalctl _PID=1039
```

Show messages belonging to a specific user ID:

```
# journalctl _UID=1000
```

Show messages from the kernel ring buffer (the same as **`dmesg`** produces):

```
# journalctl _TRANSPORT=kernel
```

Show messages from the service's standard or error output:

```
# journalctl _TRANSPORT=stdout
```

Show messages produced by a specified service only:

```
# journalctl _SYSTEMD_UNIT=avahi-daemon.service
```

If two different fields are specified, only entries that match both expressions at the same time are shown:

```
# journalctl _SYSTEMD_UNIT=avahi-daemon.service _PID=1488
```

If two matches refer to the same field, all entries matching either expression are shown:

```
# journalctl _SYSTEMD_UNIT=avahi-daemon.service _SYSTEMD_UNIT=dbus.service
```

You can use the '+' separator to combine two expressions in a logical 'OR'. The following example shows all messages from the Avahi service process with the process ID 1480 together with all messages from the D-Bus service:

```
# journalctl _SYSTEMD_UNIT=avahi-daemon.service _PID=1480 + _SYSTEMD_UNIT=dbus.service
```

16.4 Investigating systemd Errors

This section introduces a simple example to illustrate how to find and fix the error reported by `systemd` during **apache2** start-up.

1. Try to start the apache2 service:

```
# systemctl start apache2
Job for apache2.service failed. See 'systemctl status apache2' and 'journalctl -xn'
 for details.
```

2. Let us see what the service's status says:

```
# systemctl status apache2
apache2.service - The Apache Webserver
   Loaded: loaded (/usr/lib/systemd/system/apache2.service; disabled)
   Active: failed (Result: exit-code) since Tue 2014-06-03 11:08:13 CEST; 7min ago
  Process: 11026 ExecStop=/usr/sbin/start_apache2 -D SYSTEMD -DFOREGROUND \
           -k graceful-stop (code=exited, status=1/FAILURE)
```

The ID of the process causing the failure is 11026.

3. Show the verbose version of messages related to process ID 11026:

```
# journalctl -o verbose _PID=11026
[...]
MESSAGE=AH00526: Syntax error on line 6 of /etc/apache2/default-server.conf:
```

```
[...]
MESSAGE=Invalid command 'DocumenttRoot', perhaps misspelled or defined by a module
[...]
```

4. Fix the typo inside `/etc/apache2/default-server.conf`, start the apache2 service, and print its status:

```
# systemctl start apache2 && systemctl status apache2
apache2.service - The Apache Webserver
   Loaded: loaded (/usr/lib/systemd/system/apache2.service; disabled)
   Active: active (running) since Tue 2014-06-03 11:26:24 CEST; 4ms ago
  Process: 11026 ExecStop=/usr/sbin/start_apache2 -D SYSTEMD -DFOREGROUND
           -k graceful-stop (code=exited, status=1/FAILURE)
 Main PID: 11263 (httpd2-prefork)
   Status: "Processing requests..."
   CGroup: /system.slice/apache2.service
           ├─11263 /usr/sbin/httpd2-prefork -f /etc/apache2/httpd.conf -D [...]
           ├─11280 /usr/sbin/httpd2-prefork -f /etc/apache2/httpd.conf -D [...]
           ├─11281 /usr/sbin/httpd2-prefork -f /etc/apache2/httpd.conf -D [...]
           ├─11282 /usr/sbin/httpd2-prefork -f /etc/apache2/httpd.conf -D [...]
           ├─11283 /usr/sbin/httpd2-prefork -f /etc/apache2/httpd.conf -D [...]
           └─11285 /usr/sbin/httpd2-prefork -f /etc/apache2/httpd.conf -D [...]
```

16.5 Journald Configuration

The behavior of the systemd-journald service can be adjusted by modifying `/etc/systemd/journald.conf`. This section introduces only basic option settings. For a complete file description, see **`man 5 journald.conf`**. Note that you need to restart the journal for the changes to take effect with

```
# systemctl restart systemd-journald
```

16.5.1 Changing the Journal Size Limit

If the journal log data is saved to a persistent location (see *Section 16.1, "Making the Journal Persistent"*), it uses up to 10% of the file system the `/var/log/journal` resides on. For example, if `/var/log/journal` is located on a 30 GB `/var` partition, the journal may use up to 3 GB of the disk space. To change this limit, change (and uncomment) the `SystemMaxUse` option:

```
SystemMaxUse=50M
```

16.5.2 Forwarding the Journal to /dev/ttyX

You can forward the journal to a terminal device to inform you about system messages on a preferred terminal screen, for example `/dev/tty12`. Change the following journald options to

```
ForwardToConsole=yes
TTYPath=/dev/tty12
```

16.5.3 Forwarding the Journal to Syslog Facility

Journald is backward compatible with traditional syslog implementations such as `rsyslog`. Make sure the following is valid:

- rsyslog is installed.

```
# rpm -q rsyslog
rsyslog-7.4.8-2.16.x86_64
```

- rsyslog service is enabled.

```
# systemctl is-enabled rsyslog
enabled
```

- Forwarding to syslog is enabled in `/etc/systemd/journald.conf`.

```
ForwardToSyslog=yes
```

16.6 Using YaST to Filter the systemd Journal

For an easy way of filtering the systemd journal (without having to deal with the journalctl syntax), you can use the YaST journal module. After installing it with **`sudo zypper in yast2-journal`**, start it from YaST by selecting *System › Systemd Journal*. Alternatively, start it from command line by entering **`sudo yast2 journal`**.

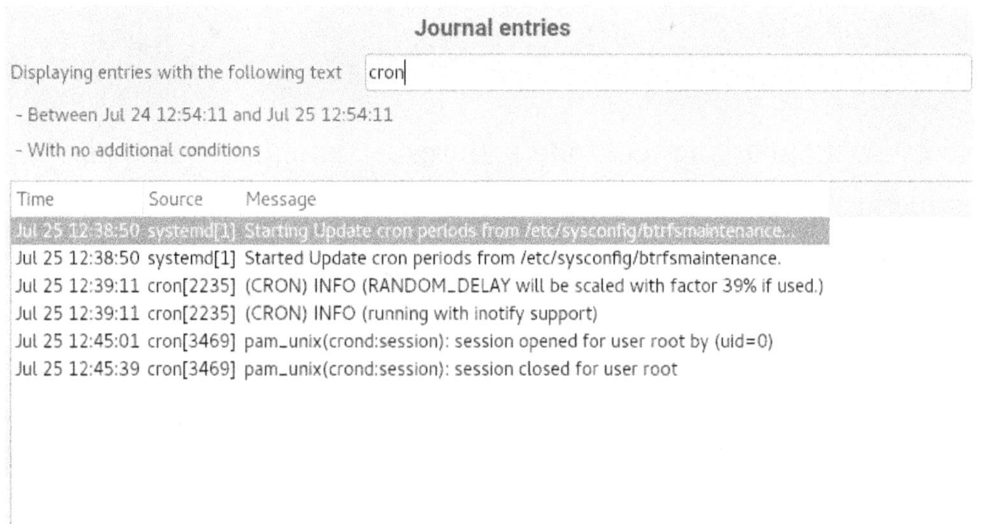

FIGURE 16.1: YAST SYSTEMD JOURNAL

The module displays the log entries in a table. The search box on top allows you to search for entries that contain certain characters, similar to using **grep**. To filter the entries by date and time, unit, file, or priority, click *Change filters* and set the respective options.

17 Basic Networking

Linux offers the necessary networking tools and features for integration into all types of network structures. Network access using a network card can be configured with YaST. Manual configuration is also possible. In this chapter only the fundamental mechanisms and the relevant network configuration files are covered.

Linux and other Unix operating systems use the TCP/IP protocol. It is not a single network protocol, but a family of network protocols that offer various services. The protocols listed in *Several Protocols in the TCP/IP Protocol Family*, are provided for exchanging data between two machines via TCP/IP. Networks combined by TCP/IP, comprising a worldwide network, are also called "the Internet."

RFC stands for *Request for Comments*. RFCs are documents that describe various Internet protocols and implementation procedures for the operating system and its applications. The RFC documents describe the setup of Internet protocols. For more information about RFCs, see http://www.ietf.org/rfc.html ↗.

SEVERAL PROTOCOLS IN THE TCP/IP PROTOCOL FAMILY

TCP

Transmission Control Protocol: a connection-oriented secure protocol. The data to transmit is first sent by the application as a stream of data and converted into the appropriate format by the operating system. The data arrives at the respective application on the destination host in the original data stream format it was initially sent. TCP determines whether any data has been lost or jumbled during the transmission. TCP is implemented wherever the data sequence matters.

UDP

User Datagram Protocol: a connectionless, insecure protocol. The data to transmit is sent in the form of packets generated by the application. The order in which the data arrives at the recipient is not guaranteed and data loss is possible. UDP is suitable for record-oriented applications. It features a smaller latency period than TCP.

ICMP

Internet Control Message Protocol: This is not a protocol for the end user, but a special control protocol that issues error reports and can control the behavior of machines participating in TCP/IP data transfer. In addition, it provides a special echo mode that can be viewed using the program ping.

IGMP

Internet Group Management Protocol: This protocol controls machine behavior when implementing IP multicast.

As shown in *Figure 17.1, "Simplified Layer Model for TCP/IP"*, data exchange takes place in different layers. The actual network layer is the insecure data transfer via IP (Internet protocol). On top of IP, TCP (transmission control protocol) guarantees, to a certain extent, security of the data transfer. The IP layer is supported by the underlying hardware-dependent protocol, such as Ethernet.

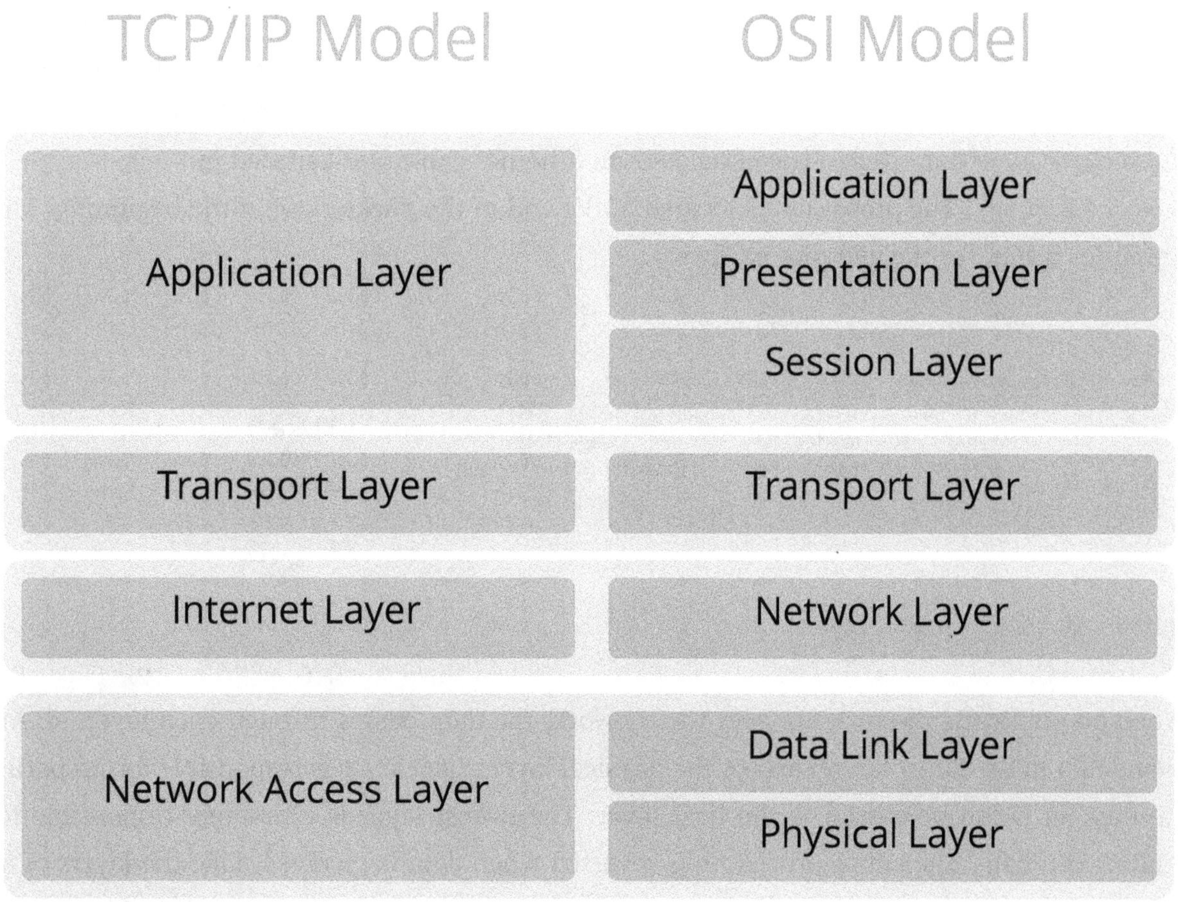

FIGURE 17.1: SIMPLIFIED LAYER MODEL FOR TCP/IP

The diagram provides one or two examples for each layer. The layers are ordered according to *abstraction levels*. The lowest layer is very close to the hardware. The uppermost layer, however, is almost a complete abstraction from the hardware. Every layer has its own special function. The special functions of each layer are mostly implicit in their description. The data link and physical layers represent the physical network used, such as Ethernet.

Almost all hardware protocols work on a packet-oriented basis. The data to transmit is collected into *packets* (it cannot be sent all at once). The maximum size of a TCP/IP packet is approximately 64 KB. Packets are normally quite smaller, as the network hardware can be a limiting factor. The maximum size of a data packet on an Ethernet is about fifteen hundred bytes. The size of a TCP/IP packet is limited to this amount when the data is sent over an Ethernet. If more data is transferred, more data packets need to be sent by the operating system.

For the layers to serve their designated functions, additional information regarding each layer must be saved in the data packet. This takes place in the *header* of the packet. Every layer attaches a small block of data, called the protocol header, to the front of each emerging packet. A sample TCP/IP data packet traveling over an Ethernet cable is illustrated in Figure 17.2, "TCP/IP Ethernet Packet". The proof sum is located at the end of the packet, not at the beginning. This simplifies things for the network hardware.

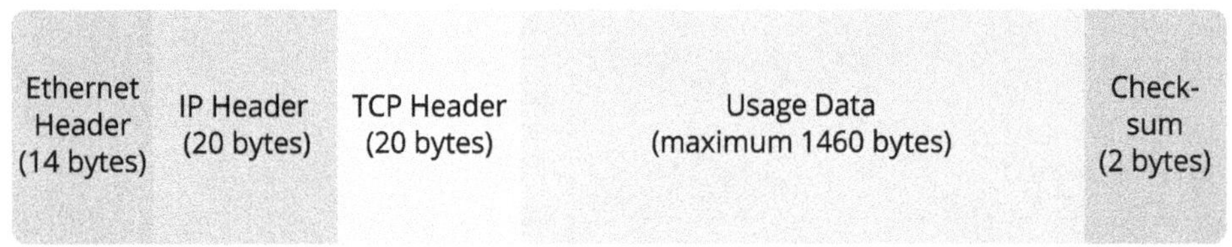

FIGURE 17.2: TCP/IP ETHERNET PACKET

When an application sends data over the network, the data passes through each layer, all implemented in the Linux kernel except the physical layer. Each layer is responsible for preparing the data so it can be passed to the next layer. The lowest layer is ultimately responsible for sending the data. The entire procedure is reversed when data is received. Like the layers of an onion, in each layer the protocol headers are removed from the transported data. Finally, the transport layer is responsible for making the data available for use by the applications at the destination. In this manner, one layer only communicates with the layer directly above or below it. For applications, it is irrelevant whether data is transmitted via a 100 Mbit/s FDDI network or via a 56-Kbit/s modem line. Likewise, it is irrelevant for the data line which kind of data is transmitted, as long as packets are in the correct format.

17.1 IP Addresses and Routing

The discussion in this section is limited to IPv4 networks. For information about IPv6 protocol, the successor to IPv4, refer to Section 17.2, "IPv6—The Next Generation Internet".

17.1.1 IP Addresses

Every computer on the Internet has a unique 32-bit address. These 32 bits (or 4 bytes) are normally written as illustrated in the second row in Example 17.1, "Writing IP Addresses".

EXAMPLE 17.1: WRITING IP ADDRESSES

```
IP Address (binary):  11000000 10101000 00000000 00010100
IP Address (decimal):      192.     168.       0.      20
```

In decimal form, the four bytes are written in the decimal number system, separated by periods. The IP address is assigned to a host or a network interface. It can be used only once throughout the world. There are exceptions to this rule, but these are not relevant to the following passages.

The points in IP addresses indicate the hierarchical system. Until the 1990s, IP addresses were strictly categorized in classes. However, this system proved too inflexible and was discontinued. Now, *classless routing* (CIDR, classless interdomain routing) is used.

17.1.2 Netmasks and Routing

Netmasks are used to define the address range of a subnet. If two hosts are in the same subnet, they can reach each other directly. If they are not in the same subnet, they need the address of a gateway that handles all the traffic for the subnet. To check if two IP addresses are in the same subnet, simply "AND" both addresses with the netmask. If the result is identical, both IP addresses are in the same local network. If there are differences, the remote IP address, and thus the remote interface, can only be reached over a gateway.

To understand how the netmask works, look at Example 17.2, "Linking IP Addresses to the Netmask". The netmask consists of 32 bits that identify how much of an IP address belongs to the network. All those bits that are `1` mark the corresponding bit in the IP address as belonging to the network. All bits that are `0` mark bits inside the subnet. This means that the more bits are `1`, the smaller the subnet is. Because the netmask always consists of several successive `1` bits, it is also possible to count the number of bits in the netmask. In Example 17.2, "Linking IP Addresses to the Netmask" the first net with 24 bits could also be written as `192.168.0.0/24`.

EXAMPLE 17.2: LINKING IP ADDRESSES TO THE NETMASK

```
IP address (192.168.0.20):  11000000 10101000 00000000 00010100
Netmask   (255.255.255.0):  11111111 11111111 11111111 00000000
---------------------------------------------------------------
Result of the link:         11000000 10101000 00000000 00000000
In the decimal system:           192.     168.       0.       0

IP address (213.95.15.200): 11010101 10111111 00001111 11001000
Netmask    (255.255.255.0): 11111111 11111111 11111111 00000000
---------------------------------------------------------------
Result of the link:         11010101 10111111 00001111 00000000
In the decimal system:           213.      95.      15.       0
```

To give another example: all machines connected with the same Ethernet cable are usually located in the same subnet and are directly accessible. Even when the subnet is physically divided by switches or bridges, these hosts can still be reached directly.

IP addresses outside the local subnet can only be reached if a gateway is configured for the target network. In the most common case, there is only one gateway that handles all traffic that is external. However, it is also possible to configure several gateways for different subnets.

If a gateway has been configured, all external IP packets are sent to the appropriate gateway. This gateway then attempts to forward the packets in the same manner—from host to host—until it reaches the destination host or the packet's TTL (time to live) expires.

SPECIFIC ADDRESSES

Base Network Address

This is the netmask AND any address in the network, as shown in *Example 17.2, "Linking IP Addresses to the Netmask"* under `Result`. This address cannot be assigned to any hosts.

Broadcast Address

This could be paraphrased as: "Access all hosts in this subnet." To generate this, the netmask is inverted in binary form and linked to the base network address with a logical OR. The above example therefore results in 192.168.0.255. This address cannot be assigned to any hosts.

Local Host

The address `127.0.0.1` is assigned to the "loopback device" on each host. A connection can be set up to your own machine with this address and with all addresses from the complete `127.0.0.0/8` loopback network as defined with IPv4. With IPv6 there is only one loopback address (`::1`).

Because IP addresses must be unique all over the world, you cannot select random addresses. There are three address domains to use if you want to set up a private IP-based network. These cannot get any connection from the rest of the Internet, because they cannot be transmitted over the Internet. These address domains are specified in RFC 1597 and listed in *Table 17.1, "Private IP Address Domains"*.

TABLE 17.1: PRIVATE IP ADDRESS DOMAINS

Network/Netmask	Domain
`10.0.0.0/255.0.0.0`	`10.x.x.x`
`172.16.0.0/255.240.0.0`	`172.16.x.x – 172.31.x.x`
`192.168.0.0/255.255.0.0`	`192.168.x.x`

17.2 IPv6—The Next Generation Internet

Due to the emergence of the World Wide Web (WWW), the Internet has experienced explosive growth, with an increasing number of computers communicating via TCP/IP in the past fifteen years. Since Tim Berners-Lee at CERN (http://public.web.cern.ch) invented the WWW in 1990, the number of Internet hosts has grown from a few thousand to about a hundred million.

As mentioned, an IPv4 address consists of only 32 bits. Also, quite a few IP addresses are lost —they cannot be used because of the way in which networks are organized. The number of addresses available in your subnet is two to the power of the number of bits, minus two. A subnet has, for example, 2, 6, or 14 addresses available. To connect 128 hosts to the Internet, for example, you need a subnet with 256 IP addresses, from which only 254 are usable, because two IP addresses are needed for the structure of the subnet itself: the broadcast and the base network address.

Under the current IPv4 protocol, DHCP or NAT (network address translation) are the typical mechanisms used to circumvent the potential address shortage. Combined with the convention to keep private and public address spaces separate, these methods can certainly mitigate the shortage. The problem with them lies in their configuration, which is a chore to set up and a burden to maintain. To set up a host in an IPv4 network, you need several address items, such as the host's own IP address, the subnetmask, the gateway address and maybe a name server address. All these items need to be known and cannot be derived from somewhere else.

With IPv6, both the address shortage and the complicated configuration should be a thing of the past. The following sections tell more about the improvements and benefits brought by IPv6 and about the transition from the old protocol to the new one.

17.2.1 Advantages

The most important and most visible improvement brought by the new protocol is the enormous expansion of the available address space. An IPv6 address is made up of 128 bit values instead of the traditional 32 bits. This provides for as many as several quadrillion IP addresses.

However, IPv6 addresses are not only different from their predecessors with regard to their length. They also have a different internal structure that may contain more specific information about the systems and the networks to which they belong. More details about this are found in *Section 17.2.2, "Address Types and Structure"*.

The following is a list of other advantages of the new protocol:

Autoconfiguration

IPv6 makes the network "plug and play" capable, which means that a newly set up system integrates into the (local) network without any manual configuration. The new host uses its automatic configuration mechanism to derive its own address from the information made available by the neighboring routers, relying on a protocol called the *neighbor discovery* (ND) protocol. This method does not require any intervention on the administrator's part and there is no need to maintain a central server for address allocation—an additional advantage over IPv4, where automatic address allocation requires a DHCP server.

Nevertheless if a router is connected to a switch, the router should send periodic advertisements with flags telling the hosts of a network how they should interact with each other. For more information, see RFC 2462 and the `radvd.conf(5)` man page, and RFC 3315.

Mobility

IPv6 makes it possible to assign several addresses to one network interface at the same time. This allows users to access several networks easily, something that could be compared with the international roaming services offered by mobile phone companies. When you take your mobile phone abroad, the phone automatically logs in to a foreign service when it enters the corresponding area, so you can be reached under the same number everywhere and can place an outgoing call, as you would in your home area.

Secure Communication

With IPv4, network security is an add-on function. IPv6 includes IPsec as one of its core features, allowing systems to communicate over a secure tunnel to avoid eavesdropping by outsiders on the Internet.

Backward Compatibility

Realistically, it would be impossible to switch the entire Internet from IPv4 to IPv6 at one time. Therefore, it is crucial that both protocols can coexist not only on the Internet, but also on one system. This is ensured by compatible addresses (IPv4 addresses can easily be translated into IPv6 addresses) and by using several tunnels. See *Section 17.2.3, "Coexistence of IPv4 and IPv6"*. Also, systems can rely on a *dual stack IP* technique to support both protocols at the same time, meaning that they have two network stacks that are completely separate, such that there is no interference between the two protocol versions.

Custom Tailored Services through Multicasting

With IPv4, some services, such as SMB, need to broadcast their packets to all hosts in the local network. IPv6 allows a much more fine-grained approach by enabling servers to address hosts through *multicasting*, that is by addressing several hosts as parts of a group. This is different from addressing all hosts through *broadcasting* or each host individually through *unicasting*). Which hosts are addressed as a group may depend on the concrete application. There are some predefined groups to address all name servers (the *all name servers multicast group*), for example, or all routers (the *all routers multicast group*).

17.2.2 Address Types and Structure

As mentioned, the current IP protocol has two major limitations: there is an increasing shortage of IP addresses, and configuring the network and maintaining the routing tables is becoming a more complex and burdensome task. IPv6 solves the first problem by expanding the address space to 128 bits. The second one is mitigated by introducing a hierarchical address structure combined with sophisticated techniques to allocate network addresses, and *multihoming* (the ability to assign several addresses to one device, giving access to several networks).

When dealing with IPv6, it is useful to know about three different types of addresses:

Unicast

Addresses of this type are associated with exactly one network interface. Packets with such an address are delivered to only one destination. Accordingly, unicast addresses are used to transfer packets to individual hosts on the local network or the Internet.

Multicast

Addresses of this type relate to a group of network interfaces. Packets with such an address are delivered to all destinations that belong to the group. Multicast addresses are mainly used by certain network services to communicate with certain groups of hosts in a well-directed manner.

Anycast

Addresses of this type are related to a group of interfaces. Packets with such an address are delivered to the member of the group that is closest to the sender, according to the principles of the underlying routing protocol. Anycast addresses are used to make it easier for hosts to find out about servers offering certain services in the given network area. All servers of the same type have the same anycast address. Whenever a host requests a service, it receives a reply from the server with the closest location, as determined by the routing protocol. If this server should fail for some reason, the protocol automatically selects the second closest server, then the third one, and so forth.

An IPv6 address is made up of eight four-digit fields, each representing 16 bits, written in hexadecimal notation. They are separated by colons (:). Any leading zero bytes within a given field may be dropped, but zeros within the field or at its end may not. Another convention is that more than four consecutive zero bytes may be collapsed into a double colon. However, only one such `::` is allowed per address. This kind of shorthand notation is shown in *Example 17.3, "Sample IPv6 Address"*, where all three lines represent the same address.

EXAMPLE 17.3: SAMPLE IPV6 ADDRESS

```
fe80 : 0000 : 0000 : 0000 : 0000 : 10 : 1000 : 1a4
fe80 :    0 :    0 :    0 :    0 : 10 : 1000 : 1a4
fe80 :                           : 10 : 1000 : 1a4
```

Each part of an IPv6 address has a defined function. The first bytes form the prefix and specify the type of address. The center part is the network portion of the address, but it may be unused. The end of the address forms the host part. With IPv6, the netmask is defined by indicating the length of the prefix after a slash at the end of the address. An address, as shown in *Example 17.4, "IPv6 Address Specifying the Prefix Length"*, contains the information that the first 64 bits form the network part of the address and the last 64 form its host part. In other words, the `64` means that the netmask is filled with 64 1-bit values from the left. As with IPv4, the IP address is combined with AND with the values from the netmask to determine whether the host is located in the same subnet or in another one.

EXAMPLE 17.4: IPV6 ADDRESS SPECIFYING THE PREFIX LENGTH

```
fe80::10:1000:1a4/64
```

IPv6 knows about several predefined types of prefixes. Some are shown in Various IPv6 Prefixes.

VARIOUS IPV6 PREFIXES

`00`

IPv4 addresses and IPv4 over IPv6 compatibility addresses. These are used to maintain compatibility with IPv4. Their use still requires a router able to translate IPv6 packets into IPv4 packets. Several special addresses, such as the one for the loopback device, have this prefix as well.

`2` or `3` as the first digit

Aggregatable global unicast addresses. As is the case with IPv4, an interface can be assigned to form part of a certain subnet. Currently, there are the following address spaces: `2001::/16` (production quality address space) and `2002::/16` (6to4 address space).

`fe80::/10`

Link-local addresses. Addresses with this prefix should not be routed and should therefore only be reachable from within the same subnet.

`fec0::/10`

Site-local addresses. These may be routed, but only within the network of the organization to which they belong. In effect, they are the IPv6 equivalent of the current private network address space, such as `10.x.x.x`.

`ff`

These are multicast addresses.

A unicast address consists of three basic components:

Public Topology

The first part (which also contains one of the prefixes mentioned above) is used to route packets through the public Internet. It includes information about the company or institution that provides the Internet access.

Site Topology

The second part contains routing information about the subnet to which to deliver the packet.

Interface ID

The third part identifies the interface to which to deliver the packet. This also allows for the MAC to form part of the address. Given that the MAC is a globally unique, fixed identifier coded into the device by the hardware maker, the configuration procedure is substantially simplified. In fact, the first 64 address bits are consolidated to form the `EUI-64` token, with the last 48 bits taken from the MAC, and the remaining 24 bits containing special information about the token type. This also makes it possible to assign an `EUI-64` token to interfaces that do not have a MAC, such as those based on PPP.

On top of this basic structure, IPv6 distinguishes between five different types of unicast addresses:

`::` (unspecified)

This address is used by the host as its source address when the interface is initialized for the first time (at which point, the address cannot yet be determined by other means).

`::1` (loopback)

The address of the loopback device.

IPv4 Compatible Addresses

The IPv6 address is formed by the IPv4 address and a prefix consisting of 96 zero bits. This type of compatibility address is used for tunneling (see *Section 17.2.3, "Coexistence of IPv4 and IPv6"*) to allow IPv4 and IPv6 hosts to communicate with others operating in a pure IPv4 environment.

IPv4 Addresses Mapped to IPv6

This type of address specifies a pure IPv4 address in IPv6 notation.

Local Addresses

There are two address types for local use:

link-local

This type of address can only be used in the local subnet. Packets with a source or target address of this type should not be routed to the Internet or other subnets. These addresses contain a special prefix (`fe80::/10`) and the interface ID of the network card, with the middle part consisting of zero bytes. Addresses of this type are used during automatic configuration to communicate with other hosts belonging to the same subnet.

site-local

Packets with this type of address may be routed to other subnets, but not to the wider Internet—they must remain inside the organization's own network. Such addresses are used for intranets and are an equivalent of the private address space defined by IPv4. They contain a special prefix (`fec0::/10`), the interface ID, and a 16 bit field specifying the subnet ID. Again, the rest is filled with zero bytes.

As a completely new feature introduced with IPv6, each network interface normally gets several IP addresses, with the advantage that several networks can be accessed through the same interface. One of these networks can be configured completely automatically using the MAC and a known prefix with the result that all hosts on the local network can be reached when IPv6 is enabled (using the link-local address). With the MAC forming part of it, any IP address used in the world is unique. The only variable parts of the address are those specifying the *site topology* and the *public topology*, depending on the actual network in which the host is currently operating.

For a host to go back and forth between different networks, it needs at least two addresses. One of them, the *home address*, not only contains the interface ID but also an identifier of the home network to which it normally belongs (and the corresponding prefix). The home address is a static address and, as such, it does not normally change. Still, all packets destined to the mobile host can be delivered to it, regardless of whether it operates in the home network or somewhere outside. This is made possible by the completely new features introduced with IPv6, such as *stateless autoconfiguration* and *neighbor discovery*. In addition to its home address, a mobile host gets one or more additional addresses that belong to the foreign networks where it is roaming. These are called *care-of* addresses. The home network has a facility that forwards any packets destined to the host when it is roaming outside. In an IPv6 environment, this task is performed by the *home agent*, which takes all packets destined to the home address and relays them through a tunnel. On the other hand, those packets destined to the care-of address are directly transferred to the mobile host without any special detours.

17.2.3 Coexistence of IPv4 and IPv6

The migration of all hosts connected to the Internet from IPv4 to IPv6 is a gradual process. Both protocols will coexist for some time to come. The coexistence on one system is guaranteed where there is a *dual stack* implementation of both protocols. That still leaves the question of how an IPv6 enabled host should communicate with an IPv4 host and how IPv6 packets should be transported by the current networks, which are predominantly IPv4-based. The best solutions offer tunneling and compatibility addresses (see *Section 17.2.2, "Address Types and Structure"*).

IPv6 hosts that are more or less isolated in the (worldwide) IPv4 network can communicate through tunnels: IPv6 packets are encapsulated as IPv4 packets to move them across an IPv4 network. Such a connection between two IPv4 hosts is called a *tunnel*. To achieve this, packets must include the IPv6 destination address (or the corresponding prefix) and the IPv4 address of the remote host at the receiving end of the tunnel. A basic tunnel can be configured manually according to an agreement between the hosts' administrators. This is also called *static tunneling*.

However, the configuration and maintenance of static tunnels is often too labor-intensive to use them for daily communication needs. Therefore, IPv6 provides for three different methods of *dynamic tunneling*:

6over4

IPv6 packets are automatically encapsulated as IPv4 packets and sent over an IPv4 network capable of multicasting. IPv6 is tricked into seeing the whole network (Internet) as a huge local area network (LAN). This makes it possible to determine the receiving end of the IPv4 tunnel automatically. However, this method does not scale very well and is also hampered because IP multicasting is far from widespread on the Internet. Therefore, it only provides a solution for smaller corporate or institutional networks where multicasting can be enabled. The specifications for this method are laid down in RFC 2529.

6to4

With this method, IPv4 addresses are automatically generated from IPv6 addresses, enabling isolated IPv6 hosts to communicate over an IPv4 network. However, several problems have been reported regarding the communication between those isolated IPv6 hosts and the Internet. The method is described in RFC 3056.

IPv6 Tunnel Broker

This method relies on special servers that provide dedicated tunnels for IPv6 hosts. It is described in RFC 3053.

17.2.4 Configuring IPv6

To configure IPv6, you normally do not need to make any changes on the individual workstations. IPv6 is enabled by default. To disable or enable IPv6 on an installed system, use the YaST *Network Settings* module. On the *Global Options* tab, check or uncheck the *Enable IPv6* option as necessary. To enable it temporarily until the next reboot, enter `modprobe -i ipv6` as `root`. It is impossible to unload the IPv6 module after it has been loaded.

Because of the autoconfiguration concept of IPv6, the network card is assigned an address in the *link-local* network. Normally, no routing table management takes place on a workstation. The network routers can be queried by the workstation, using the *router advertisement protocol*, for what prefix and gateways should be implemented. The radvd program can be used to set up an IPv6 router. This program informs the workstations which prefix to use for the IPv6 addresses and which routers. Alternatively, use zebra/quagga for automatic configuration of both addresses and routing.

For information about how to set up various types of tunnels using the `/etc/sysconfig/network` files, see the man page of `ifcfg-tunnel` (**`man ifcfg-tunnel`**).

17.2.5 For More Information

The above overview does not cover the topic of IPv6 comprehensively. For a more in-depth look at the new protocol, refer to the following online documentation and books:

http://www.ipv6.org/ ↗
: The starting point for everything about IPv6.

http://www.ipv6day.org ↗
: All information needed to start your own IPv6 network.

http://www.ipv6-to-standard.org/ ↗
: The list of IPv6-enabled products.

http://www.bieringer.de/linux/IPv6/ ↗
: Here, find the Linux IPv6-HOWTO and many links related to the topic.

RFC 2460
: The fundamental RFC about IPv6.

IPv6 Essentials
: A book describing all the important aspects of the topic is *IPv6 Essentials* by Silvia Hagen (ISBN 0-596-00125-8).

17.3 Name Resolution

DNS assists in assigning an IP address to one or more names and assigning a name to an IP address. In Linux, this conversion is usually carried out by a special type of software known as bind. The machine that takes care of this conversion is called a *name server*. The names make up a hierarchical system in which each name component is separated by a period. The name hierarchy is, however, independent of the IP address hierarchy described above.

Consider a complete name, such as `jupiter.example.com`, written in the format `hostname.domain`. A full name, called a *fully qualified domain name* (FQDN), consists of a host name and a domain name (`example.com`). The latter also includes the *top level domain* or TLD (`com`).

TLD assignment has become quite confusing for historical reasons. Traditionally, three-letter domain names are used in the USA. In the rest of the world, the two-letter ISO national codes are the standard. In addition to that, longer TLDs were introduced in 2000 that represent certain spheres of activity (for example, `.info`, `.name`, `.museum`).

In the early days of the Internet (before 1990), the file `/etc/hosts` was used to store the names of all the machines represented over the Internet. This quickly proved to be impractical in the face of the rapidly growing number of computers connected to the Internet. For this reason, a decentralized database was developed to store the host names in a widely distributed manner. This database, similar to the name server, does not have the data pertaining to all hosts in the Internet readily available, but can dispatch requests to other name servers.

The top of the hierarchy is occupied by *root name servers*. These root name servers manage the top level domains and are run by the Network Information Center (NIC). Each root name server knows about the name servers responsible for a given top level domain. Information about top level domain NICs is available at http://www.internic.net ↗.

DNS can do more than resolve host names. The name server also knows which host is receiving e-mails for an entire domain—the *mail exchanger (MX)*.

For your machine to resolve an IP address, it must know about at least one name server and its IP address. Easily specify such a name server using YaST.

The protocol `whois` is closely related to DNS. With this program, quickly find out who is responsible for a given domain.

Note: MDNS and .local Domain Names

The `.local` top level domain is treated as link-local domain by the resolver. DNS requests are send as multicast DNS requests instead of normal DNS requests. If you already use the `.local` domain in your name server configuration, you must switch this option off in `/etc/host.conf`. For more information, see the `host.conf` manual page.

If you want to switch off MDNS during installation, use `nomdns=1` as a boot parameter.

For more information on multicast DNS, see http://www.multicastdns.org.

17.4 Configuring a Network Connection with YaST

There are many supported networking types on Linux. Most of them use different device names and the configuration files are spread over several locations in the file system. For a detailed overview of the aspects of manual network configuration, see *Section 17.6, "Configuring a Network Connection Manually"*.

On SUSE Linux Enterprise Desktop, where NetworkManager is active by default, all network cards are configured. If NetworkManager is not active, only the first interface with link up (with a network cable connected) is automatically configured. Additional hardware can be configured any time on the installed system. The following sections describe the network configuration for all types of network connections supported by SUSE Linux Enterprise Desktop.

17.4.1 Configuring the Network Card with YaST

To configure your Ethernet or Wi-Fi/Bluetooth card in YaST, select *System* › *Network Settings*. After starting the module, YaST displays the *Network Settings* dialog with four tabs: *Global Options*, *Overview*, *Hostname/DNS* and *Routing*.

The *Global Options* tab allows you to set general networking options such as the network setup method, IPv6, and general DHCP options. For more information, see *Section 17.4.1.1, "Configuring Global Networking Options"*.

The *Overview* tab contains information about installed network interfaces and configurations. Any properly detected network card is listed with its name. You can manually configure new cards, remove or change their configuration in this dialog. To manually configure a card that was not automatically detected, see *Section 17.4.1.3, "Configuring an Undetected Network Card"*. If you want to change the configuration of an already configured card, see *Section 17.4.1.2, "Changing the Configuration of a Network Card"*.

The *Hostname/DNS* tab allows to set the host name of the machine and name the servers to be used. For more information, see *Section 17.4.1.4, "Configuring Host Name and DNS"*.

The *Routing* tab is used for the configuration of routing. See *Section 17.4.1.5, "Configuring Routing"* for more information.

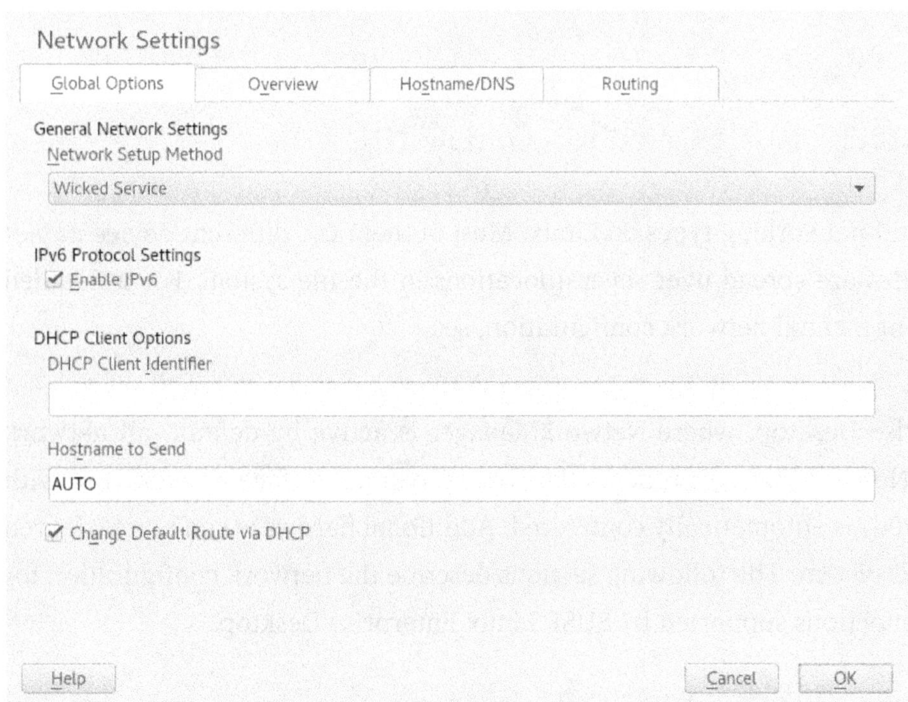

FIGURE 17.3: CONFIGURING NETWORK SETTINGS

17.4.1.1 Configuring Global Networking Options

The *Global Options* tab of the YaST *Network Settings* module allows you to set important global networking options, such as the use of NetworkManager, IPv6 and DHCP client options. These settings are applicable for all network interfaces.

In the *Network Setup Method* choose the way network connections are managed. If you want a NetworkManager desktop applet to manage connections for all interfaces, choose *NetworkManager Service*. NetworkManager is well suited for switching between multiple wired and wireless networks. If you do not run a desktop environment, or if your computer is a Xen server, virtual system, or provides network services such as DHCP or DNS in your network, use the *Wicked*

Service method. If NetworkManager is used, `nm-applet` should be used to configure network options and the *Overview, Hostname/DNS* and *Routing* tabs of the *Network Settings* module are disabled. For more information on NetworkManager, see Chapter 30, Using NetworkManager.

In the *IPv6 Protocol Settings* choose whether to use the IPv6 protocol. It is possible to use IPv6 together with IPv4. By default, IPv6 is enabled. However, in networks not using IPv6 protocol, response times can be faster with IPv6 protocol disabled. To disable IPv6, deactivate *Enable IPv6*. If IPv6 is disabled, the kernel no longer loads the IPv6 module automatically. This setting will be applied after reboot.

In the *DHCP Client Options* configure options for the DHCP client. The *DHCP Client Identifier* must be different for each DHCP client on a single network. If left empty, it defaults to the hardware address of the network interface. However, if you are running several virtual machines using the same network interface and, therefore, the same hardware address, specify a unique free-form identifier here.

The *Hostname to Send* specifies a string used for the host name option field when the DHCP client sends messages to DHCP server. Some DHCP servers update name server zones (forward and reverse records) according to this host name (Dynamic DNS). Also, some DHCP servers require the *Hostname to Send* option field to contain a specific string in the DHCP messages from clients. Leave `AUTO` to send the current host name (that is the one defined in `/etc/HOSTNAME`). Make the option field empty for not sending any host name.

If you do not want to change the default route according to the information from DHCP, deactivate *Change Default Route via DHCP*.

17.4.1.2 Changing the Configuration of a Network Card

To change the configuration of a network card, select a card from the list of the detected cards in *Network Settings › Overview* in YaST and click *Edit*. The *Network Card Setup* dialog appears in which to adjust the card configuration using the *General, Address* and *Hardware* tabs.

17.4.1.2.1 Configuring IP Addresses

You can set the IP address of the network card or the way its IP address is determined in the *Address* tab of the *Network Card Setup* dialog. Both IPv4 and IPv6 addresses are supported. The network card can have *No IP Address* (which is useful for bonding devices), a *Statically Assigned IP Address* (IPv4 or IPv6) or a *Dynamic Address* assigned via *DHCP* or *Zeroconf* or both.

If using *Dynamic Address*, select whether to use *DHCP Version 4 Only* (for IPv4), *DHCP Version 6 Only* (for IPv6) or *DHCP Both Version 4 and 6*.

If possible, the first network card with link that is available during the installation is automatically configured to use automatic address setup via DHCP. On SUSE Linux Enterprise Desktop, where NetworkManager is active by default, all network cards are configured.

DHCP should also be used if you are using a DSL line but with no static IP assigned by the ISP (Internet Service Provider). If you decide to use DHCP, configure the details in *DHCP Client Options* in the *Global Options* tab of the *Network Settings* dialog of the YaST network card configuration module. If you have a virtual host setup where different hosts communicate through the same interface, an *DHCP Client Identifier* is necessary to distinguish them.

DHCP is a good choice for client configuration but it is not ideal for server configuration. To set a static IP address, proceed as follows:

1. Select a card from the list of detected cards in the *Overview* tab of the YaST network card configuration module and click *Edit*.
2. In the *Address* tab, choose *Statically Assigned IP Address*.
3. Enter the *IP Address*. Both IPv4 and IPv6 addresses can be used. Enter the network mask in *Subnet Mask*. If the IPv6 address is used, use *Subnet Mask* for prefix length in format `/64`. Optionally, you can enter a fully qualified *Hostname* for this address, which will be written to the `/etc/hosts` configuration file.
4. Click *Next*.
5. To activate the configuration, click *OK*.

Note: Interface Activation and Link Detection

During activation of a network interface, **`wicked`** checks for a carrier and only applies the IP configuration when a link has been detected. If you need to apply the configuration regardless of the link status (for example, when you want to test a service listening to a certain address), you can skip link detection by adding the variable `LINK_REQUIRED=no` to the configuration file of the interface in `/etc/sysconfig/network/ifcfg`.

Additionally, you can use the variable `LINK_READY_WAIT=5` to specify the timeout for waiting for a link in seconds.

For more information about the `ifcfg-*` configuration files, refer to *Section 17.6.2.5, "/etc/sysconfig/network/ifcfg-*"* and **`man 5 ifcfg`**.

If you use the static address, the name servers and default gateway are not configured automatically. To configure name servers, proceed as described in *Section 17.4.1.4, "Configuring Host Name and DNS"*. To configure a gateway, proceed as described in *Section 17.4.1.5, "Configuring Routing"*.

17.4.1.2.2 Configuring Multiple Addresses

One network device can have multiple IP addresses.

Note: Aliases Are a Compatibility Feature

These so-called aliases or labels, respectively, work with IPv4 only. With IPv6 they will be ignored. Using `iproute2` network interfaces can have one or more addresses.

Using YaST to set additional addresses for your network card, proceed as follows:

1. Select a card from the list of detected cards in the *Overview* tab of the YaST *Network Settings* dialog and click *Edit*.
2. In the *Address › Additional Addresses* tab, click *Add*.
3. Enter *IPv4 Address Label*, *IP Address*, and *Netmask*. Do not include the interface name in the alias name.
4. To activate the configuration, confirm the settings.

17.4.1.2.3 Changing the Device Name and Udev Rules

It is possible to change the device name of the network card when it is used. It is also possible to determine whether the network card should be identified by udev via its hardware (MAC) address or via the bus ID. The later option is preferable in large servers to simplify hotplugging of cards. To set these options with YaST, proceed as follows:

1. Select a card from the list of detected cards in the *Overview* tab of the YaST *Network Settings* dialog and click *Edit*.
2. Go to the *Hardware* tab. The current device name is shown in *Udev Rules*. Click *Change*.
3. Select whether udev should identify the card by its *MAC Address* or *Bus ID*. The current MAC address and bus ID of the card are shown in the dialog.

4. To change the device name, check the *Change Device Name* option and edit the name.
5. To activate the configuration, confirm the settings.

17.4.1.2.4 Changing Network Card Kernel Driver

For some network cards, several kernel drivers may be available. If the card is already configured, YaST allows you to select a kernel driver to be used from a list of available suitable drivers. It is also possible to specify options for the kernel driver. To set these options with YaST, proceed as follows:

1. Select a card from the list of detected cards in the *Overview* tab of the YaST Network Settings module and click *Edit*.
2. Go to the *Hardware* tab.
3. Select the kernel driver to be used in *Module Name*. Enter any options for the selected driver in *Options* in the form `=` = *`VALUE`*. If more options are used, they should be space-separated.
4. To activate the configuration, confirm the settings.

17.4.1.2.5 Activating the Network Device

If you use the method with **`wicked`**, you can configure your device to either start during boot, on cable connection, on card detection, manually, or never. To change device start-up, proceed as follows:

1. In YaST select a card from the list of detected cards in *System › Network Settings* and click *Edit*.
2. In the *General* tab, select the desired entry from *Device Activation*.
   Choose *At Boot Time* to start the device during the system boot. With *On Cable Connection*, the interface is watched for any existing physical connection. With *On Hotplug*, the interface is set when available. It is similar to the *At Boot Time* option, and only differs in that no error occurs if the interface is not present at boot time. Choose *Manually* to control the interface manually with **`ifup`**. Choose *Never* to not start the device. The *On NFSroot* is similar to *At Boot Time*, but the interface does not shut down with the **`systemctl stop network`** command; the `network` service also cares about the `wicked` service if **`wicked`** is active. Use this if you use an NFS or iSCSI root file system.

3. To activate the configuration, confirm the settings.

Tip: NFS as a Root File System

On (diskless) systems where the root partition is mounted via network as an NFS share, you need to be careful when configuring the network device with which the NFS share is accessible.

When shutting down or rebooting the system, the default processing order is to turn off network connections, then unmount the root partition. With NFS root, this order causes problems as the root partition cannot be cleanly unmounted as the network connection to the NFS share is already not activated. To prevent the system from deactivating the relevant network device, open the network device configuration tab as described in *Section 17.4.1.2.5, "Activating the Network Device"* and choose *On NFSroot* in the *Device Activation* pane.

17.4.1.2.6 Setting Up Maximum Transfer Unit Size

You can set a maximum transmission unit (MTU) for the interface. MTU refers to the largest allowed packet size in bytes. A higher MTU brings higher bandwidth efficiency. However, large packets can block up a slow interface for some time, increasing the lag for further packets.

1. In YaST select a card from the list of detected cards in *System* › *Network Settings* and click *Edit*.
2. In the *General* tab, select the desired entry from the *Set MTU* list.
3. To activate the configuration, confirm the settings.

17.4.1.2.7 PCIe Multifunction Devices

Multifunction devices that support LAN, iSCSI, and FCoE are supported. YaST FCoE client (`yast2 fcoe-client`) shows the private flags in additional columns to allow the user to select the device meant for FCoE. YaST network module (`yast2 lan`) excludes "storage only devices" for network configuration.

17.4.1.2.8 Infiniband Configuration for IP-over-InfiniBand (IPoIB)

1. In YaST select the InfiniBand device in *System › Network Settings* and click *Edit*.
2. In the *General* tab, select one of the *IP-over-InfiniBand* (IPoIB) modes: *connected* (default) or *datagram*.
3. To activate the configuration, confirm the settings.

For more information about InfiniBand, see `/usr/src/linux/Documentation/infiniband/ipoib.txt`.

17.4.1.2.9 Configuring the Firewall

Without having to enter the detailed firewall setup as described in *Book "Security Guide", Chapter 15 "Masquerading and Firewalls", Section 15.4.1 "Configuring the Firewall with YaST"*, you can determine the basic firewall configuration for your device as part of the device setup. Proceed as follows:

1. Open the YaST *System › Network Settings* module. In the *Overview* tab, select a card from the list of detected cards and click *Edit*.
2. Enter the *General* tab of the *Network Settings* dialog.
3. Determine the *Firewall Zone* to which your interface should be assigned. The following options are available:

   Firewall Disabled

   This option is available only if the firewall is disabled and the firewall does not run. Only use this option if your machine is part of a greater network that is protected by an outer firewall.

   Automatically Assign Zone

   This option is available only if the firewall is enabled. The firewall is running and the interface is automatically assigned to a firewall zone. The zone which contains the keyword `any` or the external zone will be used for such an interface.

Internal Zone (Unprotected)

The firewall is running, but does not enforce any rules to protect this interface. Use this option if your machine is part of a greater network that is protected by an outer firewall. It is also useful for the interfaces connected to the internal network, when the machine has more network interfaces.

Demilitarized Zone

A demilitarized zone is an additional line of defense in front of an internal network and the (hostile) Internet. Hosts assigned to this zone can be reached from the internal network and from the Internet, but cannot access the internal network.

External Zone

The firewall is running on this interface and fully protects it against other—presumably hostile—network traffic. This is the default option.

4. To activate the configuration, confirm the settings.

17.4.1.3 Configuring an Undetected Network Card

If a network card is not detected correctly, the card is not included in the list of detected cards. If you are sure that your system includes a driver for your card, you can configure it manually. You can also configure special network device types, such as bridge, bond, TUN or TAP. To configure an undetected network card (or a special device) proceed as follows:

1. In the *System › Network Settings › Overview* dialog in YaST click *Add*.
2. In the *Hardware* dialog, set the *Device Type* of the interface from the available options and *Configuration Name*. If the network card is a PCMCIA or USB device, activate the respective check box and exit this dialog with *Next*. Otherwise, you can define the kernel *Module Name* to be used for the card and its *Options*, if necessary.
   In *Ethtool Options*, you can set **`ethtool`** options used by **`ifup`** for the interface. For information about available options, see the **`ethtool`** manual page.
   If the option string starts with a `-` (for example, `-K INTERFACE_NAME rx on`), the second word in the string is replaced with the current interface name. Otherwise (for example, `autoneg off speed 10`) **`ifup`** adds `-s INTERFACE_NAME` to the beginning.
3. Click *Next*.

4. Configure any needed options, such as the IP address, device activation or firewall zone for the interface in the *General*, *Address*, and *Hardware* tabs. For more information about the configuration options, see Section 17.4.1.2, "Changing the Configuration of a Network Card".

5. If you selected *Wireless* as the device type of the interface, configure the wireless connection in the next dialog.

6. To activate the new network configuration, confirm the settings.

17.4.1.4 Configuring Host Name and DNS

If you did not change the network configuration during installation and the Ethernet card was already available, a host name was automatically generated for your computer and DHCP was activated. The same applies to the name service information your host needs to integrate into a network environment. If DHCP is used for network address setup, the list of domain name servers is automatically filled with the appropriate data. If a static setup is preferred, set these values manually.

To change the name of your computer and adjust the name server search list, proceed as follows:

1. Go to the *Network Settings* › *Hostname/DNS* tab in the *System* module in YaST.

2. Enter the *Hostname* and, if needed, the *Domain Name*. The domain is especially important if the machine is a mail server. Note that the host name is global and applies to all set network interfaces.

   If you are using DHCP to get an IP address, the host name of your computer will be automatically set by the DHCP. You should disable this behavior if you connect to different networks, because they may assign different host names and changing the host name at runtime may confuse the graphical desktop. To disable using DHCP to get an IP address deactivate *Change Hostname via DHCP*.

   Assign Hostname to Loopback IP associates your host name with `127.0.0.2` (loopback) IP address in `/etc/hosts`. This is a useful option if you want to have the host name resolvable at all times, even without active network.

3. In *Modify DNS Configuration*, select the way the DNS configuration (name servers, search list, the content of the `/etc/resolv.conf` file) is modified.

If the *Use Default Policy* option is selected, the configuration is handled by the **`netconfig`** script which merges the data defined statically (with YaST or in the configuration files) with data obtained dynamically (from the DHCP client or NetworkManager). This default policy is usually sufficient.

If the *Only Manually* option is selected, **`netconfig`** is not allowed to modify the `/etc/resolv.conf` file. However, this file can be edited manually.

If the *Custom Policy* option is selected, a *Custom Policy Rule* string defining the merge policy should be specified. The string consists of a comma-separated list of interface names to be considered a valid source of settings. Except for complete interface names, basic wild cards to match multiple interfaces are allowed, as well. For example, `eth* ppp?` will first target all eth and then all ppp0-ppp9 interfaces. There are two special policy values that indicate how to apply the static settings defined in the `/etc/sysconfig/network/config` file:

`STATIC`
: The static settings need to be merged together with the dynamic settings.

`STATIC_FALLBACK`
: The static settings are used only when no dynamic configuration is available.

For more information, see the man page of **`netconfig`**(8) (**`man 8 netconfig`**).

4. Enter the *Name Servers* and fill in the *Domain Search* list. Name servers must be specified by IP addresses, such as 192.168.1.116, not by host names. Names specified in the *Domain Search* tab are domain names used for resolving host names without a specified domain. If more than one *Domain Search* is used, separate domains with commas or white space.

5. To activate the configuration, confirm the settings.

It is also possible to edit the host name using YaST from the command line. The changes made by YaST take effect immediately (which is not the case when editing the `/etc/HOSTNAME` file manually). To change the host name, use the following command:

```
yast dns edit hostname=HOSTNAME
```

To change the name servers, use the following commands:

```
yast dns edit nameserver1=192.168.1.116
yast dns edit nameserver2=192.168.1.117
yast dns edit nameserver3=192.168.1.118
```

17.4.1.5 Configuring Routing

To make your machine communicate with other machines and other networks, routing information must be given to make network traffic take the correct path. If DHCP is used, this information is automatically provided. If a static setup is used, this data must be added manually.

1. In YaST go to *Network Settings* › *Routing*.
2. Enter the IP address of the *Default Gateway* (IPv4 and IPv6 if necessary). The default gateway matches every possible destination, but if a routing table entry exists that matches the required address, this will be used instead of the default route via the Default Gateway.
3. More entries can be entered in the *Routing Table*. Enter the *Destination* network IP address, *Gateway* IP address and the *Netmask*. Select the *Device* through which the traffic to the defined network will be routed (the minus sign stands for any device). To omit any of these values, use the minus sign `-`. To enter a default gateway into the table, use `default` in the *Destination* field.

Note: Route Prioritization

If more default routes are used, it is possible to specify the metric option to determine which route has a higher priority. To specify the metric option, enter `-metric NUMBER` in *Options*. The route with the highest metric is used as default. If the network device is disconnected, its route will be removed and the next one will be used. However, the current kernel does not use metric in static routing, only routing daemons like `multipathd` do.

4. If the system is a router, enable *IPv4 Forwarding* and *IPv6 Forwarding* in the *Network Settings* as needed.
5. To activate the configuration, confirm the settings.

17.5 NetworkManager

NetworkManager is the ideal solution for laptops and other portable computers. With NetworkManager, you do not need to worry about configuring network interfaces and switching between networks when you are moving.

17.5.1 NetworkManager and `wicked`

However, NetworkManager is not a suitable solution for all cases, so you can still choose between the `wicked` controlled method for managing network connections and NetworkManager. If you want to manage your network connection with NetworkManager, enable NetworkManager in the YaST Network Settings module as described in *Section 30.2, "Enabling or Disabling NetworkManager"* and configure your network connections with NetworkManager. For a list of use cases and a detailed description of how to configure and use NetworkManager, refer to *Chapter 30, Using NetworkManager*.

Some differences between wicked and NetworkManager:

`root` Privileges

If you use NetworkManager for network setup, you can easily switch, stop or start your network connection at any time from within your desktop environment using an applet. NetworkManager also makes it possible to change and configure wireless card connections without requiring `root` privileges. For this reason, NetworkManager is the ideal solution for a mobile workstation.

`wicked` also provides some ways to switch, stop or start the connection with or without user intervention, like user-managed devices. However, this always requires `root` privileges to change or configure a network device. This is often a problem for mobile computing, where it is not possible to preconfigure all the connection possibilities.

Types of Network Connections

Both `wicked` and NetworkManager can handle network connections with a wireless network (with WEP, WPA-PSK, and WPA-Enterprise access) and wired networks using DHCP and static configuration. They also support connection through dial-up and VPN. With NetworkManager you can also connect a mobile broadband (3G) modem or set up a DSL connection, which is not possible with the traditional configuration.

NetworkManager tries to keep your computer connected at all times using the best connection available. If the network cable is accidentally disconnected, it tries to reconnect. It can find the network with the best signal strength from the list of your wireless connections and automatically use it to connect. To get the same functionality with `wicked`, more configuration effort is required.

17.5.2 NetworkManager Functionality and Configuration Files

The individual network connection settings created with NetworkManager are stored in configuration profiles. The *system* connections configured with either NetworkManager or YaST are saved in `/etc/networkmanager/system-connections/*` or in `/etc/sysconfig/network/ifcfg-*`. For GNOME, all user-defined connections are stored in GConf.

In case no profile is configured, NetworkManager automatically creates one and names it `Auto $INTERFACE-NAME`. That is made in an attempt to work without any configuration for as many cases as (securely) possible. If the automatically created profiles do not suit your needs, use the network connection configuration dialogs provided by GNOME to modify them as desired. For more information, see *Section 30.3, "Configuring Network Connections"*.

17.5.3 Controlling and Locking Down NetworkManager Features

On centrally administered machines, certain NetworkManager features can be controlled or disabled with PolKit, for example if a user is allowed to modify administrator defined connections or if a user is allowed to define his own network configurations. To view or change the respective NetworkManager policies, start the graphical *Authorizations* tool for PolKit. In the tree on the left side, find them below the *network-manager-settings* entry. For an introduction to PolKit and details on how to use it, refer to *Book "Security Guide", Chapter 9 "Authorization with PolKit"*.

17.6 Configuring a Network Connection Manually

Manual configuration of the network software should be the last alternative. Using YaST is recommended. However, this background information about the network configuration can also assist your work with YaST.

17.6.1 The **wicked** Network Configuration

The tool and library called **`wicked`** provides a new framework for network configuration.

One of the challenges with traditional network interface management is that different layers of network management get jumbled together into one single script, or at most two different scripts. These scripts interact with each other in a way that is not well-defined. This leads to unpredictable issues, obscure constraints and conventions, etc. Several layers of special hacks for a variety of different scenarios increase the maintenance burden. Address configuration protocols are being used that are implemented via daemons like dhcpcd, which interact rather poorly with the rest of the infrastructure. Funky interface naming schemes that require heavy udev support are introduced to achieve persistent identification of interfaces.

The idea of wicked is to decompose the problem in several ways. None of them is entirely novel, but trying to put ideas from different projects together is hopefully going to create a better solution overall.

One approach is to use a client/server model. This allows wicked to define standardized facilities for things like address configuration that are well integrated with the overall framework. For example, using a specific address configuration, the administrator may request that an interface should be configured via DHCP or IPv4 zeroconf. In this case, the address configuration service simply obtains the lease from its server and passes it on to the wicked server process that installs the requested addresses and routes.

The other approach to decomposing the problem is to enforce the layering aspect. For any type of network interface, it is possible to define a dbus service that configures the network interface's device layer—a VLAN, a bridge, a bonding, or a paravirtualized device. Common functionality, such as address configuration, is implemented by joint services that are layered on top of these device specific services without having to implement them specifically.

The wicked framework implements these two aspects by using a variety of dbus services, which get attached to a network interface depending on its type. Here is a rough overview of the current object hierarchy in wicked.

Each network interface is represented via a child object of `/org/opensuse/Network/Interfaces`. The name of the child object is given by its ifindex. For example, the loopback interface, which usually gets ifindex 1, is `/org/opensuse/Network/Interfaces/1`, the first Ethernet interface registered is `/org/opensuse/Network/Interfaces/2`.

Each network interface has a "class" associated with it, which is used to select the dbus interfaces it supports. By default, each network interface is of class `netif`, and `wickedd` will automatically attach all interfaces compatible with this class. In the current implementation, this includes the following interfaces:

org.opensuse.Network.Interface

Generic network interface functions, such as taking the link up or down, assigning an MTU, etc.

org.opensuse.Network.Addrconf.ipv4.dhcp, org.opensuse.Network.Addrconf.ipv6.dhcp, org.opensuse.Network.Addrconf.ipv4.auto

Address configuration services for DHCP, IPv4 zeroconf, etc.

Beyond this, network interfaces may require or offer special configuration mechanisms. For an Ethernet device, for example, you should be able to control the link speed, offloading of checksumming, etc. To achieve this, Ethernet devices have a class of their own, called `netif-ethernet`, which is a subclass of `netif`. As a consequence, the dbus interfaces assigned to an Ethernet interface include all the services listed above, plus the `org.opensuse.Network.Ethernet` service available only to objects belonging to the `netif-ethernet` class.

Similarly, there exist classes for interface types like bridges, VLANs, bonds, or infinibands.

How do you interact with an interface like VLAN (which is really a virtual network interface that sits on top of an Ethernet device) that needs to be created first? For this, wicked defines factory interfaces, such as `org.opensuse.Network.VLAN.Factory`. Such a factory interface offers a single function that lets you create an interface of the requested type. These factory interfaces are attached to the `/org/opensuse/Network/Interfaces` list node.

17.6.1.1 wicked Architecture and Features

The `wicked` service comprises several parts as depicted in *Figure 17.4, "wicked architecture"*.

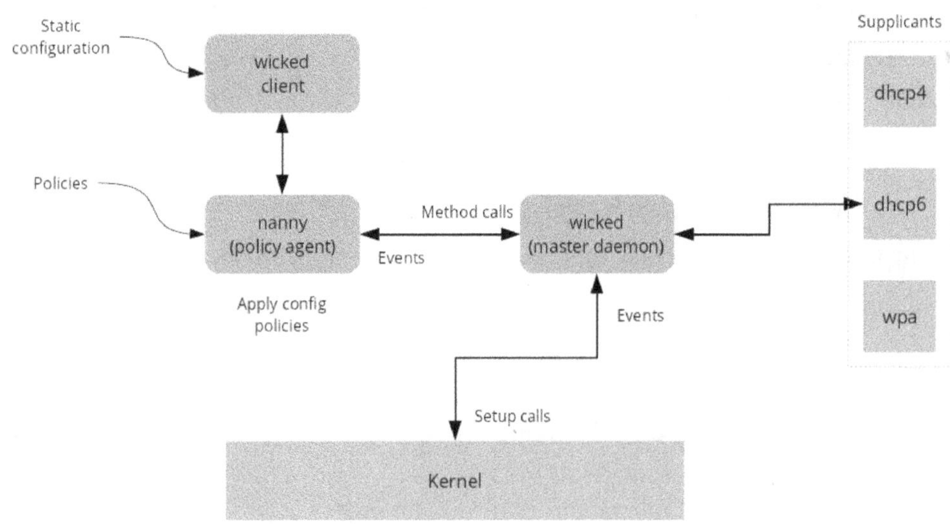

FIGURE 17.4: wicked **ARCHITECTURE**

`wicked` currently supports the following:

- Configuration file back-ends to parse SUSE style `/etc/sysconfig/network` files.
- An internal configuration back-end to represent network interface configuration in XML.
- Bring up and shutdown of "normal" network interfaces such as Ethernet or InfiniBand, VLAN, bridge, bonds, tun, tap, dummy, macvlan, macvtap, hsi, qeth, iucv, and wireless (currently limited to one wpa-psk/eap network) devices.
- A built-in DHCPv4 client and a built-in DHCPv6 client.
- The nanny daemon (enabled by default) helps to automatically bring up configured interfaces when the device is available (interface hotplugging) and set up the IP configuration when a link (carrier) is detected. See *Section 17.6.1.3, "Nanny"* for more information.
- `wicked` was implemented as a group of DBus services that are integrated with systemd. So the usual **`systemctl`** commands will apply to `wicked`.

17.6.1.2 Using wicked

On SUSE Linux Enterprise, `wicked` is running by default. If you want to check what is currently enabled and whether it is running, call:

On openSUSE Leap `wicked` is running by default on desktop or server hardware. On mobile hardware NetworkManager is running by default. If you want to check what is currently enabled and whether it is running, call:

```
systemctl status network
```

If `wicked` is enabled, you will see something along these lines:

```
wicked.service - wicked managed network interfaces
    Loaded: loaded (/usr/lib/systemd/system/wicked.service; enabled)
    ...
```

In case something different is running (for example, NetworkManager) and you want to switch to `wicked`, first stop what is running and then enable `wicked`:

```
systemctl is-active network && \
systemctl stop      network
systemctl enable --force wicked
```

This enables the wicked services, creates the `network.service` to `wicked.service` alias link, and starts the network at the next boot.

Starting the server process:

```
systemctl start wickedd
```

This starts **`wickedd`** (the main server) and associated supplicants:

```
/usr/lib/wicked/bin/wickedd-auto4 --systemd --foreground
/usr/lib/wicked/bin/wickedd-dhcp4 --systemd --foreground
/usr/lib/wicked/bin/wickedd-dhcp6 --systemd --foreground
/usr/sbin/wickedd --systemd --foreground
/usr/sbin/wickedd-nanny --systemd --foreground
```

Then bringing up the network:

```
systemctl start wicked
```

Alternatively use the `network.service` alias:

```
systemctl start network
```

These commands are using the default or system configuration sources as defined in `/etc/wicked/client.xml`.

To enable debugging, set `WICKED_DEBUG` in `/etc/sysconfig/network/config`, for example:

```
WICKED_DEBUG="all"
```

Or, to omit some:

```
WICKED_DEBUG="all,-dbus,-objectmodel,-xpath,-xml"
```

Use the client utility to display interface information for all interfaces or the interface specified with *`IFNAME`*:

```
wicked show all
wicked show IFNAME
```

In XML output:

```
wicked show-xml all
wicked show-xml IFNAME
```

Bringing up one interface:

```
wicked ifup eth0
wicked ifup wlan0
...
```

Because there is no configuration source specified, the wicked client checks its default sources of configuration defined in `/etc/wicked/client.xml`:

1. `firmware:` iSCSI Boot Firmware Table (iBFT)
2. `compat:` `ifcfg` files—implemented for compatibility

Whatever `wicked` gets from those sources for a given interface is applied. The intended order of importance is `firmware`, then `compat`—this may be changed in the future.

For more information, see the **`wicked`** man page.

17.6.1.3 Nanny

Nanny is an event and policy driven daemon that is responsible for asynchronous or unsolicited scenarios such as hotplugging devices. Thus the nanny daemon helps with starting or restarting delayed or temporarily gone devices. Nanny monitors device and link changes, and integrates new devices defined by the current policy set. Nanny continues to set up even if **`ifup`** already exited because of specified timeout constraints.

By default, the nanny daemon is active on the system. It is enabled in the `/etc/wicked/common.xml` configuration file:

```
<config>
  ...
  <use-nanny>true</use-nanny>
</config>
```

This setting causes ifup and ifreload to apply a policy with the effective configuration to the nanny daemon; then, nanny configures `wickedd` and thus ensures hotplug support. It waits in the background for events or changes (such as new devices or carrier on).

17.6.1.4 Bringing Up Multiple Interfaces

For bonds and bridges, it may make sense to define the entire device topology in one file (ifcfg-bondX), and bring it up in one go. wicked then can bring up the whole configuration if you specify the top level interface names (of the bridge or bond):

```
wicked ifup br0
```

This command automatically sets up the bridge and its dependencies in the appropriate order without the need to list the dependencies (ports, etc.) separately.

To bring up multiple interfaces in one command:

```
wicked ifup bond0 br0 br1 br2
```

Or also all interfaces:

```
wicked ifup all
```

17.6.1.5 Using Tunnels with Wicked

When you need to use tunnels with Wicked, the `TUNNEL_DEVICE` is used for this. It permits to specify an optional device name to bind the tunnel to the device. The tunneled packets will only be routed via this device.

For more information, refer to **`man 5 ifcfg-tunnel`**.

17.6.1.6 Handling Incremental Changes

With **`wicked`**, there is no need to actually take down an interface to reconfigure it (unless it is required by the kernel). For example, to add another IP address or route to a statically configured network interface, add the IP address to the interface definition, and do another "ifup" operation. The server will try hard to update only those settings that have changed. This applies to link-level options such as the device MTU or the MAC address, and network-level settings, such as addresses, routes, or even the address configuration mode (for example, when moving from a static configuration to DHCP).

Things get tricky of course with virtual interfaces combining several real devices such as bridges or bonds. For bonded devices, it is not possible to change certain parameters while the device is up. Doing that will result in an error.

However, what should still work, is the act of adding or removing the child devices of a bond or bridge, or choosing a bond's primary interface.

17.6.1.7 Wicked Extensions: Address Configuration

`wicked` is designed to be extensible with shell scripts. These extensions can be defined in the `config.xml` file.

Currently, several classes of extensions are supported:

- link configuration: these are scripts responsible for setting up a device's link layer according to the configuration provided by the client, and for tearing it down again.
- address configuration: these are scripts responsible for managing a device's address configuration. Usually address configuration and DHCP are managed by **`wicked`** itself, but can be implemented by means of extensions.
- firewall extension: these scripts can apply firewall rules.

Typically, extensions have a start and a stop command, an optional “pid file”, and a set of environment variables that get passed to the script.

To illustrate how this is supposed to work, look at a firewall extension defined in `etc/server.xml`:

```
<dbus-service interface="org.opensuse.Network.Firewall">
 <action name="firewallUp"   command="/etc/wicked/extensions/firewall up"/>
 <action name="firewallDown" command="/etc/wicked/extensions/firewall down"/>

 <!-- default environment for all calls to this extension script -->
 <putenv name="WICKED_OBJECT_PATH" value="$object-path"/>
 <putenv name="WICKED_INTERFACE_NAME" value="$property:name"/>
 <putenv name="WICKED_INTERFACE_INDEX" value="$property:index"/>
</dbus-service>
```

The extension is attached to the `<dbus-service>` tag and defines commands to execute for the actions of this interface. Further, the declaration can define and initialize environment variables passed to the actions.

17.6.1.8 Wicked Extensions: Configuration Files

You can extend the handling of configuration files with scripts as well. For example, DNS updates from leases are ultimately handled by the `extensions/resolver` script, with behavior configured in `server.xml`:

```
<system-updater name="resolver">
 <action name="backup" command="/etc/wicked/extensions/resolver backup"/>
 <action name="restore" command="/etc/wicked/extensions/resolver restore"/>
 <action name="install" command="/etc/wicked/extensions/resolver install"/>
 <action name="remove" command="/etc/wicked/extensions/resolver remove"/>
</system-updater>
```

When an update arrives in `wickedd`, the system updater routines parse the lease and call the appropriate commands (`backup`, `install`, etc.) in the resolver script. This in turn configures the DNS settings using **`/sbin/netconfig`**, or by manually writing `/etc/resolv.conf` as a fallback.

17.6.2 Configuration Files

This section provides an overview of the network configuration files and explains their purpose and the format used.

17.6.2.1 `/etc/wicked/common.xml`

The `/etc/wicked/common.xml` file contains common definitions that should be used by all applications. It is sourced/included by the other configuration files in this directory. Although you can use this file to enable debugging across all `wicked` components, we recommend to use the file `/etc/wicked/local.xml` for this purpose. After applying maintenance updates you might lose your changes as the `/etc/wicked/common.xml` might be overwritten. The `/etc/wicked/common.xml` file includes the `/etc/wicked/local.xml` in the default installation, thus you typically do not need to modify the `/etc/wicked/common.xml`.

In case you want to disable `nanny` by setting the `<use-nanny>` to `false`, restart the `wickedd.service` and then run the following command to apply all configurations and policies:

```
wicked ifup all
```

Note: Configuration Files

The `wickedd`, `wicked`, or `nanny` programs try to read `/etc/wicked/common.xml` if their own configuration files do not exist.

17.6.2.2 /etc/wicked/server.xml

The file `/etc/wicked/server.xml` is read by the `wickedd` server process at start-up. The file stores extensions to the `/etc/wicked/common.xml`. On top of that this file configures handling of a resolver and receiving information from `addrconf` supplicants, for example DHCP.

We recommend to add changes required to this file into a separate file `/etc/wicked/server-local.xml`, that gets included by `/etc/wicked/server.xml`. By using a separate file you avoid overwriting of your changes during maintenance updates.

17.6.2.3 /etc/wicked/client.xml

The `/etc/wicked/client.xml` is used by the **`wicked`** command. The file specifies the location of a script used when discovering devices managed by ibft and configures locations of network interface configurations.

We recommend to add changes required to this file into a separate file `/etc/wicked/client-local.xml`, that gets included by `/etc/wicked/server.xml`. By using a separate file you avoid overwriting of your changes during maintenance updates.

17.6.2.4 /etc/wicked/nanny.xml

The `/etc/wicked/nanny.xml` configures types of link layers. We recommend to add specific configuration into a separate file: `/etc/wicked/nanny-local.xml` to avoid losing the changes during maintenance updates.

17.6.2.5 /etc/sysconfig/network/ifcfg-*

These files contain the traditional configurations for network interfaces. In SUSE Linux Enterprise 11, this was the only supported format besides iBFT firmware.

Note: **wicked** and the `ifcfg-*` Files

wicked reads these files if you specify the `compat:` prefix. According to the SUSE Linux Enterprise Desktop default configuration in `/etc/wicked/client.xml`, **wicked** tries these files before the XML configuration files in `/etc/wicked/ifconfig`.

The `--ifconfig` switch is provided mostly for testing only. If specified, default configuration sources defined in `/etc/wicked/ifconfig` are not applied.

The `ifcfg-*` files include information such as the start mode and the IP address. Possible parameters are described in the manual page of `ifup`. Additionally, most variables from the `dhcp` and `wireless` files can be used in the `ifcfg-*` files if a general setting should be used for only one interface. However, most of the `/etc/sysconfig/network/config` variables are global and cannot be overridden in ifcfg-files. For example, `NETCONFIG_*` variables are global.

For configuring `macvlan` and `macvtab` interfaces, see the `ifcfg-macvlan` and `ifcfg-macvtap` man pages. For example, for a macvlan interface provide a `ifcfg-macvlan0` with settings as follows:

```
STARTMODE='auto'
MACVLAN_DEVICE='eth0'
#MACVLAN_MODE='vepa'
#LLADDR=02:03:04:05:06:aa
```

For `ifcfg.template`, see *Section 17.6.2.6, "/etc/sysconfig/network/config, /etc/sysconfig/network/dhcp, and /etc/sysconfig/network/wireless"*.

17.6.2.6 /etc/sysconfig/network/config, /etc/sysconfig/network/dhcp, and /etc/sysconfig/network/wireless

The file `config` contains general settings for the behavior of **ifup**, **ifdown** and **ifstatus**. `dhcp` contains settings for DHCP and `wireless` for wireless LAN cards. The variables in all three configuration files are commented. Some variables from `/etc/sysconfig/network/config` can also be used in `ifcfg-*` files, where they are given a higher priority. The `/etc/sysconfig/network/ifcfg.template` file lists variables that can be specified in a per interface scope. However, most of the `/etc/sysconfig/network/config` variables are global and cannot be overridden in ifcfg-files. For example, `NETWORKMANAGER` or `NETCONFIG_*` variables are global.

Note: Using DHCPv6

In SUSE Linux Enterprise 11, DHCPv6 used to work even on networks where IPv6 Router Advertisements (RAs) were not configured properly. Starting with SUSE Linux Enterprise 12, DHCPv6 will correctly require that at least one of the routers on the network sends out RAs that indicate that this network is managed by DHCPv6.

For networks where the router cannot be configured correctly, the `ifcfg` option allows the user to override this behavior by specifying `DHCLIENT6_MODE='managed'` in the `ifcfg` file. You can also activate this workaround with a boot parameter in the installation system:

```
ifcfg=eth0=dhcp6,DHCLIENT6_MODE=managed
```

17.6.2.7 /etc/sysconfig/network/routes and /etc/sysconfig/network/ifroute-*

The static routing of TCP/IP packets is determined by the `/etc/sysconfig/network/routes` and `/etc/sysconfig/network/ifroute-*` files. All the static routes required by the various system tasks can be specified in `/etc/sysconfig/network/routes`: routes to a host, routes to a host via a gateway and routes to a network. For each interface that needs individual routing, define an additional configuration file: `/etc/sysconfig/network/ifroute-*`. Replace the wild card (`*`) with the name of the interface. The entries in the routing configuration files look like this:

```
# Destination     Gateway             Netmask            Interface  Options
```

The route's destination is in the first column. This column may contain the IP address of a network or host or, in the case of *reachable* name servers, the fully qualified network or host name. The network should be written in CIDR notation (address with the associated routing prefix-length) such as 10.10.0.0/16 for IPv4 or fc00::/7 for IPv6 routes. The keyword `default` indicates that the route is the default gateway in the same address family as the gateway. For devices without a gateway use explicit 0.0.0.0/0 or ::/0 destinations.

The second column contains the default gateway or a gateway through which a host or network can be accessed.

The third column is deprecated; it used to contain the IPv4 netmask of the destination. For IPv6 routes, the default route, or when using a prefix-length (CIDR notation) in the first column, enter a dash (`-`) here.

The fourth column contains the name of the interface. If you leave it empty using a dash (`-`), it can cause unintended behavior in `/etc/sysconfig/network/routes`. For more information, see the `routes` man page.

An (optional) fifth column can be used to specify special options. For details, see the `routes` man page.

EXAMPLE 17.5: COMMON NETWORK INTERFACES AND SOME STATIC ROUTES

```
# --- IPv4 routes in CIDR prefix notation:
# Destination     [Gateway]          -                   Interface
127.0.0.0/8       -                  -                   lo
204.127.235.0/24  -                  -                   eth0
default           204.127.235.41     -                   eth0
207.68.156.51/32  207.68.145.45      -                   eth1
192.168.0.0/16    207.68.156.51      -                   eth1

# --- IPv4 routes in deprecated netmask notation"
# Destination     [Dummy/Gateway]    Netmask             Interface
#
127.0.0.0         0.0.0.0            255.255.255.0       lo
204.127.235.0     0.0.0.0            255.255.255.0       eth0
default           204.127.235.41     0.0.0.0             eth0
207.68.156.51     207.68.145.45      255.255.255.255     eth1
192.168.0.0       207.68.156.51      255.255.0.0         eth1

# --- IPv6 routes are always using CIDR notation:
# Destination     [Gateway]                 -            Interface
2001:DB8:100::/64 -                         -            eth0
2001:DB8:100::/32 fe80::216:3eff:fe6d:c042 -            eth0
```

17.6.2.8 /etc/resolv.conf

The domain to which the host belongs is specified in `/etc/resolv.conf` (keyword `search`). Up to six domains with a total of 256 characters can be specified with the `search` option. When resolving a name that is not fully qualified, an attempt is made to generate one by attaching the individual `search` entries. Up to 3 name servers can be specified with the `nameserver` option, each on a line of its own. Comments are preceded by hash mark or semicolon signs (`#` or `;`). As an example, see *Example 17.6, "/etc/resolv.conf"*.

However, the `/etc/resolv.conf` should not be edited by hand. Instead, it is generated by the **`netconfig`** script. To define static DNS configuration without using YaST, edit the appropriate variables manually in the `/etc/sysconfig/network/config` file:

`NETCONFIG_DNS_STATIC_SEARCHLIST`

list of DNS domain names used for host name lookup

`NETCONFIG_DNS_STATIC_SERVERS`

list of name server IP addresses to use for host name lookup

`NETCONFIG_DNS_FORWARDER`

the name of the DNS forwarder that needs to be configured, for example `bind` or `resolver`

`NETCONFIG_DNS_RESOLVER_OPTIONS`

arbitrary options that will be written to `/etc/resolv.conf`, for example:

```
debug attempts:1 timeout:10
```

For more information, see the `resolv.conf` man page.

`NETCONFIG_DNS_RESOLVER_SORTLIST`

list of up to 10 items, for example:

```
130.155.160.0/255.255.240.0 130.155.0.0
```

For more information, see the `resolv.conf` man page.

To disable DNS configuration using netconfig, set `NETCONFIG_DNS_POLICY=''`. For more information about **`netconfig`**, see the `netconfig(8)` man page (**`man 8 netconfig`**).

EXAMPLE 17.6: `/etc/resolv.conf`

```
# Our domain
search example.com
#
# We use dns.example.com (192.168.1.116) as nameserver
nameserver 192.168.1.116
```

17.6.2.9 /sbin/netconfig

netconfig is a modular tool to manage additional network configuration settings. It merges statically defined settings with settings provided by autoconfiguration mechanisms as DHCP or PPP according to a predefined policy. The required changes are applied to the system by calling the netconfig modules that are responsible for modifying a configuration file and restarting a service or a similar action.

netconfig recognizes three main actions. The **netconfig modify** and **netconfig remove** commands are used by daemons such as DHCP or PPP to provide or remove settings to netconfig. Only the **netconfig update** command is available for the user:

modify

The **netconfig modify** command modifies the current interface and service specific dynamic settings and updates the network configuration. Netconfig reads settings from standard input or from a file specified with the `--lease-file` *FILENAME* option and internally stores them until a system reboot (or the next modify or remove action). Already existing settings for the same interface and service combination are overwritten. The interface is specified by the `-i` *INTERFACE_NAME* parameter. The service is specified by the `-s` *SERVICE_NAME* parameter.

remove

The **netconfig remove** command removes the dynamic settings provided by a modificatory action for the specified interface and service combination and updates the network configuration. The interface is specified by the `-i` *INTERFACE_NAME* parameter. The service is specified by the `-s` *SERVICE_NAME* parameter.

update

The **netconfig update** command updates the network configuration using current settings. This is useful when the policy or the static configuration has changed. Use the `-m` *MODULE_TYPE* parameter, if you want to update a specified service only (`dns`, `nis`, or `ntp`).

The netconfig policy and the static configuration settings are defined either manually or using YaST in the `/etc/sysconfig/network/config` file. The dynamic configuration settings provided by autoconfiguration tools such as DHCP or PPP are delivered directly by these tools with the **netconfig modify** and **netconfig remove** actions. When NetworkManager is enabled, netconfig (in policy mode `auto`) uses only NetworkManager settings, ignoring settings from any other interfaces configured using the traditional ifup method. If NetworkManager does not provide any setting, static settings are used as a fallback. A mixed usage of NetworkManager and the **wicked** method is not supported.

For more information about **netconfig**, see **man 8 netconfig**.

17.6.2.10 /etc/hosts

In this file, shown in *Example 17.7, "/etc/hosts"*, IP addresses are assigned to host names. If no name server is implemented, all hosts to which an IP connection will be set up must be listed here. For each host, enter a line consisting of the IP address, the fully qualified host name, and the host name into the file. The IP address must be at the beginning of the line and the entries separated by blanks and tabs. Comments are always preceded by the # sign.

EXAMPLE 17.7: /etc/hosts

```
127.0.0.1 localhost
192.168.2.100 jupiter.example.com jupiter
192.168.2.101 venus.example.com venus
```

17.6.2.11 /etc/networks

Here, network names are converted to network addresses. The format is similar to that of the hosts file, except the network names precede the addresses. See *Example 17.8, "/etc/networks"*.

EXAMPLE 17.8: /etc/networks

```
loopback     127.0.0.0
localnet     192.168.0.0
```

17.6.2.12 /etc/host.conf

Name resolution—the translation of host and network names via the *resolver* library—is controlled by this file. This file is only used for programs linked to libc4 or libc5. For current glibc programs, refer to the settings in /etc/nsswitch.conf. Each parameter must always be entered on a separate line. Comments are preceded by a # sign. *Table 17.2, "Parameters for /etc/host.conf"* shows the parameters available. A sample /etc/host.conf is shown in *Example 17.9, "/etc/host.conf"*.

TABLE 17.2: PARAMETERS FOR /ETC/HOST.CONF

order *hosts, bind*	Specifies in which order the services are accessed for the name resolution. Available arguments are (separated by blank spaces or commas):
	hosts: searches the `/etc/hosts` file
	bind: accesses a name server
	nis: uses NIS
multi *on/off*	Defines if a host entered in `/etc/hosts` can have multiple IP addresses.
nospoof *on* spoofalert *on/off*	These parameters influence the name server *spoofing* but do not exert any influence on the network configuration.
trim *domainname*	The specified domain name is separated from the host name after host name resolution (as long as the host name includes the domain name). This option is useful only if names from the local domain are in the `/etc/hosts` file, but should still be recognized with the attached domain names.

EXAMPLE 17.9: `/etc/host.conf`

```
# We have named running
order hosts bind
# Allow multiple address
multi on
```

17.6.2.13 /etc/nsswitch.conf

The introduction of the GNU C Library 2.0 was accompanied by the introduction of the *Name Service Switch* (NSS). Refer to the `nsswitch.conf(5)` man page and *The GNU C Library Reference Manual* for details.

The order for queries is defined in the file `/etc/nsswitch.conf`. A sample `nsswitch.conf` is shown in *Example 17.10, "/etc/nsswitch.conf"*. Comments are preceded by `#` signs. In this example, the entry under the `hosts` database means that a request is sent to `/etc/hosts` (`files`) via DNS.

EXAMPLE 17.10: /etc/nsswitch.conf

```
passwd:     compat
group:      compat

hosts:      files dns
networks:   files dns

services:   db files
protocols:  db files
rpc:        files
ethers:     files
netmasks:   files
netgroup:   files nis
publickey:  files

bootparams: files
automount:  files nis
aliases:    files nis
shadow:     compat
```

The "databases" available over NSS are listed in *Table 17.3, "Databases Available via /etc/nsswitch.conf"*.

The configuration options for NSS databases are listed in *Table 17.4, "Configuration Options for NSS "Databases""*.

TABLE 17.3: DATABASES AVAILABLE VIA /ETC/NSSWITCH.CONF

`aliases`	Mail aliases implemented by `sendmail`; see **man** `5 aliases`.
`ethers`	Ethernet addresses.

`netmasks`	List of networks and their subnet masks. Only needed, if you use subnetting.
`group`	User groups used by `getgrent`. See also the man page for **`group`**.
`hosts`	Host names and IP addresses, used by `gethostbyname` and similar functions.
`netgroup`	Valid host and user lists in the network for controlling access permissions; see the `netgroup(5)` man page.
`networks`	Network names and addresses, used by `getnetent`.
`publickey`	Public and secret keys for Secure_RPC used by NFS and NIS+.
`passwd`	User passwords, used by `getpwent`; see the `passwd(5)` man page.
`protocols`	Network protocols, used by `getprotoent`; see the `protocols(5)` man page.
`rpc`	Remote procedure call names and addresses, used by `getrpcbyname` and similar functions.
`services`	Network services, used by `getservent`.
`shadow`	Shadow passwords of users, used by `getspnam`; see the `shadow(5)` man page.

TABLE 17.4: CONFIGURATION OPTIONS FOR NSS "DATABASES"

`files`	directly access files, for example, `/etc/aliases`
`db`	access via a database

nis, nisplus	NIS, see also *Book "Security Guide", Chapter 3 "Using NIS"*
dns	can only be used as an extension for hosts and networks
compat	can only be used as an extension for passwd, shadow and group

17.6.2.14 /etc/nscd.conf

This file is used to configure nscd (name service cache daemon). See the nscd(8) and nscd.conf(5) man pages. By default, the system entries of passwd, groups and hosts are cached by nscd. This is important for the performance of directory services, like NIS and LDAP, because otherwise the network connection needs to be used for every access to names, groups or hosts.

If the caching for passwd is activated, it usually takes about fifteen seconds until a newly added local user is recognized. Reduce this waiting time by restarting nscd with:

```
systemctl restart nscd
```

17.6.2.15 /etc/HOSTNAME

/etc/HOSTNAME contains the fully qualified host name (FQHN). The fully qualified host name is the host name with the domain name attached. This file must contain only one line (in which the host name is set). It is read while the machine is booting.

17.6.3 Testing the Configuration

Before you write your configuration to the configuration files, you can test it. To set up a test configuration, use the **ip** command. To test the connection, use the **ping** command.

The command **ip** changes the network configuration directly without saving it in the configuration file. Unless you enter your configuration in the correct configuration files, the changed network configuration is lost on reboot.

Note: **ifconfig** and **route** Are Obsolete

The **ifconfig** and **route** tools are obsolete. Use **ip** instead. **ifconfig**, for example, limits interface names to 9 characters.

17.6.3.1 Configuring a Network Interface with ip

ip is a tool to show and configure network devices, routing, policy routing, and tunnels.

ip is a very complex tool. Its common syntax is **ip** *OPTIONS OBJECT COMMAND*. You can work with the following objects:

link

This object represents a network device.

address

This object represents the IP address of device.

neighbor

This object represents an ARP or NDISC cache entry.

route

This object represents the routing table entry.

rule

This object represents a rule in the routing policy database.

maddress

This object represents a multicast address.

mroute

This object represents a multicast routing cache entry.

tunnel

This object represents a tunnel over IP.

If no command is given, the default command is used (usually **list**).

Change the state of a device with the command **ip link set** *DEVICE_NAME* . For example, to deactivate device eth0, enter **ip link set** eth0 down. To activate it again, use **ip link set** eth0 up.

After activating a device, you can configure it. To set the IP address, use **ip addr add** *IP_ADDRESS* + dev *DEVICE_NAME*. For example, to set the address of the interface eth0 to 192.168.12.154/30 with standard broadcast (option `brd`), enter **ip addr** `add 192.168.12.154/30 brd + dev eth0`.

To have a working connection, you must also configure the default gateway. To set a gateway for your system, enter **ip route add** `gateway_ip_address`. To translate one IP address to another, use **nat**: **ip route add nat** `ip_address` **via** `other_ip_address`.

To display all devices, use **ip link ls**. To display the running interfaces only, use **ip link ls up**. To print interface statistics for a device, enter **ip -s link ls** `device_name`. To view addresses of your devices, enter **ip addr**. In the output of the **ip addr**, also find information about MAC addresses of your devices. To show all routes, use **ip route show**.

For more information about using **ip**, enter **ip** `help` or see the `ip(8)` man page. The `help` option is also available for all **ip** subcommands. If, for example, you need help for **ip** `addr`, enter **ip** `addr help`. Find the **ip** manual in `/usr/share/doc/packages/iproute2/ip-cref.pdf`.

17.6.3.2 Testing a Connection with ping

The **ping** command is the standard tool for testing whether a TCP/IP connection works. It uses the ICMP protocol to send a small data packet, ECHO_REQUEST datagram, to the destination host, requesting an immediate reply. If this works, **ping** displays a message to that effect. This indicates that the network link is functioning.

ping does more than only test the function of the connection between two computers: it also provides some basic information about the quality of the connection. In *Example 17.11, "Output of the Command ping"*, you can see an example of the **ping** output. The second-to-last line contains information about the number of transmitted packets, packet loss, and total time of **ping** running.

As the destination, you can use a host name or IP address, for example, **ping** `example.com` or **ping** `192.168.3.100`. The program sends packets until you press Ctrl – C.

If you only need to check the functionality of the connection, you can limit the number of the packets with the `-c` option. For example to limit ping to three packets, enter **ping** `-c 3 example.com`.

EXAMPLE 17.11: OUTPUT OF THE COMMAND PING

```
ping -c 3 example.com
```

```
PING example.com (192.168.3.100) 56(84) bytes of data.
64 bytes from example.com (192.168.3.100): icmp_seq=1 ttl=49 time=188 ms
64 bytes from example.com (192.168.3.100): icmp_seq=2 ttl=49 time=184 ms
64 bytes from example.com (192.168.3.100): icmp_seq=3 ttl=49 time=183 ms
--- example.com ping statistics ---
3 packets transmitted, 3 received, 0% packet loss, time 2007ms
rtt min/avg/max/mdev = 183.417/185.447/188.259/2.052 ms
```

The default interval between two packets is one second. To change the interval, ping provides the option `-i`. For example, to increase the ping interval to ten seconds, enter **`ping`** `-i 10 example.com`.

In a system with multiple network devices, it is sometimes useful to send the ping through a specific interface address. To do so, use the `-I` option with the name of the selected device, for example, **`ping`** `-I wlan1 example.com`.

For more options and information about using ping, enter **`ping`** `-h` or see the `ping (8)` man page.

Tip: Pinging IPv6 Addresses

For IPv6 addresses use the **`ping6`** command. Note, to ping link-local addresses, you must specify the interface with `-I`. The following command works, if the address is reachable via `eth1`:

```
ping6 -I eth1 fe80::117:21ff:feda:a425
```

17.6.4 Unit Files and Start-Up Scripts

Apart from the configuration files described above, there are also systemd unit files and various scripts that load the network services while the machine is booting. These are started when the system is switched to the `multi-user.target` target. Some of these unit files and scripts are described in *Some Unit Files and Start-Up Scripts for Network Programs*. For more information about `systemd`, see *Chapter 14, The* `systemd` *Daemon* and for more information about the `systemd` targets, see the man page of `systemd.special` (**`man systemd.special`**).

`network.target`

`network.target` is the systemd target for networking, but its mean depends on the settings provided by the system administrator.

For more information, see http://www.freedesktop.org/wiki/Software/systemd/NetworkTarget/ ↗.

`multi-user.target`

`multi-user.target` is the systemd target for a multiuser system with all required network services.

`xinetd`

Starts xinetd. xinetd can be used to make server services available on the system. For example, it can start vsftpd whenever an FTP connection is initiated.

`rpcbind`

Starts the rpcbind utility that converts RPC program numbers to universal addresses. It is needed for RPC services, such as an NFS server.

`ypserv`

Starts the NIS server.

`ypbind`

Starts the NIS client.

`/etc/init.d/nfsserver`

Starts the NFS server.

`/etc/init.d/postfix`

Controls the postfix process.

17.7 Setting Up Bonding Devices

For some systems, there is a desire to implement network connections that comply to more than the standard data security or availability requirements of a typical Ethernet device. In these cases, several Ethernet devices can be aggregated to a single bonding device.

The configuration of the bonding device is done by means of bonding module options. The behavior is mainly affected by the mode of the bonding device. By default, this is `mode=active-backup` which means that a different slave device will become active if the active slave fails.

Tip: Bonding and Xen

Using bonding devices is only of interest for machines where you have multiple real network cards available. In most configurations, this means that you should use the bonding configuration only in Dom0. Only if you have multiple network cards assigned to a VM Guest system it may also be useful to set up the bond in a VM Guest.

To configure a bonding device, use the following procedure:

1. Run *YaST* › *System* › *Network Settings*.
2. Use *Add* and change the *Device Type* to *Bond*. Proceed with *Next*.

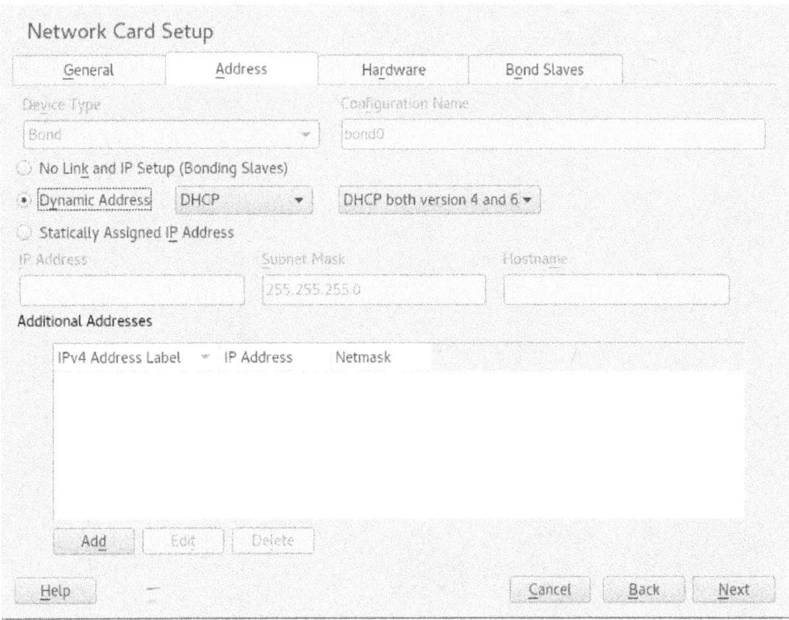

3. Select how to assign the IP address to the bonding device. Three methods are at your disposal:

    - No IP Address
    - Dynamic Address (with DHCP or Zeroconf)
    - Statically assigned IP Address

   Use the method that is appropriate for your environment.

4. In the *Bond Slaves* tab, select the Ethernet devices that should be included into the bond by activating the related check box.

5. Edit the *Bond Driver Options*. The modes that are available for configuration are the following:

    - balance-rr
    - active-backup
    - balance-xor
    - broadcast
    - 802.3ad
      `802.3ad` is the standardized LACP "IEEE 802.3ad Dynamic link aggregation" mode.
    - balance-tlb
    - balance-alb

6. Make sure that the parameter `miimon=100` is added to the *Bond Driver Options*. Without this parameter, the data integrity is not checked regularly.

7. Click *Next* and leave YaST with *OK* to create the device.

All modes, and many more options are explained in detail in the *Linux Ethernet Bonding Driver HOWTO* found at `/usr/src/linux/Documentation/networking/bonding.txt` after installing the package `kernel-source`.

17.7.1 Hotplugging of Bonding Slaves

In specific network environments (such as High Availability), there are cases when you need to replace a bonding slave interface with another one. The reason may be a constantly failing network device. The solution is to set up hotplugging of bonding slaves.

The bond is configured as usual (according to **`man 5 ifcfg-bonding`**), for example:

```
ifcfg-bond0
          STARTMODE='auto' # or 'onboot'
          BOOTPROTO='static'
          IPADDR='192.168.0.1/24'
          BONDING_MASTER='yes'
          BONDING_SLAVE_0='eth0'
          BONDING_SLAVE_1='eth1'
          BONDING_MODULE_OPTS='mode=active-backup miimon=100'
```

The slaves are specified with `STARTMODE=hotplug` and `BOOTPROTO=none`:

```
ifcfg-eth0
          STARTMODE='hotplug'
          BOOTPROTO='none'

ifcfg-eth1
          STARTMODE='hotplug'
          BOOTPROTO='none'
```

`BOOTPROTO=none` uses the **`ethtool`** options (when provided), but does not set the link up on **`ifup eth0`**. The reason is that the slave interface is controlled by the bond master.

`STARTMODE=hotplug` causes the slave interface to join the bond automatically when it is available.

The `udev` rules in `/etc/udev/rules.d/70-persistent-net.rules` need to be changed to match the device by bus ID (udev `KERNELS` keyword equal to "SysFS BusID" as visible in **`hwinfo --netcard`**) instead of by MAC address. This allows replacement of defective hardware (a network card in the same slot but with a different MAC) and prevents confusion when the bond changes the MAC address of all its slaves.

For example:

```
SUBSYSTEM=="net", ACTION=="add", DRIVERS=="?*",
KERNELS=="0000:00:19.0", ATTR{dev_id}=="0x0", ATTR{type}=="1",
KERNEL=="eth*", NAME="eth0"
```

At boot time, the systemd `network.service` does not wait for the hotplug slaves, but for the bond to become ready, which requires at least one available slave. When one of the slave interfaces gets removed (unbind from NIC driver, **`rmmod`** of the NIC driver or true PCI hotplug remove) from the system, the kernel removes it from the bond automatically. When a new card is added to the system (replacement of the hardware in the slot), `udev` renames it using the bus-based persistent name rule to the name of the slave, and calls **`ifup`** for it. The **`ifup`** call automatically joins it into the bond.

17.8 Setting Up Team Devices for Network Teaming

The term "link aggregation" is the general term which describes combining (or aggregating) a network connection to provide a logical layer. Sometimes you find the terms "channel teaming", "Ethernet bonding", "port truncating", etc. which are synonyms and refer to the same concept.

This concept is widely known as "bonding" and was originally integrated into the Linux kernel (see *Section 17.7, "Setting Up Bonding Devices"* for the original implementation). The term *Network Teaming* is used to refer to the new implementation of this concept.

The main difference between bonding and Network Teaming is that teaming supplies a set of small kernel modules responsible for providing an interface for teamd instances. Everything else is handled in user space. This is different from the original bonding implementation which contains all of its functionality exclusively in the kernel. For a comparison refer to *Table 17.5, "Feature Comparison between Bonding and Team"*.

TABLE 17.5: FEATURE COMPARISON BETWEEN BONDING AND TEAM

Feature	Bonding	Team
broadcast, round-robin TX policy	yes	yes
active-backup TX policy	yes	yes
LACP (802.3ad) support	yes	yes
hash-based TX policy	yes	yes
user can set hash function	no	yes
Source: http://libteam.org/files/teamdev.pp.pdf		

Feature	Bonding	Team
TX load-balancing support (TLB)	yes	yes
TX load-balancing support for LACP	no	yes
Ethtool link monitoring	yes	yes
ARP link monitoring	yes	yes
NS/NA (IPV6) link monitoring	no	yes
RCU locking on TX/RX paths	no	yes
port prio and stickiness	no	yes
separate per-port link monitoring setup	no	yes
multiple link monitoring setup	limited	yes
VLAN support	yes	yes
multiple device stacking	yes	yes
Source: http://libteam.org/files/teamdev.pp.pdf ↗		

Both implementations, bonding and Network Teaming, can be used in parallel. Network Teaming is an alternative to the existing bonding implementation. It does not replace bonding.

Network Teaming can be used for different use cases. The two most important use cases are explained later and involve:

- Load balancing between different network devices.
- Failover from one network device to another in case one of the devices should fail.

Currently, there is no YaST module to support creating a teaming device. You need to configure Network Teaming manually. The general procedure is shown below which can be applied for all your Network Teaming configurations:

PROCEDURE 17.1: GENERAL PROCEDURE

1. Make sure you have all the necessary packages installed. Install the packages `libteam-tools`, `libteamdctl0`, and `python-libteam`.

2. Create a configuration file under `/etc/sysconfig/network/`. Usually it will be `ifcfg-team0`. If you need more than one Network Teaming device, give them ascending numbers. This configuration file contains several variables which are explained in the man pages (see **`man ifcfg`** and **`man ifcfg-team`**). An example configuration can be found in your system in the file `/etc/sysconfig/network/ifcfg.template`.

3. Remove the configuration files of the interfaces which will be used for the teaming device (usually `ifcfg-eth0` and `ifcfg-eth1`).
   It is recommended to make a backup and remove both files. Wicked will re-create the configuration files with the necessary parameters for teaming.

4. Optionally, check if everything is included in Wicked's configuration file:

   ```
   wicked show-config
   ```

5. Start the Network Teaming device `team0`:

   ```
   wicked ifup all team0
   ```

   In case you need additional debug information, use the option `--debug all` after the **`all`** subcommand.

6. Check the status of the Network Teaming device. This can be done by the following commands:

   - Get the state of the teamd instance from Wicked:

     ```
     wicked ifstatus --verbose team0
     ```

   - Get the state of the entire instance:

     ```
     teamdctl team0 state
     ```

   - Get the systemd state of the teamd instance:

     ```
     systemctl status teamd@team0
     ```

   Each of them shows a slightly different view depending on your needs.

7. In case you need to change something in the `ifcfg-team0` file afterward, reload its configuration with:

   ```
   wicked ifreload team0
   ```

Do *not* use **`systemctl`** for starting or stopping the teaming device! Instead, use the **`wicked`** command as shown above.

To completely remove the team device, use this procedure:

PROCEDURE 17.2: REMOVING A TEAM DEVICE

1. Stop the Network Teaming device `team0`:

   ```
   wicked ifdown team0
   ```

2. Rename the file `/etc/sysconfig/network/ifcfg-team0` to `/etc/sysconfig/network/.ifcfg-team0`. Inserting a dot in front of the file name makes it "invisible" for wicked. If you really do not need the configuration anymore, you can also remove the file.

3. Reload the configuration:

   ```
   wicked ifreload all
   ```

17.8.1 Use Case: Loadbalancing with Network Teaming

Loadbalancing is used to improve bandwidth. Use the following configuration file to create a Network Teaming device with loadbalancing capabilities. Proceed with *Procedure 17.1, "General Procedure"* to set up the device. Check the output with **`teamdctl`**.

EXAMPLE 17.12: CONFIGURATION FOR LOADBALANCING WITH NETWORK TEAMING

```
STARTMODE=auto ①
BOOTPROTO=static ②
IPADDRESS="192.168.1.1/24" ②
IPADDR6="fd00:deca:fbad:50::1/64" ②

TEAM_RUNNER="loadbalance" ③
TEAM_LB_TX_HASH="ipv4,ipv6,eth,vlan"
TEAM_LB_TX_BALANCER_NAME="basic"
TEAM_LB_TX_BALANCER_INTERVAL="100"

TEAM_PORT_DEVICE_0="eth0" ④
TEAM_PORT_DEVICE_1="eth1" ④

TEAM_LW_NAME="ethtool" ⑤
TEAM_LW_ETHTOOL_DELAY_UP="10" ⑥
TEAM_LW_ETHTOOL_DELAY_DOWN="10" ⑥
```

① Controls the start of the teaming device. The value of `auto` means, the interface will be set up when the network service is available and will be started automatically on every reboot. In case you need to control the device yourself (and prevent it from starting automatically), set `STARTMODE` to `manual`.

② Sets a static IP address (here `192.168.1.1` for IPv4 and `fd00:deca:fbad:50::1` for IPv6). If the Network Teaming device should use a dynamic IP address, set `BOOTPROTO="dhcp"` and remove (or comment) the line with `IPADDRESS` and `IPADDR6`.

③ Sets `TEAM_RUNNER` to `loadbalance` to activate the loadbalancing mode.

④ Specifies one or more devices which should be aggregated to create the Network Teaming device.

⑤ Defines a link watcher to monitor the state of subordinate devices. The default value `ethtool` checks only if the device is up and accessible. This makes this check fast enough. However, it does not check if the device can really send or receive packets.
If you need a higher confidence in the connection, use the `arp_ping` option. This sends pings to an arbitrary host (configured in the `TEAM_LW_ARP_PING_TARGET_HOST` variable). Only if the replies are received, the Network Teaming device is considered to be up.

6 Defines the delay in milliseconds between the link coming up (or down) and the runner being notified.

17.8.2 Use Case: Failover with Network Teaming

Failover is used to ensure high availability of a critical Network Teaming device by involving a parallel backup network device. The backup network device is running all the time and takes over if and when the main device fails.

Use the following configuration file to create a Network Teaming device with failover capabilities. Proceed with *Procedure 17.1, "General Procedure"* to set up the device. Check the output with **`teamdctl`**.

EXAMPLE 17.13: CONFIGURATION FOR DHCP NETWORK TEAMING DEVICE

```
STARTMODE=auto ①
BOOTPROTO=static ②
IPADDR="192.168.1.2/24" ②
IPADDR6="fd00:deca:fbad:50::2/64" ②

TEAM_RUNNER=activebackup ③
TEAM_PORT_DEVICE_0="eth0" ④
TEAM_PORT_DEVICE_1="eth1" ④

TEAM_LW_NAME=ethtool ⑤
TEAM_LW_ETHTOOL_DELAY_UP="10" ⑥
TEAM_LW_ETHTOOL_DELAY_DOWN="10" ⑥
```

1 Controls the start of the teaming device. The value of `auto` means, the interface will be set up when the network service is available and will be started automatically on every reboot. In case you need to control the device yourself (and prevent it from starting automatically), set `STARTMODE` to `manual`.

2 Sets a static IP address (here `192.168.1.2` for IPv4 and `fd00:deca:fbad:50::2` for IPv6). If the Network Teaming device should use a dynamic IP address, set `BOOTPROTO="dhcp"` and remove (or comment) the line with `IPADDRESS` and `IPADDR6`.

3 Sets `TEAM_RUNNER` to `activebackup` to activate the failover mode.

4 Specifies one or more devices which should be aggregated to create the Network Teaming device.

5. Defines a link watcher to monitor the state of subordinate devices. The default value `ethtool` checks only if the device is up and accessible. This makes this check fast enough. However, it does not check if the device can really send or receive packets.
   If you need a higher confidence in the connection, use the `arp_ping` option. This sends pings to an arbitrary host (configured in the `TEAM_LW_ARP_PING_TARGET_HOST` variable). Only if the replies are received, the Network Teaming device is considered to be up.
6. Defines the delay in milliseconds between the link coming up (or down) and the runner being notified.

17.8.3 Use Case: VLAN over Team Device

VLAN is an abbreviation of *Virtual Local Area Network*. It allows the running of multiple *logical* (virtual) ethernets over one single physical ethernet. It logically splits the network into different broadcast domains so that packets are only switched between ports that are designated for the same VLAN.

The following use case creates two static VLANs on top of a team device:

- `vlan0`, bound to the IP address `192.168.10.1`
- `vlan1`, bound to the IP address `192.168.20.1`

Proceed as follows:

1. Enable the VLAN tags on your switch. If you want to use loadbalancing for your team device, your switch needs to be capable of *Link Aggregation Control Protocol* (LACP) (802.3ad). Consult your hardware manual about the details.
2. Decide if you want to use loadbalancing or failover for your team device. Set up your team device as described in *Section 17.8.1, "Use Case: Loadbalancing with Network Teaming"* or *Section 17.8.2, "Use Case: Failover with Network Teaming"*.
3. In `/etc/sysconfig/network` create a file `ifcfg-vlan0` with the following content:

```
STARTMODE="auto"
BOOTPROTO="static" ❶
IPADDR='192.168.10.1/24' ❷
ETHERDEVICE="team0" ❸
VLAN_ID="0" ❹
VLAN='yes'
```

1. Defines a fixed IP address, specified in `IPADDR`.
2. Defines the IP address, here with its netmask.
3. Contains the real interface to use for the VLAN interface, here our team device (`team0`).
4. Specifies a unique ID for the VLAN. Preferably, the file name and the `VLAN_ID` corresponds to the name `ifcfg-vlan`*`VLAN_ID`*. In our case `VLAN_ID` is `0` which leads to the filename `ifcfg-vlan0`.

4. Copy the file `/etc/sysconfig/network/ifcfg-vlan0` to `/etc/sysconfig/network/ifcfg-vlan1` and change the following values:

   - `IPADDR` from `192.168.10.1/24` to `192.168.20.1/24`.
   - `VLAN_ID` from `0` to `1`.

5. Start the two VLANs:

```
root # wicked ifup vlan0 vlan1
```

6. Check the output of **`ifconfig`**:

```
root # ifconfig -a
[...]
vlan0     Link encap:Ethernet  HWaddr 08:00:27:DC:43:98
          inet addr:192.168.10.1 Bcast:192.168.10.255 Mask:255.255.255.0
          inet6 addr: fe80::a00:27ff:fedc:4398/64 Scope:Link
          UP BROADCAST RUNNING MULTICAST  MTU:1500  Metric:1
          RX packets:0 errors:0 dropped:0 overruns:0 frame:0
          TX packets:12 errors:0 dropped:0 overruns:0 carrier:0
          collisions:0 txqueuelen:1000
          RX bytes:0 (0.0 b)  TX bytes:816 (816.0 b)

vlan1     Link encap:Ethernet  HWaddr 08:00:27:DC:43:98
          inet addr:192.168.20.1 Bcast:192.168.20.255 Mask:255.255.255.0
          inet6 addr: fe80::a00:27ff:fedc:4398/64 Scope:Link
          UP BROADCAST RUNNING MULTICAST  MTU:1500  Metric:1
          RX packets:0 errors:0 dropped:0 overruns:0 frame:0
          TX packets:12 errors:0 dropped:0 overruns:0 carrier:0
          collisions:0 txqueuelen:1000
          RX bytes:0 (0.0 b)  TX bytes:816 (816.0 b)
```

18 Printer Operation

SUSE® Linux Enterprise Desktop supports printing with many types of printers, including remote network printers. Printers can be configured manually or with YaST. For configuration instructions, refer to *Book "Deployment Guide", Chapter 7 "Setting Up Hardware Components with YaST", Section 7.3 "Setting Up a Printer"*. Both graphical and command line utilities are available for starting and managing print jobs. If your printer does not work as expected, refer to *Section 18.8, "Troubleshooting"*.

CUPS (Common Unix Printing System) is the standard print system in SUSE Linux Enterprise Desktop.

Printers can be distinguished by interface, such as USB or network, and printer language. When buying a printer, make sure that the printer has an interface that is supported (USB, Ethernet, or Wi-Fi) and a suitable printer language. Printers can be categorized on the basis of the following three classes of printer languages:

PostScript Printers

PostScript is the printer language in which most print jobs in Linux and Unix are generated and processed by the internal print system. If PostScript documents can be processed directly by the printer and do not need to be converted in additional stages in the print system, the number of potential error sources is reduced.

Currently PostScript is being replaced by PDF as the standard print job format. PostScript +PDF printers that can directly print PDF (in addition to PostScript) already exist. For traditional PostScript printers PDF needs to be converted to PostScript in the printing workflow.

Standard Printers (Languages Like PCL and ESC/P)

In the case of known printer languages, the print system can convert PostScript jobs to the respective printer language with Ghostscript. This processing stage is called interpreting. The best-known languages are PCL (which is mostly used by HP printers and their clones) and ESC/P (which is used by Epson printers). These printer languages are usually supported by Linux and produce an adequate print result. Linux may not be able to address some special printer functions. Except for HP and Epson, there are currently no printer manufacturers who develop Linux drivers and make them available to Linux distributors under an open source license.

Proprietary Printers (Also Called GDI Printers)

These printers do not support any of the common printer languages. They use their own undocumented printer languages, which are subject to change when a new edition of a model is released. Usually only Windows drivers are available for these printers. See *Section 18.8.1, "Printers without Standard Printer Language Support"* for more information.

Before you buy a new printer, refer to the following sources to check how well the printer you intend to buy is supported:

http://www.linuxfoundation.org/OpenPrinting/ ↗

The OpenPrinting home page with the printer database. The database shows the latest Linux support status. However, a Linux distribution can only integrate the drivers available at production time. Accordingly, a printer currently rated as "perfectly supported" may not have had this status when the latest SUSE Linux Enterprise Desktop version was released. Thus, the databases may not necessarily indicate the correct status, but only provide an approximation.

http://pages.cs.wisc.edu/~ghost/ ↗

The Ghostscript Web page.

`/usr/share/doc/packages/ghostscript/catalog.devices`

List of built-in Ghostscript drivers.

18.1 The CUPS Workflow

The user creates a print job. The print job consists of the data to print plus information for the spooler. This includes the name of the printer or the name of the print queue, and optionally, information for the filter, such as printer-specific options.

At least one dedicated print queue exists for every printer. The spooler holds the print job in the queue until the desired printer is ready to receive data. When the printer is ready, the spooler sends the data through the filter and back-end to the printer.

The filter converts the data generated by the application that is printing (usually PostScript or PDF, but also ASCII, JPEG, etc.) into printer-specific data (PostScript, PCL, ESC/P, etc.). The features of the printer are described in the PPD files. A PPD file contains printer-specific options with the parameters needed to enable them on the printer. The filter system makes sure that options selected by the user are enabled.

If you use a PostScript printer, the filter system converts the data into printer-specific PostScript. This does not require a printer driver. If you use a non-PostScript printer, the filter system converts the data into printer-specific data. This requires a printer driver suitable for your printer. The back-end receives the printer-specific data from the filter then passes it to the printer.

18.2 Methods and Protocols for Connecting Printers

There are various possibilities for connecting a printer to the system. The configuration of CUPS does not distinguish between a local printer and a printer connected to the system over the network. For more information about the printer connection, read the article *CUPS in a Nutshell* at http://en.opensuse.org/SDB:CUPS_in_a_Nutshell.

Warning: Changing Cable Connections in a Running System

When connecting the printer to the machine, do not forget that only USB devices can be plugged in or unplugged during operation. To avoid damaging your system or printer, shut down the system before changing any connections that are not USB.

18.3 Installing the Software

PPD (PostScript printer description) is the computer language that describes the properties, like resolution, and options, such as the availability of a duplex unit. These descriptions are required for using various printer options in CUPS. Without a PPD file, the print data would be forwarded to the printer in a "raw" state, which is usually not desired.

To configure a PostScript printer, the best approach is to get a suitable PPD file. Many PPD files are available in the packages `manufacturer-PPDs` and `OpenPrintingPPDs-postscript`. See *Section 18.7.3, "PPD Files in Various Packages"* and *Section 18.8.2, "No Suitable PPD File Available for a PostScript Printer"*.

New PPD files can be stored in the directory `/usr/share/cups/model/` or added to the print system with YaST as described in *Book "Deployment Guide", Chapter 7 "Setting Up Hardware Components with YaST", Section 7.3.1.1 "Adding Drivers with YaST"*. Subsequently, the PPD file can be selected during the printer setup.

Be careful if a printer manufacturer wants you to install entire software packages. This kind of installation may result in the loss of the support provided by SUSE Linux Enterprise Desktop. Also, print commands may work differently and the system may no longer be able to address devices of other manufacturers. For this reason, the installation of manufacturer software is not recommended.

18.4 Network Printers

A network printer can support various protocols, some even concurrently. Although most of the supported protocols are standardized, some manufacturers modify the standard. Manufacturers then provide drivers for only a few operating systems. Unfortunately, Linux drivers are rarely provided. The current situation is such that you cannot act on the assumption that every protocol works smoothly in Linux. Therefore, you may need to experiment with various options to achieve a functional configuration.

CUPS supports the `socket`, `LPD`, `IPP` and `smb` protocols.

socket

Socket refers to a connection in which the plain print data is sent directly to a TCP socket. Some socket port numbers that are commonly used are `9100` or `35`. The device URI (uniform resource identifier) syntax is: socket://*`IP.OF.THE.PRINTER`*:*`PORT`*, for example: `socket://192.168.2.202:9100/`.

LPD (Line Printer Daemon)

The LPD protocol is described in RFC 1179. Under this protocol, some job-related data, such as the ID of the print queue, is sent before the actual print data is sent. Therefore, a print queue must be specified when configuring the LPD protocol. The implementations of diverse printer manufacturers are flexible enough to accept any name as the print queue. If necessary, the printer manual should indicate what name to use. LPT, LPT1, LP1 or similar names are often used. The port number for an LPD service is `515`. An example device URI is `lpd://192.168.2.202/LPT1`.

IPP (Internet Printing Protocol)

IPP is a relatively new protocol (1999) based on the HTTP protocol. With IPP, more job-related data is transmitted than with the other protocols. CUPS uses IPP for internal data transmission. The name of the print queue is necessary to configure IPP correctly. The port number for IPP is `631`. Example device URIs are `ipp://192.168.2.202/ps` and `ipp://192.168.2.202/printers/ps`.

SMB (Windows Share)

CUPS also supports printing on printers connected to Windows shares. The protocol used for this purpose is SMB. SMB uses the port numbers `137`, `138` and `139`. Example device URIs are `smb://user:password@workgroup/smb.example.com/printer`, `smb://user:password@smb.example.com/printer`, and `smb://smb.example.com/printer`.

The protocol supported by the printer must be determined before configuration. If the manufacturer does not provide the needed information, the command **`nmap`** (which comes with the `nmap` package) can be used to ascertain the protocol. **`nmap`** checks a host for open ports. For example:

```
nmap -p 35,137-139,515,631,9100-10000 IP.OF.THE.PRINTER
```

18.5 Configuring CUPS with Command Line Tools

CUPS can be configured with command line tools like **`lpinfo`**, **`lpadmin`** and **`lpoptions`**. You need a device URI consisting of a back-end, such as USB, and parameters. To determine valid device URIs on your system use the command **`lpinfo -v | grep ":/"`**:

```
# lpinfo -v | grep ":/"
direct usb://ACME/FunPrinter%20XL
network socket://192.168.2.253
```

With **`lpadmin`** the CUPS server administrator can add, remove or manage print queues. To add a print queue, use the following syntax:

```
lpadmin -p QUEUE -v DEVICE-URI -P PPD-FILE -E
```

Then the device (`-v`) is available as *`QUEUE`* (`-p`), using the specified PPD file (`-P`). This means that you must know the PPD file and the device URI to configure the printer manually.

Do not use `-E` as the first option. For all CUPS commands, `-E` as the first argument sets use of an encrypted connection. To enable the printer, `-E` must be used as shown in the following example:

```
lpadmin -p ps -v usb://ACME/FunPrinter%20XL -P \
/usr/share/cups/model/Postscript.ppd.gz -E
```

The following example configures a network printer:

```
lpadmin -p ps -v socket://192.168.2.202:9100/ -P \
```

```
/usr/share/cups/model/Postscript-level1.ppd.gz -E
```

For more options of **lpadmin**, see the man page of lpadmin(8).

During printer setup, certain options are set as default. These options can be modified for every print job (depending on the print tool used). Changing these default options with YaST is also possible. Using command line tools, set default options as follows:

1. First, list all options:

   ```
   lpoptions -p QUEUE -l
   ```

   Example:

   ```
   Resolution/Output Resolution: 150dpi *300dpi 600dpi
   ```

   The activated default option is identified by a preceding asterisk (*).

2. Change the option with **lpadmin**:

   ```
   lpadmin -p QUEUE -o Resolution=600dpi
   ```

3. Check the new setting:

   ```
   lpoptions -p QUEUE -l

   Resolution/Output Resolution: 150dpi 300dpi *600dpi
   ```

When a normal user runs **lpoptions**, the settings are written to ~/.cups/lpoptions. However, root settings are written to /etc/cups/lpoptions.

18.6 Printing from the Command Line

To print from the command line, enter **lp -d** *QUEUENAME* *FILENAME*, substituting the corresponding names for *QUEUENAME* and *FILENAME*.

Some applications rely on the **lp** command for printing. In this case, enter the correct command in the application's print dialog, usually without specifying *FILENAME*, for example, **lp -d** *QUEUENAME*.

18.7 Special Features in SUSE Linux Enterprise Desktop

Several CUPS features have been adapted for SUSE Linux Enterprise Desktop. Some of the most important changes are covered here.

18.7.1 CUPS and Firewall

After having performed a default installation of SUSE Linux Enterprise Desktop, SuSEFirewall2 is active and the network interfaces are configured to be in the `External Zone` which blocks incoming traffic. More information about the SuSEFirewall2 configuration is available in *Book "Security Guide", Chapter 15 "Masquerading and Firewalls", Section 15.4 "SuSEFirewall2"* and at http://en.opensuse.org/SDB:CUPS_and_SANE_Firewall_settings ↗.

18.7.1.1 CUPS Client

Normally, a CUPS client runs on a regular workstation located in a trusted network environment behind a firewall. In this case it is recommended to configure the network interface to be in the `Internal Zone`, so the workstation is reachable from within the network.

18.7.1.2 CUPS Server

If the CUPS server is part of a trusted network environment protected by a firewall, the network interface should be configured to be in the `Internal Zone` of the firewall. It is not recommended to set up a CUPS server in an untrusted network environment unless you ensure that it is protected by special firewall rules and secure settings in the CUPS configuration.

18.7.2 Browsing for Network Printers

CUPS servers regularly announce the availability and status information of shared printers over the network. Clients can access this information to display a list of available printers in printing dialogs, for example. This is called "browsing".

CUPS servers announce their print queues over the network either via the traditional CUPS browsing protocol or via Bonjour/DND-SD. To be able to browse network print queues, the service `cups-browsed` needs to run on all clients that print via CUPS servers. `cups-browsed` is not started by default. To start it for the active session, use **`sudo systemctl start cups-browsed`**. To ensure it is automatically started after booting, enable it with **`sudo systemctl enable cups-browsed`** on all clients.

In case browsing does not work after having started `cups-browsed`, the CUPS server(s) probably announce the network print queues via Bonjour/DND-SD. In this case you need to additionally install the package `avahi` and start the associated service with **`sudo systemctl start avahi-daemon`** on all clients.

18.7.3 PPD Files in Various Packages

The YaST printer configuration sets up the queues for CUPS using the PPD files installed in `/usr/share/cups/model`. To find the suitable PPD files for the printer model, YaST compares the vendor and model determined during hardware detection with the vendors and models in all PPD files. For this purpose, the YaST printer configuration generates a database from the vendor and model information extracted from the PPD files.

The configuration using only PPD files and no other information sources has the advantage that the PPD files in `/usr/share/cups/model` can be modified freely. For example, if you have PostScript printers the PPD files can be copied directly to `/usr/share/cups/model` (if they do not already exist in the `manufacturer-PPDs` or `OpenPrintingPPDs-postscript` packages) to achieve an optimum configuration for your printers.

Additional PPD files are provided by the following packages:

- gutenprint: the Gutenprint driver and its matching PPDs
- splix: the SpliX driver and its matching PPDs
- OpenPrintingPPDs-ghostscript: PPDs for Ghostscript built-in drivers
- OpenPrintingPPDs-hpijs: PPDs for the HPIJS driver for non-HP printers

18.8 Troubleshooting

The following sections cover some of the most frequently encountered printer hardware and software problems and ways to solve or circumvent these problems. Among the topics covered are GDI printers, PPD files and port configuration. Common network printer problems, defective printouts, and queue handling are also addressed.

18.8.1 Printers without Standard Printer Language Support

These printers do not support any common printer language and can only be addressed with special proprietary control sequences. Therefore they can only work with the operating system versions for which the manufacturer delivers a driver. GDI is a programming interface developed by Microsoft* for graphics devices. Usually the manufacturer delivers drivers only for Windows, and since the Windows driver uses the GDI interface these printers are also called *GDI printers*. The actual problem is not the programming interface, but that these printers can only be addressed with the proprietary printer language of the respective printer model.

Some GDI printers can be switched to operate either in GDI mode or in one of the standard printer languages. See the manual of the printer whether this is possible. Some models require special Windows software to do the switch (note that the Windows printer driver may always switch the printer back into GDI mode when printing from Windows). For other GDI printers there are extension modules for a standard printer language available.

Some manufacturers provide proprietary drivers for their printers. The disadvantage of proprietary printer drivers is that there is no guarantee that these work with the installed print system or that they are suitable for the various hardware platforms. In contrast, printers that support a standard printer language do not depend on a special print system version or a special hardware platform.

Instead of spending time trying to make a proprietary Linux driver work, it may be more cost-effective to purchase a printer which supports a standard printer language (preferably PostScript). This would solve the driver problem once and for all, eliminating the need to install and configure special driver software and obtain driver updates that may be required because of new developments in the print system.

18.8.2 No Suitable PPD File Available for a PostScript Printer

If the `manufacturer-PPDs` or `OpenPrintingPPDs-postscript` packages do not contain a suitable PPD file for a PostScript printer, it should be possible to use the PPD file from the driver CD of the printer manufacturer or download a suitable PPD file from the Web page of the printer manufacturer.

If the PPD file is provided as a zip archive (.zip) or a self-extracting zip archive (`.exe`), unpack it with **`unzip`**. First, review the license terms of the PPD file. Then use the **`cupstestppd`** utility to check if the PPD file complies with “Adobe PostScript Printer Description File Format

Specification, version 4.3." If the utility returns "FAIL," the errors in the PPD files are serious and are likely to cause major problems. The problem spots reported by **cupstestppd** should be eliminated. If necessary, ask the printer manufacturer for a suitable PPD file.

18.8.3 Network Printer Connections

Identifying Network Problems

Connect the printer directly to the computer. For test purposes, configure the printer as a local printer. If this works, the problems are related to the network.

Checking the TCP/IP Network

The TCP/IP network and name resolution must be functional.

Checking a Remote lpd

Use the following command to test if a TCP connection can be established to **lpd** (port 515) on *HOST*:

```
netcat -z HOST 515 && echo ok || echo failed
```

If the connection to **lpd** cannot be established, **lpd** may not be active or there may be basic network problems.

Provided that the respective **lpd** is active and the host accepts queries, run the following command as root to query a status report for *QUEUE* on remote *HOST*:

```
echo -e "\004queue" \
| netcat -w 2 -p 722 HOST 515
```

If **lpd** does not respond, it may not be active or there may be basic network problems. If **lpd** responds, the response should show why printing is not possible on the queue on host. If you receive a response like that shown in *Example 18.1, "Error Message from lpd"*, the problem is caused by the remote **lpd**.

EXAMPLE 18.1: ERROR MESSAGE FROM lpd

```
lpd: your host does not have line printer access
lpd: queue does not exist
printer: spooling disabled
printer: printing disabled
```

Checking a Remote `cupsd`

A CUPS network server can broadcast its queues by default every 30 seconds on UDP port `631`. Accordingly, the following command can be used to test whether there is a broadcasting CUPS network server in the network. Make sure to stop your local CUPS daemon before executing the command.

```
netcat -u -l -p 631 & PID=$! ; sleep 40 ; kill $PID
```

If a broadcasting CUPS network server exists, the output appears as shown in Example 18.2, "Broadcast from the CUPS Network Server".

EXAMPLE 18.2: BROADCAST FROM THE CUPS NETWORK SERVER

```
ipp://192.168.2.202:631/printers/queue
```

The following command can be used to test if a TCP connection can be established to **`cupsd`** (port `631`) on *`HOST`*:

```
netcat -z HOST 631 && echo ok || echo failed
```

If the connection to **`cupsd`** cannot be established, **`cupsd`** may not be active or there may be basic network problems. **`lpstat -h`** *`HOST`* -l -t returns a (possibly very long) status report for all queues on *`HOST`*, provided the respective **`cupsd`** is active and the host accepts queries.

The next command can be used to test if the *`QUEUE`* on *`HOST`* accepts a print job consisting of a single carriage-return character. Nothing should be printed. Possibly, a blank page may be ejected.

```
echo -en "\r" \
| lp -d queue -h HOST
```

Troubleshooting a Network Printer or Print Server Machine

Spoolers running in a print server machine sometimes cause problems when they need to deal with multiple print jobs. Since this is caused by the spooler in the print server machine, there no way to resolve this issue. As a work-around, circumvent the spooler in the print server machine by addressing the printer connected to the print server machine directly with the TCP socket. See Section 18.4, "Network Printers".

In this way, the print server machine is reduced to a converter between the various forms of data transfer (TCP/IP network and local printer connection). To use this method, you need to know the TCP port on the print server machine. If the printer is connected to the print server machine and turned on, this TCP port can usually be determined with the **nmap** utility from the `nmap` package some time after the print server machine is powered up. For example, **nmap** *IP-address* may deliver the following output for a print server machine:

```
Port      State      Service
23/tcp    open       telnet
80/tcp    open       http
515/tcp   open       printer
631/tcp   open       cups
9100/tcp  open       jetdirect
```

This output indicates that the printer connected to the print server machine can be addressed via TCP socket on port `9100`. By default, **nmap** only checks several commonly known ports listed in `/usr/share/nmap/nmap-services`. To check all possible ports, use the command **nmap -p** *FROM_PORT-TO_PORT* *IP_ADDRESS*. This may take some time. For further information, refer to the man page of **nmap**.

Enter a command like

```
echo -en "\rHello\r\f" | netcat -w 1 IP-address port
cat file | netcat -w 1 IP-address port
```

to send character strings or files directly to the respective port to test if the printer can be addressed on this port.

18.8.4 Defective Printouts without Error Message

For the print system, the print job is completed when the CUPS back-end completes the data transfer to the recipient (printer). If further processing on the recipient fails (for example, if the printer is not able to print the printer-specific data) the print system does not notice this. If the printer cannot print the printer-specific data, select a PPD file that is more suitable for the printer.

18.8.5 Disabled Queues

If the data transfer to the recipient fails entirely after several attempts, the CUPS back-end, such as `USB` or `socket`, reports an error to the print system (to **cupsd**). The back-end determines how many unsuccessful attempts are appropriate until the data transfer is reported as impossible.

As further attempts would be in vain, `cupsd` disables printing for the respective queue. After eliminating the cause of the problem, the system administrator must re-enable printing with the command `cupsenable`.

18.8.6 CUPS Browsing: Deleting Print Jobs

If a CUPS network server broadcasts its queues to the client hosts via browsing and a suitable local `cupsd` is active on the client hosts, the client `cupsd` accepts print jobs from applications and forwards them to the `cupsd` on the server. When `cupsd` on the server accepts a print job, it is assigned a new job number. Therefore, the job number on the client host is different from the job number on the server. As a print job is usually forwarded immediately, it cannot be deleted with the job number on the client host This is because the client `cupsd` regards the print job as completed when it has been forwarded to the server `cupsd`.

To delete the print job on the server, use a command such as `lpstat -h cups.example.com -o` to determine the job number on the server. This assumes that the server has not already completed the print job (that is, sent it completely to the printer). Use the obtained job number to delete the print job on the server as follows:

```
cancel -h cups.example.com QUEUE-JOBNUMBER
```

18.8.7 Defective Print Jobs and Data Transfer Errors

If you switch the printer off or shut down the computer during the printing process, print jobs remain in the queue. Printing resumes when the computer (or the printer) is switched back on. Defective print jobs must be removed from the queue with `cancel`.

If a print job is corrupted or an error occurs in the communication between the host and the printer, the printer cannot process the data correctly and prints numerous sheets of paper with unintelligible characters. To fix the problem, follow these steps:

1. To stop printing, remove all paper from ink jet printers or open the paper trays of laser printers. High-quality printers have a button for canceling the current printout.

2. The print job may still be in the queue, because jobs are only removed after they are sent completely to the printer. Use `lpstat -o` or `lpstat -h cups.example.com -o` to check which queue is currently printing. Delete the print job with `cancel` *`QUEUE-JOBNUMBER`* or `cancel -h cups.example.com` *`QUEUE-JOBNUMBER`*.

3. Some data may still be transferred to the printer even though the print job has been deleted from the queue. Check if a CUPS back-end process is still running for the respective queue and terminate it.

4. Reset the printer completely by switching it off for some time. Then insert the paper and turn on the printer.

18.8.8 Debugging CUPS

Use the following generic procedure to locate problems in CUPS:

1. Set **`LogLevel debug`** in `/etc/cups/cupsd.conf`.

2. Stop **`cupsd`**.

3. Remove `/var/log/cups/error_log*` to avoid having to search through very large log files.

4. Start **`cupsd`**.

5. Repeat the action that led to the problem.

6. Check the messages in `/var/log/cups/error_log*` to identify the cause of the problem.

18.8.9 For More Information

In-depth information about printing on SUSE Linux is presented in the openSUSE Support Database at http://en.opensuse.org/Portal:Printing. Solutions to many specific problems are presented in the SUSE Knowledgebase (http://www.suse.com/support/). Locate the relevant articles with a text search for `CUPS`.

19 The X Window System

The X Window System (X11) is the de facto standard for graphical user interfaces in Unix. X is network-based, enabling applications started on one host to be displayed on another host connected over any kind of network (LAN or Internet). This chapter provides basic information on the X configuration, and background information about the use of fonts in SUSE® Linux Enterprise Desktop.

Usually, the X Window System needs no configuration. The hardware is dynamically detected during X start-up. The use of `xorg.conf` is therefore deprecated. If you still need to specify custom options to change the way X behaves, you can still do so by modifying configuration files under `/etc/X11/xorg.conf.d/`.

19.1 Installing and Configuring Fonts

Fonts in Linux can be categorized into two parts:

Outline or Vector Fonts

Contains a mathematical description as drawing instructions about the shape of a glyph. As such, each glyph can be scaled to arbitrary sizes without loss of quality. Before such a font (or glyph) can be used, the mathematical descriptions need to be transformed into a raster (grid). This process is called *font rasterization. Font hinting* (embedded inside the font) improves and optimizes the rendering result for a particular size. Rasterization and hinting is done with the FreeType library.

Common formats under Linux are PostScript Type 1 and Type 2, TrueType, and OpenType.

Bitmap or Raster Fonts

Consists of an array of pixels designed for a specific font size. Bitmap fonts are extremely fast and simple to render. However, compared to vector fonts, bitmap fonts cannot be scaled without losing quality. As such, these fonts are usually distributed in different sizes. These days, bitmap fonts are still used in the Linux console and sometimes in terminals.

Under Linux, Portable Compiled Format (PCF) or Glyph Bitmap Distribution Format (BDF) are the most common formats.

The appearance of these fonts can be influenced by two main aspects:

- choosing a suitable font family,
- rendering the font with an algorithm that achieves results comfortable for the receiver's eyes.

The last point is only relevant to vector fonts. Although the above two points are highly subjective, some defaults need to be created.

Linux font rendering systems consist of several libraries with different relations. The basic font rendering library is FreeType (http://www.freetype.org/) ↗, which converts font glyphs of supported formats into optimized bitmap glyphs. The rendering process is controlled by an algorithm and its parameters (which may be subject to patent issues).

Every program or library which uses FreeType should consult the Fontconfig (http://www.fontconfig.org/) ↗ library. This library gathers font configuration from users and from the system. When a user amends his Fontconfig setting, this change will result in Fontconfig-aware applications.

More sophisticated OpenType shaping needed for scripts such as Arabic, Han or Phags-Pa and other higher level text processing is done using Harfbuzz (http://www.harfbuzz.org/) ↗ or Pango (http://www.pango.org/) ↗.

19.1.1 Showing Installed Fonts

To get an overview about which fonts are installed on your system, ask the commands **`rpm`** or **`fc-list`**. Both will give you a good answer, but may return a different list depending on system and user configuration:

`rpm`

Invoke **`rpm`** to see which software packages containing fonts are installed on your system:

```
rpm -qa '*fonts*'
```

Every font package should satisfy this expression. However, the command may return some false positives like `fonts-config` (which is neither a font nor does it contain fonts).

fc-list

Invoke **fc-list** to get an overview about what font families can be accessed, whether they are installed on the system or in your home:

```
fc-list ':' family
```

Note: Command **fc-list**

The command **fc-list** is a wrapper to the Fontconfig library. It is possible to query a lot of interesting information from Fontconfig—or, to be more precise, from its cache. See **man 1 fc-list** for more details.

19.1.2 Viewing Fonts

If you want to know what an installed font family looks like, either use the command **ftview** (package ft2demos) or visit http://fontinfo.opensuse.org/ ↗. For example, to display the FreeMono font in 14 point, use **ftview** like this:

```
ftview 14 /usr/share/fonts/truetype/FreeMono.ttf
```

If you need further information, go to http://fontinfo.opensuse.org/ ↗ to find out which styles (regular, bold, italic, etc.) and languages are supported.

19.1.3 Querying Fonts

To query which font is used when a pattern is given, use the **fc-match** command.

For example, if your pattern contains an already installed font, **fc-match** returns the file name, font family, and the style:

```
tux > fc-match 'Liberation Serif'
LiberationSerif-Regular.ttf: "Liberation Serif" "Regular"
```

If the desired font does not exist on your system, Fontconfig's matching rules take place and try to find the most similar fonts available. This means, your request is substituted:

```
tux > fc-match 'Foo Family'
DejaVuSans.ttf: "DejaVu Sans" "Book"
```

Fontconfig supports *aliases*: a name is substituted with another family name. A typical example are the generic names such as "sans-serif", "serif", and "monospace". These alias names can be substituted by real family names or even a preference list of family names:

```
tux > for font in serif sans mono; do fc-match "$font" ; done
DejaVuSerif.ttf: "DejaVu Serif" "Book"
DejaVuSans.ttf: "DejaVu Sans" "Book"
DejaVuSansMono.ttf: "DejaVu Sans Mono" "Book"
```

The result may vary on your system, depending on which fonts are currently installed.

Note: Similarity Rules according to Fontconfig

Fontconfig *always* returns a real family (if at least one is installed) according to the given request, as similar as possible. "Similarity" depends on Fontconfig's internal metrics and on the user's or administrator's Fontconfig settings.

19.1.4 Installing Fonts

To install a new font there are these major methods:

1. Manually install the font files such as `*.ttf` or `*.otf` to a known font directory. If it needs to be system-wide, use the standard directory `/usr/share/fonts`. For installation in your home directory, use `~/.config/fonts`.
   If you want to deviate from the standard directories, Fontconfig allows you to choose another one. Let Fontconfig know by using the `<dir>` element, see *Section 19.1.5.2, "Diving into Fontconfig XML"* for details.

2. Install fonts using **`zypper`**. Lots of fonts are already available as a package, be it on your SUSE distribution or in the M17N:fonts (http://download.opensuse.org/repositories/M17N:/fonts/) repository. Add the repository to your list using the following command. For example, to add a repository for SLE 12:

   ```
   sudo zypper ar
        http://download.opensuse.org/repositories/M17N:/fonts/SLE_12_SP3/
   ```

   To search for your *`FONT_FAMILY_NAME`* use this command:

   ```
   sudo zypper se 'FONT_FAMILY_NAME*fonts'
   ```

19.1.5 Configuring the Appearance of Fonts

Depending on the rendering medium, and font size, the result may be unsatisfactory. For example, an average monitor these days has a resolution of 100dpi which makes pixels too big and glyphs look clunky.

There are several algorithms available to deal with low resolutions, such as anti-aliasing (grayscale smoothing), hinting (fitting to the grid), or subpixel rendering (tripling resolution in one direction). These algorithms can also differ from one font format to another.

> **Important: Patent Issues with Subpixel Rendering**
>
> Subpixel rendering is not used in SUSE distributions. Although FreeType2 has support for this algorithm, it is covered by several patents expiring at the end of the year 2019. Therefore, setting subpixel rendering options in Fontconfig has no effect unless the system has a FreeType2 library with subpixel rendering compiled in.

Via Fontconfig, it is possible to select a rendering algorithms for every font individually or for a set of fonts.

19.1.5.1 Configuring Fonts via `sysconfig`

SUSE Linux Enterprise Desktop comes with a `sysconfig` layer above Fontconfig. This is a good starting point for experimenting with font configuration. To change the default settings, edit the configuration file `/etc/sysconfig/fonts-config`. (or use the YaST sysconfig module). After you have edited the file, run **`fonts-config`**:

```
sudo /usr/sbin/fonts-config
```

Restart the application to make the effect visible. Keep in mind the following issues:

- A few applications do need not to be restarted. For example, Firefox re-reads Fontconfig configuration from time to time. Newly created or reloaded tabs get new font configurations later.
- The **`fonts-config`** script is called automatically after every package installation or removal (if not, it is a bug of the font software package).
- Every sysconfig variable can be temporarily overridden by the **`fonts-config`** command line option. See **`fonts-config --help`** for details.

There are several sysconfig variables which can be altered. See **`man 1 fonts-config`** or the help page of the YaST sysconfig module. The following variables are examples:

Usage of Rendering Algorithms

Consider `FORCE_HINTSTYLE`, `FORCE_AUTOHINT`, `FORCE_BW`, `FORCE_BW_MONOSPACE`, `USE_EMBEDDED_BITMAPS` and `EMBEDDED_BITMAP_LANGAGES`

Preference Lists of Generic Aliases

Use `PREFER_SANS_FAMILIES`, `PREFER_SERIF_FAMILIES`, `PREFER_MONO_FAMILIES` and `SEARCH_METRIC_COMPATIBLE`

The following list provides some configuration examples, sorted from the “most readable” fonts (more contrast) to “most beautiful” (more smoothed).

Bitmap Fonts

Prefer bitmap fonts via the `PREFER_*_FAMILIES` variables. Follow the example in the help section for these variables. Be aware that these fonts are rendered black and white, not smoothed and that bitmap fonts are available in several sizes only. Consider using

```
SEARCH_METRIC_COMPATIBLE="no"
```

to disable metric compatibility-driven family name substitutions.

Scalable Fonts Rendered Black and White

Scalable fonts rendered without antialiasing can result in a similar outcome to bitmap fonts, while maintaining font scalability. Use well hinted fonts like the Liberation families. Unfortunately, there is a lack of well hinted fonts though. Set the following variable to force this method:

```
FORCE_BW="yes"
```

Monospaced Fonts Rendered Black and White

Render monospaced fonts without antialiasing only, otherwise use default settings:

```
FORCE_BW_MONOSPACE="yes"
```

Default Settings

All fonts are rendered with antialiasing. Well hinted fonts will be rendered with the *byte code interpreter* (BCI) and the rest with autohinter (`hintstyle=hintslight`). Leave all relevant sysconfig variables to the default setting.

CFF Fonts

Use fonts in CFF format. They can be considered also more readable than the default TrueType fonts given the current improvements in FreeType2. Try them out by following the example of `PREFER_*_FAMILIES`. Possibly make them more dark and bold with:

```
SEARCH_METRIC_COMPATIBLE="no"
```

as they are rendered by `hintstyle=hintslight` by default. Also consider using:

```
SEARCH_METRIC_COMPATIBLE="no"
```

Autohinter Exclusively

Even for a well hinted font, use FreeType2's autohinter. That can lead to thicker, sometimes fuzzier letter shapes with lower contrast. Set the following variable to activate this:

```
FORCE_AUTOHINTER="yes"
```

Use `FORCE_HINTSTYLE` to control the level of hinting.

19.1.5.2 Diving into Fontconfig XML

Fontconfig's configuration format is the *eXtensible Markup Language* (XML). These few examples are not a complete reference, but a brief overview. Details and other inspiration can be found in **`man 5 fonts-conf`** or in `/etc/fonts/conf.d/`.

The central Fontconfig configuration file is `/etc/fonts/fonts.conf`, which—along other work—includes the whole `/etc/fonts/conf.d/` directory. To customize Fontconfig, there are two places where you can insert your changes:

FONTCONFIG CONFIGURATION FILES

1. **System-wide changes.** Edit the file `/etc/fonts/local.conf` (by default, it contains an empty `fontconfig` element).

2. **User-specific changes.** Edit the file `~/.config/fontconfig/fonts.conf`. Place Fontconfig configuration files in the `~/.config/fontconfig/conf.d/` directory.

User-specific changes overwrite any system-wide settings.

Note: Deprecated User Configuration File

The file `~/.fonts.conf` is marked as deprecated and should not be used anymore. Use `~/.config/fontconfig/fonts.conf` instead.

Every configuration file needs to have a `fontconfig` element. As such, the minimal file looks like this:

```
<?xml version="1.0"?>
   <!DOCTYPE fontconfig SYSTEM "fonts.dtd">
   <fontconfig>
   <!-- Insert your changes here -->
   </fontconfig>
```

If the default directories are not enough, insert the `dir` element with the respective directory:

```
<dir>/usr/share/fonts2</dir>
```

Fontconfig searches *recursively* for fonts.

Font-rendering algorithms can be chosen with following Fontconfig snippet (see *Example 19.1, "Specifying Rendering Algorithms"*):

EXAMPLE 19.1: SPECIFYING RENDERING ALGORITHMS

```
<match target="font">
 <test name="family">
  <string>FAMILY_NAME</string>
 </test>
 <edit name="antialias" mode="assign">
  <bool>true</bool>
 </edit>
 <edit name="hinting" mode="assign">
  <bool>true</bool>
 </edit>
 <edit name="autohint" mode="assign">
  <bool>false</bool>
 </edit>
 <edit name="hintstyle" mode="assign">
  <const>hintfull</const>
 </edit>
</match>
```

Various properties of fonts can be tested. For example, the `<test>` element can test for the font family (as shown in the example), size interval, spacing, font format, and others. When abandoning `<test>` completely, all `<edit>` elements will be applied to every font (global change).

EXAMPLE 19.2: ALIASES AND FAMILY NAME SUBSTITUTIONS

Rule 1

```
<alias>
 <family>Alegreya SC</family>
 <default>
  <family>serif</family>
 </default>
</alias>
```

Rule 2

```
<alias>
 <family>serif</family>
 <prefer>
  <family>Droid Serif</family>
 </prefer>
</alias>
```

Rule 3

```
<alias>
 <family>serif</family>
 <accept>
  <family>STIXGeneral</family>
 </accept>
</alias>
```

The rules from *Example 19.2, "Aliases and Family Name Substitutions"* create a ***prioritized family list*** (PFL). Depending on the element, different actions are performed:

`<default>` from *Rule 1*

This rule adds a `serif` family name *at the end* of the PFL.

`<prefer>` from *Rule 2*

This rule adds "Droid Serif" *just before* the first occurrence of `serif` in the PFL, whenever `Alegreya SC` is in PFL.

`<accept>` from *Rule 3*

This rule adds a "STIXGeneral" family name *just after* the first occurrence of the `serif` family name in the PFL.

Putting this together, when snippets occur in the order *Rule 1* - *Rule 2* - *Rule 3* and the user requests "Alegreya SC", then the PFL is created as depicted in *Table 19.1, "Generating PFL from Fontconfig rules"*.

TABLE 19.1: GENERATING PFL FROM FONTCONFIG RULES

Order	Current PFL
Request	`Alegreya SC`
Rule 1	`Alegreya SC`, `serif`
Rule 2	`Alegreya SC`, `Droid Serif`, `serif`
Rule 3	`Alegreya SC`, `Droid Serif`, `serif`, `STIXGeneral`

In Fontconfig's metrics, the family name has the highest priority over other patterns, like style, size, etc. Fontconfig checks which family is currently installed on the system. If "Alegreya SC" is installed, then Fontconfig returns it. If not, it asks for "Droid Serif", etc.

Be careful. When the order of Fontconfig snippets is changed, Fontconfig can return different results, as depicted in *Table 19.2, "Results from Generating PFL from Fontconfig Rules with Changed Order"*.

TABLE 19.2: RESULTS FROM GENERATING PFL FROM FONTCONFIG RULES WITH CHANGED ORDER

Order	Current PFL	Note
Request	`Alegreya SC`	Same request performed.
Rule 2	`Alegreya SC`	`serif` not in FPL, nothing is substituted
Rule 3	`Alegreya SC`	`serif` not in FPL, nothing is substituted
Rule 1	`Alegreya SC`, `serif`	`Alegreya SC` present in FPL, substitution is performed

Note: Implication.

Think of the `<default>` alias as a classification or inclusion of this group (if not installed). As the example shows, `<default>` should always precede the `<prefer>` and `<accept>` aliases of that group.

`<default>` classification is not limited to the generic aliases serif, sans-serif and monospace. See `/usr/share/fontconfig/conf.avail/30-metric-aliases.conf` for a complex example.

The following Fontconfig snippet in *Example 19.3, "Aliases and Family Name Substitutions"* creates a `serif` group. Every family in this group could substitute others when a former font is not installed.

EXAMPLE 19.3: ALIASES AND FAMILY NAME SUBSTITUTIONS

```
<alias>
 <family>Alegreya SC</family>
 <default>
  <family>serif</family>
 </default>
</alias>
<alias>
 <family>Droid Serif</family>
 <default>
  <family>serif</family>
 </default>
</alias>
<alias>
 <family>STIXGeneral</family>
 <default>
  <family>serif</family>
 </default>
</alias>
<alias>
 <family>serif</family>
 <accept>
  <family>Droid Serif</family>
  <family>STIXGeneral</family>
  <family>Alegreya SC</family>
 </accept>
</alias>
```

Priority is given by the order in the `<accept>` alias. Similarly, stronger `<prefer>` aliases can be used.

Example 19.2, "Aliases and Family Name Substitutions" is expanded by *Example 19.4, "Aliases and Family Names Substitutions"*.

EXAMPLE 19.4: ALIASES AND FAMILY NAMES SUBSTITUTIONS

Rule 4

```
<alias>
 <family>serif</family>
 <accept>
  <family>Liberation Serif</family>
 </accept>
</alias>
```

Rule 5

```
<alias>
 <family>serif</family>
 <prefer>
  <family>DejaVu Serif</family>
 </prefer>
</alias>
```

The expanded configuration from *Example 19.4, "Aliases and Family Names Substitutions"* would lead to the following PFL evolution:

TABLE 19.3: RESULTS FROM GENERATING PFL FROM FONTCONFIG RULES

Order	Current PFL
Request	`Alegreya SC`
Rule 1	`Alegreya SC`, `serif`
Rule 2	`Alegreya SC`, `Droid Serif`, `serif`
Rule 3	`Alegreya SC`, `Droid Serif`, `serif`, `STIXGeneral`
Rule 4	`Alegreya SC`, `Droid Serif`, `serif`, `Liberation Serif`, `STIX-General`
Rule 5	`Alegreya SC`, `Droid Serif`, `DejaVu Serif`, `serif`, `Liberation Serif`, `STIXGeneral`

- In case multiple `<accept>` declarations for the same generic name exist, the declaration that is parsed last “wins”. If possible, do not use `<accept>` **after** user (`/etc/fonts/conf.d/*-user.conf`) when creating a system-wide configuration.
- In case multiple `<prefer` declarations for the same generic name exist, the declaration that is parsed last “wins”. If possible, do not use `<prefer>` **before** user in the system-wide configuration.
- Every `<prefer>` declaration overwrites `<accept>` declarations for the same generic name. If the administrator wants to allow the user to utilize even `<accept>` and not only `<prefer>`,the administrator should not use `<prefer>` in the system-wide configuration. On the other hand, as users mostly use `<prefer>`, this should not have any detrimental effect. We also see the use of `<prefer>` also in system wide configurations.

19.2 For More Information

Install the packages `xorg-docs` to get more in-depth information about X11. **`man 5 xorg.conf`** tells you more about the format of the manual configuration (if needed). More information on the X11 development can be found on the project's home page at http://www.x.org ↗.

Drivers are found in `xf86-video-*` packages, for example `xf86-video-nv`. Many of the drivers delivered with these packages are described in detail in the related manual page. For example, if you use the `nv` driver, find more information about this driver in **`man 4 nv`**.

Information about third-party drivers should be available in `/usr/share/doc/packages/<package_name>`. For example, the documentation of `x11-video-nvidiaG03` is available in `/usr/share/doc/packages/x11-video-nvidiaG03` after the package was installed.

20 Accessing File Systems with FUSE

FUSE is the acronym for *file system in user space*. This means you can configure and mount a file system as an unprivileged user. Normally, you need to be `root` for this task. FUSE alone is a kernel module. Combined with plug-ins, it allows you to extend FUSE to access almost all file systems like remote SSH connections, ISO images, and more.

20.1 Configuring FUSE

Before you can use FUSE, you need to install the package `fuse`. Depending which file system you want to use, you need additional plug-ins available as separate packages.

Generally you do not need to configure FUSE. However, it is a good idea to create a directory where all your mount points are combined. For example, you can create a directory `~/mounts` and insert your subdirectories for your different file systems there.

20.2 Mounting an NTFS Partition

NTFS, the *New Technology File System*, is the default file system of Windows. Since under normal circumstances the unprivileged user cannot mount NTFS block devices using the external FUSE library, the process of mounting a Windows partition described below requires root privileges.

1. Become `root` and install the package `ntfs-3g`.
2. Create a directory that is to be used as a mount point, for example `~/mounts/windows`.
3. Find out which Windows partition you need. Use YaST and start the partitioner module to see which partition belongs to Windows, but do not modify anything. Alternatively, become `root` and execute **`/sbin/fdisk`** `-l`. Look for partitions with a partition type of `HPFS/NTFS`.
4. Mount the partition in read-write mode. Replace the placeholder *`DEVICE`* with your respective Windows partition:

   ```
   ntfs-3g /dev/DEVICE MOUNT POINT
   ```

To use your Windows partition in read-only mode, append `-o ro`:

```
ntfs-3g /dev/DEVICE MOUNT POINT -o ro
```

The command **ntfs-3g** uses the current user (UID) and group (GID) to mount the given device. If you want to set the write permissions to a different user, use the command **id** `USER` to get the output of the UID and GID values. Set it with:

```
id tux
uid=1000(tux) gid=100(users) groups=100(users),16(dialout),33(video)
ntfs-3g /dev/DEVICE MOUNT POINT -o uid=1000,gid=100
```

Find additional options in the man page.

To unmount the resource, run **fusermount -u** *MOUNT POINT*.

20.3 For More Information

See the home page http://fuse.sourceforge.net ↗ of FUSE for more information.

21 Managing Kernel Modules

Although Linux is a monolithic kernel, it can be extended using kernel modules. These are special objects that can be inserted into the kernel and removed on demand. In practical terms, kernel modules make it possible to add and remove drivers and interfaces that are not included in the kernel itself. Linux provides several commands for managing kernel modules.

21.1 Listing Loaded Modules with lsmod and modinfo

Use the **lsmod** command to view what kernel modules are currently loaded. The output of the command may look as follows:

```
tux >  lsmod
Module                  Size  Used by
snd_usb_audio         188416  2
snd_usbmidi_lib        36864  1 snd_usb_audio
hid_plantronics        16384  0
snd_rawmidi            36864  1 snd_usbmidi_lib
snd_seq_device         16384  1 snd_rawmidi
fuse                  106496  3
nfsv3                  45056  1
nfs_acl                16384  1 nfsv3
```

The output is divided into three columns. The `Module` column lists the names of the loaded modules, while the `Size` column displays the size of each module. The `Used by` column shows the number of referring modules and their names. Note that this list may be incomplete.

To view detailed information about a specific kernel module, use the **modinfo** *MODULE_NAME* command, where *MODULE_NAME* is the name of the desired kernel module. Note that the **modinfo** binary resides in the `/sbin` directory that is not in the user's PATH environment variable. This means that you must specify the full path to the binary when running **modinfo** command as a regular user:

```
$ /sbin/modinfo kvm
filename:       /lib/modules/4.4.57-18.3-default/kernel/arch/x86/kvm/kvm.ko
license:        GPL
author:         Qumranet
srcversion:     BDFD8098BEEA517CB75959B
depends:        irqbypass
```

```
intree:         Y
vermagic:       4.4.57-18.3-default SMP mod_unload modversions
signer:         openSUSE Secure Boot Signkey
sig_key:        03:32:FA:9C:BF:0D:88:BF:21:92:4B:0D:E8:2A:09:A5:4D:5D:EF:C8
sig_hashalgo:   sha256
parm:           ignore_msrs:bool
parm:           min_timer_period_us:uint
parm:           kvmclock_periodic_sync:bool
parm:           tsc_tolerance_ppm:uint
parm:           lapic_timer_advance_ns:uint
parm:           halt_poll_ns:uint
parm:           halt_poll_ns_grow:int
parm:           halt_poll_ns_shrink:int
```

21.2 Adding and Removing Kernel Modules

While it is possible to use `insmod` and `rmmod` to add and remove kernel modules, it is recommended to use the `modprobe` tool instead. `modprobe` offers several important advantages, including automatic dependency resolution and blacklisting.

When used without any parameters, the `modprobe` command installs a specified kernel module. `modprobe` must be run with root privileges:

```
tux > sudo modprobe acpi
```

To remove a kernel module, use the `-r` parameter:

```
sudo modprobe -r acpi
```

21.2.1 Loading Kernel Modules Automatically on Boot

Instead of loading kernel modules manually, you can load them automatically during the boot process using the `system-modules-load.service` service. To enable a kernel module, add a `.conf` file to the `/etc/modules-load.d/` directory. It is good practice to give the configuration file the same name as the module, for example:

```
/etc/modules-load.d/rt2800usb.conf
```

The configuration file must contain the name of the desired kernel module (for example, `rt2800usb`).

The described technique allows you to load kernel modules without any parameters. If you need to load a kernel module with specific options, add a configuration file to the `/etc/modprobe.d/` directory instead. The file must have the `.conf` extension. The name of the file should adhere to the following naming convention: `priority-modulename.conf`, for example: `50-thinkfan.conf`. The configuration file must contain the name of the kernel module and the desired parameters. You can use the example command below to create a configuration file containing the name of the kernel module and its parameters:

```
echo "options thinkpad_acpi fan_control=1" | sudo tee /etc/modprobe.d/thinkfan.conf
```

Note: Loading Kernel Modules

Most kernel modules are loaded by the system automatically when a device is detected or user space requests specific functionality. Thus, adding modules manually to `/etc/modules-load.d/` is rarely required.

21.2.2 Blacklisting Kernel Modules with modprobe

Blacklisting a kernel module prevents it from loading during the boot process. This can be useful when you want to disable a module that you suspect is causing problems on your system. Note that you can still load blacklisted kernel modules manually using the `insmod` or `modprobe` tools.

To blacklist a module, add the `blacklist` *`MODULE_NAME`* line to the `/etc/modprobe.d/50-blacklist.conf` file. For example:

```
blacklist nouveau
```

Run the **`mkinitrd`** command as root to generate a new `initrd` image, then reboot your machine. These steps can be performed using the following command:

```
su
echo "blacklist nouveau" >> /etc/modprobe.d/50-blacklist.conf && mkinitrd && reboot
```

To disable a kernel module temporarily only, blacklist it on-the-fly during the boot. To do this, press the E key when you see the boot screen. This drops you into a minimal editor that allows you to modify boot parameters. Locate the line that looks as follows:

```
linux /boot/vmlinuz...splash= silent quiet showopts
```

Add the **modprobe.blacklist=*MODULE_NAME*** command to the end of the line. For example:

```
linux /boot/vmlinuz...splash= silent quiet showopts modprobe.blacklist=nouveau
```

Press F10 or Ctrl–X to boot with the specified configuration.

To blacklist a kernel module permanently via GRUB, open the /etc/default/grub file for editing, and add the **modprobe.blacklist=*MODULE_NAME*** option to the **GRUB_CMD_LINUX** command. Then run the **sudo grub2-mkconfig -o /boot/grub2/grub.cfg** command to enable the changes.

22 Dynamic Kernel Device Management with udev

The kernel can add or remove almost any device in a running system. Changes in the device state (whether a device is plugged in or removed) need to be propagated to user space. Devices need to be configured when they are plugged in and recognized. Users of a certain device need to be informed about any changes in this device's recognized state. `udev` provides the needed infrastructure to dynamically maintain the device node files and symbolic links in the `/dev` directory. `udev` rules provide a way to plug external tools into the kernel device event processing. This allows you to customize `udev` device handling by adding certain scripts to execute as part of kernel device handling, or request and import additional data to evaluate during device handling.

22.1 The /dev Directory

The device nodes in the `/dev` directory provide access to the corresponding kernel devices. With `udev`, the `/dev` directory reflects the current state of the kernel. Every kernel device has one corresponding device file. If a device is disconnected from the system, the device node is removed.

The content of the `/dev` directory is kept on a temporary file system and all files are rendered at every system start-up. Manually created or modified files do not, by design, survive a reboot. Static files and directories that should always be in the `/dev` directory regardless of the state of the corresponding kernel device can be created with systemd-tmpfiles. The configuration files are found in `/usr/lib/tmpfiles.d/` and `/etc/tmpfiles.d/`; for more information, see the `systemd-tmpfiles(8)` man page.

22.2 Kernel uevents and udev

The required device information is exported by the `sysfs` file system. For every device the kernel has detected and initialized, a directory with the device name is created. It contains attribute files with device-specific properties.

Every time a device is added or removed, the kernel sends a uevent to notify `udev` of the change. The `udev` daemon reads and parses all provided rules from the `/etc/udev/rules.d/*.rules` files once at start-up and keeps them in memory. If rules files are changed, added or removed, the daemon can reload the in-memory representation of all rules with the command **`udevadm control --reload`**. For more details on `udev` rules and their syntax, refer to *Section 22.6, "Influencing Kernel Device Event Handling with* udev *Rules"*.

Every received event is matched against the set of provides rules. The rules can add or change event environment keys, request a specific name for the device node to create, add symbolic links pointing to the node or add programs to run after the device node is created. The driver core `uevents` are received from a kernel netlink socket.

22.3 Drivers, Kernel Modules and Devices

The kernel bus drivers probe for devices. For every detected device, the kernel creates an internal device structure while the driver core sends a uevent to the `udev` daemon. Bus devices identify themselves by a specially-formatted ID, which tells what kind of device it is. Usually these IDs consist of vendor and product ID and other subsystem-specific values. Every bus has its own scheme for these IDs, called `MODALIAS`. The kernel takes the device information, composes a `MODALIAS` ID string from it and sends that string along with the event. For a USB mouse, it looks like this:

```
MODALIAS=usb:v046DpC03Ed2000dc00dsc00dp00ic03isc01ip02
```

Every device driver carries a list of known aliases for devices it can handle. The list is contained in the kernel module file itself. The program depmod reads the ID lists and creates the file `modules.alias` in the kernel's `/lib/modules` directory for all currently available modules. With this infrastructure, module loading is as easy as calling **`modprobe`** for every event that carries a `MODALIAS` key. If **`modprobe $MODALIAS`** is called, it matches the device alias composed for the device with the aliases provided by the modules. If a matching entry is found, that module is loaded. All this is automatically triggered by `udev`.

22.4 Booting and Initial Device Setup

All device events happening during the boot process before the `udev` daemon is running are lost, because the infrastructure to handle these events resides on the root file system and is not available at that time. To cover that loss, the kernel provides a `uevent` file located in the device directory of every device in the `sysfs` file system. By writing `add` to that file, the kernel resends the same event as the one lost during boot. A simple loop over all `uevent` files in `/sys` triggers all events again to create the device nodes and perform device setup.

As an example, a USB mouse present during boot may not be initialized by the early boot logic, because the driver is not available at that time. The event for the device discovery was lost and failed to find a kernel module for the device. Instead of manually searching for connected devices, `udev` requests all device events from the kernel after the root file system is available, so the event for the USB mouse device runs again. Now it finds the kernel module on the mounted root file system and the USB mouse can be initialized.

From user space, there is no visible difference between a device coldplug sequence and a device discovery during runtime. In both cases, the same rules are used to match and the same configured programs are run.

22.5 Monitoring the Running udev Daemon

The program **`udevadm monitor`** can be used to visualize the driver core events and the timing of the `udev` event processes.

```
UEVENT[1185238505.276660] add   /devices/pci0000:00/0000:00:1d.2/usb3/3-1 (usb)
UDEV  [1185238505.279198] add   /devices/pci0000:00/0000:00:1d.2/usb3/3-1 (usb)
UEVENT[1185238505.279527] add   /devices/pci0000:00/0000:00:1d.2/usb3/3-1/3-1:1.0 (usb)
UDEV  [1185238505.285573] add   /devices/pci0000:00/0000:00:1d.2/usb3/3-1/3-1:1.0 (usb)
UEVENT[1185238505.298878] add   /devices/pci0000:00/0000:00:1d.2/usb3/3-1/3-1:1.0/input/
input10 (input)
UDEV  [1185238505.305026] add   /devices/pci0000:00/0000:00:1d.2/usb3/3-1/3-1:1.0/input/
input10 (input)
UEVENT[1185238505.305442] add   /devices/pci0000:00/0000:00:1d.2/usb3/3-1/3-1:1.0/input/
input10/mouse2 (input)
UEVENT[1185238505.306440] add   /devices/pci0000:00/0000:00:1d.2/usb3/3-1/3-1:1.0/input/
input10/event4 (input)
UDEV  [1185238505.325384] add   /devices/pci0000:00/0000:00:1d.2/usb3/3-1/3-1:1.0/input/
input10/event4 (input)
UDEV  [1185238505.342257] add   /devices/pci0000:00/0000:00:1d.2/usb3/3-1/3-1:1.0/input/
input10/mouse2 (input)
```

The `UEVENT` lines show the events the kernel has sent over netlink. The `UDEV` lines show the finished `udev` event handlers. The timing is printed in microseconds. The time between `UEVENT` and `UDEV` is the time `udev` took to process this event or the `udev` daemon has delayed its execution to synchronize this event with related and already running events. For example, events for hard disk partitions always wait for the main disk device event to finish, because the partition events may rely on the data that the main disk event has queried from the hardware.

udevadm monitor --env shows the complete event environment:

```
ACTION=add
DEVPATH=/devices/pci0000:00/0000:00:1d.2/usb3/3-1/3-1:1.0/input/input10
SUBSYSTEM=input
SEQNUM=1181
NAME="Logitech USB-PS/2 Optical Mouse"
PHYS="usb-0000:00:1d.2-1/input0"
UNIQ=""
EV=7
KEY=70000 0 0 0 0
REL=103
MODALIAS=input:b0003v046DpC03Ee0110-e0,1,2,k110,111,112,r0,1,8,amlsfw
```

udev also sends messages to syslog. The default syslog priority that controls which messages are sent to syslog is specified in the udev configuration file /etc/udev/udev.conf. The log priority of the running daemon can be changed with **udevadm control --log_priority=** *LEVEL/NUMBER*.

22.6 Influencing Kernel Device Event Handling with udev Rules

A udev rule can match any property the kernel adds to the event itself or any information that the kernel exports to sysfs. The rule can also request additional information from external programs. Every event is matched against all provided rules. All rules are located in the /etc/udev/rules.d directory.

Every line in the rules file contains at least one key value pair. There are two kinds of keys, match and assignment keys. If all match keys match their values, the rule is applied and the assignment keys are assigned the specified value. A matching rule may specify the name of the device node, add symbolic links pointing to the node or run a specified program as part of the event handling. If no matching rule is found, the default device node name is used to create the device node. Detailed information about the rule syntax and the provided keys to match or import data are described in the udev man page. The following example rules provide a basic introduction to udev rule syntax. The example rules are all taken from the udev default rule set that is located under /etc/udev/rules.d/50-udev-default.rules.

EXAMPLE 22.1: EXAMPLE udev RULES

```
# console
KERNEL=="console", MODE="0600", OPTIONS="last_rule"

# serial devices
KERNEL=="ttyUSB*", ATTRS{product}=="[Pp]alm*Handheld*", SYMLINK+="pilot"

# printer
SUBSYSTEM=="usb", KERNEL=="lp*", NAME="usb/%k", SYMLINK+="usb%k", GROUP="lp"

# kernel firmware loader
SUBSYSTEM=="firmware", ACTION=="add", RUN+="firmware.sh"
```

The `console` rule consists of three keys: one match key (`KERNEL`) and two assign keys (`MODE`, `OPTIONS`). The `KERNEL` match rule searches the device list for any items of the type `console`. Only exact matches are valid and trigger this rule to be executed. The `MODE` key assigns special permissions to the device node, in this case, read and write permissions to the owner of this device only. The `OPTIONS` key makes this rule the last rule to be applied to any device of this type. Any later rule matching this particular device type does not have any effect.

The `serial devices` rule is not available in `50-udev-default.rules` anymore, but it is still worth considering. It consists of two match keys (`KERNEL` and `ATTRS`) and one assign key (`SYMLINK`). The `KERNEL` key searches for all devices of the `ttyUSB` type. Using the `*` wild card, this key matches several of these devices. The second match key, `ATTRS`, checks whether the `product` attribute file in `sysfs` for any `ttyUSB` device contains a certain string. The assign key (`SYMLINK`) triggers the addition of a symbolic link to this device under `/dev/pilot`. The operator used in this key (`+=`) tells `udev` to additionally perform this action, even if previous or later rules add other symbolic links. As this rule contains two match keys, it is only applied if both conditions are met.

The `printer` rule deals with USB printers and contains two match keys which must both apply to get the entire rule applied (`SUBSYSTEM` and `KERNEL`). Three assign keys deal with the naming for this device type (`NAME`), the creation of symbolic device links (`SYMLINK`) and the group membership for this device type (`GROUP`). Using the `*` wild card in the `KERNEL` key makes it match several `lp` printer devices. Substitutions are used in both, the `NAME` and the `SYMLINK` keys to extend these strings by the internal device name. For example, the symbolic link to the first `lp` USB printer would read `/dev/usblp0`.

The `kernel firmware loader` rule makes `udev` load additional firmware by an external helper script during runtime. The `SUBSYSTEM` match key searches for the `firmware` subsystem. The `ACTION` key checks whether any device belonging to the `firmware` subsystem has been added. The `RUN+=` key triggers the execution of the `firmware.sh` script to locate the firmware that is to be loaded.

Some general characteristics are common to all rules:

- Each rule consists of one or more key value pairs separated by a comma.
- A key's operation is determined by the operator. `udev` rules support several operators.
- Each given value must be enclosed by quotation marks.
- Each line of the rules file represents one rule. If a rule is longer than one line, use `\` to join the different lines as you would do in shell syntax.
- `udev` rules support a shell-style pattern that matches the `*`, `?`, and `[]` patterns.
- `udev` rules support substitutions.

22.6.1 Using Operators in udev Rules

Creating keys you can choose from several operators, depending on the type of key you want to create. Match keys will normally be used to find a value that either matches or explicitly mismatches the search value. Match keys contain either of the following operators:

`==`

Compare for equality. If the key contains a search pattern, all results matching this pattern are valid.

`!=`

Compare for non-equality. If the key contains a search pattern, all results matching this pattern are valid.

Any of the following operators can be used with assign keys:

`=`

Assign a value to a key. If the key previously consisted of a list of values, the key resets and only the single value is assigned.

`+=`

Add a value to a key that contains a list of entries.

`:=`

Assign a final value. Disallow any later change by later rules.

22.6.2 Using Substitutions in udev Rules

`udev` rules support the use of placeholders and substitutions. Use them in a similar fashion as you would do in any other scripts. The following substitutions can be used with `udev` rules:

`%r`, `$root`

The device directory, `/dev` by default.

`%p`, `$devpath`

The value of `DEVPATH`.

`%k`, `$kernel`

The value of `KERNEL` or the internal device name.

`%n`, `$number`

The device number.

`%N`, `$tempnode`

The temporary name of the device file.

`%M`, `$major`

The major number of the device.

`%m`, `$minor`

The minor number of the device.

`%s{ATTRIBUTE}`, `$attr{ATTRIBUTE}`

The value of a `sysfs` attribute (specified by *`ATTRIBUTE`*).

`%E{VARIABLE}`, `$attr{VARIABLE}`

The value of an environment variable (specified by *`VARIABLE`*).

`%c`, `$result`

The output of `PROGRAM`.

`%%`

The `%` character.

`$$`

The `$` character.

22.6.3 Using udev Match Keys

Match keys describe conditions that must be met before a `udev` rule can be applied. The following match keys are available:

`ACTION`

The name of the event action, for example, `add` or `remove` when adding or removing a device.

`DEVPATH`

The device path of the event device, for example, `DEVPATH=/bus/pci/drivers/ipw3945` to search for all events related to the ipw3945 driver.

`KERNEL`

The internal (kernel) name of the event device.

`SUBSYSTEM`

The subsystem of the event device, for example, `SUBSYSTEM=usb` for all events related to USB devices.

`ATTR{FILENAME}`

`sysfs` attributes of the event device. To match a string contained in the `vendor` attribute file name, you could use `ATTR{vendor}=="On[sS]tream"`, for example.

`KERNELS`

Let `udev` search the device path upwards for a matching device name.

`SUBSYSTEMS`

Let `udev` search the device path upwards for a matching device subsystem name.

`DRIVERS`

Let `udev` search the device path upwards for a matching device driver name.

`ATTRS{FILENAME}`

Let `udev` search the device path upwards for a device with matching `sysfs` attribute values.

`ENV{KEY}`

The value of an environment variable, for example, `ENV{ID_BUS}="ieee1394` to search for all events related to the FireWire bus ID.

`PROGRAM`

Let `udev` execute an external program. To be successful, the program must return with exit code zero. The program's output, printed to STDOUT, is available to the `RESULT` key.

`RESULT`

Match the output string of the last `PROGRAM` call. Either include this key in the same rule as the `PROGRAM` key or in a later one.

22.6.4 Using udev Assign Keys

In contrast to the match keys described above, assign keys do not describe conditions that must be met. They assign values, names and actions to the device nodes maintained by `udev`.

`NAME`

The name of the device node to be created. After a rule has set a node name, all other rules with a `NAME` key for this node are ignored.

`SYMLINK`

The name of a symbolic link related to the node to be created. Multiple matching rules can add symbolic links to be created with the device node. You can also specify multiple symbolic links for one node in one rule using the space character to separate the symbolic link names.

`OWNER, GROUP, MODE`

The permissions for the new device node. Values specified here overwrite anything that has been compiled in.

`ATTR{KEY}`

Specify a value to be written to a `sysfs` attribute of the event device. If the `==` operator is used, this key is also used to match against the value of a `sysfs` attribute.

`ENV{KEY}`

Tell `udev` to export a variable to the environment. If the `==` operator is used, this key is also used to match against an environment variable.

`RUN`

Tell `udev` to add a program to the list of programs to be executed for this device. Keep in mind to restrict this to very short tasks to avoid blocking further events for this device.

`LABEL`

Add a label where a `GOTO` can jump to.

`GOTO`

Tell `udev` to skip several rules and continue with the one that carries the label referenced by the `GOTO` key.

`IMPORT{TYPE}`

Load variables into the event environment such as the output of an external program. `udev` imports variables of several types. If no type is specified, `udev` tries to determine the type itself based on the executable bit of the file permissions.

- `program` tells `udev` to execute an external program and import its output.
- `file` tells `udev` to import a text file.
- `parent` tells `udev` to import the stored keys from the parent device.

`WAIT_FOR_SYSFS`

Tells `udev` to wait for the specified `sysfs` file to be created for a certain device. For example, `WAIT_FOR_SYSFS="ioerr_cnt"` informs `udev` to wait until the `ioerr_cnt` file has been created.

`OPTIONS`

The `OPTION` key may have several values:

- `last_rule` tells `udev` to ignore all later rules.
- `ignore_device` tells `udev` to ignore this event completely.
- `ignore_remove` tells `udev` to ignore all later remove events for the device.
- `all_partitions` tells `udev` to create device nodes for all available partitions on a block device.

22.7 Persistent Device Naming

The dynamic device directory and the udev rules infrastructure make it possible to provide stable names for all disk devices—regardless of their order of recognition or the connection used for the device. Every appropriate block device the kernel creates is examined by tools with special knowledge about certain buses, drive types or file systems. Along with the dynamic kernel-provided device node name, udev maintains classes of persistent symbolic links pointing to the device:

```
/dev/disk
|-- by-id
|   |-- scsi-SATA_HTS726060M9AT00_MRH453M4HWHG7B -> ../../sda
|   |-- scsi-SATA_HTS726060M9AT00_MRH453M4HWHG7B-part1 -> ../../sda1
|   |-- scsi-SATA_HTS726060M9AT00_MRH453M4HWHG7B-part6 -> ../../sda6
|   |-- scsi-SATA_HTS726060M9AT00_MRH453M4HWHG7B-part7 -> ../../sda7
|   |-- usb-Generic_STORAGE_DEVICE_02773 -> ../../sdd
|   `-- usb-Generic_STORAGE_DEVICE_02773-part1 -> ../../sdd1
|-- by-label
|   |-- Photos -> ../../sdd1
|   |-- SUSE10 -> ../../sda7
|   `-- devel -> ../../sda6
|-- by-path
|   |-- pci-0000:00:1f.2-scsi-0:0:0:0 -> ../../sda
|   |-- pci-0000:00:1f.2-scsi-0:0:0:0-part1 -> ../../sda1
|   |-- pci-0000:00:1f.2-scsi-0:0:0:0-part6 -> ../../sda6
|   |-- pci-0000:00:1f.2-scsi-0:0:0:0-part7 -> ../../sda7
|   |-- pci-0000:00:1f.2-scsi-1:0:0:0 -> ../../sr0
|   |-- usb-02773:0:0:2 -> ../../sdd
|   |-- usb-02773:0:0:2-part1 -> ../../sdd1
`-- by-uuid
    |-- 159a47a4-e6e6-40be-a757-a629991479ae -> ../../sda7
    |-- 3e999973-00c9-4917-9442-b7633bd95b9e -> ../../sda6
    `-- 4210-8F8C -> ../../sdd1
```

22.8 Files used by udev

/sys/*

Virtual file system provided by the Linux kernel, exporting all currently known devices. This information is used by udev to create device nodes in /dev

`/dev/*`

Dynamically created device nodes and static content created with systemd-tmpfiles; for more information, see the `systemd-tmpfiles(8)` man page.

The following files and directories contain the crucial elements of the `udev` infrastructure:

`/etc/udev/udev.conf`

Main `udev` configuration file.

`/etc/udev/rules.d/*`

`udev` event matching rules.

`/usr/lib/tmpfiles.d/` **and** `/etc/tmpfiles.d/`

Responsible for static `/dev` content.

`/usr/lib/udev/*`

Helper programs called from `udev` rules.

22.9 For More Information

For more information about the `udev` infrastructure, refer to the following man pages:

`udev`

General information about `udev`, keys, rules and other important configuration issues.

`udevadm`

`udevadm` can be used to control the runtime behavior of `udev`, request kernel events, manage the event queue and provide simple debugging mechanisms.

`udevd`

Information about the `udev` event managing daemon.

23 Live Patching the Linux Kernel Using kGraft

This document describes the basic principles of the kGraft live patching technology and provides usage guidelines for the SLE Live Patching service.

kGraft is a live patching technology for runtime patching of the Linux kernel, without stopping the kernel. This maximizes system uptime, and thus system availability, which is important for mission-critical systems. By allowing dynamic patching of the kernel, the technology also encourages users to install critical security updates without deferring them to a scheduled downtime.

A kGraft patch is a kernel module, intended for replacing whole functions in the kernel. kGraft primarily offers in-kernel infrastructure for integration of the patched code with base kernel code at runtime.

SLE Live Patching is a service provided on top of regular SUSE Linux Enterprise Server maintenance. kGraft patches distributed through SLE Live Patching supplement regular SLES maintenance updates. Common update stack and procedures can be used for SLE Live Patching deployment.

Information provided further are related to the AMD64/Intel 64 architecture only. In case you use a different architecture, the procedures may differ.

23.1 Advantages of kGraft

Live kernel patching using kGraft is especially useful for quick response in emergencies (when serious vulnerabilities are known and should be fixed when possible or there are serious system stability issues with a known fix). It is not used for scheduled updates where time is not critical.

Typical use cases for kGraft include systems like memory databases with huge amounts of RAM, where boot-up times of 15 minutes or more are not uncommon, large simulations that need weeks or months without a restart, or infrastructure building blocks providing continuous service to a many consumers.

The main advantage of kGraft is that it never requires stopping the kernel, not even for a short time period.

A kGraft patch is a `.ko` kernel module in a KMP RPM package. It is inserted into the kernel using the **`insmod`** command when the RPM package is installed or updated. kGraft replaces whole functions in the kernel, even if they are being executed. An updated kGraft module can replace an existing patch if necessary.

kGraft is also lean—it contains only a small amount of code, because it leverages other standard Linux technologies.

23.2 Low-level Function of kGraft

kGraft uses the ftrace infrastructure to perform patching. The following describes the implementation on the AMD64/Intel 64 architecture.

To patch a kernel function, kGraft needs some space at the start of the function to insert a jump to a new function. This space is allocated during kernel compilation by GCC with function profiling turned on. In particular, a 5-byte call instruction is injected to the start of kernel functions. When such instrumented kernel is booting, profiling calls are replaced by 5-byte NOP (no operation) instructions.

After patching starts, the first byte is replaced by the INT3 (breakpoint) instruction. This ensures atomicity of the 5-byte instruction replacement. The other four bytes are replaced by the address to the new function. Finally, the first byte is replaced by the JMP (long jump) opcode.

Inter-processor non-maskable interrupts (IPI NMI) are used throughout the process to flush speculative decoding queues of other CPUs in the system. This allows switching to the new function without ever stopping the kernel, not even for a very short moment. The interruptions by IPI NMIs can be measured in microseconds and are not considered service interruptions as they happen while the kernel is running in any case.

Callers are never patched. Instead, the callee's NOPs are replaced by a JMP to the new function. JMP instructions remain forever. This takes care of function pointers, including in structures, and does not require saving any old data for the possibility of un-patching.

However, these steps alone would not be good enough: since the functions would be replaced non-atomically, a new fixed function in one part of the kernel could still be calling an old function elsewhere or vice versa. If the semantics of the function interfaces changed in the patch, chaos would ensue.

Thus, until all functions are replaced, kGraft uses an approach based on trampolines and similar to RCU (read-copy-update), to ensure a consistent view of the world to each user space thread, kernel thread and kernel interrupt. A per-thread flag is set on each kernel entry and exit. This way, an old function would always call another old function and a new function always a new one. Once all processes have the "new universe" flag set, patching is complete, trampolines can be removed and the code can operate at full speed without performance impact other than an extra-long jump for each patched function.

23.3 Installing kGraft Patches

This section describes the activation of the SUSE Linux Enterprise Live Patching extension and the installation of kGraft patches.

23.3.1 Activation of SLE Live Patching

To activate SLE Live Patching on your system, follow these steps:

1. If your SLES system is not yet registered, register it. Registration can be done during the system installation or later using the YaST *Product Registration* module (`yast2 registration`). After registration, click *Yes* to see the list of available online updates.
   If your SLES system is already registered, but SLE Live Patching is not yet activated, open the YaST *Product Registration* module (`yast2 registration`) and click *Select Extensions*.
2. Select *SUSE Linux Enterprise Live Patching 12* in the list of available extensions and click *Next*.
3. Confirm the license terms and click *Next*.
4. Enter the SLE Live Patching registration code and click *Next*.
5. Check the *Installation Summary* and selected *Patterns*. The pattern `Live Patching` should be selected for installation.
6. Click *Accept* to complete the installation. This will install the base kGraft components on your system together with the initial live patch.

23.3.2 Updating System

1. SLE Live Patching updates are distributed in a form that allows using standard SLE update stack for patch application. The initial live patch can be updated using `zypper patch`, YaST Online Update or equivalent method.

2. The kernel is patched automatically during the package installation. However, invocations of the old kernel functions are not completely eliminated until all sleeping processes wake up and get out of the way. This can take a considerable amount of time. Despite this, sleeping processes that use the old kernel functions are not considered a security issue. Nevertheless, in the current version of kGraft, it is not possible to apply another kGraft patch until all processes cross the kernel-user space boundary to use patched functions from the previous patch.
   To see the global status of patching, check the flag in `/sys/kernel/kgraft/in_progress`. The value `1` signifies the existence of sleeping processes that still need to be woken (the patching is still in progress). The value `0` signifies that all processes are using solely the patched functions and patching has finished already. Alternatively, use the **`kgr status`** command to obtain the same information.
   The flag can be checked on a per-process basis too. Check the number in `/proc/`*`PROCESS_NUMBER`*`/kgr_in_progress` for each process individually. Again, the value `1` signifies sleeping process that still needs to be woken. Alternatively, use the **`kgr blocking`** command to output the list of sleeping processes.

23.4 Patch Lifecycle

Expiration dates of live patches can be accessed with **`zypper lifecycle`**. Make sure that the package `lifecycle-data-sle-live-patching` is installed.

```
tux > zypper lifecycle

Product end of support
Codestream: SUSE Linux Enterprise Server 12                 2024-10-31
SUSE Linux Enterprise Server 12 SP2                         n/a*

Extension end of support
SUSE Linux Enterprise Live Patching                         2017-10-31

Package end of support if different from product:
SUSEConnect                                   Now, installed 0.2.41-18.1, update available
 0.2.42-19.3.1
apache2-utils                                 Now


*) See https://www.suse.com/lifecycle  for latest information
```

When the expiration date of a patch is reached, no further live patches for this kernel version will be supplied. Plan an update of your kernel before the end of the live patch lifecycle period.

23.5 Removing a kGraft Patch

To remove a kGraft patch, use the following procedure:

1. First remove the patch itself using Zypper:

```
zypper rm kgraft-patch-3_12_32-25-default
```

2. Then reboot the machine.

23.6 Stuck Kernel Execution Threads

Kernel threads need to be prepared to handle kGraft. Third-party software may not be ready for kGraft adoption and its kernel modules may spawn kernel execution threads. These threads will block the patching process indefinitely. As an emergency measure kGraft offers the possibility to force finishing of the patching process without waiting for all execution threads to cross the safety checkpoint. This can be achieved by writing `0` into `/sys/kernel/kgraft/in_progress`. Consult SUSE Support before performing this procedure.

23.7 The **kgr** Tool

Several kGraft management tasks can be simplified with the **`kgr`** tool. The available commands are:

`kgr status`

Displays the overall status of kGraft patching (`ready` or `in_progress`).

`kgr patches`

Displays the list of loaded kGraft patches.

`kgr blocking`

Lists processes that are preventing kGraft patching from finishing. By default only the PIDs are listed. Specifying `-v` prints command lines if available. Another `-v` displays also stack traces.

For detailed information, see `man kgr`.

23.8 Scope of kGraft Technology

kGraft is based on replacing functions. Data structure alteration can be accomplished only indirectly with kGraft. As a result, changes to kernel data structure require special care and, if the change is too large, rebooting might be required. kGraft also might not be able to handle situations where one compiler is used to compile the old kernel and another compiler is used for compiling the patch.

Because of the way kGraft works, support for third-party modules that are spawning kernel threads is limited.

23.9 Scope of SLE Live Patching

Fixes for SUSE CVSS (Common Vulnerability Scoring System) level 6+ vulnerabilities and bug fixes related to system stability or data corruption will be shipped in the scope of SLE Live Patching. It might not be possible to produce a live patch for all kinds of fixes fulfilling the above criteria. SUSE reserves the right to skip fixes where production of a kernel live patch is unviable because of technical reasons. For more information on CVSS, which is the base for the SUSE CVSS rating, see http://nvd.nist.gov/cvss.cfm/ ↗.

23.10 Interaction with the Support Processes

While resolving a technical difficulty with SUSE Support, you may receive a so-called Program Temporary Fix (PTF). PTFs may be issued for various packages including those forming the base of SLE Live Patching.

kGraft PTFs complying with the conditions described in the previous section can be installed as usual and SUSE will ensure that the system in question does not need to be rebooted and that future live updates are applied cleanly.

PTFs issued for the base kernel disrupt the live patching process. First, installing the PTF kernel means a reboot as the kernel cannot be replaced as a whole at runtime. Second, another reboot is needed to replace the PTF with any regular maintenance updates for which the live patches are issued.

PTFs for other packages in SLE Live Patching can be treated like regular PTFs with the usual guarantees.

24 Special System Features

This chapter starts with information about various software packages, the virtual consoles and the keyboard layout. We talk about software components like `bash`, `cron` and `logrotate`, because they were changed or enhanced during the last release cycles. Even if they are small or considered of minor importance, users should change their default behavior, because these components are often closely coupled with the system. The chapter concludes with a section about language and country-specific settings (I18N and L10N).

24.1 Information about Special Software Packages

The programs `bash`, `cron`, `logrotate`, `locate`, `ulimit` and `free` are very important for system administrators and many users. Man pages and info pages are two useful sources of information about commands, but both are not always available. GNU Emacs is a popular and very configurable text editor.

24.1.1 The bash Package and /etc/profile

Bash is the default system shell. When used as a login shell, it reads several initialization files. Bash processes them in the order they appear in this list:

1. `/etc/profile`
2. `~/.profile`
3. `/etc/bash.bashrc`
4. `~/.bashrc`

Make custom settings in `~/.profile` or `~/.bashrc`. To ensure the correct processing of these files, it is necessary to copy the basic settings from `/etc/skel/.profile` or `/etc/skel/.bashrc` into the home directory of the user. It is recommended to copy the settings from `/etc/skel` after an update. Execute the following shell commands to prevent the loss of personal adjustments:

```
mv ~/.bashrc ~/.bashrc.old
```

```
cp /etc/skel/.bashrc ~/.bashrc
mv ~/.profile ~/.profile.old
cp /etc/skel/.profile ~/.profile
```

Then copy personal adjustments back from the `*.old` files.

24.1.2 The cron Package

Use cron to run commands automatically in the background at predefined time. cron uses specially formatted time tables, and the tool comes with several default ones. Users can also specify custom tables, if needed.

The cron tables are located in `/var/spool/cron/tabs`. `/etc/crontab` serves as a systemwide cron table. Enter the user name to run the command directly after the time table and before the command. In *Example 24.1, "Entry in /etc/crontab"*, `root` is entered. Package-specific tables, located in `/etc/cron.d`, have the same format. See the **`cron`** man page (**`man cron`**).

EXAMPLE 24.1: ENTRY IN /ETC/CRONTAB

```
1-59/5 * * * *   root   test -x /usr/sbin/atrun && /usr/sbin/atrun
```

You cannot edit `/etc/crontab` by calling the command **`crontab -e`**. This file must be loaded directly into an editor, then modified and saved.

A number of packages install shell scripts to the directories `/etc/cron.hourly`, `/etc/cron.daily`, `/etc/cron.weekly` and `/etc/cron.monthly`, whose execution is controlled by `/usr/lib/cron/run-crons`. `/usr/lib/cron/run-crons` is run every 15 minutes from the main table (`/etc/crontab`). This guarantees that processes that may have been neglected can be run at the proper time.

To run the `hourly`, `daily` or other periodic maintenance scripts at custom times, remove the time stamp files regularly using `/etc/crontab` entries (see *Example 24.2, "/etc/crontab: Remove Time Stamp Files"*, which removes the `hourly` one before every full hour, the `daily` one once a day at 2:14 a.m., etc.).

EXAMPLE 24.2: /ETC/CRONTAB: REMOVE TIME STAMP FILES

```
59 *  * * *     root  rm -f /var/spool/cron/lastrun/cron.hourly
14 2  * * *     root  rm -f /var/spool/cron/lastrun/cron.daily
29 2  * * 6     root  rm -f /var/spool/cron/lastrun/cron.weekly
```

```
44 2  1 * *     root  rm -f /var/spool/cron/lastrun/cron.monthly
```

Or you can set `DAILY_TIME` in `/etc/sysconfig/cron` to the time at which `cron.daily` should start. The setting of `MAX_NOT_RUN` ensures that the daily tasks get triggered to run, even if the user did not turn on the computer at the specified `DAILY_TIME` for a longer time. The maximum value of `MAX_NOT_RUN` is 14 days.

The daily system maintenance jobs are distributed to various scripts for reasons of clarity. They are contained in the package `aaa_base`. `/etc/cron.daily` contains, for example, the components `suse.de-backup-rpmdb`, `suse.de-clean-tmp` or `suse.de-cron-local`.

24.1.3 Stopping Cron Status Messages

To avoid the mail-flood caused by cron status messages, the default value of `SEND_MAIL_ON_NO_ERROR` in `/etc/sysconfig/cron` is set to "`no`" for new installations. Even with this setting to "`no`", cron data output will still be sent to the `MAILTO` address, as documented in the cron man page.

In the update case it is recommended to set these values according to your needs.

24.1.4 Log Files: Package logrotate

There are several system services (*daemons*) that, along with the kernel itself, regularly record the system status and specific events onto log files. This way, the administrator can regularly check the status of the system at a certain point in time, recognize errors or faulty functions and troubleshoot them with pinpoint precision. These log files are normally stored in `/var/log` as specified by FHS and grow on a daily basis. The `logrotate` package helps control the growth of these files. For more details refer to *Book "System Analysis and Tuning Guide", Chapter 3 "Analyzing and Managing System Log Files", Section 3.3 "Managing Log Files with* **`logrotate`**".

24.1.5 The locate Command

`locate`, a command for quickly finding files, is not included in the standard scope of installed software. If desired, install the package `mlocate`, the successor of the package `findutils-locate`. The updatedb process is started automatically every night or about 15 minutes after booting the system.

24.1.6 The ulimit Command

With the **ulimit** (*user limits*) command, it is possible to set limits for the use of system resources and to have these displayed. **ulimit** is especially useful for limiting available memory for applications. With this, an application can be prevented from co-opting too much of the system resources and slowing or even hanging up the operating system.

ulimit can be used with various options. To limit memory usage, use the options listed in *Table 24.1, "ulimit: Setting Resources for the User"*.

TABLE 24.1: ulimit: SETTING RESOURCES FOR THE USER

-m	The maximum resident set size
-v	The maximum amount of virtual memory available to the shell
-s	The maximum size of the stack
-c	The maximum size of core files created
-a	All current limits are reported

Systemwide default entries are set in /etc/profile. Editing this file directly is not recommended, because changes will be overwritten during system upgrades. To customize systemwide profile settings, use /etc/profile.local. Per-user settings should be made in *~USER*/.bashrc.

EXAMPLE 24.3: ULIMIT: SETTINGS IN ~/.BASHRC

```
# Limits maximum resident set size (physical memory):
ulimit -m 98304

# Limits of virtual memory:
ulimit -v 98304
```

Memory allocations must be specified in KB. For more detailed information, see **man bash**.

Not all shells support **ulimit** directives. PAM (for example, pam_limits) offers comprehensive adjustment possibilities as an alternative to **ulimit**.

24.1.7 The free Command

The **free** command displays the total amount of free and used physical memory as well as swap space in the system and the buffers and cache consumed by the kernel. The concept of *available RAM* dates back to before the days of unified memory management. The slogan *free memory is bad memory* applies well to Linux. As a result, Linux has always made the effort to balance out caches without actually allowing free or unused memory.

The kernel does not have direct knowledge of any applications or user data. Instead, it manages applications and user data in a *page cache.* If memory runs short, parts of it are written to the swap partition or to files, from which they can initially be read using the **mmap** command (see **man mmap**).

The kernel also contains other caches, such as the *slab cache*, where the caches used for network access are stored. This may explain the differences between the counters in `/proc/meminfo`. Most, but not all, of them can be accessed via `/proc/slabinfo`.

However, if your goal is to find out how much RAM is currently being used, find this information in `/proc/meminfo`.

24.1.8 Man Pages and Info Pages

For some GNU applications (such as tar), the man pages are no longer maintained. For these commands, use the `--help` option to get a quick overview of the info pages, which provide more in-depth instructions. Info is GNU's hypertext system. Read an introduction to this system by entering **info** `info`. Info pages can be viewed with Emacs by entering **emacs** `-f info` or directly in a console with **info**. You can also use tkinfo, xinfo or the help system to view info pages.

24.1.9 Selecting Man Pages Using the **man** Command

To read a man page enter **man** *`MAN_PAGE`*. If a man page with the same name exists in different sections, they will all be listed with the corresponding section numbers. Select the one to display. If you do not enter a section number within a few seconds, the first man page will be displayed.

To change this to the default system behavior, set `MAN_POSIXLY_CORRECT=1` in a shell initialization file such as `~/.bashrc`.

24.1.10 Settings for GNU Emacs

GNU Emacs is a complex work environment. The following sections cover the configuration files processed when GNU Emacs is started. More information is available at http://www.gnu.org/software/emacs/.

On start-up, Emacs reads several files containing the settings of the user, system administrator and distributor for customization or preconfiguration. The initialization file `~/.emacs` is installed to the home directories of the individual users from `/etc/skel`. `.emacs`, in turn, reads the file `/etc/skel/.gnu-emacs`. To customize the program, copy `.gnu-emacs` to the home directory (with **`cp /etc/skel/.gnu-emacs ~/.gnu-emacs`**) and make the desired settings there.

`.gnu-emacs` defines the file `~/.gnu-emacs-custom` as `custom-file`. If users make settings with the `customize` options in Emacs, the settings are saved to `~/.gnu-emacs-custom`.

With SUSE Linux Enterprise Desktop, the `emacs` package installs the file `site-start.el` in the directory `/usr/share/emacs/site-lisp`. The file `site-start.el` is loaded before the initialization file `~/.emacs`. Among other things, `site-start.el` ensures that special configuration files distributed with Emacs add-on packages, such as `psgml`, are loaded automatically. Configuration files of this type are located in `/usr/share/emacs/site-lisp`, too, and always begin with `suse-start-`. The local system administrator can specify systemwide settings in `default.el`.

More information about these files is available in the Emacs info file under *Init File*: `info:/emacs/InitFile`. Information about how to disable the loading of these files (if necessary) is also provided at this location.

The components of Emacs are divided into several packages:

- The base package `emacs`.
- `emacs-x11` (usually installed): the program *with* X11 support.
- `emacs-nox`: the program *without* X11 support.
- `emacs-info`: online documentation in info format.

- `emacs-el`: the uncompiled library files in Emacs Lisp. These are not required at runtime.
- Numerous add-on packages can be installed if needed: `emacs-auctex` (LaTeX), `psgml` (SGML and XML), `gnuserv` (client and server operation) and others.

24.2 Virtual Consoles

Linux is a multiuser and multitasking system. The advantages of these features can be appreciated even on a stand-alone PC system. In text mode, there are six virtual consoles available. Switch between them using Alt–F1 through Alt–F6. The seventh console is reserved for X and the tenth console shows kernel messages.

To switch to a console from X without shutting it down, use Ctrl–Alt–F1 to Ctrl–Alt–F6. To return to X, press Alt–F7.

24.3 Keyboard Mapping

To standardize the keyboard mapping of programs, changes were made to the following files:

```
/etc/inputrc
/etc/X11/Xmodmap
/etc/skel/.emacs
/etc/skel/.gnu-emacs
/etc/skel/.vimrc
/etc/csh.cshrc
/etc/termcap
/usr/share/terminfo/x/xterm
/usr/share/X11/app-defaults/XTerm
/usr/share/emacs/VERSION/site-lisp/term/*.el
```

These changes only affect applications that use **`terminfo`** entries or whose configuration files are changed directly (**`vi`**, **`emacs`**, etc.). Applications not shipped with the system should be adapted to these defaults.

Under X, the compose key (multikey) can be enabled as explained in `/etc/X11/Xmodmap`.

Further settings are possible using the X Keyboard Extension (XKB). This extension is also used by the desktop environment GNOME (gswitchit).

Tip: For More Information

Information about XKB is available in the documents listed in `/usr/share/doc/packages/xkeyboard-config` (part of the `xkeyboard-config` package).

24.4 Language and Country-Specific Settings

The system is, to a very large extent, internationalized and can be modified for local needs. Internationalization (*I18N*) allows specific localization (*L10N*). The abbreviations I18N and L10N are derived from the first and last letters of the words and, in between, the number of letters omitted.

Settings are made with `LC_` variables defined in the file `/etc/sysconfig/language`. This refers not only to *native language support*, but also to the categories *Messages* (Language), *Character Set*, *Sort Order*, *Time and Date*, *Numbers* and *Money*. Each of these categories can be defined directly with its own variable or indirectly with a master variable in the file `language` (see the **`locale`** man page).

`RC_LC_MESSAGES`, `RC_LC_CTYPE`, `RC_LC_COLLATE`, `RC_LC_TIME`, `RC_LC_NUMERIC`, `RC_LC_MONETARY`

These variables are passed to the shell without the `RC_` prefix and represent the listed categories. The shell profiles concerned are listed below. The current setting can be shown with the command **`locale`**.

`RC_LC_ALL`

This variable, if set, overwrites the values of the variables already mentioned.

`RC_LANG`

If none of the previous variables are set, this is the fallback. By default, only `RC_LANG` is set. This makes it easier for users to enter their own values.

`ROOT_USES_LANG`

A `yes` or `no` variable. If set to `no`, `root` always works in the POSIX environment.

The variables can be set with the YaST sysconfig editor. The value of such a variable contains the language code, country code, encoding and modifier. The individual components are connected by special characters:

```
LANG=<language>[[_<COUNTRY>].<Encoding>[@<Modifier>]]
```

24.4.1 Some Examples

You should always set the language and country codes together. Language settings follow the standard ISO 639 available at http://www.evertype.com/standards/iso639/iso639-en.html and http://www.loc.gov/standards/iso639-2/. Country codes are listed in ISO 3166, see http://en.wikipedia.org/wiki/ISO_3166.

It only makes sense to set values for which usable description files can be found in `/usr/lib/locale`. Additional description files can be created from the files in `/usr/share/i18n` using the command **`localedef`**. The description files are part of the `glibc-i18ndata` package. A description file for `en_US.UTF-8` (for English and United States) can be created with:

```
localedef -i en_US -f UTF-8 en_US.UTF-8
```

`LANG=en_US.UTF-8`

This is the default setting if American English is selected during installation. If you selected another language, that language is enabled but still with UTF-8 as the character encoding.

`LANG=en_US.ISO-8859-1`

This sets the language to English, country to United States and the character set to `ISO-8859-1`. This character set does not support the Euro sign, but it can be useful sometimes for programs that have not been updated to support `UTF-8`. The string defining the charset (`ISO-8859-1` in this case) is then evaluated by programs like Emacs.

`LANG=en_IE@euro`

The above example explicitly includes the Euro sign in a language setting. This setting is obsolete now, as UTF-8 also covers the Euro symbol. It is only useful if an application supports ISO-8859-15 and not UTF-8.

Changes to `/etc/sysconfig/language` are activated by the following process chain:

- For the Bash: `/etc/profile` reads `/etc/profile.d/lang.sh` which, in turn, analyzes `/etc/sysconfig/language`.
- For tcsh: At login, `/etc/csh.login` reads `/etc/profile.d/lang.csh` which, in turn, analyzes `/etc/sysconfig/language`.

This ensures that any changes to /etc/sysconfig/language are available at the next login to the respective shell, without having to manually activate them.

Users can override the system defaults by editing their ~/.bashrc accordingly. For example, if you do not want to use the system-wide en_US for program messages, include LC_MESSAGES=es_ES so that messages are displayed in Spanish instead.

24.4.2 Locale Settings in ~/.i18n

If you are not satisfied with locale system defaults, change the settings in ~/.i18n according to the Bash scripting syntax. Entries in ~/.i18n override system defaults from /etc/sysconfig/language. Use the same variable names but without the RC_ name space prefixes. For example, use LANG instead of RC_LANG:

```
LANG=cs_CZ.UTF-8
LC_COLLATE=C
```

24.4.3 Settings for Language Support

Files in the category *Messages* are, as a rule, only stored in the corresponding language directory (like en) to have a fallback. If you set LANG to en_US and the message file in /usr/share/locale/en_US/LC_MESSAGES does not exist, it falls back to /usr/share/locale/en/LC_MESSAGES.

A fallback chain can also be defined, for example, for Breton to French or for Galician to Spanish to Portuguese:

LANGUAGE="br_FR:fr_FR"

LANGUAGE="gl_ES:es_ES:pt_PT"

If desired, use the Norwegian variants Nynorsk and Bokmål instead (with additional fallback to no):

LANG="nn_NO"

LANGUAGE="nn_NO:nb_NO:no"

or

LANG="nb_NO"

LANGUAGE="nb_NO:nn_NO:no"

Note that in Norwegian, LC_TIME is also treated differently.

One problem that can arise is a separator used to delimit groups of digits not being recognized properly. This occurs if `LANG` is set to only a two-letter language code like `de`, but the definition file glibc uses is located in `/usr/share/lib/de_DE/LC_NUMERIC`. Thus `LC_NUMERIC` must be set to `de_DE` to make the separator definition visible to the system.

24.4.4 For More Information

- *The GNU C Library Reference Manual*, Chapter "Locales and Internationalization". It is included in `glibc-info`. The package is available from the SUSE Linux Enterprise SDK. The SDK is a module for SUSE Linux Enterprise and is available via an online channel from the SUSE Customer Center. Alternatively, go to http://download.suse.com/ ↗, search for `SUSE Linux Enterprise Software Development Kit` and download it from there. Refer to *Book "Deployment Guide", Chapter 10 "Installing Modules, Extensions, and Third Party Add-On Products"* for details.
- Markus Kuhn, *UTF-8 and Unicode FAQ for Unix/Linux*, currently at http://www.cl.cam.ac.uk/~mgk25/unicode.html ↗.
- *Unicode-HOWTO* by Bruno Haible, available at http://tldp.org/HOWTO/Unicode-HOWTO-1.html ↗.

IV Services

25 Time Synchronization with NTP

The NTP (network time protocol) mechanism is a protocol for synchronizing the system time over the network. First, a machine can obtain the time from a server that is a reliable time source. Second, a machine can itself act as a time source for other computers in the network. The goal is twofold—maintaining the absolute time and synchronizing the system time of all machines within a network.

Maintaining an exact system time is important in many situations. The built-in hardware clock does often not meet the requirements of applications such as databases or clusters. Manual correction of the system time would lead to severe problems because, for example, a backward leap can cause malfunction of critical applications. Within a network, it is usually necessary to synchronize the system time of all machines, but manual time adjustment is a bad approach. NTP provides a mechanism to solve these problems. The NTP service continuously adjusts the system time with reliable time servers in the network. It further enables the management of local reference clocks, such as radio-controlled clocks.

Note

To enable time synchronization by means of active directory, follow the instructions found at *Book "Security Guide", Chapter 7 "Active Directory Support", Section 7.3.3 "Joining Active Directory Using Windows Domain Membership ", Joining an Active Directory Domain Using Windows Domain Membership* .

25.1 Configuring an NTP Client with YaST

The NTP daemon (`ntpd`) coming with the `ntp` package is preset to use the local computer clock as a time reference. Using the hardware clock, however, only serves as a fallback for cases where no time source of better precision is available. YaST simplifies the configuration of an NTP client.

25.1.1 Basic Configuration

The YaST NTP client configuration (*Network Services › NTP Configuration*) consists of tabs. Set the start mode of `ntpd` and the server to query on the *General Settings* tab.

Only Manually

Select *Only Manually*, if you want to manually start the `ntpd` daemon.

Synchronize without Daemon

Select *Synchronize without Daemon* to set the system time periodically without a permanently running `ntpd`. You can set the *Interval of the Synchronization in Minutes*.

Now and On Boot

Select *Now and On Boot* to start `ntpd` automatically when the system is booted. This setting is recommended.

25.1.2 Changing Basic Configuration

The servers and other time sources for the client to query are listed in the lower part of the *General Settings* tab. Modify this list as needed with *Add*, *Edit*, and *Delete*. *Display Log* provides the possibility to view the log files of your client.

Click *Add* to add a new source of time information. In the following dialog, select the type of source with which the time synchronization should be made. The following options are available:

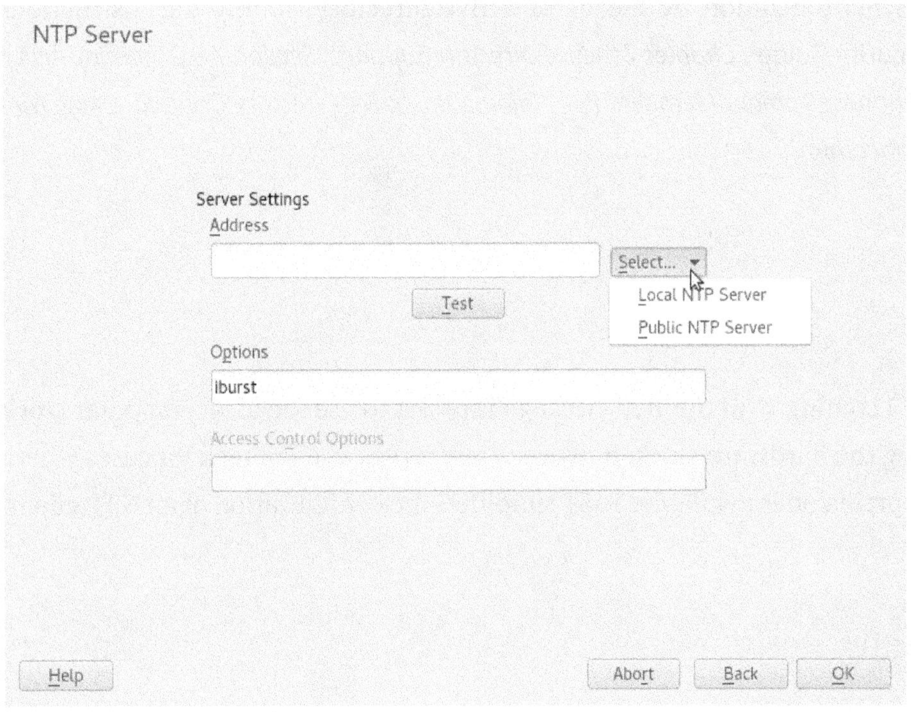

FIGURE 25.1: YAST: NTP SERVER

Server

In the drop-down *Select* list (see Figure 25.1, "YaST: NTP Server"), determine whether to set up time synchronization using a time server from your local network (*Local NTP Server*) or an Internet-based time server that takes care of your time zone (*Public NTP Server*). For a local time server, click *Lookup* to start an SLP query for available time servers in your network. Select the most suitable time server from the list of search results and exit the dialog with *OK*. For a public time server, select your country (time zone) and a suitable server from the list under *Public NTP Server* then exit the dialog with *OK*. In the main dialog, test the availability of the selected server with *Test*. *Options* allows you to specify additional options for `ntpd`.

Using *Access Control Options*, you can restrict the actions that the remote computer can perform with the daemon running on your computer. This field is enabled only after checking *Restrict NTP Service to Configured Servers Only* on the *Security Settings* tab (see Figure 25.2, "Advanced NTP Configuration: Security Settings"). The options correspond to the `restrict` clauses in `/etc/ntp.conf`. For example, `nomodify notrap noquery` disallows the server to modify NTP settings of your computer and to use the trap facility (a remote event logging feature) of your NTP daemon. Using these restrictions is recommended for servers out of your control (for example, on the Internet).

Refer to `/usr/share/doc/packages/ntp-doc` (part of the `ntp-doc` package) for detailed information.

Peer

A peer is a machine to which a symmetric relationship is established: it acts both as a time server and as a client. To use a peer in the same network instead of a server, enter the address of the system. The rest of the dialog is identical to the *Server* dialog.

Radio Clock

To use a radio clock in your system for the time synchronization, enter the clock type, unit number, device name, and other options in this dialog. Click *Driver Calibration* to fine-tune the driver. Detailed information about the operation of a local radio clock is available in `/usr/share/doc/packages/ntp-doc/refclock.html`.

Outgoing Broadcast

Time information and queries can also be transmitted by broadcast in the network. In this dialog, enter the address to which such broadcasts should be sent. Do not activate broadcasting unless you have a reliable time source like a radio controlled clock.

Incoming Broadcast

If you want your client to receive its information via broadcast, enter the address from which the respective packets should be accepted in this fields.

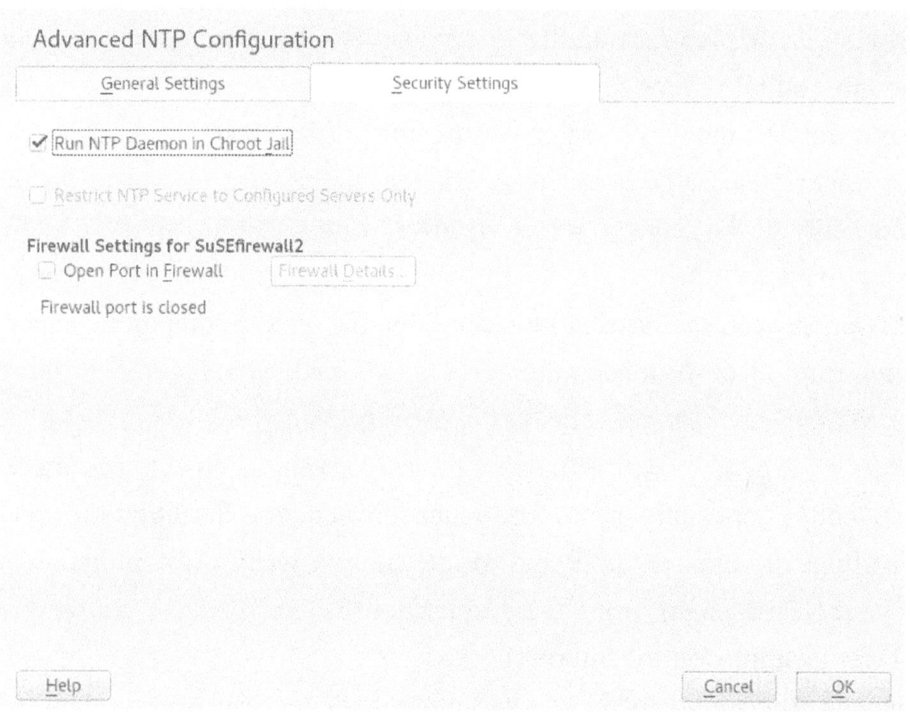

FIGURE 25.2: ADVANCED NTP CONFIGURATION: SECURITY SETTINGS

In the *Security Settings* tab (see *Figure 25.2, "Advanced NTP Configuration: Security Settings"*), determine whether `ntpd` should be started in a chroot jail. By default, *Run NTP Daemon in Chroot Jail* is not activated. The chroot jail option increases the security in the event of an attack over `ntpd`, as it prevents the attacker from compromising the entire system.

Restrict NTP Service to Configured Servers Only increases the security of your system by disallowing remote computers to view and modify NTP settings of your computer and to use the trap facility for remote event logging. After being enabled, these restrictions apply to all remote computers, unless you override the access control options for individual computers in the list of time sources in the *General Settings* tab. For all other remote computers, only querying for local time is allowed.

Enable *Open Port in Firewall* if SuSEFirewall2 is active (which it is by default). If you leave the port closed, it is not possible to establish a connection to the time server.

25.2 Manually Configuring NTP in the Network

The easiest way to use a time server in the network is to set server parameters. For example, if a time server called `ntp.example.com` is reachable from the network, add its name to the file `/etc/ntp.conf` by adding the following line:

```
server ntp.example.com
```

To add more time servers, insert additional lines with the keyword `server`. After initializing `ntpd` with the command **`systemctl start ntp`**, it takes about one hour until the time is stabilized and the drift file for correcting the local computer clock is created. With the drift file, the systematic error of the hardware clock can be computed when the computer is powered on. The correction is used immediately, resulting in a higher stability of the system time.

There are two possible ways to use the NTP mechanism as a client: First, the client can query the time from a known server in regular intervals. With many clients, this approach can cause a high load on the server. Second, the client can wait for NTP broadcasts sent out by broadcast time servers in the network. This approach has the disadvantage that the quality of the server is unknown and a server sending out wrong information can cause severe problems.

If the time is obtained via broadcast, you do not need the server name. In this case, enter the line `broadcastclient` in the configuration file `/etc/ntp.conf`. To use one or more known time servers exclusively, enter their names in the line starting with `servers`.

25.3 Dynamic Time Synchronization at Runtime

If the system boots without network connection, `ntpd` starts up, but it cannot resolve DNS names of the time servers set in the configuration file. This can happen if you use NetworkManager with an encrypted Wi-Fi.

If you want `ntpd` to resolve DNS names at runtime, you must set the `dynamic` option. When a network connection is established after booting, `ntpd` looks up the names again and can reach the time servers to get the time.

Manually edit `/etc/ntp.conf` and add `dynamic` to one or more `server` entries:

```
server ntp.example.com dynamic
```

Or use YaST and proceed as follows:

1. In YaST click *Network Services › NTP Configuration.*

2. Select the server you want to configure. Then click *Edit*.
3. Activate the *Options* field and add `dynamic`. Separate it with a space, if there are already other options entered.
4. Click *Ok* to close the edit dialog. Repeat the previous step to change all servers as wanted.
5. Finally click *Ok* to save the settings.

25.4 Setting Up a Local Reference Clock

The software package `ntpd` contains drivers for connecting local reference clocks. A list of supported clocks is available in the `ntp-doc` package in the file `/usr/share/doc/packages/ntp-doc/refclock.html`. Every driver is associated with a number. In NTP, the actual configuration takes place by means of pseudo IP addresses. The clocks are entered in the file `/etc/ntp.conf` as though they existed in the network. For this purpose, they are assigned special IP addresses in the form `127.127.T.U`. Here, `T` stands for the type of the clock and determines which driver is used and `U` for the unit, which determines the interface used.

Normally, the individual drivers have special parameters that describe configuration details. The file `/usr/share/doc/packages/ntp-doc/drivers/driverNN.html` (where `NN` is the number of the driver) provides information about the particular type of clock. For example, the "type 8" clock (radio clock over serial interface) requires an additional mode that specifies the clock more precisely. The Conrad DCF77 receiver module, for example, has mode 5. To use this clock as a preferred reference, specify the keyword `prefer`. The complete `server` line for a Conrad DCF77 receiver module would be:

```
server 127.127.8.0 mode 5 prefer
```

Other clocks follow the same pattern. Following the installation of the `ntp-doc` package, the documentation for NTP is available in the directory `/usr/share/doc/packages/ntp-doc`. The file `/usr/share/doc/packages/ntp-doc/refclock.html` provides links to the driver pages describing the driver parameters.

25.5 Clock Synchronization to an External Time Reference (ETR)

Support for clock synchronization to an external time reference (ETR) is available. The external time reference sends an oscillator signal and a synchronization signal every 2**20 (2 to the power of 20) microseconds to keep TOD clocks of all connected servers synchronized.

For availability two ETR units can be connected to a machine. If the clock deviates for more than the sync-check tolerance all CPUs get a machine check that indicates that the clock is out of sync. If this happens, all DASD I/O to XRC enabled devices is stopped until the clock is synchronized again.

The ETR support is activated via two `sysfs` attributes; run the following commands as `root`:

```
echo 1 > /sys/devices/system/etr/etr0/online
echo 1 > /sys/devices/system/etr/etr1/online
```

26 Sharing File Systems with NFS

Distributing and sharing file systems over a network is a common task in corporate environments. The well-proven network file system (*NFS*) works with *NIS*, the yellow pages protocol. For a more secure protocol that works with *LDAP* and Kerberos, check *NFSv4* (default). Combined with pNFS, you can eliminate performance bottlenecks.

NFS with NIS makes a network transparent to the user. With NFS, it is possible to distribute arbitrary file systems over the network. With an appropriate setup, users always find themselves in the same environment regardless of the terminal they currently use.

26.1 Terminology

The following are terms used in the YaST module.

Exports

A directory *exported* by an NFS server, which clients can integrate it into their system.

NFS Client

The NFS client is a system that uses NFS services from an NFS server over the Network File System protocol. The TCP/IP protocol is already integrated into the Linux kernel; there is no need to install any additional software.

NFS Server

The NFS server provides NFS services to clients. A running server depends on the following daemons: `nfsd` (worker), `idmapd` (ID-to-name mapping for NFSv4, needed for certain scenarios only), `statd` (file locking), and `mountd` (mount requests).

NFSv3

NFSv3 is the version 3 implementation, the “old” stateless NFS that supports client authentication.

NFSv4

NFSv4 is the new version 4 implementation that supports secure user authentication via kerberos. NFSv4 requires one single port only and thus is better suited for environments behind a firewall than NFSv3.

The protocol is specified as http://tools.ietf.org/html/rfc3530.

pNFS

Parallel NFS, a protocol extension of NFSv4. Any pNFS clients can directly access the data on an NFS server.

26.2 Installing NFS Server

For installing and configuring an NFS server, see the SUSE Linux Enterprise Server documentation.

26.3 Configuring Clients

To configure your host as an NFS client, you do not need to install additional software. All needed packages are installed by default.

26.3.1 Importing File Systems with YaST

Authorized users can mount NFS directories from an NFS server into the local file tree using the YaST NFS client module. Proceed as follows:

PROCEDURE 26.1: IMPORTING NFS DIRECTORIES

1. Start the YaST NFS client module.
2. Click *Add* in the *NFS Shares* tab. Enter the host name of the NFS server, the directory to import, and the mount point at which to mount this directory locally.
3. When using NFSv4, select *Enable NFSv4* in the *NFS Settings* tab. Additionally, the *NFSv4 Domain Name* must contain the same value as used by the NFSv4 server. The default domain is `localdomain`.
4. To use Kerberos authentication for NFS, GSS security must be enabled. Select *Enable GSS Security*.
5. Enable *Open Port in Firewall* in the *NFS Settings* tab if you use a Firewall and want to allow access to the service from remote computers. The firewall status is displayed next to the check box.

6. Click *OK* to save your changes.

The configuration is written to `/etc/fstab` and the specified file systems are mounted. When you start the YaST configuration client at a later time, it also reads the existing configuration from this file.

Tip: NFS as a Root File System

On (diskless) systems, where the root partition is mounted via network as an NFS share, you need to be careful when configuring the network device with which the NFS share is accessible.

When shutting down or rebooting the system, the default processing order is to turn off network connections, then unmount the root partition. With NFS root, this order causes problems as the root partition cannot be cleanly unmounted as the network connection to the NFS share is already not activated. To prevent the system from deactivating the relevant network device, open the network device configuration tab as described in *Section 17.4.1.2.5, "Activating the Network Device"* and choose *On NFSroot* in the *Device Activation* pane.

26.3.2 Importing File Systems Manually

The prerequisite for importing file systems manually from an NFS server is a running RPC port mapper. The `nfs` service takes care to start it properly; thus, start it by entering **`systemctl start nfs`** as `root`. Then remote file systems can be mounted in the file system like local partitions using **`mount`**:

```
tux > sudo mount HOST:REMOTE-PATHLOCAL-PATH
```

To import user directories from the `nfs.example.com` machine, for example, use:

```
tux > sudo mount nfs.example.com:/home /home
```

26.3.2.1 Using the Automount Service

The autofs daemon can be used to mount remote file systems automatically. Add the following entry to the `/etc/auto.master` file:

```
/nfsmounts /etc/auto.nfs
```

Now the `/nfsmounts` directory acts as the root for all the NFS mounts on the client if the `auto.nfs` file is filled appropriately. The name `auto.nfs` is chosen for the sake of convenience—you can choose any name. In `auto.nfs` add entries for all the NFS mounts as follows:

```
localdata -fstype=nfs server1:/data
nfs4mount -fstype=nfs4 server2:/
```

Activate the settings with **`systemctl start autofs`** as `root`. In this example, `/nfsmounts/localdata`, the `/data` directory of `server1`, is mounted with NFS and `/nfsmounts/nfs4mount` from `server2` is mounted with NFSv4.

If the `/etc/auto.master` file is edited while the service autofs is running, the automounter must be restarted for the changes to take effect with **`systemctl restart autofs`**.

26.3.2.2 Manually Editing /etc/fstab

A typical NFSv3 mount entry in `/etc/fstab` looks like this:

```
nfs.example.com:/data /local/path nfs rw,noauto 0 0
```

For NFSv4 mounts, use `nfs4` instead of `nfs` in the third column:

```
nfs.example.com:/data /local/pathv4 nfs4 rw,noauto 0 0
```

The `noauto` option prevents the file system from being mounted automatically at start-up. If you want to mount the respective file system manually, it is possible to shorten the mount command specifying the mount point only:

```
tux > sudo mount /local/path
```

Note: Mounting at Start-Up

If you do not enter the `noauto` option, the init scripts of the system will handle the mount of those file systems at start-up.

26.3.3 Parallel NFS (pNFS)

NFS is one of the oldest protocols, developed in the '80s. As such, NFS is usually sufficient if you want to share small files. However, when you want to transfer big files or large numbers of clients want to access data, an NFS server becomes a bottleneck and has a significant impact on the system performance. This is because of files quickly getting bigger, whereas the relative speed of your Ethernet has not fully kept up.

When you request a file from a regular NFS server, the server looks up the file metadata, collects all the data and transfers it over the network to your client. However, the performance bottleneck becomes apparent no matter how small or big the files are:

- With small files most of the time is spent collecting the metadata.
- With big files most of the time is spent on transferring the data from server to client.

pNFS, or parallel NFS, overcomes this limitation as it separates the file system metadata from the location of the data. As such, pNFS requires two types of servers:

- A *metadata* or *control server* that handles all the non-data traffic
- One or more *storage server(s)* that hold(s) the data

The metadata and the storage servers form a single, logical NFS server. When a client wants to read or write, the metadata server tells the NFSv4 client which storage server to use to access the file chunks. The client can access the data directly on the server.

SUSE Linux Enterprise Desktop supports pNFS on the client side only.

26.3.3.1 Configuring pNFS Client With YaST

Proceed as described in *Procedure 26.1, "Importing NFS Directories"*, but click the ***pNFS (v4.1)*** check box and optionally *NFSv4 share.* YaST will do all the necessary steps and will write all the required options in the file `/etc/exports`.

26.3.3.2 Configuring pNFS Client Manually

Refer to *Section 26.3.2, "Importing File Systems Manually"* to start. Most of the configuration is done by the NFSv4 server. For pNFS, the only difference is to add the `minorversion` option and the metadata server *`MDS_SERVER`* to your **`mount`** command:

```
tux > sudo mount -t nfs4 -o minorversion=1 MDS_SERVER MOUNTPOINT
```

To help with debugging, change the value in the `/proc` file system:

```
tux > sudo echo 32767 > /proc/sys/sunrpc/nfsd_debug
tux > sudo echo 32767 > /proc/sys/sunrpc/nfs_debug
```

26.4 For More Information

In addition to the man pages of **`exports`**, **`nfs`**, and **`mount`**, information about configuring an NFS server and client is available in `/usr/share/doc/packages/nfsidmap/README`. For further documentation online refer to the following Web sites:

- Find the detailed technical documentation online at SourceForge (http://nfs.sourceforge.net/) ↗.
- For instructions for setting up kerberized NFS, refer to NFS Version 4 Open Source Reference Implementation (http://www.citi.umich.edu/projects/nfsv4/linux/krb5-setup.html) ↗.
- If you have questions on NFSv4, refer to the Linux NFSv4 FAQ (http://www.citi.umich.edu/projects/nfsv4/linux/faq/) ↗.

27 Samba

Using Samba, a Unix machine can be configured as a file and print server for macOS, Windows, and OS/2 machines. Samba has developed into a fully-fledged and rather complex product. Configure Samba with YaST, or by editing the configuration file manually.

27.1 Terminology

The following are some terms used in Samba documentation and in the YaST module.

SMB protocol

Samba uses the SMB (server message block) protocol that is based on the NetBIOS services. Microsoft released the protocol so other software manufacturers could establish connections to a Microsoft domain network. With Samba, the SMB protocol works on top of the TCP/IP protocol, so the TCP/IP protocol must be installed on all clients.

CIFS protocol

CIFS (common Internet file system) protocol is another protocol supported by Samba. CIFS defines a standard remote file system access protocol for use over the network, enabling groups of users to work together and share documents across the network.

NetBIOS

NetBIOS is a software interface (API) designed for communication between machines providing a name service. It enables machines connected to the network to reserve names for themselves. After reservation, these machines can be addressed by name. There is no central process that checks names. Any machine on the network can reserve as many names as it wants as long as the names are not already in use. The NetBIOS interface can be implemented for different network architectures. An implementation that works relatively closely with network hardware is called NetBEUI, but this is often called NetBIOS. Network protocols implemented with NetBIOS are IPX from Novell (NetBIOS via TCP/IP) and TCP/IP.

The NetBIOS names sent via TCP/IP have nothing in common with the names used in `/etc/hosts` or those defined by DNS. NetBIOS uses its own, completely independent naming convention. However, it is recommended to use names that correspond to DNS host names to make administration easier or use DNS natively. This is the default used by Samba.

Samba server

Samba server provides SMB/CIFS services and NetBIOS over IP naming services to clients. For Linux, there are three daemons for Samba server: smbd for SMB/CIFS services, nmbd for naming services, and winbind for authentication.

Samba client

The Samba client is a system that uses Samba services from a Samba server over the SMB protocol. Common operating systems, such as Windows and macOS support the SMB protocol. The TCP/IP protocol must be installed on all computers. Samba provides a client for the different Unix flavors. For Linux, there is a kernel module for SMB that allows the integration of SMB resources on the Linux system level. You do not need to run any daemon for the Samba client.

Shares

SMB servers provide resources to the clients by means of shares. Shares are printers and directories with their subdirectories on the server. It is exported by means of a name and can be accessed by its name. The share name can be set to any name—it does not need to be the name of the export directory. A printer is also assigned a name. Clients can access the printer by its name.

DC

A domain controller (DC) is a server that handles accounts in a domain. For data replication, additional domain controllers are available in one domain.

27.2 Installing a Samba Server

To install a Samba server, start YaST and select *Software* › *Software Management*. Choose *View* › *Patterns* and select *File Server*. Confirm the installation of the required packages to finish the installation process.

27.3 Configuring a Samba Server

For configuring a Samba server, see the SUSE Linux Enterprise Server documentation.

27.4 Configuring Clients

Clients can only access the Samba server via TCP/IP. NetBEUI and NetBIOS via IPX cannot be used with Samba.

27.4.1 Configuring a Samba Client with YaST

Configure a Samba client to access resources (files or printers) on the Samba or Windows server. Enter the NT or Active Directory domain or workgroup in the dialog *Network Services › Windows Domain Membership*. If you activate *Also Use SMB Information for Linux Authentication*, the user authentication runs over the Samba, NT or Kerberos server.

Click *Expert Settings* for advanced configuration options. For example, use the *Mount Server Directories* table to enable mounting server home directory automatically with authentication. This way users can access their home directories when hosted on CIFS. For details, see the `pam_mount` man page.

After completing all settings, confirm the dialog to finish the configuration.

27.5 Samba as Login Server

In networks where predominantly Windows clients are found, it is often preferable that users may only register with a valid account and password. In a Windows-based network, this task is handled by a primary domain controller (PDC). You can use a Windows NT server configured as PDC, but this task can also be done with a Samba server. The entries that must be made in the `[global]` section of `smb.conf` are shown in *Example 27.1, "Global Section in smb.conf"*.

EXAMPLE 27.1: GLOBAL SECTION IN SMB.CONF

```
[global]
    workgroup = WORKGROUP
    domain logons = Yes
```

```
domain master = Yes
```

It is necessary to prepare user accounts and passwords in an encryption format that conforms with Windows. Do this with the command **smbpasswd** -a name. Create the domain account for the computers, required by the Windows domain concept, with the following commands:

```
useradd hostname\$
smbpasswd -a -m hostname
```

With the **useradd** command, a dollar sign is added. The command **smbpasswd** inserts this automatically when the parameter -m is used. The commented configuration example (/usr/share/doc/packages/samba/examples/smb.conf.SUSE) contains settings that automate this task.

```
add machine script = /usr/sbin/useradd -g nogroup -c "NT Machine Account" \
-s /bin/false %m\$
```

To make sure that Samba can execute this script correctly, choose a Samba user with the required administrator permissions and add it to the ntadmin group. Then all users belonging to this Linux group can be assigned Domain Admin status with the command:

```
net groupmap add ntgroup="Domain Admins" unixgroup=ntadmin
```

27.6 Advanced Topics

This section introduces more advanced techniques to manage both the client and server part of the Samba suite.

27.6.1 Transparent File Compression on Btrfs

Samba allows clients to remotely manipulate file and directory compression flags for shares placed on the Btrfs file system. Windows Explorer provides the ability to flag files/directories for transparent compression via the *File* › *Properties* › *Advanced* dialog:

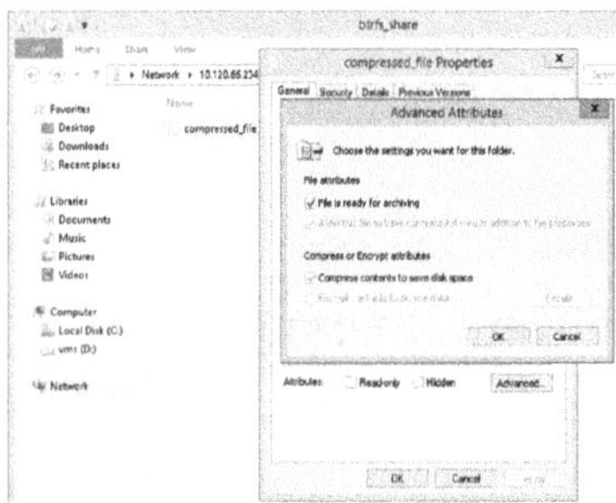

FIGURE 27.1: WINDOWS EXPLORER *ADVANCED ATTRIBUTES* DIALOG

Files flagged for compression are transparently compressed and decompressed by the underlying file system when accessed or modified. This normally results in storage capacity savings at the expense of extra CPU overhead when accessing the file. New files and directories inherit the compression flag from the parent directory, unless created with the FILE_NO_COMPRESSION option.

Windows Explorer presents compressed files and directories visually differently to those that are not compressed:

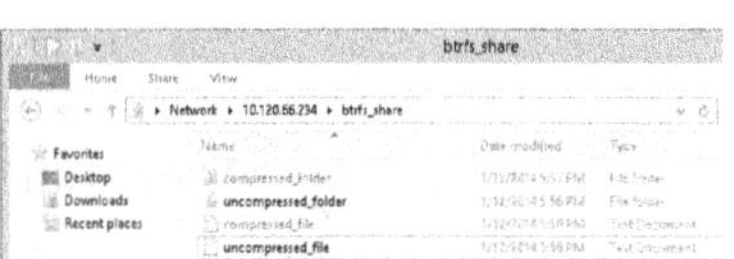

FIGURE 27.2: WINDOWS EXPLORER DIRECTORY LISTING WITH COMPRESSED FILES

You can enable Samba share compression either manually by adding

```
vfs objects = btrfs
```

to the share configuration in `/etc/samba/smb.conf`, or using YaST: *Network Services* › *Samba Server* › *Add*, and checking *Utilize Btrfs Features*.

27.6.2 Snapshots

Snapshots, also called Shadow Copies, are copies of the state of a file system subvolume at a certain point of time. Snapper is the tool to manage these snapshots in Linux. Snapshots are supported on the Btrfs file system or thin-provisioned LVM volumes. The Samba suite supports managing of remote snapshots through the FSRVP protocol on both the server and client side.

27.6.2.1 Previous Versions

Snapshots on a Samba server can be exposed to remote Windows clients as file or directory previous versions.

To enable snapshots on a Samba server, the following conditions must be fulfilled:

- The SMB network share resides on a Btrfs subvolume.
- The SMB network share path has a related snapper configuration file. You can create the snapper file with

  ```
  snapper -c <cfg_name> create-config /path/to/share
  ```

  For more information on snapper, see *Chapter 7, System Recovery and Snapshot Management with Snapper*.
- The snapshot directory tree must allow access for relevant users. For more information, see the PERMISSIONS section of the vfs_snapper manual page (**`man 8 vfs_snapper`**).

To support remote snapshots, you need to modify the `/etc/samba/smb.conf` file. You can do it either with *YaST › Network Services › Samba Server*, or manually by enhancing the relevant share section with

```
vfs objects = snapper
```

Note that you need to restart the Samba service for manual `smb.conf` changes to take effect:

```
systemctl restart nmb smb
```

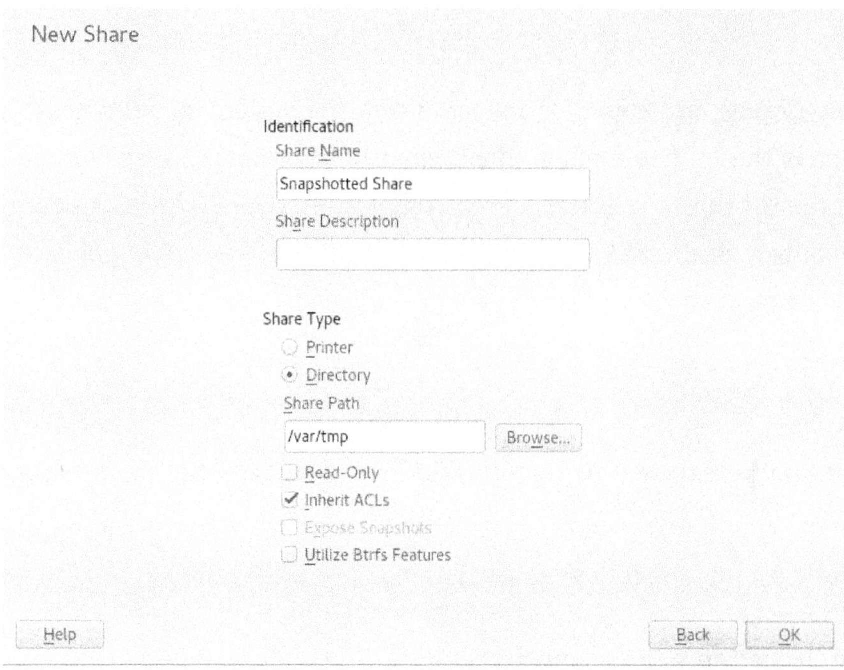

FIGURE 27.3: ADDING A NEW SAMBA SHARE WITH SNAPSHOTTING ENABLED

After being configured, snapshots created by snapper for the Samba share path can be accessed from Windows Explorer from a file or directory's *Previous Versions* tab.

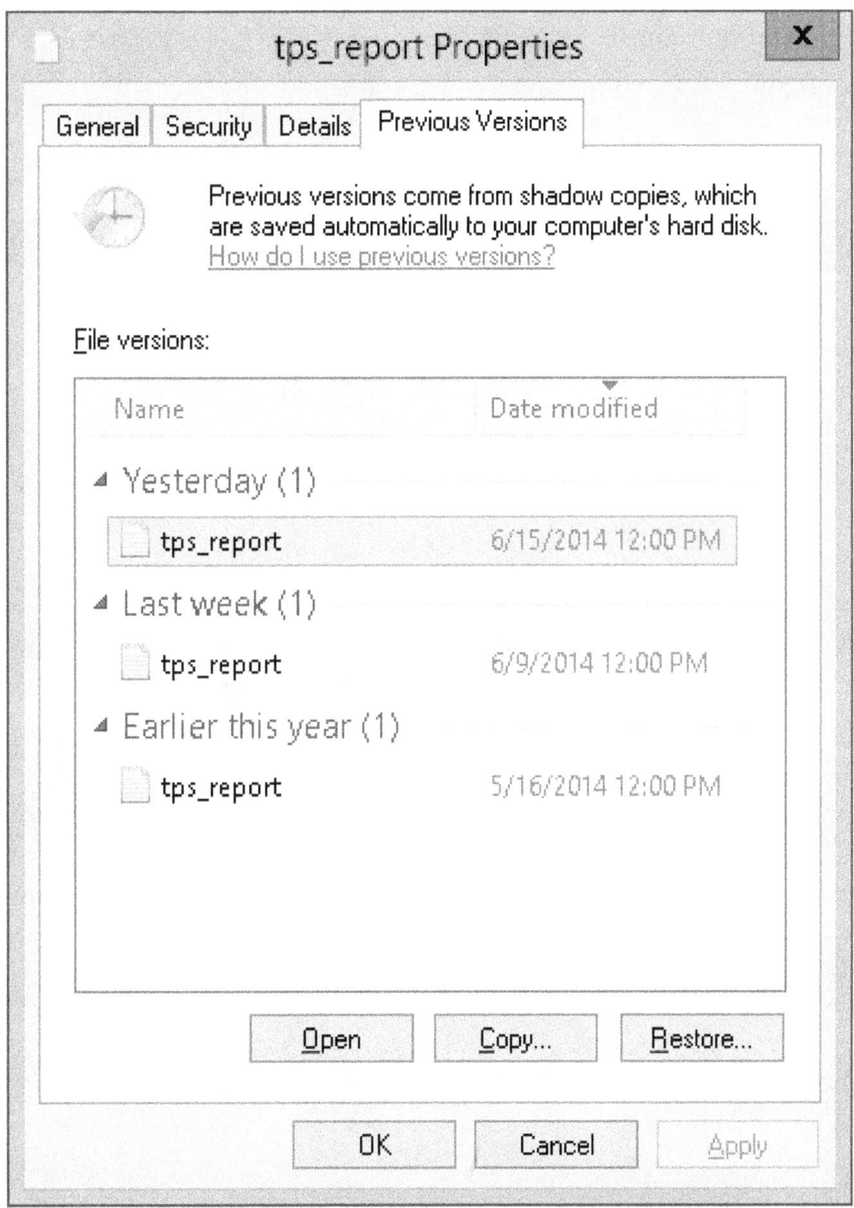

FIGURE 27.4: THE *PREVIOUS VERSIONS* TAB IN WINDOWS EXPLORER

27.6.2.2 Remote Share Snapshots

By default, snapshots can only be created and deleted on the Samba server locally, via the snapper command line utility, or using snapper's time line feature.

Samba can be configured to process share snapshot creation and deletion requests from remote hosts using the File Server Remote VSS Protocol (FSRVP).

In addition to the configuration and prerequisites documented in *Section 27.6.2.1, "Previous Versions"*, the following global configuration is required in `/etc/samba/smb.conf`:

```
[global]
rpc_daemon:fssd = fork
registry shares = yes
include = registry
```

FSRVP clients, including Samba's **`rpcclient`** and Windows Server 2012 **`DiskShadow.exe`**, can then instruct Samba to create or delete a snapshot for a given share, and expose the snapshot as a new share.

27.6.2.3 Managing Snapshots Remotely from Linux with `rpcclient`

The `samba-client` package contains an FSRVP client that can remotely request a Windows/Samba server to create and expose a snapshot of a given share. You can then use existing tools in SUSE Linux Enterprise Desktop to mount the exposed share and back up its files. Requests to the server are sent using the **`rpcclient`** binary.

EXAMPLE 27.2: USING `rpcclient` TO REQUEST A WINDOWS SERVER 2012 SHARE SNAPSHOT

Connect to `win-server.example.com` server as an administrator in an `EXAMPLE` domain:

```
# rpcclient -U 'EXAMPLE\Administrator' ncacn_np:win-server.example.com[ndr64,sign]
Enter EXAMPLE/Administrator's password:
```

Check that the SMB share is visible for **`rpcclient`**:

```
rpcclient $> netshareenum
netname: windows_server_2012_share
remark:
path:   C:\Shares\windows_server_2012_share
password:       (null)
```

Check that the SMB share supports snapshot creation:

```
rpcclient $> fss_is_path_sup windows_server_2012_share \
UNC \\WIN-SERVER\windows_server_2012_share\ supports shadow copy requests
```

Request the creation of a share snapshot:

```
rpcclient $> fss_create_expose backup ro windows_server_2012_share
13fe880e-e232-493d-87e9-402f21019fb6: shadow-copy set created
13fe880e-e232-493d-87e9-402f21019fb6(1c26544e-8251-445f-be89-d1e0a3938777): \
```

```
\\WIN-SERVER\windows_server_2012_share\ shadow-copy added to set
13fe880e-e232-493d-87e9-402f21019fb6: prepare completed in 0 secs
13fe880e-e232-493d-87e9-402f21019fb6: commit completed in 1 secs
13fe880e-e232-493d-87e9-402f21019fb6(1c26544e-8251-445f-be89-d1e0a3938777): \
share windows_server_2012_share@{1C26544E-8251-445F-BE89-D1E0A3938777} \
exposed as a snapshot of \\WIN-SERVER\windows_server_2012_share\
```

Confirm that the snapshot share is exposed by the server:

```
rpcclient $> netshareenum
netname: windows_server_2012_share
remark:
path:   C:\Shares\windows_server_2012_share
password:       (null)

netname: windows_server_2012_share@{1C26544E-8251-445F-BE89-D1E0A3938777}
remark: (null)
path:   \\?\GLOBALROOT\Device\HarddiskVolumeShadowCopy{F6E6507E-F537-11E3-9404-
B8AC6F927453}\Shares\windows_server_2012_share\
password:       (null)
```

Attempt to delete the snapshot share:

```
rpcclient $> fss_delete windows_server_2012_share \
13fe880e-e232-493d-87e9-402f21019fb6 1c26544e-8251-445f-be89-d1e0a3938777
13fe880e-e232-493d-87e9-402f21019fb6(1c26544e-8251-445f-be89-d1e0a3938777): \
\\WIN-SERVER\windows_server_2012_share\ shadow-copy deleted
```

Confirm that the snapshot share has been removed by the server:

```
rpcclient $> netshareenum
netname: windows_server_2012_share
remark:
path:   C:\Shares\windows_server_2012_share
password:       (null)
```

27.6.2.4 Managing Snapshots Remotely from Windows with `DiskShadow.exe`

You can manage snapshots of SMB shares on the Linux Samba server from the Windows environment acting as a client as well. Windows Server 2012 includes the **`DiskShadow.exe`** utility that can manage remote shares similar to the **`rpcclient`** described in *Section 27.6.2.3, "Managing Snapshots Remotely from Linux with `rpcclient`"*. Note that you need to carefully set up the Samba server first.

Following is an example procedure to set up the Samba server so that the Windows Server client can manage its share's snapshots. Note that *EXAMPLE* is the Active Directory domain used in the testing environment, `fsrvp-server.example.com` is the host name of the Samba server, and `/srv/smb` is the path to the SMB share.

PROCEDURE 27.1: DETAILED SAMBA SERVER CONFIGURATION

1. Join Active Directory domain via YaST.
2. Ensure that the Active Domain DNS entry was correct:

```
fsrvp-server:~ # net -U 'Administrator' ads dns register \
fsrvp-server.example.com <IP address>
Successfully registered hostname with DNS
```

3. Create Btrfs subvolume at `/srv/smb`

```
fsrvp-server:~ # btrfs subvolume create /srv/smb
```

4. Create snapper configuration file for path `/srv/smb`

```
fsrvp-server:~ # snapper -c <snapper_config> create-config /srv/smb
```

5. Create new share with path `/srv/smb`, and YaST *Expose Snapshots* check box enabled. Make sure to add the following snippets to the global section of `/etc/samba/smb.conf` as mentioned in *Section 27.6.2.2, "Remote Share Snapshots"*:

```
[global]
 rpc_daemon:fssd = fork
 registry shares = yes
 include = registry
```

6. Restart Samba with **`systemctl restart nmb smb`**
7. Configure snapper permissions:

```
fsrvp-server:~ # snapper -c <snapper_config> set-config \
ALLOW_USERS="EXAMPLE\\\\Administrator EXAMPLE\\\\win-client$"
```

Ensure that any ALLOW_USERS are also permitted traversal of the `.snapshots` subdirectory.

```
fsrvp-server:~ # snapper -c <snapper_config> set-config SYNC_ACL=yes
```

 Important: Path Escaping

Be careful about the '\' escapes! Escape twice to ensure that the value stored in `/etc/snapper/configs/<snapper_config>` is escaped once.

"EXAMPLE\win-client$" corresponds to the Windows client computer account. Windows issues initial FSRVP requests while authenticated with this account.

8. Grant Windows client account necessary privileges:

```
fsrvp-server:~ # net -U 'Administrator' rpc rights grant \
"EXAMPLE\\win-client$" SeBackupPrivilege
Successfully granted rights.
```

The previous command is not needed for the "EXAMPLE\Administrator" user, which has privileges already granted.

PROCEDURE 27.2: WINDOWS CLIENT SETUP AND `DiskShadow.exe` IN ACTION

1. Boot Windows Server 2012 (example host name WIN-CLIENT).
2. Join the same Active Directory domain EXAMPLE as with the SUSE Linux Enterprise Desktop.
3. Reboot.
4. Open Powershell.
5. Start **`DiskShadow.exe`** and begin the backup procedure:

```
PS C:\Users\Administrator.EXAMPLE> diskshadow.exe
Microsoft DiskShadow version 1.0
Copyright (C) 2012 Microsoft Corporation
On computer:  WIN-CLIENT,  6/17/2014 3:53:54 PM

DISKSHADOW> begin backup
```

6. Specify that shadow copy persists across program exit, reset or reboot:

```
DISKSHADOW> set context PERSISTENT
```

7. Check whether the specified share supports snapshots, and create one:

```
DISKSHADOW> add volume \\fsrvp-server\sles_snapper
```

```
DISKSHADOW> create
Alias VSS_SHADOW_1 for shadow ID {de4ddca4-4978-4805-8776-cdf82d190a4a} set as \
 environment variable.
Alias VSS_SHADOW_SET for shadow set ID {c58e1452-c554-400e-a266-d11d5c837cb1} \
 set as environment variable.

Querying all shadow copies with the shadow copy set ID \
 {c58e1452-c554-400e-a266-d11d5c837cb1}

 * Shadow copy ID = {de4ddca4-4978-4805-8776-cdf82d190a4a}      %VSS_SHADOW_1%
    - Shadow copy set: {c58e1452-c554-400e-a266-d11d5c837cb1}  %VSS_SHADOW_SET%
    - Original count of shadow copies = 1
    - Original volume name: \\FSRVP-SERVER\SLES_SNAPPER\ \
      [volume not on this machine]
    - Creation time: 6/17/2014 3:54:43 PM
    - Shadow copy device name:
      \\FSRVP-SERVER\SLES_SNAPPER@{31afd84a-44a7-41be-b9b0-751898756faa}
    - Originating machine: FSRVP-SERVER
    - Service machine: win-client.example.com
    - Not exposed
    - Provider ID: {89300202-3cec-4981-9171-19f59559e0f2}
    - Attributes:  No_Auto_Release Persistent FileShare

Number of shadow copies listed: 1
```

8. Finish the backup procedure:

```
DISKSHADOW> end backup
```

9. After the snapshot was created, try to delete it and verify the deletion:

```
DISKSHADOW> delete shadows volume \\FSRVP-SERVER\SLES_SNAPPER\
Deleting shadow copy {de4ddca4-4978-4805-8776-cdf82d190a4a} on volume \
 \\FSRVP-SERVER\SLES_SNAPPER\ from provider \
{89300202-3cec-4981-9171-19f59559e0f2} [Attributes: 0x04000009]...

Number of shadow copies deleted: 1

DISKSHADOW> list shadows all

Querying all shadow copies on the computer ...
No shadow copies found in system.
```

27.7 For More Information

Documentation for Samba ships with the `samba-doc` package which is not installed by default. Install it with **`zypper install samba-doc`**. Enter **`apropos`** `samba` at the command line to display some manual pages or browse the `/usr/share/doc/packages/samba` directory for more online documentation and examples. Find a commented example configuration (`smb.conf.SUSE`) in the `examples` subdirectory. Another file to look for Samba related information is `/usr/share/doc/packages/samba/README.SUSE`.

The Samba HOWTO (see https://wiki.samba.org) provided by the Samba team includes a section about troubleshooting. In addition to that, Part V of the document provides a step-by-step guide to checking your configuration.

28 On-Demand Mounting with Autofs

`autofs` is a program that automatically mounts specified directories on an on-demand basis. It is based on a kernel module for high efficiency, and can manage both local directories and network shares. These automatic mount points are mounted only when they are accessed, and unmounted after a certain period of inactivity. This on-demand behavior saves bandwidth and results in better performance than static mounts managed by `/etc/fstab`. While `autofs` is a control script, **`automount`** is the command (daemon) that does the actual auto-mounting.

28.1 Installation

`autofs` is not installed on SUSE Linux Enterprise Desktop by default. To use its auto-mounting capabilities, first install it with

```
sudo zypper install autofs
```

28.2 Configuration

You need to configure `autofs` manually by editing its configuration files with a text editor, such as **`vim`**. There are two basic steps to configure `autofs`—the *master* map file, and specific map files.

28.2.1 The Master Map File

The default master configuration file for `autofs` is `/etc/auto.master`. You can change its location by changing the value of the `DEFAULT_MASTER_MAP_NAME` option in `/etc/sysconfig/autofs`. Here is the content of the default one for SUSE Linux Enterprise Desktop:

```
#
# Sample auto.master file
# This is an automounter map and it has the following format
# key [ -mount-options-separated-by-comma ] location
# For details of the format look at autofs(5). ❶
#
#/misc  /etc/auto.misc❷
```

```
#/net -hosts
#
# Include /etc/auto.master.d/*.autofs❸
#
#+dir:/etc/auto.master.d
#
# Include central master map if it can be found using
# nsswitch sources.
#
# Note that if there are entries for /net or /misc (as
# above) in the included master map any keys that are the
# same will not be seen as the first read key seen takes
# precedence.
#
+auto.master❹
```

❶ The `autofs` manual page (**`man 5 autofs`**) offers a lot of valuable information on the format of the automounter maps.

❷ Although commented out (#) by default, this is an example of a simple automounter mapping syntax.

❸ In case you need to split the master map into several files, uncomment the line, and put the mappings (suffixed with `.autofs`) in the `/etc/auto.master.d/` directory.

❹ `+auto.master` ensures that those using NIS will still find their master map.

Entries in `auto.master` have three fields with the following syntax:

```
mount point      map name      options
```

mount point

The base location where to mount the `autofs` file system, such as `/home`.

map name

The name of a map source to use for mounting. For the syntax of the maps files, see *Section 28.2.2, "Map Files"*.

options

These options (if specified) will apply as defaults to all entries in the given map.

Tip: For More Information

For more detailed information on the specific values of the optional `map-type`, `format`, and `options`, see the *auto.master* manual page (**`man 5 auto.master`**).

The following entry in `auto.master` tells `autofs` to look in `/etc/auto.smb`, and create mount points in the `/smb` directory.

```
/smb    /etc/auto.smb
```

28.2.1.1 Direct Mounts

Direct mounts create a mount point at the path specified inside the relevant map file. Instead of specifying the mount point in `auto.master`, replace the mount point field with `/-`. For example, the following line tells `autofs` to create a mount point at the place specified in `auto.smb`:

```
/-        /etc/auto.smb
```

Tip: Maps without Full Path

If the map file is not specified with its full local or network path, it is located using the Name Service Switch (NSS) configuration:

```
/-        auto.smb
```

28.2.2 Map Files

Important: Other Types of Maps

Although *files* are the most common types of maps for auto-mounting with `autofs`, there are other types as well. A map specification can be the output of a command, or a result of a query in LDAP or database. For more detailed information on map types, see the manual page **`man 5 auto.master`**.

Map files specify the (local or network) source location, and the mount point where to mount the source locally. The general format of maps is similar to the master map. The difference is that the *options* appear between the mount point and the location instead of at the end of the entry:

```
mount point      options      location
```

mount point

Specifies where to mount the source location. This can be either a single directory name (so-called *indirect* mount) to be added to the base mount point specified in `auto.master`, or the full path of the mount point (direct mount, see Section 28.2.1.1, "Direct Mounts").

options

Specifies optional comma-separated list of mount options for the relevant entries. If `auto.master` contains options for this map file as well, theses are appended.

location

Specifies from where the file system is to be mounted. It is usually an NFS or SMB volume in the usual notation `host_name:path_name`. If the file system to be mounted begins with a '/' (such as local `/dev` entries or smbfs shares), a colon symbol ':' needs to be prefixed, such as `:/dev/sda1.`

28.3 Operation and Debugging

This section introduces information on how to control the `autofs` service operation, and how to view more debugging information when tuning the automounter operation.

28.3.1 Controlling the autofs Service

The operation of the `autofs` service is controlled by `systemd`. The general syntax of the **`systemctl`** command for `autofs` is

```
sudo systemctl SUB_COMMAND autofs
```

where *`SUB_COMMAND`* is one of:

enable

Starts the automounter daemon at boot.

start

Starts the automounter daemon.

stop

Stops the automounter daemon. Automatic mount points are not accessible.

status

Prints the current status of the `autofs` service together with a part of a relevant log file.

restart

Stops and starts the automounter, terminating all running daemons and starting new ones.

reload

Checks the current `auto.master` map, restarts those daemons whose entries have changed, and starts new ones for new entries.

28.3.2 Debugging the Automounter Problems

If you experience problems when mounting directories with `autofs`, it is useful to run the **`automount`** daemon manually and watch its output messages:

1. Stop `autofs`.

```
sudo systemctl stop autofs
```

2. From one terminal, run **`automount`** manually in the foreground, producing verbose output.

```
sudo automount -f -v
```

3. From another terminal, try to mount the auto-mounting file systems by accessing the mount points (for example by **`cd`** or **`ls`**).

4. Check the output of **`automount`** from the first terminal for more information why the mount failed, or why it was not even attempted.

28.4 Auto-Mounting an NFS Share

The following procedure illustrates how to configure `autofs` to auto-mount an NFS share available on your network. It makes use of the information mentioned above, and assumes you are familiar with NFS exports. For more information on NFS, see *Chapter 26, Sharing File Systems with NFS*.

1. Edit the master map file `/etc/auto.master`:

```
sudo vim /etc/auto.master
```

Add a new entry for the new NFS mount at the end of `/etc/auto.master`:

```
/nfs       /etc/auto.nfs       --timeout=10
```

It tells `autofs` that the base mount point is `/nfs`, the NFS shares are specified in the `/etc/auto.nfs` map, and that all shares in this map will be automatically unmounted after 10 seconds of inactivity.

2. Create a new map file for NFS shares:

```
sudo vim /etc/auto.nfs
```

`/etc/auto.nfs` normally contains a separate line for each NFS share. Its format is described in *Section 28.2.2, "Map Files"*. Add the line describing the mount point and the NFS share network address:

```
export      jupiter.com:/home/geeko/doc/export
```

The above line means that the `/home/geeko/doc/export` directory on the `jupiter.com` host will be auto-mounted to the `/nfs/export` directory on the local host (`/nfs` is taken from the `auto.master` map) when requested. The `/nfs/export` directory will be created automatically by `autofs`.

3. Optionally comment out the related line in `/etc/fstab` if you previously mounted the same NFS share statically. The line should look similar to this:

```
#jupiter.com:/home/geeko/doc/export /nfs/export nfs defaults 0 0
```

4. Reload `autofs` and check if it works:

```
sudo systemctl restart autofs
```

```
# ls -l /nfs/export
total 20
drwxr-xr-x  6 1001 users 4096 Oct 25 08:56 ./
drwxr-xr-x  3 root root     0 Apr  1 09:47 ../
drwxr-xr-x  5 1001 users 4096 Jan 14  2013 .images/
drwxr-xr-x 10 1001 users 4096 Aug 16  2013 .profiled/
drwxr-xr-x  3 1001 users 4096 Aug 30  2013 .tmp/
drwxr-xr-x  4 1001 users 4096 Oct 25 08:56 SLE-12-manual/
```

If you can see the list of files on the remote share, then `autofs` is functioning.

28.5 Advanced Topics

This section describes topics that are beyond the basic introduction to `autofs`—auto-mounting of NFS shares that are available on your network, using wild cards in map files, and information specific to the CIFS file system.

28.5.1 /net Mount Point

This helper mount point is useful if you use a lot of NFS shares. `/net` auto-mounts all NFS shares on your local network on demand. The entry is already present in the `auto.master` file, so all you need to do is uncomment it and restart `autofs`:

```
/net      -hosts
```

```
systemctl restart autofs
```

For example, if you have a server named `jupiter` with an NFS share called `/export`, you can mount it by typing

```
# cd /net/jupiter/export
```

on the command line.

28.5.2 Using Wild Cards to Auto-Mount Subdirectories

If you have a directory with subdirectories that you need to auto-mount individually—the typical case is the `/home` directory with individual users' home directories inside— `autofs` offers a clever solution for that.

In case of home directories, add the following line in `auto.master`:

```
/home      /etc/auto.home
```

Now you need to add the correct mapping to the `/etc/auto.home` file, so that the users' home directories are mounted automatically. One solution is to create separate entries for each directory:

```
wilber      jupiter.com:/home/wilber
penguin      jupiter.com:/home/penguin
```

```
tux        jupiter.com:/home/tux
[...]
```

This is very awkward as you need to manage the list of users inside `auto.home`. You can use the asterisk '*' instead of the mount point, and the ampersand '&' instead of the directory to be mounted:

```
*       jupiter:/home/&
```

28.5.3 Auto-Mounting CIFS File System

If you want to auto-mount an SMB/CIFS share (see *Chapter 27, Samba* for more information on the SMB/CIFS protocol), you need to modify the syntax of the map file. Add `-fstype=cifs` in the option field, and prefix the share location with a colon ':'.

```
mount point      -fstype=cifs      ://jupiter.com/export
```

V Mobile Computers

29 Mobile Computing with Linux

Mobile computing is mostly associated with laptops, PDAs and cellular phones (and the data exchange between them). Mobile hardware components, such as external hard disks, flash disks, or digital cameras, can be connected to laptops or desktop systems. A number of software components are involved in mobile computing scenarios and some applications are tailor-made for mobile use.

29.1 Laptops

The hardware of laptops differs from that of a normal desktop system. This is because criteria like exchangeability, space requirements and power consumption must be taken into account. The manufacturers of mobile hardware have developed standard interfaces like PCMCIA (Personal Computer Memory Card International Association), Mini PCI and Mini PCIe that can be used to extend the hardware of laptops. The standards cover memory cards, network interface cards, and external hard disks.

29.1.1 Power Conservation

The inclusion of energy-optimized system components during laptop manufacturing contributes to their suitability for use without access to the electrical power grid. Their contribution to conservation of power is at least as important as that of the operating system. SUSE® Linux Enterprise Desktop supports various methods that control the power consumption of a laptop and have varying effects on the operating time under battery power. The following list is in descending order of contribution to power conservation:

- Throttling the CPU speed.
- Switching off the display illumination during pauses.
- Manually adjusting the display illumination.
- Disconnecting unused, hotplug-enabled accessories (USB CD-ROM, external mouse, unused PCMCIA cards, Wi-Fi, etc.).
- Spinning down the hard disk when idling.

Detailed background information about power management in SUSE Linux Enterprise Desktop is provided in *Chapter 31, Power Management*.

29.1.2 Integration in Changing Operating Environments

Your system needs to adapt to changing operating environments when used for mobile computing. Many services depend on the environment and the underlying clients must be reconfigured. SUSE Linux Enterprise Desktop handles this task for you.

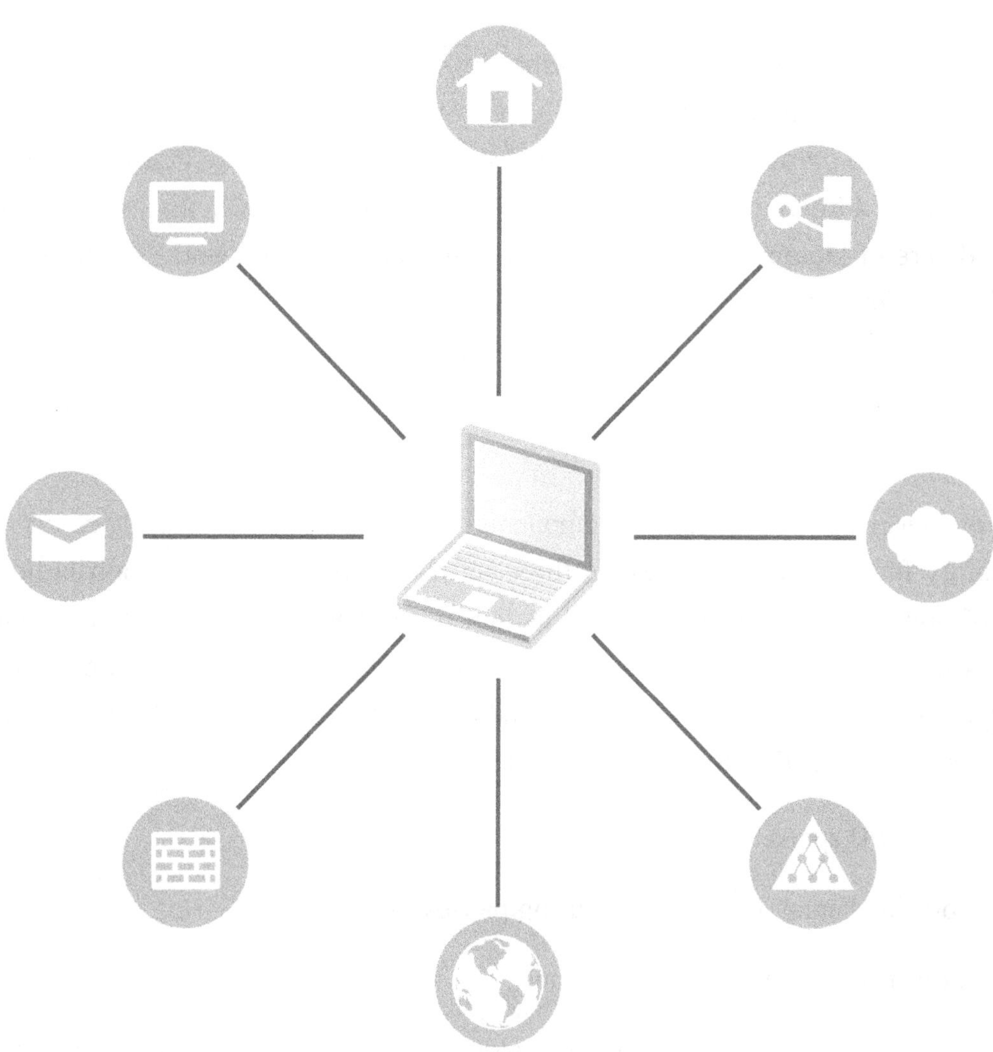

FIGURE 29.1: INTEGRATING A MOBILE COMPUTER IN AN EXISTING ENVIRONMENT

The services affected in the case of a laptop commuting back and forth between a small home network and an office network are:

Network
: This includes IP address assignment, name resolution, Internet connectivity and connectivity to other networks.

Printing
: A current database of available printers and an available print server must be present, depending on the network.

E-Mail and Proxies
: As with printing, the list of the corresponding servers must be current.

X (Graphical Environment)
: If your laptop is temporarily connected to a projector or an external monitor, different display configurations must be available.

SUSE Linux Enterprise Desktop offers several ways of integrating laptops into existing operating environments:

NetworkManager
: NetworkManager is especially tailored for mobile networking on laptops. It provides a means to easily and automatically switch between network environments or different types of networks such as mobile broadband (such as GPRS, EDGE, or 3G), wireless LAN, and Ethernet. NetworkManager supports WEP and WPA-PSK encryption in wireless LANs. It also supports dial-up connections. The GNOME desktop includes a front-end for NetworkManager. For more information, see Section 30.3, "Configuring Network Connections".

TABLE 29.1: USE CASES FOR NETWORKMANAGER

My computer...	Use NetworkManager
is a laptop	Yes
is sometimes attached to different networks	Yes
provides network services (such as DNS or DHCP)	No

My computer...	Use NetworkManager
only uses a static IP address	No

Use the YaST tools to configure networking whenever NetworkManager should not handle network configuration.

Tip: DNS Configuration and Various Types of Network Connections

If you travel frequently with your laptop and change different types of network connections, NetworkManager works fine when all DNS addresses are assigned correctly assigned with DHCP. If some connections use static DNS address(es), add it to the `NETCONFIG_DNS_STATIC_SERVERS` option in `/etc/sysconfig/network/config`.

SLP

The service location protocol (SLP) simplifies the connection of a laptop to an existing network. Without SLP, the administrator of a laptop usually requires detailed knowledge of the services available in a network. SLP broadcasts the availability of a certain type of service to all clients in a local network. Applications that support SLP can process the information dispatched by SLP and be configured automatically. SLP can also be used to install a system, minimizing the effort of searching for a suitable installation source.

29.1.3 Software Options

There are various task areas in mobile use that are covered by dedicated software: system monitoring (especially the battery charge), data synchronization, and wireless communication with peripherals and the Internet. The following sections cover the most important applications that SUSE Linux Enterprise Desktop provides for each task.

29.1.3.1 System Monitoring

Two system monitoring tools are provided by SUSE Linux Enterprise Desktop:

Power Management

Power Management is an application that lets you adjust the energy saving related behavior of the GNOME desktop. You can typically access it via *Computer* › *Control Center* › *System* › *Power Management*.

System Monitor

The *System Monitor* gathers measurable system parameters into one monitoring environment. It presents the output information in three tabs by default. *Processes* gives detailed information about currently running processes, such as CPU load, memory usage, or process ID number and priority. The presentation and filtering of the collected data can be customized—to add a new type of process information, left-click the process table header and choose which column to hide or add to the view. It is also possible to monitor different system parameters in various data pages or collect the data of various machines in parallel over the network. The *Resources* tab shows graphs of CPU, memory and network history and the *File System* tab lists all partitions and their usage.

29.1.3.2 Synchronizing Data

When switching between working on a mobile machine disconnected from the network and working at a networked workstation in an office, it is necessary to keep processed data synchronized across all instances. This could include e-mail folders, directories and individual files that need to be present for work on the road and at the office. The solution in both cases is as follows:

Synchronizing E-Mail

Use an IMAP account for storing your e-mails in the office network. Then access the e-mails from the workstation using any disconnected IMAP-enabled e-mail client, like Mozilla Thunderbird or Evolution as described in *Book* "GNOME User Guide". The e-mail client must be configured so that the same folder is always accessed for `Sent messages`. This ensures that all messages are available along with their status information after the synchronization process has completed. Use an SMTP server implemented in the mail client for sending messages instead of the system-wide MTA postfix or sendmail to receive reliable feedback about unsent mail.

Synchronizing Files and Directories

There are several utilities suitable for synchronizing data between a laptop and a workstation. One of the most widely used is a command-line tool called `rsync`. For more information, see its manual page (`man 1 rsync`).

29.1.3.3 Wireless Communication: Wi-Fi

With the largest range of these wireless technologies, Wi-Fi is the only one suitable for the operation of large and sometimes even spatially separate networks. Single machines can connect with each other to form an independent wireless network or access the Internet. Devices called *access points* act as base stations for Wi-Fi-enabled devices and act as intermediaries for access to the Internet. A mobile user can switch among access points depending on location and which access point is offering the best connection. Like in cellular telephony, a large network is available to Wi-Fi users without binding them to a specific location for accessing it.

Wi-Fi cards communicate using the 802.11 standard, prepared by the IEEE organization. Originally, this standard provided for a maximum transmission rate of 2 Mbit/s. Meanwhile, several supplements have been added to increase the data rate. These supplements define details such as the modulation, transmission output, and transmission rates (see *Table 29.2, "Overview of Various Wi-Fi Standards"*). Additionally, many companies implement hardware with proprietary or draft features.

TABLE 29.2: OVERVIEW OF VARIOUS WI-FI STANDARDS

Name (802.11)	Frequency (GHz)	Maximum Transmission Rate (Mbit/s)	Note
a	5	54	Less interference-prone
b	2.4	11	Less common
g	2.4	54	Widespread, backward-compatible with 11b
n	2.4 and/or 5	300	Common

Name (802.11)	Frequency (GHz)	Maximum Transmission Rate (Mbit/s)	Note
ac	5	up to ~865	Expected to be common in 2015
ad	60	up to appr. 7000	Released 2012, currently less common; not supported in SUSE Linux Enterprise Desktop

802.11 Legacy cards are not supported by SUSE® Linux Enterprise Desktop. Most cards using 802.11 a/b/g/n are supported. New cards usually comply with the 802.11n standard, but cards using 802.11g are still available.

29.1.3.3.1 Operating Modes

In wireless networking, various techniques and configurations are used to ensure fast, high-quality, and secure connections. Usually your Wi-Fi card operates in *managed mode*. However, different operating types need different setups. Wireless networks can be classified into four network modes:

Managed Mode (Infrastructure Mode), via Access Point (default mode)

Managed networks have a managing element: the access point. In this mode (also called infrastructure or default mode), all connections of the Wi-Fi stations in the network run through the access point, which may also serve as a connection to an Ethernet. To make sure only authorized stations can connect, various authentication mechanisms (WPA, etc.) are used. This is also the main mode that consumes the least amount of energy.

Ad-hoc Mode (Peer-to-Peer Network)

Ad-hoc networks do not have an access point. The stations communicate directly with each other, therefore an ad-hoc network is usually slower than a managed network. However, the transmission range and number of participating stations are greatly limited in ad-hoc networks. They also do not support WPA authentication. Additionally, not all cards support ad-hoc mode reliably.

Master Mode

In master mode, your Wi-Fi card is used as the access point, assuming your card supports this mode. Find out the details of your Wi-Fi card at http://linux-wless.passys.nl ↗.

Mesh Mode

Wireless mesh networks are organized in a *mesh topology*. A wireless mesh network's connection is spread among all wireless mesh *nodes*. Each node belonging to this network is connected to other nodes to share the connection, possibly over a large area.

29.1.3.3.2 Authentication

Because a wireless network is much easier to intercept and compromise than a wired network, the various standards include authentication and encryption methods.

Old Wi-Fi cards support only WEP (Wired Equivalent Privacy). However, because WEP has proven to be insecure, the Wi-Fi industry has defined an extension called WPA, which is supposed to eliminate the weaknesses of WEP. WPA, sometimes synonymous with WPA2, should be the default authentication method.

Usually the user cannot choose the authentication method. For example, when a card operates in managed mode the authentication is set by the access point. NetworkManager shows the authentication method.

29.1.3.3.3 Encryption

There are various encryption methods to ensure that no unauthorized person can read the data packets that are exchanged in a wireless network or gain access to the network:

WEP (defined in IEEE 802.11)

This standard uses the RC4 encryption algorithm, originally with a key length of 40 bits, later also with 104 bits. Often, the length is declared as 64 bits or 128 bits, depending on whether the 24 bits of the initialization vector are included. However, this standard has some weaknesses. Attacks against the keys generated by this system may be successful. Nevertheless, it is better to use WEP than not to encrypt the network.
Some vendors have implemented the non-standard “Dynamic WEP”. It works exactly as WEP and shares the same weaknesses, except that the key is periodically changed by a key management service.

TKIP (defined in WPA/IEEE 802.11i)

This key management protocol defined in the WPA standard uses the same encryption algorithm as WEP, but eliminates its weakness. Because a new key is generated for every data packet, attacks against these keys are fruitless. TKIP is used together with WPA-PSK.

CCMP (defined in IEEE 802.11i)

CCMP describes the key management. Usually, it is used in connection with WPA-EAP, but it can also be used with WPA-PSK. The encryption takes place according to AES and is stronger than the RC4 encryption of the WEP standard.

29.1.3.4 Wireless Communication: Bluetooth

Bluetooth has the broadest application spectrum of all wireless technologies. It can be used for communication between computers (laptops) and PDAs or cellular phones, as can IrDA. It can also be used to connect various computers within range. Bluetooth is also used to connect wireless system components, like a keyboard or a mouse. The range of this technology is, however, not sufficient to connect remote systems to a network. Wi-Fi is the technology of choice for communicating through physical obstacles like walls.

29.1.3.5 Wireless Communication: IrDA

IrDA is the wireless technology with the shortest range. Both communication parties must be within viewing distance of each other. Obstacles like walls cannot be overcome. One possible application of IrDA is the transmission of a file from a laptop to a cellular phone. The short path from the laptop to the cellular phone is then covered using IrDA. Long-range transmission of the file to the recipient is handled by the mobile network. Another application of IrDA is the wireless transmission of printing jobs in the office.

29.1.4 Data Security

Ideally, you protect data on your laptop against unauthorized access in multiple ways. Possible security measures can be taken in the following areas:

Protection against Theft

Always physically secure your system against theft whenever possible. Various securing tools (like chains) are available in retail stores.

Strong Authentication

Use biometric authentication in addition to standard authentication via login and password. SUSE Linux Enterprise Desktop supports fingerprint authentication.

Securing Data on the System

Important data should not only be encrypted during transmission, but also on the hard disk. This ensures its safety in case of theft. The creation of an encrypted partition with SUSE Linux Enterprise Desktop is described in *Book* "Security Guide", *Chapter 11 "Encrypting Partitions and Files"*. Another possibility is to create encrypted home directories when adding the user with YaST.

Important: Data Security and Suspend to Disk

Encrypted partitions are not unmounted during a suspend to disk event. Thus, all data on these partitions is available to any party who manages to steal the hardware and issue a resume of the hard disk.

Network Security

Any transfer of data should be secured, no matter how the transfer is done. Find general security issues regarding Linux and networks in *Book* "Security Guide", *Chapter 1 "Security and Confidentiality"*.

29.2 Mobile Hardware

SUSE Linux Enterprise Desktop supports the automatic detection of mobile storage devices over FireWire (IEEE 1394) or USB. The term *mobile storage device* applies to any kind of FireWire or USB hard disk, flash disk, or digital camera. These devices are automatically detected and configured when they are connected with the system over the corresponding interface. The file manager of GNOME offers flexible handling of mobile hardware items. To unmount any of these media safely, use the *Unmount Volume* (GNOME) feature of the file manager. For more details refer to *Book* "GNOME User Guide".

External Hard Disks (USB and FireWire)

When an external hard disk is correctly recognized by the system, its icon appears in the file manager. Clicking the icon displays the contents of the drive. It is possible to create directories and files here and edit or delete them. To rename a hard disk, select the corresponding menu item from the right-click contextual menu. This name change is limited to display in the file manager. The descriptor by which the device is mounted in `/media` remains unaffected.

USB Flash Disks

These devices are handled by the system like external hard disks. It is similarly possible to rename the entries in the file manager.

Digital Cameras (USB and FireWire)

Digital cameras recognized by the system also appear as external drives in the overview of the file manager. The images can then be processed using Shotwell. For advanced photo processing use The GIMP. For a short introduction to The GIMP, see *Book* "GNOME User Guide", *Chapter 18 "GIMP: Manipulating Graphics"*.

29.3 Cellular Phones and PDAs

A desktop system or a laptop can communicate with a cellular phone via Bluetooth or IrDA. Some models support both protocols and some only one of the two. The usage areas for the two protocols and the corresponding extended documentation has already been mentioned in *Section 29.1.3.3, "Wireless Communication: Wi-Fi"*. The configuration of these protocols on the cellular phones themselves is described in their manuals.

29.4 For More Information

The central point of reference for all questions regarding mobile devices and Linux is http://tuxmobil.org/ ↗. Various sections of that Web site deal with the hardware and software aspects of laptops, PDAs, cellular phones and other mobile hardware.

A similar approach to that of http://tuxmobil.org/ ↗ is made by http://www.linux-on-laptops.com/ ↗. Information about laptops and handhelds can be found here.

SUSE maintains a mailing list in German dedicated to the subject of laptops. See http://lists.opensuse.org/opensuse-mobile-de/ ↗. On this list, users and developers discuss all aspects of mobile computing with SUSE Linux Enterprise Desktop. Postings in English are answered, but the majority of the archived information is only available in German. Use http://lists.opensuse.org/opensuse-mobile/ ↗ for English postings.

30 Using NetworkManager

NetworkManager is the ideal solution for laptops and other portable computers. It supports state-of-the-art encryption types and standards for network connections, including connections to 802.1X protected networks. 802.1X is the “IEEE Standard for Local and Metropolitan Area Networks—Port-Based Network Access Control”. With NetworkManager, you need not worry about configuring network interfaces and switching between wired or wireless networks when you are moving. NetworkManager can automatically connect to known wireless networks or manage several network connections in parallel—the fastest connection is then used as default. Furthermore, you can manually switch between available networks and manage your network connection using an applet in the system tray.

Instead of only one connection being active, multiple connections may be active at once. This enables you to unplug your laptop from an Ethernet and remain connected via a wireless connection.

30.1 Use Cases for NetworkManager

NetworkManager provides a sophisticated and intuitive user interface, which enables users to easily switch their network environment. However, NetworkManager is not a suitable solution in the following cases:

- Your computer provides network services for other computers in your network, for example, it is a DHCP or DNS server.
- Your computer is a Xen server or your system is a virtual system inside Xen.

30.2 Enabling or Disabling NetworkManager

On laptop computers, NetworkManager is enabled by default. However, it can be at any time enabled or disabled in the YaST Network Settings module.

1. Run YaST and go to *System › Network Settings*.
2. The *Network Settings* dialog opens. Go to the *Global Options* tab.

3. To configure and manage your network connections with NetworkManager:

   a. In the *Network Setup Method* field, select *User Controlled with NetworkManager.*

   b. Click *OK* and close YaST.

   c. Configure your network connections with NetworkManager as described in *Section 30.3, "Configuring Network Connections"*.

4. To deactivate NetworkManager and control the network with your own configuration

   a. In the *Network Setup Method* field, choose *Controlled by wicked.*

   b. Click *OK.*

   c. Set up your network card with YaST using automatic configuration via DHCP or a static IP address.
      Find a detailed description of the network configuration with YaST in *Section 17.4, "Configuring a Network Connection with YaST"*.

30.3 Configuring Network Connections

After having enabled NetworkManager in YaST, configure your network connections with the NetworkManager front-end available in GNOME. It shows tabs for all types of network connections, such as wired, wireless, mobile broadband, DSL, and VPN connections.

To open the network configuration dialog in GNOME, open the settings menu via the status menu and click the *Network* entry.

Note: Availability of Options

Depending on your system setup, you may not be allowed to configure connections. In a secured environment, some options may be locked or require `root` permission. Ask your system administrator for details.

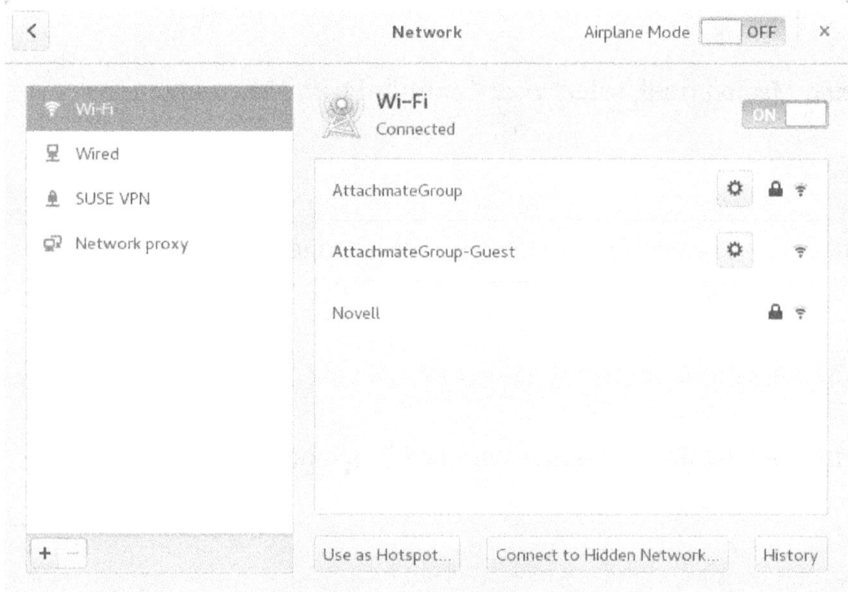

FIGURE 30.1: GNOME NETWORK CONNECTIONS DIALOG

PROCEDURE 30.1: ADDING AND EDITING CONNECTIONS

1. Open the NetworkManager configuration dialog.
2. To add a Connection:
   a. Click the + icon in the lower left corner.
   b. Select your preferred connection type and follow the instructions.
   c. When you are finished click *Add*.
   d. After having confirmed your changes, the newly configured network connection appears in the list of available networks you get by opening the Status Menu.
3. To edit a connection:
   a. Select the entry to edit.
   b. Click the gear icon to open the *Connection Settings* dialog.
   c. Insert your changes and click *Apply* to save them.
   d. To Make your connection available as system connection go to the *Identity* tab and set the check box *Make available to other users*. For more information about User and System Connections, see Section 30.4.1, "User and System Connections".

30.3.1 Managing Wired Network Connections

If your computer is connected to a wired network, use the NetworkManager applet to manage the connection.

1. Open the Status Menu and click *Wired* to change the connection details or to switch it off.
2. To change the settings click *Wired Settings* and then click the gear icon.
3. To switch off all network connections, activate the *Airplane Mode* setting.

30.3.2 Managing Wireless Network Connections

Visible wireless networks are listed in the GNOME NetworkManager applet menu under *Wireless Networks*. The signal strength of each network is also shown in the menu. Encrypted wireless networks are marked with a shield icon.

PROCEDURE 30.2: CONNECTING TO A VISIBLE WIRELESS NETWORK

1. To connect to a visible wireless network, open the Status Menu and click *Wi-Fi*.
2. Click *Turn On* to enable it.
3. Click *Select Network*, select your Wi-Fi Network and click *Connect*.
4. If the network is encrypted, a configuration dialog opens. It shows the type of encryption the network uses and text boxes for entering the login credentials.

PROCEDURE 30.3: CONNECTING TO AN INVISIBLE WIRELESS NETWORK

1. To connect to a network that does not broadcast its service set identifier (SSID or ESSID) and therefore cannot be detected automatically, open the Status Menu and click *Wi-Fi*.
2. Click *Wi-Fi Settings* to open the detailed settings menu.
3. Make sure your Wi-Fi is enabled and click *Connect to Hidden Network*.
4. In the dialog that opens, enter the SSID or ESSID in *Network Name* and set encryption parameters if necessary.

A wireless network that has been chosen explicitly will remain connected as long as possible. If a network cable is plugged in during that time, any connections that have been set to *Stay connected when possible* will be connected, while the wireless connection remains up.

30.3.3 Enabling Wireless Captive Portal Detection

On the initial connection, many public wireless hotspots force users to visit a landing page (the *captive portal*). Before you have logged in or agreed to the terms and conditions, all your HTTP requests are redirected to the provider's captive portal.

When connecting to a wireless network with a captive portal, NetworkManager and GNOME will automatically show the login page as part of the connection process. This ensures that you always know when you are connected, and helps you to get set up as quickly as possible without using the browser to login.

To enable this feature, install the package `NetworkManager-branding-SLE` and restart NetworkManager with:

```
tux > sudo systemctl restart network
```

Whenever you connect to a network with a captive portal, NetworkManager (or GNOME) will open the captive portal login page for you. Login with your credentials to get access to the Internet.

30.3.4 Configuring Your Wi-Fi/Bluetooth Card as an Access Point

If your Wi-Fi/Bluetooth card supports access point mode, you can use NetworkManager for the configuration.

1. Open the Status Menu and click *Wi-Fi*.
2. Click *Wi-Fi Settings* to open the detailed settings menu.
3. Click *Use as Hotspot* and follow the instructions.
4. Use the credentials shown in the resulting dialog to connect to the hotspot from a remote machine.

30.3.5 NetworkManager and VPN

NetworkManager supports several Virtual Private Network (VPN) technologies. For each technology, SUSE Linux Enterprise Desktop comes with a base package providing the generic support for NetworkManager. In addition to that, you also need to install the respective desktop-specific package for your applet.

OpenVPN

To use this VPN technology, install:

- `NetworkManager-openvpn`
- `NetworkManager-openvpn-gnome`

vpnc (Cisco AnyConnect)

To use this VPN technology, install:

- `NetworkManager-vpnc`
- `NetworkManager-vpnc-gnome`

PPTP (Point-to-Point Tunneling Protocol)

To use this VPN technology, install:

- `NetworkManager-pptp`
- `NetworkManager-pptp-gnome`

The following procedure describes how to set up your computer as an OpenVPN client using NetworkManager. Setting up other types of VPNs works analogously.

Before you begin, make sure that the package `NetworkManager-openvpn-gnome` is installed and all dependencies have been resolved.

PROCEDURE 30.4: SETTING UP OPENVPN WITH NETWORKMANAGER

1. Open the application *Settings* by clicking the status icons at the right end of the panel and clicking the *wrench and screwdriver* icon. In the window *All Settings*, choose *Network*.
2. Click the + icon.
3. Select *VPN* and then *OpenVPN*.
4. Choose the *Authentication* type. Depending on the setup of your OpenVPN server, choose *Certificates (TLS)* or *Password with Certificates (TLS)*.
5. Insert the necessary values into the respective text boxes. For our example configuration, these are:

Gateway	The remote endpoint of the VPN server

User name	The user (only available when you have selected *Password with Certificates (TLS)*)
Password	The password for the user (only available when you have selected *Password with Certificates (TLS)*)
User Certificate	`/etc/openvpn/client1.crt`
CA Certificate	`/etc/openvpn/ca.crt`
Private Key	`/etc/openvpn/client1.key`

6. Finish the configuration with *Add*.

7. To enable the connection, in the *Network* panel of the *Settings* application click the switch button. Alternatively, click the status icons at the right end of the panel, click the name of your VPN and then *Connect*.

30.4 NetworkManager and Security

NetworkManager distinguishes two types of wireless connections, trusted and untrusted. A trusted connection is any network that you explicitly selected in the past. All others are untrusted. Trusted connections are identified by the name and MAC address of the access point. Using the MAC address ensures that you cannot use a different access point with the name of your trusted connection.

NetworkManager periodically scans for available wireless networks. If multiple trusted networks are found, the most recently used is automatically selected. NetworkManager waits for your selection in case that all networks are untrusted.

If the encryption setting changes but the name and MAC address remain the same, NetworkManager attempts to connect, but first you are asked to confirm the new encryption settings and provide any updates, such as a new key.

If you switch from using a wireless connection to offline mode, NetworkManager blanks the SSID or ESSID. This ensures that the card is disconnected.

30.4.1 User and System Connections

NetworkManager knows two types of connections: `user` and `system` connections. User connections are connections that become available to NetworkManager when the first user logs in. Any required credentials are asked from the user and when the user logs out, the connections are disconnected and removed from NetworkManager. Connections that are defined as system connection can be shared by all users and are made available right after NetworkManager is started—before any users log in. In case of system connections, all credentials must be provided at the time the connection is created. Such system connections can be used to automatically connect to networks that require authorization. For information how to configure user or system connections with NetworkManager, refer to *Section 30.3, "Configuring Network Connections"*.

30.4.2 Storing Passwords and Credentials

If you do not want to re-enter your credentials each time you want to connect to an encrypted network, you can use the GNOME Keyring Manager to store your credentials encrypted on the disk, secured by a master password.

NetworkManager can also retrieve its certificates for secure connections (for example, encrypted wired, wireless or VPN connections) from the certificate store. For more information, refer to *Book* "Security Guide", *Chapter 12 "Certificate Store"*.

30.5 Frequently Asked Questions

In the following, find some frequently asked questions about configuring special network options with NetworkManager.

30.5.1. *How to tie a connection to a specific device?*

By default, connections in NetworkManager are device type-specific: they apply to all physical devices with the same type. If more than one physical device per connection type is available (for example, your machine is equipped with two Ethernet cards), you can tie a connection to a certain device.

To do this in GNOME, first look up the MAC address of your device (use the *Connection Information* available from the applet, or use the output of command line tools like `nm-tool` or `wicked show all`). Then start the dialog for configuring network connections and choose the connection you want to modify. On the *Wired* or *Wireless* tab, enter the *MAC Address* of the device and confirm your changes.

30.5.2. *How to specify a certain access point in case multiple access points with the same ESSID are detected?*

When multiple access points with different wireless bands (a/b/g/n) are available, the access point with the strongest signal is automatically chosen by default. To override this, use the *BSSID* field when configuring wireless connections.

The Basic Service Set Identifier (BSSID) uniquely identifies each Basic Service Set. In an infrastructure Basic Service Set, the BSSID is the MAC address of the wireless access point. In an independent (ad-hoc) Basic Service Set, the BSSID is a locally administered MAC address generated from a 46-bit random number.

Start the dialog for configuring network connections as described in *Section 30.3, "Configuring Network Connections"*. Choose the wireless connection you want to modify and click *Edit*. On the *Wireless* tab, enter the BSSID.

30.5.3. *How to share network connections to other computers?*

The primary device (the device which is connected to the Internet) does not need any special configuration. However, you need to configure the device that is connected to the local hub or machine as follows:

1. Start the dialog for configuring network connections as described in *Section 30.3, "Configuring Network Connections"*. Choose the connection you want to modify and click *Edit*. Switch to the *IPv4 Settings* tab and from the *Method* drop-down box, activate *Shared to other computers*. That will enable IP traffic forwarding and run a DHCP server on the device. Confirm your changes in NetworkManager.

2. As the DCHP server uses port `67`, make sure that it is not blocked by the firewall: On the machine sharing the connections, start YaST and select *Security and Users › Firewall*. Switch to the *Allowed Services* category. If *DCHP Server* is not already shown as *Allowed Service*, select *DCHP Server* from *Services to Allow* and click *Add*. Confirm your changes in YaST.

30.5.4. *How to provide static DNS information with automatic (DHCP, PPP, VPN) addresses?*

In case a DHCP server provides invalid DNS information (and/or routes), you can override it. Start the dialog for configuring network connections as described in Section 30.3, "Configuring Network Connections". Choose the connection you want to modify and click *Edit*. Switch to the *IPv4 Settings* tab, and from the *Method* drop-down box, activate *Automatic (DHCP) addresses only*. Enter the DNS information in the *DNS Servers* and *Search Domains* fields. To *Ignore automatically obtained routes* click *Routes* and activate the respective check box. Confirm your changes.

30.5.5. *How to make NetworkManager connect to password protected networks before a user logs in?*

Define a `system connection` that can be used for such purposes. For more information, refer to Section 30.4.1, "User and System Connections".

30.6 Troubleshooting

Connection problems can occur. Some common problems related to NetworkManager include the applet not starting or a missing VPN option. Methods for resolving and preventing these problems depend on the tool used.

NetworkManager Desktop Applet Does Not Start

The applets starts automatically if the network is set up for NetworkManager control. If the applet does not start, check if NetworkManager is enabled in YaST as described in Section 30.2, "Enabling or Disabling NetworkManager". Then make sure that the NetworkManager-gnome package is also installed.

If the desktop applet is installed but is not running for some reason, start it manually. If the desktop applet is installed but is not running for some reason, start it manually with the command **`nm-applet`**.

NetworkManager Applet Does Not Include the VPN Option

Support for NetworkManager, applets, and VPN for NetworkManager is distributed in separate packages. If your NetworkManager applet does not include the VPN option, check if the packages with NetworkManager support for your VPN technology are installed. For more information, see Section 30.3.5, "NetworkManager and VPN".

No Network Connection Available

If you have configured your network connection correctly and all other components for the network connection (router, etc.) are also up and running, it sometimes helps to restart the network interfaces on your computer. To do so, log in to a command line as `root` and run **`systemctl restart wickeds`**.

30.7 For More Information

More information about NetworkManager can be found on the following Web sites and directories:

NetworkManager Project Page

http://projects.gnome.org/NetworkManager/ ↗

Package Documentation

Also check out the information in the following directories for the latest information about NetworkManager and the GNOME applet:

- `/usr/share/doc/packages/NetworkManager/`,
- `/usr/share/doc/packages/NetworkManager-gnome/`.

31 Power Management

Power management is especially important on laptop computers, but is also useful on other systems. ACPI (Advanced Configuration and Power Interface) is available on all modern computers (laptops, desktops, and servers). Power management technologies require suitable hardware and BIOS routines. Most laptops and many modern desktops and servers meet these requirements. It is also possible to control CPU frequency scaling to save power or decrease noise.

31.1 Power Saving Functions

Power saving functions are not only significant for the mobile use of laptops, but also for desktop systems. The main functions and their use in ACPI are:

Standby

not supported.

Suspend (to memory)

This mode writes the entire system state to the RAM. Subsequently, the entire system except the RAM is put to sleep. In this state, the computer consumes very little power. The advantage of this state is the possibility of resuming work at the same point within a few seconds without having to boot and restart applications. This function corresponds to the ACPI state `S3`.

Hibernation (suspend to disk)

In this operating mode, the entire system state is written to the hard disk and the system is powered off. There must be a swap partition at least as big as the RAM to write all the active data. Reactivation from this state takes about 30 to 90 seconds. The state prior to the suspend is restored. Some manufacturers offer useful hybrid variants of this mode, such as RediSafe in IBM Thinkpads. The corresponding ACPI state is `S4`. In Linux, suspend to disk is performed by kernel routines that are independent from ACPI.

Note: Changed UUID for Swap Partitions when Formatting via `mkswap`

Do not reformat existing swap partitions with **`mkswap`** if possible. Reformatting with **`mkswap`** will change the UUID value of the swap partition. Either reformat via YaST (will update `/etc/fstab`) or adjust `/etc/fstab` manually.

Battery Monitor

ACPI checks the battery charge status and provides information about it. Additionally, it coordinates actions to perform when a critical charge status is reached.

Automatic Power-Off

Following a shutdown, the computer is powered off. This is especially important when an automatic shutdown is performed shortly before the battery is empty.

Processor Speed Control

In connection with the CPU, energy can be saved in three different ways: frequency and voltage scaling (also known as PowerNow! or Speedstep), throttling and putting the processor to sleep (C-states). Depending on the operating mode of the computer, these methods can also be combined.

31.2 Advanced Configuration and Power Interface (ACPI)

ACPI was designed to enable the operating system to set up and control the individual hardware components. ACPI supersedes both Power Management Plug and Play (PnP) and Advanced Power Management (APM). It delivers information about the battery, AC adapter, temperature, fan and system events, like "close lid" or "battery low."

The BIOS provides tables containing information about the individual components and hardware access methods. The operating system uses this information for tasks like assigning interrupts or activating and deactivating components. Because the operating system executes commands stored in the BIOS, the functionality depends on the BIOS implementation. The tables ACPI can detect and load are reported in journald. See *Chapter 16, `journalctl`: Query the `systemd` Journal* for more information on viewing the journal log messages. See *Section 31.2.2, "Troubleshooting"* for more information about troubleshooting ACPI problems.

31.2.1 Controlling the CPU Performance

The CPU can save energy in three ways:

- Frequency and Voltage Scaling
- Throttling the Clock Frequency (T-states)
- Putting the Processor to Sleep (C-states)

Depending on the operating mode of the computer, these methods can be combined. Saving energy also means that the system heats up less and the fans are activated less frequently.

Frequency scaling and throttling are only relevant if the processor is busy, because the most economic C-state is applied anyway when the processor is idle. If the CPU is busy, frequency scaling is the recommended power saving method. Often the processor only works with a partial load. In this case, it can be run with a lower frequency. Usually, dynamic frequency scaling controlled by the kernel on-demand governor is the best approach.

Throttling should be used as the last resort, for example, to extend the battery operation time despite a high system load. However, some systems do not run smoothly when they are throttled too much. Moreover, CPU throttling does not make sense if the CPU has little to do.

For in-depth information, refer to *Book* "System Analysis and Tuning Guide", *Chapter 11 "Power Management"*.

31.2.2 Troubleshooting

There are two different types of problems. On one hand, the ACPI code of the kernel may contain bugs that were not detected in time. In this case, a solution will be made available for download. More often, the problems are caused by the BIOS. Sometimes, deviations from the ACPI specification are purposely integrated in the BIOS to circumvent errors in the ACPI implementation of other widespread operating systems. Hardware components that have serious errors in the ACPI implementation are recorded in a blacklist that prevents the Linux kernel from using ACPI for these components.

The first thing to do when problems are encountered is to update the BIOS. If the computer does not boot, one of the following boot parameters may be helpful:

pci=noacpi

Do not use ACPI for configuring the PCI devices.

acpi=ht

Only perform a simple resource configuration. Do not use ACPI for other purposes.

acpi=off

Disable ACPI.

Warning: Problems Booting without ACPI

Some newer machines (especially SMP systems and AMD64 systems) need ACPI for configuring the hardware correctly. On these machines, disabling ACPI can cause problems.

Sometimes, the machine is confused by hardware that is attached over USB or FireWire. If a machine refuses to boot, unplug all unneeded hardware and try again.

Monitor the boot messages of the system with the command **`dmesg -T`** `| grep -2i acpi` (or all messages, because the problem may not be caused by ACPI) after booting. If an error occurs while parsing an ACPI table, the most important table—the DSDT (*Differentiated System Description Table*)—can be replaced with an improved version. In this case, the faulty DSDT of the BIOS is ignored. The procedure is described in *Section 31.4, "Troubleshooting"*.

In the kernel configuration, there is a switch for activating ACPI debug messages. If a kernel with ACPI debugging is compiled and installed, detailed information is issued.

If you experience BIOS or hardware problems, it is always advisable to contact the manufacturers. Especially if they do not always provide assistance for Linux, they should be confronted with the problems. Manufacturers will only take the issue seriously if they realize that an adequate number of their customers use Linux.

31.2.2.1 For More Information

- http://tldp.org/HOWTO/ACPI-HOWTO/ ↗ (detailed ACPI HOWTO, contains DSDT patches)
- http://www.acpi.info ↗ (Advanced Configuration & Power Interface Specification)
- http://acpi.sourceforge.net/dsdt/index.php ↗ (DSDT patches by Bruno Ducrot)

31.3 Rest for the Hard Disk

In Linux, the hard disk can be put to sleep entirely if it is not needed or it can be run in a more economic or quieter mode. On modern laptops, you do not need to switch off the hard disks manually, because they automatically enter an economic operating mode whenever they are not needed. However, if you want to maximize power savings, test some of the following methods, using the **`hdparm`** command.

It can be used to modify various hard disk settings. The option `-y` instantly switches the hard disk to the standby mode. `-Y` puts it to sleep. **`hdparm`** `-S` *`X`* causes the hard disk to be spun down after a certain period of inactivity. Replace *`X`* as follows: `0` disables this mechanism, causing the hard disk to run continuously. Values from `1` to `240` are multiplied by 5 seconds. Values from `241` to `251` correspond to 1 to 11 times 30 minutes.

Internal power saving options of the hard disk can be controlled with the option `-B`. Select a value from `0` to `255` for maximum saving to maximum throughput. The result depends on the hard disk used and is difficult to assess. To make a hard disk quieter, use the option `-M`. Select a value from `128` to `254` for quiet to fast.

Often, it is not so easy to put the hard disk to sleep. In Linux, numerous processes write to the hard disk, waking it up repeatedly. Therefore, it is important to understand how Linux handles data that needs to be written to the hard disk. First, all data is buffered in the RAM. This buffer is monitored by the `pdflush` daemon. When the data reaches a certain age limit or when the buffer is filled to a certain degree, the buffer content is flushed to the hard disk. The buffer size is dynamic and depends on the size of the memory and the system load. By default, pdflush is set to short intervals to achieve maximum data integrity. It checks the buffer every 5 seconds and writes the data to the hard disk. The following variables are interesting:

`/proc/sys/vm/dirty_writeback_centisecs`
: Contains the delay until a pdflush thread wakes up (in hundredths of a second).

`/proc/sys/vm/dirty_expire_centisecs`

Defines after which timeframe a dirty page should be written out latest. Default is `3000`, which means 30 seconds.

`/proc/sys/vm/dirty_background_ratio`

Maximum percentage of dirty pages until pdflush begins to write them. Default is `5` %.

`/proc/sys/vm/dirty_ratio`

When the dirty page exceeds this percentage of the total memory, processes are forced to write dirty buffers during their time slice instead of continuing to write.

Warning: Impairment of the Data Integrity

Changes to the `pdflush` daemon settings endanger the data integrity.

Apart from these processes, journaling file systems, like `Btrfs`, `Ext3`, `Ext4` and others write their metadata independently from `pdflush`, which also prevents the hard disk from spinning down. To avoid this, a special kernel extension has been developed for mobile devices. To use the extension, install the `laptop-mode-tools` package and see `/usr/src/linux/Documentation/laptops/laptop-mode.txt` for details.

Another important factor is the way active programs behave. For example, good editors regularly write hidden backups of the currently modified file to the hard disk, causing the disk to wake up. Features like this can be disabled at the expense of data integrity.

In this connection, the mail daemon postfix uses the variable `POSTFIX_LAPTOP`. If this variable is set to `yes`, postfix accesses the hard disk far less frequently.

In SUSE Linux Enterprise Desktop these technologies are controlled by `laptop-mode-tools`.

31.4 Troubleshooting

All error messages and alerts are logged in the system journal that can be queried with the command **`journalctl`** (see *Chapter 16, `journalctl`: Query the `systemd` Journal* for more information). The following sections cover the most common problems.

31.4.1 CPU Frequency Does Not Work

Refer to the kernel sources to see if your processor is supported. You may need a special kernel module or module option to activate CPU frequency control. If the `kernel-source` package is installed, this information is available in `/usr/src/linux/Documentation/cpu-freq/*`.

31.5 For More Information

- http://en.opensuse.org/SDB:Suspend_to_RAM ↗—How to get Suspend to RAM working
- http://old-en.opensuse.org/Pm-utils ↗—How to modify the general suspend framework

VI Troubleshooting

32 Help and Documentation

SUSE® Linux Enterprise Desktop comes with various sources of information and documentation, many of which are already integrated into your installed system.

Documentation in `/usr/share/doc`

This traditional help directory holds various documentation files and release notes for your system. It contains also information of installed packages in the subdirectory `packages`. Find more detailed information in *Section 32.1, "Documentation Directory"*.

Man Pages and Info Pages for Shell Commands

When working with the shell, you do not need to know the options of the commands by heart. Traditionally, the shell provides integrated help by means of man pages and info pages. Read more in *Section 32.2, "Man Pages"* and *Section 32.3, "Info Pages"*.

Desktop Help Center

The help center of the GNOME desktop (Help) provides central access to the most important documentation resources on your system in searchable form. These resources include online help for installed applications, man pages, info pages, and the SUSE manuals delivered with your product.

Separate Help Packages for Some Applications

When installing new software with YaST, the software documentation is usually installed automatically and appears in the help center of your desktop. However, some applications, such as GIMP, may have different online help packages that can be installed separately with YaST and do not integrate into the help centers.

32.1 Documentation Directory

The traditional directory to find documentation on your installed Linux system is `/usr/share/doc`. Usually, the directory contains information about the packages installed on your system, plus release notes, manuals, and more.

Note: Contents Depends on Installed Packages

In the Linux world, many manuals and other kinds of documentation are available in the form of packages, like software. How much and which information you find in `/usr/share/docs` also depends on the (documentation) packages installed. If you cannot find the subdirectories mentioned here, check if the respective packages are installed on your system and add them with YaST, if needed.

32.1.1 SUSE Manuals

We provide HTML and PDF versions of our books in different languages. In the `manual` subdirectory, find HTML versions of most of the SUSE manuals available for your product. For an overview of all documentation available for your product refer to the preface of the manuals.

If more than one language is installed, `/usr/share/doc/manual` may contain different language versions of the manuals. The HTML versions of the SUSE manuals are also available in the help center of both desktops. For information on where to find the PDF and HTML versions of the books on your installation media, refer to the SUSE Linux Enterprise Desktop Release Notes. They are available on your installed system under `/usr/share/doc/release-notes/` or online at your product-specific Web page at http://www.suse.com/releasenotes// ↗.

32.1.2 Package Documentation

Under `packages`, find the documentation that is included in the software packages installed on your system. For every package, a subdirectory `/usr/share/doc/packages/PACKAGENAME` is created. It often contains README files for the package and sometimes examples, configuration files, or additional scripts. The following list introduces typical files to be found under `/usr/share/doc/packages`. None of these entries are mandatory and many packages might only include a few of them.

`AUTHORS`

List of the main developers.

`BUGS`

Known bugs or malfunctions. Might also contain a link to a Bugzilla Web page where you can search all bugs.

`CHANGES` ,
`ChangeLog`
: Summary of changes from version to version. Usually interesting for developers, because it is very detailed.

`COPYING` ,
`LICENSE`
: Licensing information.

`FAQ`
: Question and answers collected from mailing lists or newsgroups.

`INSTALL`
: How to install this package on your system. As the package is already installed by the time you get to read this file, you can safely ignore the contents of this file.

`README`, `README.*`
: General information on the software. For example, for what purpose and how to use it.

`TODO`
: Things that are not implemented yet, but probably will be in the future.

`MANIFEST`
: List of files with a brief summary.

`NEWS`
: Description of what is new in this version.

32.2 Man Pages

Man pages are an essential part of any Linux system. They explain the usage of a command and all available options and parameters. Man pages can be accessed with **`man`** followed by the name of the command, for example, **`man ls`**.

Man pages are displayed directly in the shell. To navigate them, move up and down with Page ↑ and Page ↓. Move between the beginning and the end of a document with Home and End. End this viewing mode by pressing Q. Learn more about the **`man`** command itself with **`man man`**. Man pages are sorted in categories as shown in *Table 32.1, "Man Pages—Categories and Descriptions"* (taken from the man page for man itself).

TABLE 32.1: MAN PAGES—CATEGORIES AND DESCRIPTIONS

Number	Description
1	Executable programs or shell commands
2	System calls (functions provided by the kernel)
3	Library calls (functions within program libraries)
4	Special files (usually found in `/dev`)
5	File formats and conventions (`/etc/fstab`)
6	Games
7	Miscellaneous (including macro packages and conventions), for example, man(7), groff(7)
8	System administration commands (usually only for `root`)
9	Kernel routines (nonstandard)

Each man page consists of several parts labeled *NAME* , *SYNOPSIS* , *DESCRIPTION* , *SEE ALSO* , *LICENSING* , and *AUTHOR* . There may be additional sections available depending on the type of command.

32.3 Info Pages

Info pages are another important source of information on your system. Usually, they are more detailed than man pages. They consist of more than command line options and contain sometimes whole tutorials or reference documentation. To view the info page for a certain command, enter **`info`** followed by the name of the command, for example, **`info ls`**. You can browse an info page with a viewer directly in the shell and display the different sections, called “nodes”. Use `Space` to move forward and `<-` to move backward. Within a node, you can also browse with Page ↑ and Page ↓ but only Space and <– will take you also to the previous or subsequent node. Press Q to end the viewing mode. Not every command comes with an info page and vice versa.

32.4 Online Resources

In addition to the online versions of the SUSE manuals installed under `/usr/share/doc`, you can also access the product-specific manuals and documentation on the Web. For an overview of all documentation available for SUSE Linux Enterprise Desktop check out your product-specific documentation Web page at http://www.suse.com/doc/ ↗.

If you are searching for additional product-related information, you can also refer to the following Web sites:

SUSE Technical Support

The SUSE Technical Support can be found at http://www.suse.com/support/ ↗ if you have questions or need solutions for technical problems.

SUSE Forums

There are several forums where you can dive in on discussions about SUSE products. See http://forums.suse.com/ ↗ for a list.

SUSE Conversations

An online community, which offers articles, tips, Q and A, and free tools to download: http://www.suse.com/communities/conversations/ ↗

GNOME Documentation

Documentation for GNOME users, administrators and developers is available at http://library.gnome.org/ ↗.

The Linux Documentation Project

The Linux Documentation Project (TLDP) is run by a team of volunteers who write Linux-related documentation (see http://www.tldp.org ↗). It is probably the most comprehensive documentation resource for Linux. The set of documents contains tutorials for beginners, but is mainly focused on experienced users and professional system administrators. TLDP publishes HOWTOs, FAQs, and guides (handbooks) under a free license. Parts of the documentation from TLDP are also available on SUSE Linux Enterprise Desktop.

You can also try general-purpose search engines. For example, use the search terms `Linux CD-RW help` or `OpenOffice file conversion problem` if you have trouble with burning CDs or LibreOffice file conversion.

33 Gathering System Information for Support

For a quick overview of all relevant system information of a machine, SUSE Linux Enterprise Desktop offers the `hostinfo` package. It also helps system administrators to check for tainted kernels (that are not supported) or any third-party packages installed on a machine.

In case of problems, a detailed system report may be created with either the **`supportconfig`** command line tool or the YaST *Support* module. Both will collect information about the system such as: current kernel version, hardware, installed packages, partition setup, and much more. The result is a TAR archive of files. After opening a Service Request (SR), you can upload the TAR archive to Global Technical Support. It will help to locate the issue you reported and to assist you in solving the problem.

Additionally, you can analyze the **`supportconfig`** output for known issues to help resolve problems faster. For this purpose, SUSE Linux Enterprise Desktop provides both an appliance and a command line tool for `Supportconfig Analysis` (SCA).

33.1 Displaying Current System Information

For a quick and easy overview of all relevant system information when logging in to a server, use the package `hostinfo`. After it has been installed on a machine, the console displays the following information to any `root` user that logs in to this machine:

EXAMPLE 33.1: OUTPUT OF `hostinfo` WHEN LOGGING IN AS `root`

```
Hostname:               earth
Current As Of:          Wed 12 Mar 2014 03:57:05 PM CET
Distribution:           SUSE Linux Enterprise Server 12
 -Service Pack:         0
Architecture:           x86_64
Kernel Version:         3.12.12-3-default
 -Installed:            Mon 10 Mar 2014 03:15:05 PM CET
 -Status:               Not Tainted
Last Updated Package:   Wed 12 Mar 2014 03:56:43 PM CET
 -Patches Needed:       0
```

```
 -Security:                0
 -3rd Party Packages:      0
IPv4 Address:              ens3 192.168.1.1
Total/Free/+Cache Memory:  983/95/383 MB (38% Free)
Hard Disk:                 /dev/sda 10 GB
```

In case the output shows a `tainted` kernel status, see *Section 33.6, "Support of Kernel Modules"* for more details.

33.2 Collecting System Information with Supportconfig

To create a TAR archive with detailed system information that you can hand over to Global Technical Support, use either the **`supportconfig`** command line tool directly or the YaST *Support* module. The command line tool is provided by the package `supportutils` which is installed by default. The YaST *Support* module is also based on the command line tool.

33.2.1 Creating a Service Request Number

Supportconfig archives can be generated at any time. However, for handing over the supportconfig data to Global Technical Support, you need to generate a service request number first. You will need it to upload the archive to support.

To create a service request, go to https://scc.suse.com/support/requests and follow the instructions on the screen. Write down your 12-digit service request number.

Note: Privacy Statement

SUSE and Micro Focus treat system reports as confidential data. For details about our privacy commitment, see https://www.suse.com/company/policies/privacy/ .

33.2.2 Upload Targets

After having created a service request number, you can upload your supportconfig archives to Global Technical Support as described in *Procedure 33.1, "Submitting Information to Support with YaST"* or *Procedure 33.2, "Submitting Information to Support from Command Line"*. Use one of the following upload targets:

- US customers: ftp://ftp.novell.com/incoming ↗
- EMEA, Europe, the Middle East, and Africa: ftp://support-ftp.suse.com/in ↗

Alternatively, you can manually attach the TAR archive to your service request using the service request URL: https://scc.suse.com/support/requests ↗.

33.2.3 Creating a Supportconfig Archive with YaST

To use YaST to gather your system information, proceed as follows:

1. Start YaST and open the *Support* module.

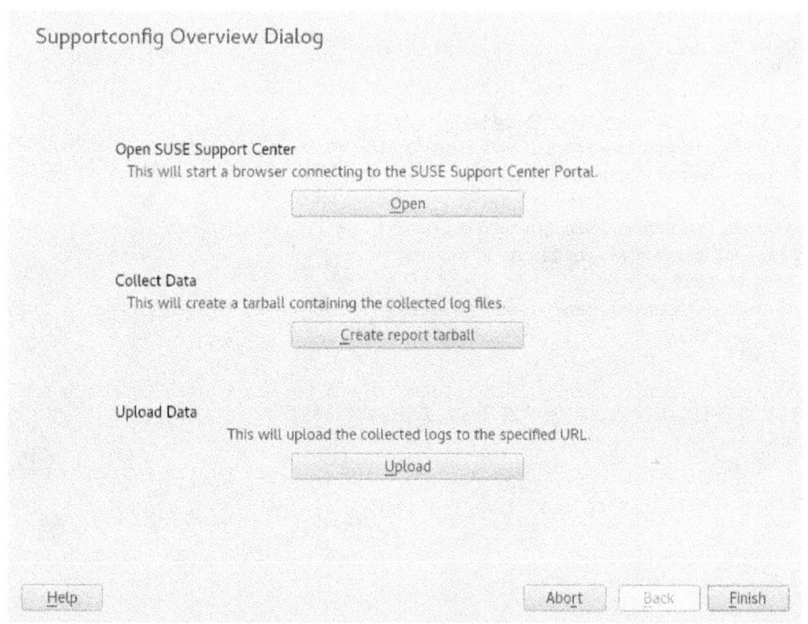

2. Click *Create report tarball.*

3. In the next window, select one of the supportconfig options from the radio button list. *Use Custom (Expert) Settings* is preselected by default. If you want to test the report function first, use *Only gather a minimum amount of info*. For some background information on the other options, refer to the **`supportconfig`** man page.
   Proceed with *Next*.
4. Enter your contact information. It will be written to a file called `basic-environment.txt` and included in the archive to be created.
5. If you want to submit the archive to Global Technical Support at the end of the information collection process, *Upload Information* is required. YaST automatically proposes an upload server. If you want to modify it, refer to Section 33.2.2, "Upload Targets" for details of which upload servers are available.
   If you want to submit the archive later on, you can leave the *Upload Information* empty for now.
6. Proceed with *Next*.
7. The information gathering begins.

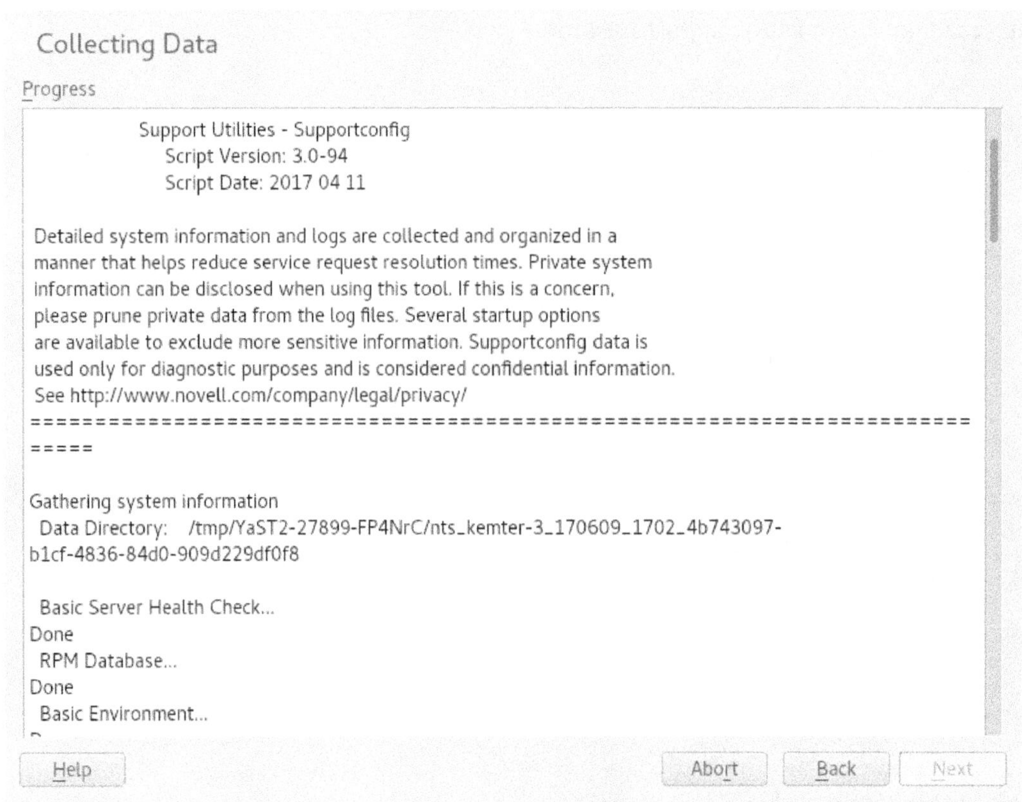

After the process is finished, continue with *Next*.

8. Review the data collection: Select the *File Name* of a log file to view its contents in YaST. To remove any files you want excluded from the TAR archive before submitting it to support, use *Remove from Data*. Continue with *Next*.

9. Save the TAR archive. If you started the YaST module as `root` user, by default YaST proposes to save the archive to `/var/log` (otherwise, to your home directory). The file name format is `nts_HOST_DATE_TIME.tbz`.

10. If you want to upload the archive to support directly, make sure *Upload log files tarball to URL* is activated. The *Upload Target* shown here is the one that YaST proposes in Step 5. If you want to modify the upload target, find detailed information of which upload servers are available in Section 33.2.2, "Upload Targets".

11. If you want to skip the upload, deactivate *Upload log files tarball to URL*.

12. Confirm your changes to close the YaST module.

33.2.4 Creating a Supportconfig Archive from Command Line

The following procedure shows how to create a supportconfig archive, but without submitting it to support directly. For uploading it, you need to run the command with certain options as described in Procedure 33.2, "Submitting Information to Support from Command Line".

1. Open a shell and become `root`.

2. Run **`supportconfig`** without any options. This gathers the default system information.

3. Wait for the tool to complete the operation.

4. The default archive location is `/var/log`, with the file name format being `nts_HOST_DATE_TIME.tbz`

33.2.5 Common Supportconfig Options

The **supportconfig** utility is usually called without any options. Display a list of all options with **supportconfig** `-h` or refer to the man page. The following list gives a brief overview of some common use cases:

Reducing the Size of the Information Being Gathered

Use the minimal option (`-m`):

```
supportconfig -m
```

Limiting the Information to a Specific Topic

If you have already localized a problem with the default **supportconfig** output and have found that it relates to a specific area or feature set only, you should limit the collected information to the specific area for the next **supportconfig** run. For example, if you detected problems with LVM and want to test a recent change that you did to the LVM configuration, it makes sense to gather the minimum supportconfig information around LVM only:

```
supportconfig -i LVM
```

For a complete list of feature keywords that you can use for limiting the collected information to a specific area, run

```
supportconfig -F
```

Including Additional Contact Information in the Output:

```
supportconfig -E tux@example.org -N "Tux Penguin" -O "Penguin Inc." ...
```

(all in one line)

Collecting Already Rotated Log Files

```
supportconfig -l
```

This is especially useful in high logging environments or after a kernel crash when syslog rotates the log files after a reboot.

33.3 Submitting Information to Global Technical Support

Use the YaST *Support* module or the **`supportconfig`** command line utility to submit system information to the Global Technical Support. When you experience a server issue and want the support's assistance, you will need to open a service request first. For details, see *Section 33.2.1, "Creating a Service Request Number"*.

The following examples use *`12345678901`* as a placeholder for your service request number. Replace *`12345678901`* with the service request number you created in *Section 33.2.1, "Creating a Service Request Number"*.

PROCEDURE 33.1: SUBMITTING INFORMATION TO SUPPORT WITH YAST

The following procedure assumes that you have already created a supportconfig archive, but have not uploaded it yet. Make sure to have included your contact information in the archive as described in *Section 33.2.3, "Creating a Supportconfig Archive with YaST", Step 4*. For instructions on how to generate and submit a supportconfig archive in one go, see *Section 33.2.3, "Creating a Supportconfig Archive with YaST"*.

1. Start YaST and open the *Support* module.
2. Click *Upload*.
3. In *Package with log files* specify the path to the existing supportconfig archive or *Browse* for it.
4. YaST automatically proposes an upload server. If you want to modify it, refer to *Section 33.2.2, "Upload Targets"* for details of which upload servers are available.

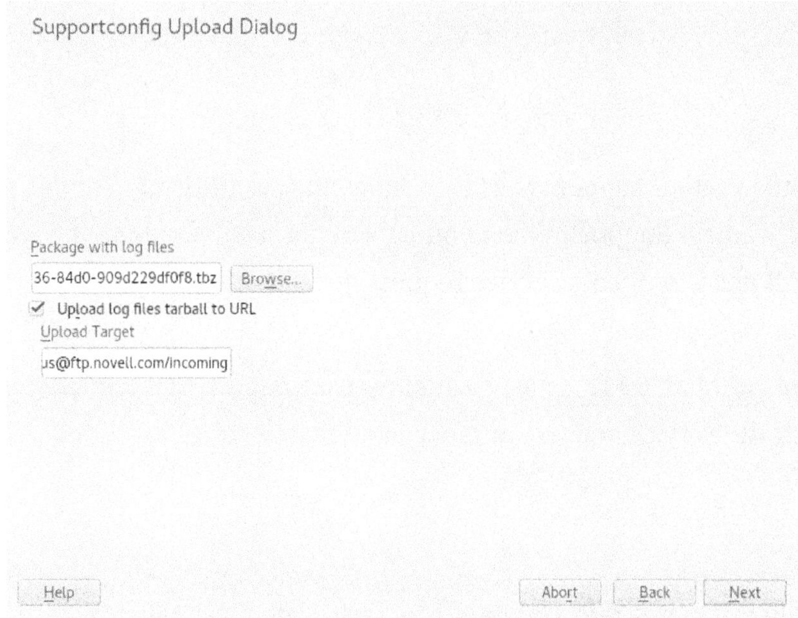

Proceed with *Next*.

5. Click *Finish*.

PROCEDURE 33.2: SUBMITTING INFORMATION TO SUPPORT FROM COMMAND LINE

The following procedure assumes that you have already created a supportconfig archive, but have not uploaded it yet. For instructions on how to generate and submit a supportconfig archive in one go, see *Section 33.2.3, "Creating a Supportconfig Archive with YaST"*.

1. Servers with Internet connectivity:

   a. To use the default upload target, run:

   ```
   supportconfig -ur 12345678901
   ```

   b. For the secure upload target, use the following:

   ```
   supportconfig -ar 12345678901
   ```

2. Servers *without* Internet connectivity

   a. Run the following:

   ```
   supportconfig -r 12345678901
   ```

b. Manually upload the `/var/log/nts_SR12345678901*tbz` archive to one of our FTP servers. Which one to use depends on your location in the world. For an overview, see Section 33.2.2, "Upload Targets".

3. After the TAR archive arrives in the incoming directory of our FTP server, it becomes automatically attached to your service request.

33.4 Analyzing System Information

System reports created with **`supportconfig`** can be analyzed for known issues to help resolve problems faster. For this purpose, SUSE Linux Enterprise Desktop provides both an appliance and a command line tool for `Supportconfig Analysis` (SCA). The SCA appliance is a server-side tool which is non-interactive. The SCA tool (**`scatool`**) runs on the client-side and is executed from command line. Both tools analyze supportconfig archives from affected servers. The initial server analysis takes place on the SCA appliance or the workstation on which scatool is running. No analysis cycles happen on the production server.

Both the appliance and the command line tool additionally need product-specific patterns that enable them to analyze the supportconfig output for the associated products. Each pattern is a script that parses and evaluates a supportconfig archive for one known issue. The patterns are available as RPM packages.

For example, if you want to analyze supportconfig archives that have been generated on a SUSE Linux Enterprise 11 machine, you need to install the package `sca-patterns-sle11` together with the SCA tool (or on the machine that you want to use as the SCA appliance server). To analyze supportconfig archives generated on a SUSE Linux Enterprise 10 machine, you need the package `sca-patterns-sle10`.

You can also develop your own patterns as briefly described in Section 33.4.3, "Developing Custom Analysis Patterns".

33.4.1 SCA Command Line Tool

The SCA command line tool lets you analyze a local machine using both **`supportconfig`** and the analysis patterns for the specific product that is installed on the local machine. The tool creates an HTML report showing its analysis results. For an example, see Figure 33.1, "HTML Report Generated by SCA Tool".

Supportconfig Analysis Report

Server Information

Analysis Date:	/4/25/2014 11:22
Archive File:	/var/log/nts_barett-2_140425_1119.html

Server Name:	barett-2	**Hardware:**	Bochs
Distribution:	SUSE Linux Enterprise Server 12 (x86_64)	**Service Pack:**	0
Hypervisor:	KVM (QEMU Virtual CPU)	**Identity:**	Virtual Machine (QEMU Virtual CPU)
Kernel Version:	3.12.14-1-default	**Supportconfig Version:**	3.0-18

Conditions Evaluated as Critical

Category			Message	Solutions
Basic Health			2 Basic Health Message(s)	
Basic Health	SLE	Kernel	Kernel Status -- Tainted: F O	TID
Basic Health	SLE	System	Last system down was not clean on Mon Mar 24 17:37:04 2014 and 1 additional failure(s)	TID TID1
SLE			2 SLE Message(s)	

Conditions Evaluated as Warning

Category			Message	Solutions
SLE			1 SLE Message(s)	

Conditions Evaluated as Recommended

Category			Message	Solutions
SLE			1 SLE Message(s)	

Conditions Evaluated as Success

Category			Message	Solutions
Security			1 Security Message(s)	
Security	SLE	AppArmor	There are no AppArmor reject messages	TID Doc
Basic Health			8 Basic Health Message(s)	
Basic Health	SLE	Kernel	Context switches per second observed: 79	TID
Basic Health	SLE	Kernel	Interrupts per second observed: 51	TID
Basic Health	SLE	CPU	Utilization: 1.00%, Idle: 99.00%	TID
Basic Health	SLE	Disk	Mount on / has highest used space: 22%	TID TID2
Basic Health	SLE	Kernel	2% CPU load within limits, CPUs: 1, Load Average: 0.02	TID Web Wikipedia
Basic Health	SLE	Memory	Memory used 29% - Swapping: No	TID
Basic Health	SLE	Processes	0 Uninterruptible processes observed	TID
Basic Health	SLE	Processes	0 Zombie processes observed	TID

FIGURE 33.1: HTML REPORT GENERATED BY SCA TOOL

The **scatool** command is provided by the sca-server-report package. It is not installed by default. Additionally, you need the sca-patterns-base package and any of the product-specific sca-patterns-* packages that matches the product installed on the machine where you want to run the **scatool** command.

Execute the **scatool** command either as root user or with **sudo**. When calling the SCA tool, you can either analyze an existing **supportconfig** TAR archive or you can let it generate and analyze a new archive in one go. The tool also provides an interactive console (with tab completion) and the possibility to run **supportconfig** on an external machine and to execute the subsequent analysis on the local machine.

Find some example commands below:

sudo scatool -s

Calls **supportconfig** and generates a new supportconfig archive on the local machine. Analyzes the archive for known issues by applying the SCA analysis patterns that match the installed product. Displays the path to the HTML report that is generated from the results of the analysis. It is usually written to the same directory where the supportconfig archive can be found.

sudo scatool -s -o */opt/sca/reports/*

Same as **sudo scatool** -s, only that the HTML report is written to the path specified with -o.

sudo scatool -a *PATH_TO_TARBALL_OR_DIR*

Analyzes the specified supportconfig archive file (or the specified directory to where the supportconfig archive has been extracted). The generated HTML report is saved in the same location as the supportconfig archive or directory.

sudo scatool -a *SLES_SERVER.COMPANY.COM*

Establishes an SSH connection to an external server *SLES_SERVER.COMPANY.COM* and runs **supportconfig** on the server. The supportconfig archive is then copied back to the local machine and is analyzed there. The generated HTML report is saved to the default /var/log directory. (Only the supportconfig archive is created on *SLES_SERVER.COMPANY.COM*).

sudo scatool -c

Starts the interactive console for **scatool**. Press →| twice to see the available commands.

For further options and information, run **sudo scatool -h** or see the **scatool** man page.

33.4.2 SCA Appliance

If you decide to use the SCA appliance for analyzing the supportconfig archives, you need to configure a dedicated server (or virtual machine) as the SCA appliance server. The SCA appliance server can then be used to analyze supportconfig archives from all machines in your enterprise running SUSE Linux Enterprise Server or SUSE Linux Enterprise Desktop. You can simply upload supportconfig archives to the appliance server for analysis. Interaction is not required. In a MariaDB database, the SCA appliance keeps track of all supportconfig archives that have been analyzed . You can read the SCA reports directly from the appliance Web interface. Alternatively, you can have the appliance send the HTML report to any administrative user via e-mail. For details, see Section 33.4.2.5.4, "Sending SCA Reports via E-Mail".

33.4.2.1 Installation Quick Start

To install and set up the SCA appliance in a very fast way from the command line, follow the instructions here. The procedure is intended for experts and focuses on the bare installation and setup commands. For more information, refer to the more detailed description in Section 33.4.2.2, "Prerequisites" to Section 33.4.2.3, "Installation and Basic Setup".

PREREQUISITES

- Web and LAMP Pattern
- Web and Scripting Module (you must register the machine to be able to select this module).

Note: `root` Privileges Required

All commands in the following procedure must be run as `root`.

PROCEDURE 33.3: INSTALLATION USING ANONYMOUS FTP FOR UPLOAD

After the appliance is set up and running, no more manual interaction is required. This way of setting up the appliance is therefore ideal for using cron jobs to create and upload supportconfig archives.

1. On the machine on which to install the appliance, log in to a console and execute the following commands:

```
zypper install sca-appliance-* sca-patterns-* vsftpd
systemctl enable apache2
systemctl start apache2
systemctl enable vsftpd
systemctl start vsftpd
yast ftp-server
```

2. In YaST FTP Server, select *Authentication* › *Enable Upload* › *Anonymous Can Upload* › *Finish* › *Yes* to *Create /srv/ftp/upload.*

3. Execute the following commands:

```
systemctl enable mysql
```

```
systemctl start mysql
mysql_secure_installation
setup-sca -f
```

The mysql_secure_installation will create a MariaDB `root` password.

PROCEDURE 33.4: INSTALLATION USING SCP/TMP FOR UPLOAD

This way of setting up the appliance requires manual interaction when typing the SSH password.

1. On the machine on which to install the appliance, log in to a console.
2. Execute the following commands:

```
zypper install sca-appliance-* sca-patterns-*
systemctl enable apache2
systemctl start apache2
sudo systemctl enable mysql
systemctl start mysql
mysql_secure_installation
setup-sca
```

33.4.2.2 Prerequisites

To run an SCA appliance server, you need the following prerequisites:

- All `sca-appliance-*` packages.
- The `sca-patterns-base` package. Additionally, any of the product-specific `sca-patterns-*` for the type of supportconfig archives that you want to analyze with the appliance.
- Apache
- PHP
- MariaDB
- anonymous FTP server (optional)

33.4.2.3 Installation and Basic Setup

As listed in *Section 33.4.2.2, "Prerequisites"*, the SCA appliance has several dependencies on other packages. Therefore you need do so some preparations before installing and setting up the SCA appliance server:

1. For Apache and MariaDB, install the `Web` and `LAMP` installation patterns.
2. Set up Apache, MariaDB, and optionally an anonymous FTP server.
3. Configure Apache and MariaDB to start at boot time:

```
sudo systemctl enable apache2 mysql
```

4. Start both services:

```
sudo systemctl start apache2 mysql
```

Now you can install the SCA appliance and set it up as described in *Procedure 33.5, "Installing and Configuring the SCA Appliance"*.

PROCEDURE 33.5: INSTALLING AND CONFIGURING THE SCA APPLIANCE

After installing the packages, use the **`setup-sca`** script for the basic configuration of the MariaDB administration and report database that is used by the SCA appliance.

It can be used to configure the following options you have for uploading the supportconfig archives from your machines to the SCA appliance:

- **`scp`**
- anonymous FTP server

1. Install the appliance and the SCA base-pattern library:

```
sudo zypper install sca-appliance-* sca-patterns-base
```

2. Additionally, install the pattern packages for the types of supportconfig archives you want to analyze. For example, if you have SUSE Linux Enterprise Server 11 and SUSE Linux Enterprise Server 12 servers in your environment, install both the `sca-patterns-sle11` and `sca-patterns-sle12` packages.
   To install all available patterns:

```
zypper install sca-patterns-*
```

3. For basic setup of the SCA appliance, use the `setup-sca` script. How to call it depends on how you want to upload the supportconfig archives to the SCA appliance server:

   - If you have configured an anonymous FTP server that uses the `/srv/ftp/upload` directory, execute the setup script with the `-f` option and follow the instructions on the screen:

     ```
     setup-sca -f
     ```

     ### Note: FTP Server Using Another Directory

     If your FTP server uses another directory than `/srv/ftp/upload`, adjust the following configuration files first to make them point to the correct directory: `/etc/sca/sdagent.conf` and `/etc/sca/sdbroker.conf` .

   - If you want to upload supportconfig files to the `/tmp` directory of the SCA appliance server via **`scp`**, call the setup script without any parameters and follow the instructions on the screen:

     ```
     setup-sca
     ```

   The setup script runs a few checks regarding its requirements and configures the needed components. It will prompt you for two passwords: the MySQL `root` password of the MariaDB that you have set up, and a Web user password with which to log in to the Web interface of the SCA appliance.

4. Enter the existing MariaDB `root` password. It will allow the SCA appliance to connect to the MariaDB.

5. Define a password for the Web user. It will be written to `/srv/www/htdocs/sca/web-config.php` and will be set as the password for the user `scdiag`. Both user name and password can be changed at any time later, see *Section 33.4.2.5.1, "Password for the Web Interface"*.

After successful installation and setup, the SCA appliance is ready for use, see *Section 33.4.2.4, "Using the SCA Appliance"*. However, you should modify some options such as changing the password for the Web interface, changing the source for the SCA pattern updates, enabling archiving mode or configuring e-mail notifications. For details on that, see *Section 33.4.2.5, "Customizing the SCA Appliance"*.

Warning: Data Protection

As the reports on the SCA appliance server contain security-relevant information of the machines whose supportconfig archives have been analyzed, make sure to protect the data on the SCA appliance server against unauthorized access.

33.4.2.4 Using the SCA Appliance

You can upload existing supportconfig archives to the SCA appliance manually or create new supportconfig archives and upload them to the SCA appliance in one step. Uploading can be done via FTP or SCP. For both, you need to know the URL where the SCA appliance can be reached. For upload via FTP, an FTP server needs to be configured for the SCA appliance, see *Procedure 33.5, "Installing and Configuring the SCA Appliance"*.

33.4.2.4.1 Uploading Supportconfig Archives to the SCA Appliance

- For creating a supportconfig archive and uploading it via (anonymous) FTP:

  ```
  sudo supportconfig -U "ftp://SCA-APPLIANCE.COMPANY.COM/upload"
  ```

- For creating a supportconfig archive and uploading it via SCP:

  ```
  sudo supportconfig -U "scp://SCA-APPLIANCE.COMPANY.COM/tmp"
  ```

  You will be prompted for the `root` user password of the server running the SCA appliance.

- If you want to manually upload one or multiple archives, copy the existing archive files (usually located at `/var/log/nts_*.tbz`) to the SCA appliance. As target, use either the appliance server's `/tmp` directory or the `/srv/ftp/upload` directory (if FTP is configured for the SCA appliance server).

33.4.2.4.2 Viewing SCA Reports

SCA reports can be viewed from any machine that has a browser installed and can access the report index page of the SCA appliance.

1. Start a Web browser and make sure that JavaScript and cookies are enabled.

2. As a URL, enter the report index page of the SCA appliance.

```
https://sca-appliance.company.com/sca
```

If in doubt, ask your system administrator.

3. You will be prompted for a user name and a password to log in.

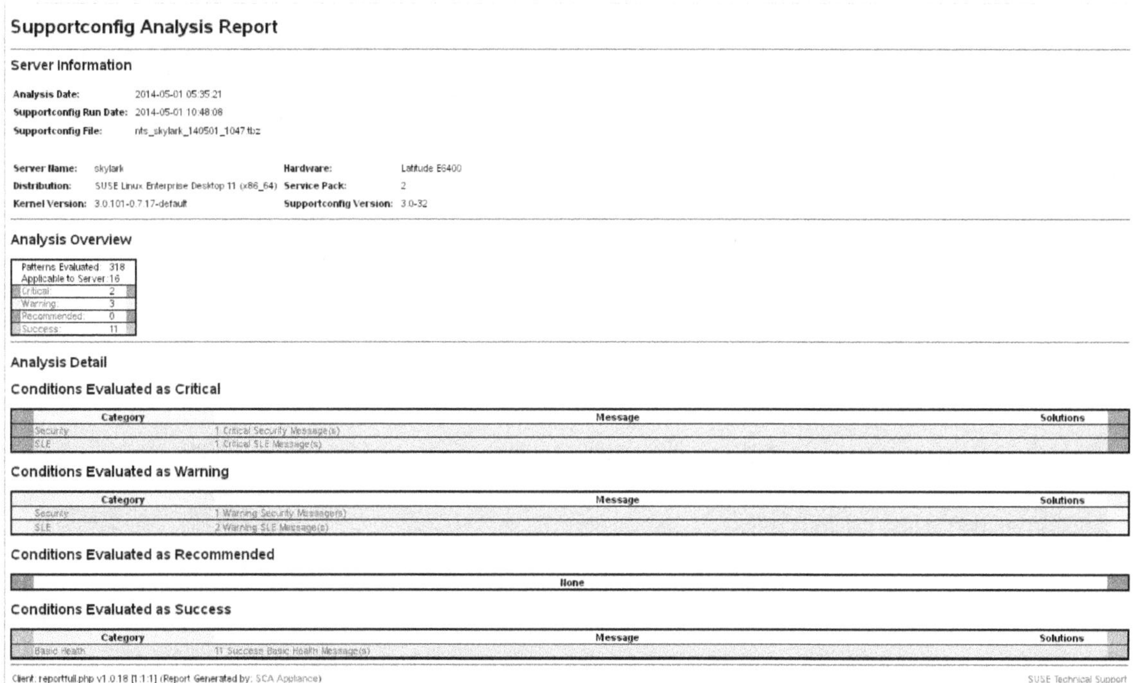

FIGURE 33.2: HTML REPORT GENERATED BY SCA APPLIANCE

4. After logging in, click the date of the report you want to read.

5. Click the *Basic Health* category first to expand it.

6. In the *Message* column, click an individual entry. This opens the corresponding article in the SUSE Knowledgebase. Read the proposed solution and follow the instructions.

7. If the *Solutions* column of the *Supportconfig Analysis Report* shows any additional entries, click them. Read the proposed solution and follow the instructions.

8. Check the SUSE Knowledgebase (http://www.suse.com/support/kb/ ↗) for results that directly relate to the problem identified by SCA. Work at resolving them.

9. Check for results that can be addressed proactively to avoid future problems.

33.4.2.5 Customizing the SCA Appliance

The following sections show how to change the password for the Web interface, how to change the source for the SCA pattern updates, how to enable archiving mode, and how to configure e-mail notifications.

33.4.2.5.1 Password for the Web Interface

The SCA Appliance Web interface requires a user name and password for logging in. The default user name is `scdiag` and the default password is `linux` (if not specified otherwise, see *Procedure 33.5, "Installing and Configuring the SCA Appliance"*). Change the default password to a secure password at the earliest possibility. You can also modify the user name.

PROCEDURE 33.6: CHANGING USER NAME OR PASSWORD FOR THE WEB INTERFACE

1. Log in as `root` user at the system console of the SCA appliance server.
2. Open `/srv/www/htdocs/sca/web-config.php` in an editor.
3. Change the values of `$username` and `$password` as desired.
4. Save the file and exit.

33.4.2.5.2 Updates of SCA Patterns

By default, all `sca-patterns-*` packages are updated regularly by a `root` cron job that executes the `sdagent-patterns` script nightly, which in turn runs **`zypper update sca-patterns-*`**. A regular system update will update all SCA appliance and pattern packages. To update the SCA appliance and patterns manually, run:

```
sudo zypper update sca-*
```

The updates are installed from the SUSE Linux Enterprise 12 SP3 update repository by default. You can change the source for the updates to an SMT server, if desired. When `sdagent-patterns` runs **`zypper update sca-patterns-*`**, it gets the updates from the currently configured update channel. If that channel is located on an SMT server, the packages will be pulled from there.

PROCEDURE 33.7: DISABLING AUTOMATIC UPDATES OF SCA PATTERNS

1. Log in as `root` user at the system console of the SCA appliance server.

2. Open `/etc/sca/sdagent-patterns.conf` in an editor.
3. Change the entry

```
UPDATE_FROM_PATTERN_REPO=1
```

to

```
UPDATE_FROM_PATTERN_REPO=0
```

4. Save the file and exit. The machine does not require any restart to apply the change.

33.4.2.5.3 Archiving Mode

All supportconfig archives are deleted from the SCA appliance after they have been analyzed and their results have been stored in the MariaDB database. However, for troubleshooting purposes it can be useful to keep copies of supportconfig archives from a machine. By default, archiving mode is disabled.

PROCEDURE 33.8: ENABLING ARCHIVING MODE IN THE SCA APPLIANCE

1. Log in as `root` user at the system console of the SCA appliance server.
2. Open `/etc/sca/sdagent.conf` in an editor.
3. Change the entry

```
ARCHIVE_MODE=0
```

to

```
ARCHIVE_MODE=1
```

4. Save the file and exit. The machine does not require any restart to apply the change.

After having enabled archive mode, the SCA appliance will save the supportconfig files to the `/var/log/archives/saved` directory, instead of deleting them.

33.4.2.5.4 Sending SCA Reports via E-Mail

The SCA appliance can e-mail a report HTML file for each supportconfig analyzed. This feature is disabled by default. When enabling it, you can define a list of e-mail addresses to which the reports should be sent, and define a level of status messages that trigger the sending of reports (`STATUS_NOTIFY_LEVEL`).

POSSIBLE VALUES FOR `STATUS_NOTIFY_LEVEL`

$STATUS_OFF

Deactivate sending of HTML reports.

$STATUS_CRITICAL

Send only SCA reports that include a CRITICAL.

$STATUS_WARNING

Send only SCA reports that include a WARNING or CRITICAL.

$STATUS_RECOMMEND

Send only SCA reports that include a RECOMMEND, WARNING or CRITICAL.

$STATUS_SUCCESS

Send SCA reports that include a SUCCESS, RECOMMEND, WARNING or CRITICAL.

PROCEDURE 33.9: CONFIGURING E-MAIL NOTIFICATIONS FOR SCA REPORTS

1. Log in as `root` user at the system console of the SCA appliance server.
2. Open `/etc/sca/sdagent.conf` in an editor.
3. Search for the entry `STATUS_NOTIFY_LEVEL`. By default, it is set to `$STATUS_OFF` (e-mail notifications are disabled).
4. To enable e-mail notifications, change `$STATUS_OFF` to the level of status messages that you want to have e-mail reports for, for example:

   ```
   STATUS_NOTIFY_LEVEL=$STATUS_SUCCESS
   ```

   For details, see *Possible Values for* `STATUS_NOTIFY_LEVEL`.
5. To define the list of recipients to which the reports should be sent:
   a. Search for the entry `EMAIL_REPORT='root'`.

b. Replace `root` with a list of e-mail addresses to which SCA reports should be sent. The e-mail addresses must be separated by spaces. For example:

```
EMAIL_REPORT='tux@my.company.com wilber@your.company.com'
```

6. Save the file and exit. The machine does not require any restart to apply the changes. All future SCA reports will be e-mailed to the specified addresses.

33.4.2.6 Backing Up and Restoring the Database

To back up and restore the MariaDB database that stores the SCA reports, use the **`scadb`** command as described below.

PROCEDURE 33.10: BACKING UP THE DATABASE

1. Log in as `root` user at the system console of the server running the SCA appliance.
2. Put the appliance into maintenance mode by executing:

```
scadb maint
```

3. Start the backup with:

```
scadb backup
```

The data is saved to a TAR archive: `sca-backup-*sql.gz`.

4. If you are using the pattern creation database to develop your own patterns (see *Section 33.4.3, "Developing Custom Analysis Patterns"*), back up this data, too:

```
sdpdb backup
```

The data is saved to a TAR archive: `sdp-backup-*sql.gz`.

5. Copy the following data to another machine or an external storage medium:

- `sca-backup-*sql.gz`
- `sdp-backup-*sql.gz`
- `/usr/lib/sca/patterns/local` (only needed if you have created custom patterns)

6. Reactivate the SCA appliance with:

```
scadb reset agents
```

PROCEDURE 33.11: RESTORING THE DATABASE

To restore the database from your backup, proceed as follows:

1. Log in as `root` user at the system console of the server running the SCA appliance.
2. Copy the newest `sca-backup-*sql.gz` and `sdp-backup-*sql.gz` TAR archives to the SCA appliance server.
3. To decompress the files, run:

```
gzip -d *-backup-*sql.gz
```

4. To import the data into the database, execute:

```
scadb import sca-backup-*sql
```

5. If you are using the pattern creation database to create your own patterns, also import the following data with:

```
sdpdb import sdp-backup-*sql
```

6. If you are using custom patterns, also restore `/usr/lib/sca/patterns/local` from your backup data.
7. Reactivate the SCA appliance with:

```
scadb reset agents
```

8. Update the pattern modules in the database with:

```
sdagent-patterns -u
```

33.4.3 Developing Custom Analysis Patterns

The SCA appliance comes with a complete pattern development environment (the SCA Pattern Database) that enables you to develop your own, custom patterns. Patterns can be written in any programming language. To make them available for the supportconfig analysis process, they need to be saved to `/usr/lib/sca/patterns/local` and to be made executable. Both the

SCA appliance and the SCA tool will then run the custom patterns against new supportconfig archives as part of the analysis report. For detailed instructions on how to create (and test) your own patterns, see http://www.suse.com/communities/conversations/sca-pattern-development/ ↗.

33.5 Gathering Information during the Installation

During the installation, **`supportconfig`** is not available. However, you can collect log files from YaST by using **`save_y2logs`**. This command will create a `.tar.xz` archive in the directory `/tmp`.

If issues appear very early during installation, you may be able to gather information from the log file created by **`linuxrc`**. **`linuxrc`** is a small command that runs before YaST starts. This log file is available at `/var/log/linuxrc.log`.

Important: Installation Log Files Not Available in the Installed System

The log files available during the installation are not available in the installed system anymore. Properly save the installation log files while the installer is still running.

33.6 Support of Kernel Modules

An important requirement for every enterprise operating system is the level of support you receive for your environment. Kernel modules are the most relevant connector between hardware ("controllers") and the operating system. Every kernel module in SUSE Linux Enterprise has a `supported` flag that can take three possible values:

- "yes", thus `supported`
- "external", thus `supported`
- "" (empty, not set), thus `unsupported`

The following rules apply:

- All modules of a self-recompiled kernel are by default marked as unsupported.
- Kernel modules supported by SUSE partners and delivered using `SUSE SolidDriver Program` are marked "external".

- If the `supported` flag is not set, loading this module will taint the kernel. Tainted kernels are not supported. Unsupported Kernel modules are included in an extra RPM package (`kernel-FLAVOR-extra`) that is only available for SUSE Linux Enterprise Desktop and the SUSE Linux Enterprise Workstation Extension. Those kernels will not be loaded by default (*FLAVOR* = `default` | `xen` |...). In addition, these unsupported modules are not available in the installer, and the `kernel-FLAVOR-extra` package is not part of the SUSE Linux Enterprise media.
- Kernel modules not provided under a license compatible to the license of the Linux kernel will also taint the kernel. For details, see `/usr/src/linux/Documentation/sysctl/kernel.txt` and the state of `/proc/sys/kernel/tainted`.

33.6.1 Technical Background

- Linux kernel: The value of `/proc/sys/kernel/unsupported` defaults to `2` on SUSE Linux Enterprise 12 SP3 (`do not warn in syslog when loading unsupported modules`). This default is used in the installer and in the installed system. See `/usr/src/linux/Documentation/sysctl/kernel.txt` for more information.
- **`modprobe`**: The **`modprobe`** utility for checking module dependencies and loading modules appropriately checks for the value of the `supported` flag. If the value is "yes" or "external" the module will be loaded, otherwise it will not. For information on how to override this behavior, see *Section 33.6.2, "Working with Unsupported Modules"*.

Note: Support

SUSE does not generally support the removal of storage modules via **`modprobe -r`**.

33.6.2 Working with Unsupported Modules

While general supportability is important, situations can occur where loading an unsupported module is required (for example, for testing or debugging purposes, or if your hardware vendor provides a hotfix).

- To override the default, edit `/etc/modprobe.d/10-unsupported-modules.conf` and change the value of the variable `allow_unsupported_modules` to `1`. If an unsupported module is needed in the initrd, do not forget to run **`dracut`** `-f` to update the initrd.

If you only want to try loading a module once, you can use the `--allow-unsupported-modules` option with **`modprobe`**. For more information, see the **`modprobe`** man page.

- During installation, unsupported modules may be added through driver update disks, and they will be loaded. To enforce loading of unsupported modules during boot and afterward, use the kernel command line option `oem-modules`. While installing and initializing the `suse-module-tools` package, the kernel flag `TAINT_NO_SUPPORT` (`/proc/sys/kernel/tainted`) will be evaluated. If the kernel is already tainted, `allow_unsupported_modules` will be enabled. This will prevent unsupported modules from failing in the system being installed. If no unsupported modules are present during installation and the other special kernel command line option (`oem-modules=1`) is not used, the default still is to disallow unsupported modules.

Remember that loading and running unsupported modules will make the kernel and the whole system unsupported by SUSE.

33.7 For More Information

- **`man supportconfig`**—The **`supportconfig`** man page.
- **`man supportconfig.conf`**—The man page of the supportconfig configuration file.
- **`man scatool`**—The **`scatool`** man page.
- **`man scadb`**—The **`scadb`** man page.
- **`man setup-sca`**—The **`setup-sca`** man page.
- https://mariadb.com/kb/en/ ↗—The MariaDB documentation.
- http://www.suse.com/communities/conversations/sca-pattern-development/ ↗—Instructions on how to create (and test) your own SCA patterns.
- http://www.suse.com/communities/conversations/basic-server-health-check-supportconfig/ ↗—A Basic Server Health Check with Supportconfig.
- https://www.novell.com/communities/coolsolutions/cool_tools/create-your-own-supportconfig-plugin/ ↗—Create Your Own Supportconfig Plugin.
- http://www.suse.com/communities/conversations/creating-a-central-supportconfig-repository/ ↗—Creating a Central Supportconfig Repository.

34 Common Problems and Their Solutions

This chapter describes a range of potential problems and their solutions. Even if your situation is not precisely listed here, there may be one similar enough to offer hints to the solution of your problem.

34.1 Finding and Gathering Information

Linux reports things in a very detailed way. There are several places to look when you encounter problems with your system, most of which are standard to Linux systems in general, and some are relevant to SUSE Linux Enterprise Desktop systems. Most log files can be viewed with YaST (*Miscellaneous › Start-Up Log*).

YaST offers the possibility to collect all system information needed by the support team. Use *Other › Support* and select the problem category. When all information is gathered, attach it to your support request.

A list of the most frequently checked log files follows with the description of their typical purpose. Paths containing `~` refer to the current user's home directory.

TABLE 34.1: LOG FILES

Log File	Description
`~/.xsession-errors`	Messages from the desktop applications currently running.
`/var/log/apparmor/`	Log files from AppArmor, see *Book* "Security Guide" for detailed information.
`/var/log/audit/audit.log`	Log file from Audit to track any access to files, directories, or resources of your system, and trace system calls. See *Book* "Security Guide" for detailed information.
`/var/log/mail.*`	Messages from the mail system.
`/var/log/NetworkManager`	Log file from NetworkManager to collect problems with network connectivity

Log File	Description
/var/log/samba/	Directory containing Samba server and client log messages.
/var/log/warn	All messages from the kernel and system log daemon with the “warning” level or higher.
/var/log/wtmp	Binary file containing user login records for the current machine session. View it with **last**.
/var/log/Xorg.*.log	Various start-up and runtime log files from the X Window System. It is useful for debugging failed X start-ups.
/var/log/YaST2/	Directory containing YaST's actions and their results.
/var/log/zypper.log	Log file of Zypper.

Apart from log files, your machine also supplies you with information about the running system. See *Table 34.2: System Information With the /proc File System*

TABLE 34.2: SYSTEM INFORMATION WITH THE /proc FILE SYSTEM

File	Description
/proc/cpuinfo	Contains processor information, including its type, make, model, and performance.
/proc/dma	Shows which DMA channels are currently being used.
/proc/interrupts	Shows which interrupts are in use, and how many of each have been in use.
/proc/iomem	Displays the status of I/O (input/output) memory.

File	Description
/proc/ioports	Shows which I/O ports are in use at the moment.
/proc/meminfo	Displays memory status.
/proc/modules	Displays the individual modules.
/proc/mounts	Displays devices currently mounted.
/proc/partitions	Shows the partitioning of all hard disks.
/proc/version	Displays the current version of Linux.

Apart from the `/proc` file system, the Linux kernel exports information with the `sysfs` module, an in-memory file system. This module represents kernel objects, their attributes and relationships. For more information about `sysfs`, see the context of udev in *Chapter 22, Dynamic Kernel Device Management with* udev. *Table 34.3* contains an overview of the most common directories under `/sys`.

TABLE 34.3: SYSTEM INFORMATION WITH THE /sys FILE SYSTEM

File	Description
/sys/block	Contains subdirectories for each block device discovered in the system. Generally, these are mostly disk type devices.
/sys/bus	Contains subdirectories for each physical bus type.
/sys/class	Contains subdirectories grouped together as a functional types of devices (like graphics, net, printer, etc.)
/sys/device	Contains the global device hierarchy.

Linux comes with several tools for system analysis and monitoring. See *Book* "System Analysis and Tuning Guide", *Chapter 2 "System Monitoring Utilities"* for a selection of the most important ones used in system diagnostics.

Each of the following scenarios begins with a header describing the problem followed by a paragraph or two offering suggested solutions, available references for more detailed solutions, and cross-references to other scenarios that are related.

34.2 Installation Problems

Installation problems are situations when a machine fails to install. It may fail entirely or it may not be able to start the graphical installer. This section highlights some typical problems you may run into, and offers possible solutions or workarounds for these kinds of situations.

34.2.1 Checking Media

If you encounter any problems using the SUSE Linux Enterprise Desktop installation media, check the integrity of your installation media. Boot from the media and choose *Check Installation Media* from the boot menu. In a running system, start YaST and choose *Software › Media Check*. To check the SUSE Linux Enterprise Desktop medium, insert it into the drive and click *Start Check* in the *Media Check* screen of YaST. This may take several minutes. If errors are detected, do not use this medium for installation. Media problems may occur when having burned the medium yourself. Burning the media at a low speed (4x) helps to avoid problems.

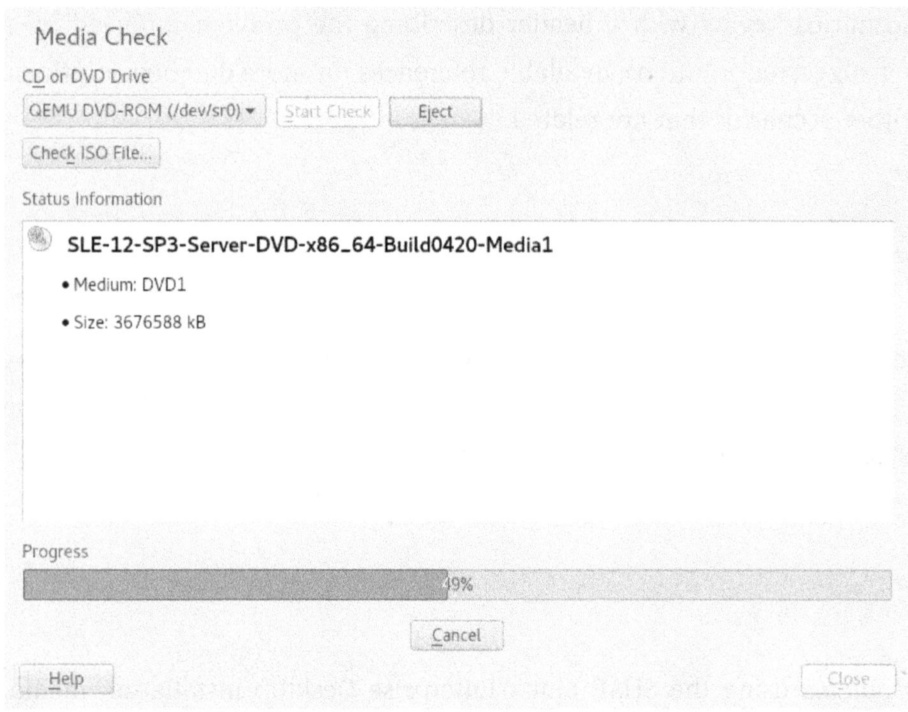

FIGURE 34.1: CHECKING MEDIA

34.2.2 No Bootable DVD Drive Available

If your computer does not contain a bootable DVD-ROM drive or if the one you have is not supported by Linux, there are several options you can install your machine without a built-in DVD drive:

Using an External Boot Device

If it is supported by your BIOS and the installation kernel, boot from external DVD drives or USB storage devices. Refer to *Book "Deployment Guide", Chapter 3 "Installation with YaST", Section 3.2.1 "PC (AMD64/Intel 64/ARM AArch64): System Start-up"* for instructions on how to create a bootable USB storage device.

Network Boot via PXE

If a machine lacks a DVD drive, but provides a working Ethernet connection, perform a completely network-based installation. See *Book "Deployment Guide", Chapter 6 "Remote Installation", Section 6.1.3 "Remote Installation via VNC—PXE Boot and Wake on LAN"* and *Book "Deployment Guide", Chapter 6 "Remote Installation", Section 6.1.6 "Remote Installation via SSH—PXE Boot and Wake on LAN"* for details.

34.2.2.1 External Boot Devices

Linux supports most existing DVD drives. If the system has no DVD drive, it is still possible that an external DVD drive, connected through USB, FireWire, or SCSI, can be used to boot the system. This depends mainly on the interaction of the BIOS and the hardware used. Sometimes a BIOS update may help if you encounter problems.

When installing from a Live CD, you can also create a "Live flash disk" to boot from.

34.2.3 Booting from Installation Media Fails

One reason a machine does not boot the installation media can be an incorrect boot sequence setting in BIOS. The BIOS boot sequence must have DVD drive set as the first entry for booting. Otherwise the machine would try to boot from another medium, typically the hard disk. Guidance for changing the BIOS boot sequence can be found the documentation provided with your mainboard, or in the following paragraphs.

The BIOS is the software that enables the very basic functions of a computer. Motherboard vendors provide a BIOS specifically made for their hardware. Normally, the BIOS setup can only be accessed at a specific time—when the machine is booting. During this initialization phase, the machine performs several diagnostic hardware tests. One of them is a memory check, indicated by a memory counter. When the counter appears, look for a line, usually below the counter or somewhere at the bottom, mentioning the key to press to access the BIOS setup. Usually the key to press is one of `Del`, `F1`, or `Esc`. Press this key until the BIOS setup screen appears.

PROCEDURE 34.1: CHANGING THE BIOS BOOT SEQUENCE

1. Enter the BIOS using the proper key as announced by the boot routines and wait for the BIOS screen to appear.

2. To change the boot sequence in an AWARD BIOS, look for the *BIOS FEATURES SETUP* entry. Other manufacturers may have a different name for this, such as *ADVANCED CMOS SETUP*. When you have found the entry, select it and confirm with `Enter`.

3. In the screen that opens, look for a subentry called *BOOT SEQUENCE* or *BOOT ORDER*. Change the settings by pressing `Page ↑` or `Page ↓` until the DVD drive is listed first.

4. Leave the BIOS setup screen by pressing `Esc`. To save the changes, select *SAVE & EXIT SETUP*, or press `F10`. To confirm that your settings should be saved, press `Y`.

PROCEDURE 34.2: CHANGING THE BOOT SEQUENCE IN AN SCSI BIOS (ADAPTEC HOST ADAPTER)

1. Open the setup by pressing Ctrl – A .
2. Select *Disk Utilities*. The connected hardware components are now displayed.
   Make note of the SCSI ID of your DVD drive.
3. Exit the menu with Esc .
4. Open *Configure Adapter Settings*. Under *Additional Options*, select *Boot Device Options* and press Enter .
5. Enter the ID of the DVD drive and press Enter again.
6. Press Esc twice to return to the start screen of the SCSI BIOS.
7. Exit this screen and confirm with *Yes* to boot the computer.

Regardless of what language and keyboard layout your final installation will be using, most BIOS configurations use the US keyboard layout as shown in the following figure:

FIGURE 34.2: US KEYBOARD LAYOUT

34.2.4 Fails to Boot

Some hardware types, mainly very old or very recent ones, fail to install. Often this may happen because support for this type of hardware is missing in the installation kernel, or because of certain functionality included in this kernel, such as ACPI, that can still cause problems on some hardware.

If your system fails to install using the standard *Installation* mode from the first installation boot screen, try the following:

1. With the DVD still in the drive, reboot the machine with `Ctrl`–`Alt`–`Del` or using the hardware reset button.
2. When the boot screen appears, press `F5`, use the arrow keys of your keyboard to navigate to *No ACPI* and press `Enter` to launch the boot and installation process. This option disables the support for ACPI power management techniques.
3. Proceed with the installation as described in *Book* "Deployment Guide", *Chapter 3 "Installation with YaST"*.

If this fails, proceed as above, but choose *Safe Settings* instead. This option disables ACPI and DMA support. Most hardware will boot with this option.

If both of these options fail, use the boot options prompt to pass any additional parameters needed to support this type of hardware to the installation kernel. For more information about the parameters available as boot options, refer to the kernel documentation located in `/usr/src/linux/Documentation/kernel-parameters.txt`.

Tip: Obtaining Kernel Documentation

Install the `kernel-source` package to view the kernel documentation.

There are other ACPI-related kernel parameters that can be entered at the boot prompt prior to booting for installation:

`acpi=off`

This parameter disables the complete ACPI subsystem on your computer. This may be useful if your computer cannot handle ACPI or if you think ACPI in your computer causes trouble.

`acpi=force`

Always enable ACPI even if your computer has an old BIOS dated before the year 2000. This parameter also enables ACPI if it is set in addition to `acpi=off`.

`acpi=noirq`

Do not use ACPI for IRQ routing.

`acpi=ht`

Run only enough ACPI to enable hyper-threading.

`acpi=strict`

Be less tolerant of platforms that are not strictly ACPI specification compliant.

`pci=noacpi`

Disable PCI IRQ routing of the new ACPI system.

`pnpacpi=off`

This option is for serial or parallel problems when your BIOS setup contains wrong interrupts or ports.

`notsc`

Disable the time stamp counter. This option can be used to work around timing problems on your systems. It is a recent feature, if you see regressions on your machine, especially time related or even total hangs, this option is worth a try.

`nohz=off`

Disable the nohz feature. If your machine hangs, this option may help. Otherwise it is of no use.

Once you have determined the right parameter combination, YaST automatically writes them to the boot loader configuration to make sure that the system boots properly next time.

If unexplainable errors occur when the kernel is loaded or during the installation, select *Memory Test* in the boot menu to check the memory. If *Memory Test* returns an error, it is usually a hardware error.

34.2.5 Fails to Launch Graphical Installer

After you insert the medium into your drive and reboot your machine, the installation screen comes up, but after you select *Installation*, the graphical installer does not start.

There are several ways to deal with this situation:

- Try to select another screen resolution for the installation dialogs.
- Select *Text Mode* for installation.
- Do a remote installation via VNC using the graphical installer.

PROCEDURE 34.3: CHANGE SCREEN RESOLUTION FOR INSTALLATION

1. Boot for installation.
2. Press F3 to open a menu from which to select a lower resolution for installation purposes.
3. Select *Installation* and proceed with the installation as described in *Book* "Deployment Guide", *Chapter 3 "Installation with YaST"*.

PROCEDURE 34.4: INSTALLATION IN TEXT MODE

1. Boot for installation.
2. Press F3 and select *Text Mode*.
3. Select *Installation* and proceed with the installation as described in *Book* "Deployment Guide", *Chapter 3 "Installation with YaST"*.

PROCEDURE 34.5: VNC INSTALLATION

1. Boot for installation.
2. Enter the following text at the boot options prompt:

```
vnc=1 vncpassword=SOME_PASSWORD
```

   Replace *SOME_PASSWORD* with the password to use for VNC installation.

3. Select *Installation* then press Enter to start the installation.
   Instead of starting right into the graphical installation routine, the system continues to run in a text mode, then halts, displaying a message containing the IP address and port number at which the installer can be reached via a browser interface or a VNC viewer application.
4. If using a browser to access the installer, launch the browser and enter the address information provided by the installation routines on the future SUSE Linux Enterprise Desktop machine and press Enter:

```
http://IP_ADDRESS_OF_MACHINE:5801
```

   A dialog opens in the browser window prompting you for the VNC password. Enter it and proceed with the installation as described in *Book* "Deployment Guide", *Chapter 3 "Installation with YaST"*.

 Important: Cross-platform Support

Installation via VNC works with any browser under any operating system, provided Java support is enabled.

Provide the IP address and password to your VNC viewer when prompted. A window opens, displaying the installation dialogs. Proceed with the installation as usual.

34.2.6 Only Minimalistic Boot Screen Started

You inserted the medium into the drive, the BIOS routines are finished, but the system does not start with the graphical boot screen. Instead it launches a very minimalistic text-based interface. This may happen on any machine not providing sufficient graphics memory for rendering a graphical boot screen.

Although the text boot screen looks minimalistic, it provides nearly the same functionality as the graphical one:

Boot Options

Unlike the graphical interface, the different boot options cannot be selected using the cursor keys of your keyboard. The boot menu of the text mode boot screen offers some keywords to enter at the boot prompt. These keywords map to the options offered in the graphical version. Enter your choice and press Enter to launch the boot process.

Custom Boot Options

After selecting a boot option, enter the appropriate keyword at the boot prompt or enter some custom boot options as described in *Section 34.2.4, "Fails to Boot"*. To launch the installation process, press Enter.

Screen Resolutions

Use the function keys (F1 ... F12) to determine the screen resolution for installation. If you need to boot in text mode, choose F3 .

34.3 Boot Problems

Boot problems are situations when your system does not boot properly (does not boot to the expected target and login screen).

34.3.1 The GRUB 2 Boot Loader Fails to Load

If the hardware is functioning properly, it is possible that the boot loader is corrupted and Linux cannot start on the machine. In this case, it is necessary to repair the boot loader. To do so, you need to start the Rescue System as described in Section 34.6.2, "Using the Rescue System" and follow the instructions in Section 34.6.2.4, "Modifying and Re-installing the Boot Loader".

Alternatively, you can use the Rescue System to fix the boot loader as follows. Boot your machine from the installation media. In the boot screen, choose *More › Boot Linux System*. Select the disk containing the installed system and kernel with the default kernel options.

When the system is booted, start YaST and switch to *System › Boot Loader*. Make sure that the *Write generic Boot Code to MRB* option is enabled, and press *OK*. This fixes the corrupted boot loader by overwriting it, or installs the boot loader if it is missing.

Other reasons for the machine not booting may be BIOS-related:

BIOS Settings

Check your BIOS for references to your hard disk. GRUB 2 may simply not be started if the hard disk itself cannot be found with the current BIOS settings.

BIOS Boot Order

Check whether your system's boot order includes the hard disk. If the hard disk option was not enabled, your system may install properly, but fails to boot when access to the hard disk is required.

34.3.2 No Login or Prompt Appears

This behavior typically occurs after a failed kernel upgrade and it is known as a *kernel panic* because of the type of error on the system console that sometimes can be seen at the final stage of the process. If, in fact, the machine has just been rebooted following a software update, the immediate goal is to reboot it using the old, proven version of the Linux kernel and associated files. This can be done in the GRUB 2 boot loader screen during the boot process as follows:

1. Reboot the computer using the reset button, or switch it off and on again.

2. When the GRUB 2 boot screen becomes visible, select the *Advanced Options* entry and choose the previous kernel from the menu. The machine will boot using the prior version of the kernel and its associated files.

3. After the boot process has completed, remove the newly installed kernel and, if necessary, set the default boot entry to the old kernel using the YaST *Boot Loader* module. For more information refer to *Section 13.3, "Configuring the Boot Loader with YaST"*. However, doing this is probably not necessary because automated update tools normally modify it for you during the rollback process.

4. Reboot.

If this does not fix the problem, boot the computer using the installation media. After the machine has booted, continue with *Step 3*.

34.3.3 No Graphical Login

If the machine starts, but does not boot into the graphical login manager, anticipate problems either with the choice of the default systemd target or the configuration of the X Window System. To check the current systemd default target run the command **`sudo systemctl get-default`**. If the value returned is *not* `graphical.target`, run the command **`sudo systemctl isolate graphical.target`**. If the graphical login screen starts, log in and start *YaST* › *System* › *Services Manager* and set the *Default System Target* to *Graphical Interface*. From now on the system should boot into the graphical login screen.

If the graphical login screen does not start even if having booted or switched to the graphical target, your desktop or X Window software is probably misconfigured or corrupted. Examine the log files at `/var/log/Xorg.*.log` for detailed messages from the X server as it attempted to start. If the desktop fails during start, it may log error messages to the system journal that can be queried with the command **`journalctl`** (see *Chapter 16, `journalctl`: Query the `systemd` Journal* for more information). If these error messages hint at a configuration problem in the X server, try to fix these issues. If the graphical system still does not come up, consider reinstalling the graphical desktop.

34.3.4 Root Btrfs Partition Cannot Be Mounted

If a `btrfs` root partition becomes corrupted, try the following options:

- Mount the partition with the `-o recovery` option.
- If that fails, run **`btrfs-zero-log`** on your root partition.

34.3.5 Force Checking Root Partitions

If the root partition becomes corrupted, use the parameter `forcefsck` on the boot prompt. This passes the option `-f` (force) to the **`fsck`** command.

34.4 Login Problems

Login problems occur when your machine does boot to the expected welcome screen or login prompt, but refuses to accept the user name and password, or accepts them but then does not behave properly (fails to start the graphic desktop, produces errors, drops to a command line, etc.).

34.4.1 Valid User Name and Password Combinations Fail

This usually occurs when the system is configured to use network authentication or directory services and, for some reason, cannot retrieve results from its configured servers. The `root` user, as the only local user, is the only user that can still log in to these machines. The following are some common reasons a machine appears functional but cannot process logins correctly:

- The network is not working. For further directions on this, turn to *Section 34.5, "Network Problems"*.
- DNS is not working at the moment (which prevents GNOME from working and the system from making validated requests to secure servers). One indication that this is the case is that the machine takes an extremely long time to respond to any action. Find more information about this topic in *Section 34.5, "Network Problems"*.

- If the system is configured to use Kerberos, the system's local time may have drifted past the accepted variance with the Kerberos server time (this is typically 300 seconds). If NTP (network time protocol) is not working properly or local NTP servers are not working, Kerberos authentication ceases to function because it depends on common clock synchronization across the network.
- The system's authentication configuration is misconfigured. Check the PAM configuration files involved for any typographical errors or misordering of directives. For additional background information about PAM and the syntax of the configuration files involved, refer to *Book "Security Guide", Chapter 2 "Authentication with PAM"*.
- The home partition is encrypted. Find more information about this topic in *Section 34.4.3, "Login to Encrypted Home Partition Fails"*.

In all cases that do not involve external network problems, the solution is to reboot the system into single-user mode and repair the configuration before booting again into operating mode and attempting to log in again. To boot into single-user mode:

1. Reboot the system. The boot screen appears, offering a prompt.
2. Press `Esc` to exit the splash screen and get to the GRUB 2 text-based menu.
3. Press `B` to enter the GRUB 2 editor.
4. Add the following parameter to the line containing the kernel parameters:

```
systemd.unit=rescue.target
```

5. Press `F10`.
6. Enter the user name and password for `root`.
7. Make all the necessary changes.
8. Boot into the full multiuser and network mode by entering **`systemctl isolate graphical.target`** at the command line.

34.4.2 Valid User Name and Password Not Accepted

This is by far the most common problem users encounter, because there are many reasons this can occur. Depending on whether you use local user management and authentication or network authentication, login failures occur for different reasons.

Local user management can fail for the following reasons:

- The user may have entered the wrong password.
- The user's home directory containing the desktop configuration files is corrupted or write protected.
- There may be problems with the X Window System authenticating this particular user, especially if the user's home directory has been used with another Linux distribution prior to installing the current one.

To locate the reason for a local login failure, proceed as follows:

1. Check whether the user remembered his password correctly before you start debugging the whole authentication mechanism. If the user may not remember his password correctly, use the YaST User Management module to change the user's password. Pay attention to the `Caps Lock` key and unlock it, if necessary.
2. Log in as `root` and check the system journal with **`journalctl -e`** for error messages of the login process and of PAM.
3. Try to log in from a console (using `Ctrl`–`Alt`–`F1`). If this is successful, the blame cannot be put on PAM, because it is possible to authenticate this user on this machine. Try to locate any problems with the X Window System or the GNOME desktop. For more information, refer to *Section 34.4.4, "Login Successful but GNOME Desktop Fails"*.
4. If the user's home directory has been used with another Linux distribution, remove the `Xauthority` file in the user's home. Use a console login via `Ctrl`–`Alt`–`F1` and run **`rm .Xauthority`** as this user. This should eliminate X authentication problems for this user. Try graphical login again.
5. If the desktop could not start because of corrupt configuration files, proceed with *Section 34.4.4, "Login Successful but GNOME Desktop Fails"*.

In the following, common reasons a network authentication for a particular user may fail on a specific machine are listed:

- The user may have entered the wrong password.
- The user name exists in the machine's local authentication files and is also provided by a network authentication system, causing conflicts.

- The home directory exists but is corrupt or unavailable. Perhaps it is write protected or is on a server that is inaccessible at the moment.
- The user does not have permission to log in to that particular host in the authentication system.
- The machine has changed host names, for whatever reason, and the user does not have permission to log in to that host.
- The machine cannot reach the authentication server or directory server that contains that user's information.
- There may be problems with the X Window System authenticating this particular user, especially if the user's home has been used with another Linux distribution prior to installing the current one.

To locate the cause of the login failures with network authentication, proceed as follows:

1. Check whether the user remembered their password correctly before you start debugging the whole authentication mechanism.
2. Determine the directory server which the machine relies on for authentication and make sure that it is up and running and properly communicating with the other machines.
3. Determine that the user's user name and password work on other machines to make sure that his authentication data exists and is properly distributed.
4. See if another user can log in to the misbehaving machine. If another user can log in without difficulty or if `root` can log in, log in and examine the system journal with **`journalctl -e`** > file. Locate the time stamps that correspond to the login attempts and determine if PAM has produced any error messages.
5. Try to log in from a console (using Ctrl–Alt–F1). If this is successful, the problem is not with PAM or the directory server on which the user's home is hosted, because it is possible to authenticate this user on this machine. Try to locate any problems with the X Window System or the GNOME desktop. For more information, refer to *Section 34.4.4, "Login Successful but GNOME Desktop Fails"*.
6. If the user's home directory has been used with another Linux distribution, remove the `Xauthority` file in the user's home. Use a console login via Ctrl–Alt–F1 and run **`rm .Xauthority`** as this user. This should eliminate X authentication problems for this user. Try graphical login again.

7. If the desktop could not start because of corrupt configuration files, proceed with *Section 34.4.4, "Login Successful but GNOME Desktop Fails"*.

34.4.3 Login to Encrypted Home Partition Fails

It is recommended to use an encrypted home partition for laptops. If you cannot log in to your laptop, the reason is usually simple: your partition could not be unlocked.

During the boot time, you need to enter the passphrase to unlock your encrypted partition. If you do not enter it, the boot process continues, leaving the partition locked.

To unlock your encrypted partition, proceed as follows:

1. Switch to the text console with `Ctrl`–`Alt`–`F1`.
2. Become `root`.
3. Restart the unlocking process again with:

   ```
   systemctl restart home.mount
   ```

4. Enter your passphrase to unlock your encrypted partition.
5. Exit the text console and switch back to the login screen with `Alt`–`F7`.
6. Log in as usual.

34.4.4 Login Successful but GNOME Desktop Fails

If this is the case, it is likely that your GNOME configuration files have become corrupted. Some symptoms may include the keyboard failing to work, the screen geometry becoming distorted, or even the screen coming up as a bare gray field. The important distinction is that if another user logs in, the machine works normally. It is then likely that the problem can be fixed relatively quickly by simply moving the user's GNOME configuration directory to a new location, which causes GNOME to initialize a new one. Although the user is forced to reconfigure GNOME, no data is lost.

1. Switch to a text console by pressing `Ctrl`–`Alt`–`F1`.
2. Log in with your user name.

3. Move the user's GNOME configuration directories to a temporary location:

```
mv .gconf  .gconf-ORIG-RECOVER
mv .gnome2 .gnome2-ORIG-RECOVER
```

4. Log out.

5. Log in again, but do not run any applications.

6. Recover your individual application configuration data (including the Evolution e-mail client data) by copying the `~/.gconf-ORIG-RECOVER/apps/` directory back into the new `~/.gconf` directory as follows:

```
cp -a .gconf-ORIG-RECOVER/apps .gconf/
```

   If this causes the login problems, attempt to recover only the critical application data and reconfigure the remainder of the applications.

34.5 Network Problems

Many problems of your system may be network-related, even though they do not seem to be at first. For example, the reason for a system not allowing users to log in may be a network problem of some kind. This section introduces a simple checklist you can apply to identify the cause of any network problem encountered.

PROCEDURE 34.6: HOW TO IDENTIFY NETWORK PROBLEMS

When checking the network connection of your machine, proceed as follows:

1. If you use an Ethernet connection, check the hardware first. Make sure that your network cable is properly plugged into your computer and router (or hub, etc.). The control lights next to your Ethernet connector are normally both be active.
   If the connection fails, check whether your network cable works with another machine. If it does, your network card causes the failure. If hubs or switches are included in your network setup, they may be faulty, as well.

2. If using a wireless connection, check whether the wireless link can be established by other machines. If not, contact the wireless network's administrator.

3. Once you have checked your basic network connectivity, try to find out which service is not responding. Gather the address information of all network servers needed in your setup. Either look them up in the appropriate YaST module or ask your system administrator. The following list gives some typical network servers involved in a setup together with the symptoms of an outage.

   DNS (Name Service)

   A broken or malfunctioning name service affects the network's functionality in many ways. If the local machine relies on any network servers for authentication and these servers cannot be found because of name resolution issues, users would not even be able to log in. Machines in the network managed by a broken name server would not be able to “see” each other and communicate.

   NTP (Time Service)

   A malfunctioning or completely broken NTP service could affect Kerberos authentication and X server functionality.

   NFS (File Service)

   If any application needs data stored in an NFS mounted directory, it cannot start or function properly if this service was down or misconfigured. In the worst case scenario, a user's personal desktop configuration would not come up if their home directory containing the `.gconf` subdirectory could not be found because of a faulty NFS server.

   Samba (File Service)

   If any application needs data stored in a directory on a faulty Samba server, it cannot start or function properly.

   NIS (User Management)

   If your SUSE Linux Enterprise Desktop system relies on a faulty NIS server to provide the user data, users cannot log in to this machine.

   LDAP (User Management)

   If your SUSE Linux Enterprise Desktop system relies on a faulty LDAP server to provide the user data, users cannot log in to this machine.

   Kerberos (Authentication)

   Authentication will not work and login to any machine fails.

CUPS (Network Printing)

Users cannot print.

4. Check whether the network servers are running and whether your network setup allows you to establish a connection:

> **Important: Limitations**
>
> The debugging procedure described below only applies to a simple network server/client setup that does not involve any internal routing. It assumes both server and client are members of the same subnet without the need for additional routing.

a. Use **`ping`** *`IP_ADDRESS/HOSTNAME`* (replace with the host name or IP address of the server) to check whether each one of them is up and responding to the network. If this command is successful, it tells you that the host you were looking for is up and running and that the name service for your network is configured correctly.
If ping fails with `destination host unreachable`, either your system or the desired server is not properly configured or down. Check whether your system is reachable by running **`ping`** *`IP address`* or *`YOUR_HOSTNAME`* from another machine. If you can reach your machine from another machine, it is the server that is not running or not configured correctly.
If ping fails with `unknown host`, the name service is not configured correctly or the host name used was incorrect. For further checks on this matter, refer to *Step 4.b*. If ping still fails, either your network card is not configured correctly or your network hardware is faulty.

b. Use **`host`** *`HOSTNAME`* to check whether the host name of the server you are trying to connect to is properly translated into an IP address and vice versa. If this command returns the IP address of this host, the name service is up and running. If the **`host`** command fails, check all network configuration files relating to name and address resolution on your host:

`/etc/resolv.conf`

This file is used to keep track of the name server and domain you are currently using. It can be modified manually or automatically adjusted by YaST or DHCP. Automatic adjustment is preferable. However, make sure that this file has the following structure and all network addresses and domain names are correct:

```
search FULLY_QUALIFIED_DOMAIN_NAME
nameserver IPADDRESS_OF_NAMESERVER
```

This file can contain more than one name server address, but at least one of them must be correct to provide name resolution to your host. If needed, adjust this file using the YaST Network Settings module (Hostname/DNS tab).

If your network connection is handled via DHCP, enable DHCP to change host name and name service information by selecting *Set Hostname via DHCP* (can be set globally for any interface or per interface) and *Update Name Servers and Search List via DHCP* in the YaST Network Settings module (Hostname/DNS tab).

`/etc/nsswitch.conf`

This file tells Linux where to look for name service information. It should look like this:

```
 ...
hosts: files dns
networks: files dns
...
```

The `dns` entry is vital. It tells Linux to use an external name server. Normally, these entries are automatically managed by YaST, but it would be prudent to check.

If all the relevant entries on the host are correct, let your system administrator check the DNS server configuration for the correct zone information. If you have made sure that the DNS configuration of your host and the DNS server are correct, proceed with checking the configuration of your network and network device.

c. If your system cannot establish a connection to a network server and you have excluded name service problems from the list of possible culprits, check the configuration of your network card.
Use the command `ip addr show` *NETWORK_DEVICE* to check whether this device was properly configured. Make sure that the `inet address` with the netmask (*/MASK*) is configured correctly. An error in the IP address or a missing bit in your network mask would render your network configuration unusable. If necessary, perform this check on the server as well.

d. If the name service and network hardware are properly configured and running, but some external network connections still get long time-outs or fail entirely, use **`traceroute`** *FULLY_QUALIFIED_DOMAIN_NAME* (executed as `root`) to track the network route these requests are taking. This command lists any gateway (hop) that a request from your machine passes on its way to its destination. It lists the response time of each hop and whether this hop is reachable. Use a combination of traceroute and ping to track down the culprit and let the administrators know.

Once you have identified the cause of your network trouble, you can resolve it yourself (if the problem is located on your machine) or let the system administrators of your network know about your findings so they can reconfigure the services or repair the necessary systems.

34.5.1 NetworkManager Problems

If you have a problem with network connectivity, narrow it down as described in *Procedure 34.6, "How to Identify Network Problems"*. If NetworkManager seems to be the culprit, proceed as follows to get logs providing hints on why NetworkManager fails:

1. Open a shell and log in as `root`.
2. Restart the NetworkManager:

```
systemctl restart Network.Manager
```

3. Open a Web page, for example, http://www.opensuse.org as normal user to see, if you can connect.
4. Collect any information about the state of NetworkManager in `/var/log/NetworkManager`.

For more information about NetworkManager, refer to *Chapter 30, Using NetworkManager*.

34.6 Data Problems

Data problems are when the machine may or may not boot properly but, in either case, it is clear that there is data corruption on the system and that the system needs to be recovered. These situations call for a backup of your critical data, enabling you to recover the system state from before your system failed.

34.6.1 Managing Partition Images

Sometimes you need to perform a backup from an entire partition or even hard disk. Linux comes with the **dd** tool which can create an exact copy of your disk. Combined with **gzip** you save some space.

PROCEDURE 34.7: BACKING UP AND RESTORING HARD DISKS

1. Start a Shell as user `root`.
2. Select your source device. Typically this is something like `/dev/sda` (labeled as *SOURCE*).
3. Decide where you want to store your image (labeled as *BACKUP_PATH*). It must be different from your source device. In other words: if you make a backup from `/dev/sda`, your image file must not to be stored under `/dev/sda`.
4. Run the commands to create a compressed image file:

```
dd if=/dev/SOURCE | gzip > /BACKUP_PATH/image.gz
```

5. Restore the hard disk with the following commands:

```
gzip -dc /BACKUP_PATH/image.gz | dd of=/dev/SOURCE
```

If you only need to back up a partition, replace the *SOURCE* placeholder with your respective partition. In this case, your image file can lie on the same hard disk, but on a different partition.

34.6.2 Using the Rescue System

There are several reasons a system could fail to come up and run properly. A corrupted file system following a system crash, corrupted configuration files, or a corrupted boot loader configuration are the most common ones.

To help you to resolve these situations, SUSE Linux Enterprise Desktop contains a rescue system that you can boot. The rescue system is a small Linux system that can be loaded into a RAM disk and mounted as root file system, allowing you to access your Linux partitions from the outside. Using the rescue system, you can recover or modify any important aspect of your system.

- Manipulate any type of configuration file.
- Check the file system for defects and start automatic repair processes.
- Access the installed system in a "change root" environment.
- Check, modify, and re-install the boot loader configuration.
- Recover from a badly installed device driver or unusable kernel.
- Resize partitions using the parted command. Find more information about this tool at the GNU Parted Web site http://www.gnu.org/software/parted/parted.html ↗.

The rescue system can be loaded from various sources and locations. The simplest option is to boot the rescue system from the original installation medium.

1. Insert the installation medium into your DVD drive.
2. Reboot the system.
3. At the boot screen, press F4 and choose *DVD-ROM*. Then choose *Rescue System* from the main menu.
4. Enter `root` at the `Rescue:` prompt. A password is not required.

If your hardware setup does not include a DVD drive, you can boot the rescue system from a network source. The following example applies to a remote boot scenario—if using another boot medium, such as a DVD, modify the `info` file accordingly and boot as you would for a normal installation.

1. Enter the configuration of your PXE boot setup and add the lines `install=PROTOCOL://INSTSOURCE` and `rescue=1`. If you need to start the repair system, use `repair=1` instead. As with a normal installation, *`PROTOCOL`* stands for any of the supported network protocols (NFS, HTTP, FTP, etc.) and *`INSTSOURCE`* for the path to your network installation source.

2. Boot the system using “Wake on LAN”, as described in *Book “Deployment Guide”, Chapter 5 “Preparing the Boot of the Target System”, Section 5.7 “Wake on LAN”*.

3. Enter `root` at the `Rescue:` prompt. A password is not required.

Once you have entered the rescue system, you can use the virtual consoles that can be reached with Alt–F1 to Alt–F6.

A shell and other useful utilities, such as the mount program, are available in the `/bin` directory. The `/sbin` directory contains important file and network utilities for reviewing and repairing the file system. This directory also contains the most important binaries for system maintenance, such as **`fdisk`**, **`mkfs`**, **`mkswap`**, **`mount`**, and **`shutdown`**, **`ip`** and **`ss`** for maintaining the network. The directory `/usr/bin` contains the vi editor, find, less, and SSH.

To see the system messages, either use the command **`dmesg`** or view the system log with **`journalctl`**.

34.6.2.1 Checking and Manipulating Configuration Files

As an example for a configuration that might be fixed using the rescue system, imagine you have a broken configuration file that prevents the system from booting properly. You can fix this using the rescue system.

To manipulate a configuration file, proceed as follows:

1. Start the rescue system using one of the methods described above.

2. To mount a root file system located under `/dev/sda6` to the rescue system, use the following command:

```
mount /dev/sda6 /mnt
```

All directories of the system are now located under `/mnt`

3. Change the directory to the mounted root file system:

```
cd /mnt
```

4. Open the problematic configuration file in the vi editor. Adjust and save the configuration.

5. Unmount the root file system from the rescue system:

```
umount /mnt
```

6. Reboot the machine.

34.6.2.2 Repairing and Checking File Systems

Generally, file systems cannot be repaired on a running system. If you encounter serious problems, you may not even be able to mount your root file system and the system boot may end with a "kernel panic". In this case, the only way is to repair the system from the outside. The system contains the utilities to check and repair the `btrfs`, `ext2`, `ext3`, `ext4`, `reiserfs`, `xfs`, `dosfs`, and `vfat` file systems. Look for the command **`fsck.`** *`FILESYSTEM`*, for example, if you need a file system check for `btrfs`, use **`fsck.btrfs`**.

34.6.2.3 Accessing the Installed System

If you need to access the installed system from the rescue system, you need to do this in a *change root* environment. For example, to modify the boot loader configuration, or to execute a hardware configuration utility.

To set up a change root environment based on the installed system, proceed as follows:

1. Run **`lsblk`** to check which node corresponds to the root partition. It is `/dev/sda2` in our example:

```
lsblk
NAME          MAJ:MIN RM   SIZE RO TYPE  MOUNTPOINT
sda             8:0    0 149,1G  0 disk
├─sda1          8:1    0     2G  0 part  [SWAP]
├─sda2          8:2    0    20G  0 part  /
└─sda3          8:3    0   127G  0 part
  └─cr_home 254:0    0   127G  0 crypt /home
```

2. Mount the root partition from the installed system:

```
mount /dev/sda2 /mnt
```

3. Mount `/proc`, `/dev`, and `/sys` partitions:

```
mount -t proc none /mnt/proc
mount --rbind /dev /mnt/dev
mount --rbind /sys /mnt/sys
```

4. Now you can "change root" into the new environment, keeping the `bash` shell:

```
chroot /mnt /bin/bash
```

5. Finally, mount the remaining partitions from the installed system:

```
mount -a
```

6. Now you have access to the installed system. Before rebooting the system, unmount the partitions with **`umount`** `-a` and leave the "change root" environment with **`exit`**.

Warning: Limitations

Although you have full access to the files and applications of the installed system, there are some limitations. The kernel that is running is the one that was booted with the rescue system, not with the change root environment. It only supports essential hardware and it is not possible to add kernel modules from the installed system unless the kernel versions are identical. Always check the version of the currently running (rescue) kernel with **`uname -r`** and then find out if a matching subdirectory exists in the `/lib/modules` directory in the change root environment. If yes, you can use the installed modules, otherwise you need to supply their correct versions on other media, such as a flash disk. Most often the rescue kernel version differs from the installed one — then you cannot simply access a sound card, for example. It is also not possible to start a graphical user interface.

Also note that you leave the "change root" environment when you switch the console with Alt–F1 to Alt–F6.

34.6.2.4 Modifying and Re-installing the Boot Loader

Sometimes a system cannot boot because the boot loader configuration is corrupted. The start-up routines cannot, for example, translate physical drives to the actual locations in the Linux file system without a working boot loader.

To check the boot loader configuration and re-install the boot loader, proceed as follows:

1. Perform the necessary steps to access the installed system as described in *Section 34.6.2.3, "Accessing the Installed System"*.

2. Check that the GRUB 2 boot loader is installed on the system. If not, install the package `grub2` and run

```
grub2-install /dev/sda
```

3. Check whether the following files are correctly configured according to the GRUB 2 configuration principles outlined in *Chapter 13, The Boot Loader GRUB 2* and apply fixes if necessary.

   - `/etc/default/grub`
   - `/boot/grub2/device.map` (optional file, only present if created manually)
   - `/boot/grub2/grub.cfg` (this file is generated, do not edit)
   - `/etc/sysconfig/bootloader`

4. Re-install the boot loader using the following command sequence:

```
grub2-mkconfig -o /boot/grub2/grub.cfg
```

5. Unmount the partitions, log out from the "change root" environment, and reboot the system:

```
umount -a
exit
reboot
```

34.6.2.5 Fixing Kernel Installation

A kernel update may introduce a new bug which can impact the operation of your system. For example a driver for a piece of hardware in your system may be faulty, which prevents you from accessing and using it. In this case, revert to the last working kernel (if available on the system) or install the original kernel from the installation media.

Tip: How to Keep Last Kernels after Update

To prevent failures to boot after a faulty kernel update, use the kernel multiversion feature and tell `libzypp` which kernels you want to keep after the update.

For example to always keep the last two kernels and the currently running one, add

```
multiversion.kernels = latest,latest-1,running
```

to the `/etc/zypp/zypp.conf` file. See *Book* "Deployment Guide", *Chapter 11 "Installing Multiple Kernel Versions"* for more information.

A similar case is when you need to re-install or update a broken driver for a device not supported by SUSE Linux Enterprise Desktop. For example when a hardware vendor uses a specific device, such as a hardware RAID controller, which needs a binary driver to be recognized by the operating system. The vendor typically releases a Driver Update Disk (DUD) with the fixed or updated version of the required driver.

In both cases you need to access the installed system in the rescue mode and fix the kernel related problem, otherwise the system may fail to boot correctly:

1. Boot from the SUSE Linux Enterprise Desktop installation media.
2. If you are recovering after a faulty kernel update, skip this step. If you need to use a driver update disk (DUD), press F6 to load the driver update after the boot menu appears, and choose the path or URL to the driver update and confirm with *Yes*.
3. Choose *Rescue System* from the boot menu and press Enter. If you chose to use DUD, you will be asked to specify where the driver update is stored.
4. Enter `root` at the `Rescue:` prompt. A password is not required.
5. Manually mount the target system and “change root” into the new environment. For more information, see *Section 34.6.2.3, "Accessing the Installed System"*.

6. If using DUD, install/re-install/update the faulty device driver package. Always make sure the installed kernel version exactly matches the version of the driver you are installing.
   If fixing faulty kernel update installation, you can install the original kernel from the installation media with the following procedure.

   a. Identify your DVD device with **`hwinfo --cdrom`** and mount it with **`mount /dev/sr0 /mnt`**.

   b. Navigate to the directory where your kernel files are stored on the DVD, for example **`cd /mnt/suse/x86_64/`**.

   c. Install required `kernel-*`, `kernel-*-base`, and `kernel-*-extra` packages of your flavor with the **`rpm -i`** command.

7. Update configuration files and reinitialize the boot loader if needed. For more information, see *Section 34.6.2.4, "Modifying and Re-installing the Boot Loader"*.

8. Remove any bootable media from the system drive and reboot.

A Documentation Updates

This chapter lists content changes for this document.

This manual was updated on the following dates:

A.1 September 2017 (Initial Release of SUSE Linux Enterprise Desktop 12 SP3)

General

- Numerous small fixes and additions to the documentation, based on technical feedback.
- Removed all references to the `faillog` package, which is no longer shipped (https://bugzilla.suse.com/show_bug.cgi?id=710788).

Chapter 4, YaST

- Added a new chapter about the YaST GUI and mentioned advanced key combinations (https://bugzilla.suse.com/show_bug.cgi?id=1010039).

Chapter 5, YaST in Text Mode

- Added *Section 5.2, "Advanced Key Combinations"* (https://bugzilla.suse.com/show_bug.cgi?id=1010039).

Chapter 6, Managing Software with Command Line Tools

- Added *Section 6.1.5.2, "Refreshing Repositories"* (Fate #319486).
- Updated *Section 6.1.3.1, "Installing All Needed Patches"* (Fate #320653).
- Added *Section 6.1.6.3, "`zypper info` Usage"* (Fate #321104).

Chapter 7, System Recovery and Snapshot Management with Snapper

- Mentioned that snapper rollback snapshots are automatically deleted. See *Section 7.3, "System Rollback by Booting from Snapshots"* and *Section 7.3.1, "Snapshots after Rollback"* (Fate #321773).
- In *Section 7.4, "Creating and Modifying Snapper Configurations"*, added in-depth information on how the minimum root file system size for enabling snapshots is calculated (https://bugzilla.suse.com/show_bug.cgi?id=1036175).
- Mentioned Btrfs default subvolume and its restrictions (https://bugzilla.suse.com/show_bug.cgi?id=1045884).

Chapter 8, Remote Access with VNC

- Fixed information about encrypted communication and added *Section 8.4, "Encrypted VNC Communication"* on how to set it up (https://bugzilla.suse.com/show_bug.cgi?id=1029117).

Chapter 9, File Copying with RSync

- Completely revised former *File Synchronization* chapter and focused on Rsync.

Chapter 14, The `systemd` *Daemon*

- Added the System V init command **`chkconfig`** to the comparison table in *Section 14.2.2.1, "Enabling/Disabling Services on the Command Line"* (Doc Comment #30251).

Chapter 17, Basic Networking

- Fixed several doc comments in *Section 17.8, "Setting Up Team Devices for Network Teaming"*.

Chapter 22, Dynamic Kernel Device Management with udev

- Fixed **`udevadm`** commands.

Chapter 23, Live Patching the Linux Kernel Using kGraft

Updated *Section 23.4, "Patch Lifecycle"* (Fate #322212).

Chapter 24, Special System Features

- Removed duplicate content from *Section 24.1.4, "Log Files: Package logrotate"*.

Part II, "Booting a Linux System"

- Reordered included chapters so that they follow the boot process order.

Bugfixes

- Replaced the command to start Apache2, **`httpd2`**, with **`apache2ctl`** (https://bugzilla.suse.com/show_bug.cgi?id=1042437).
- In *Section 17.2.5, "For More Information"*, corrected a typo in a referenced RFC document (https://bugzilla.suse.com/show_bug.cgi?id=1045881).
- In *Section 34.6, "Data Problems"*, removed a reference to a YaST module that is no longer shipped (https://bugzilla.suse.com/show_bug.cgi?id=1052675).

A.2 November 2016 (Initial Release of SUSE Linux Enterprise Desktop 12 SP2)

General

- The e-mail address for documentation feedback has changed to `doc-team@suse.com`.
- The documentation for Docker has been enhanced and renamed to *Docker Guide*.

Chapter 3, YaST Online Update

- Mentioned in *Section 3.3, "Automatic Online Update"* that the automatic online update does not automatically restart the system afterward (Doc Comment #30116).

Chapter 6, Managing Software with Command Line Tools

- **`zypper patch`** no longer installs optional patches by default. To install optional patches, use the `--with-optional` parameter (FATE#320447).

Chapter 7, System Recovery and Snapshot Management with Snapper

- Added `/var/cache` and `/var/lib/libvirt/images` to *Section 7.1.2, "Directories That Are Excluded from Snapshots"* (Fate #320834).
- Added *Section 7.6, "Automatic Snapshot Clean-Up"*, which also includes documentation on Snapper's new quota support (Fate #312751).
- Added *Q:* (Fate #318799).

Chapter 11, Introduction to the Booting Process

- Advised users to repair file system in case root file system fails on boot time (FATE#320443).

Chapter 13, The Boot Loader GRUB 2

- Added a hint on **`grub-once`** support of `/boot/grub2/custom.cfg` to *Section 13.2, "Configuration File Structure"* (Fate #319632).
- Added *Section 7.3.2, "Accessing and Identifying Snapshot Boot Entries"* (Fate #317972 and #318101).
- Added information about trusted boot support to *Section 13.3.3.3, "Boot Code Options Tab"* (Fate #316553).

Chapter 17, Basic Networking

- Added section about Network Teaming (FATE#320468), see *Section 17.8, "Setting Up Team Devices for Network Teaming"*.
- Mentioned `TUNNEL_DEVICE` for Wicked (FATE#317977, *Section 17.6.1.5, "Using Tunnels with Wicked"*).

Chapter 25, Time Synchronization with NTP

- Added information on the *Synchronize without Daemon* start-up option. Chroot jail is no longer the default (FATE #320392).

Bugfixes

- Wrong service names for NFS with Kerberos (https://bugzilla.suse.com/show_bug.cgi?id=983230 ↗).
- Live patches are released based on the SUSE CVSS score (https://bugzilla.suse.com/show_bug.cgi?id=992101 ↗).

A.3 March 2016 (Maintenance Release of SUSE Linux Enterprise Desktop 12 SP1)

Chapter 11, Introduction to the Booting Process

Added a note about initramfs migration from swap to LVM (https://bugzilla.suse.com/show_bug.cgi?id= ↗).

A.4 December 2015 (Initial Release of SUSE Linux Enterprise Desktop 12 SP1)

General

- *Book "Subscription Management Tool for SLES 12 SP3"* is now part of the documentation for SUSE Linux Enterprise Desktop.
- Add-ons provided by SUSE have been renamed as modules and extensions. The manuals have been updated to reflect this change.
- Numerous small fixes and additions to the documentation, based on technical feedback.
- The registration service has been changed from Novell Customer Center to SUSE Customer Center.
- In YaST, you will now reach *Network Settings* via the *System* group. *Network Devices* is gone (https://bugzilla.suse.com/show_bug.cgi?id=867809 ↗).

Chapter 7, System Recovery and Snapshot Management with Snapper

- Added information about the new `--sync` switch for **`snapper delete`** to *Section 7.5.4, "Deleting Snapshots"* (Fate #317066).
- Added *Section 7.3.2, "Accessing and Identifying Snapshot Boot Entries"* (Fate #317972 and Fate #318101).

- Added a tip to *Section 7.3, "System Rollback by Booting from Snapshots"* on how to do a rollback to the initial installation state or the state before a system update (Fate #317973 and Fate #317900).
- Added *Section 7.1.3.3, "Creating and Mounting New Subvolumes"* (Fate #318805, https://bugzilla.suse.com/show_bug.cgi?id=910602).

Chapter 8, Remote Access with VNC

- Turned a note into a section, added information about VNC using secured protocol by default (Fate #318936), and removed `tightvnc` as it is fully replaced by `tigervnc`. All in *Section 8.2.1, "Available Configurations"*.

Chapter 6, Managing Software with Command Line Tools

- Added *Section 6.1.4, "Identifying Processes and Services Using Deleted Files"* (Fate #318827).
- Added more examples of **`zypper list-patches --cve`** in *Section 6.1.3.1, "Installing All Needed Patches"* (Fate #319053).
- Added *Section 6.1.2.6, "Installing Packages from Disabled Repositories"* and a tip on removing all `debuginfo` packages in *Section 6.1.2, "Installing and Removing Software with Zypper"* (Fate #316287).
- Added a sentence on announcing the need for the system reboot after specific patch is applied. (Fate #317872).

Chapter 16, `journalctl`: Query the `systemd` Journal

- Added section *Section 16.6, "Using YaST to Filter the `systemd` Journal"* (Fate #318486).

Chapter 13, The Boot Loader GRUB 2

- Updated/simplified the whole chapter to match the latest GRUB version, both command line and YaST version.

Chapter 12, UEFI (Unified Extensible Firmware Interface)

- Added *Section 12.1.4, "Using Non-Inbox Drivers"* (Fate #317593).

Chapter 17, Basic Networking

- Nanny is now on by default in *Section 17.6.1.3, "Nanny"* (Fate #318977).

Available Data Synchronization Software

- Mentioned cloud computing for file synchronization.

Chapter 34, Common Problems and Their Solutions

- Improved GRUB 2 re-installation procedure in *Section 34.6.2.4, "Modifying and Re-installing the Boot Loader"*.

Part III, "System"

- Added *Chapter 23, Live Patching the Linux Kernel Using kGraft* (Fate #313296 and Fate #313438).

Bugfixes

- Removed obsolete `acpid.service` (https://bugzilla.suse.com/show_bug.cgi?id=918655 ↗).
- Added a paragraph on secure boot enabled by default in *Section 12.1.1, "Implementation on SUSE Linux Enterprise Desktop"* (https://bugzilla.suse.com/show_bug.cgi?id=879486 ↗).
- Removed documentation about VNC view-only passwords in *Section 8.3, "Persistent VNC Sessions"* because they are not available in SUSE Linux Enterprise Desktop (https://bugzilla.suse.com/show_bug.cgi?id=941307 ↗).

- Fixed procedure to access the installed system in a rescue mode in *Section 34.6.2.3, "Accessing the Installed System"* (https://bugzilla.suse.com/show_bug.cgi?id=918217).
- Added a new tip on updating the initramfs file after changing the default **`sysctl`** configuration in *Section 11.2, "`initramfs`"* (https://bugzilla.suse.com/show_bug.cgi?id=927506).
- Added a tip on preventing wicked from deactivating the network device on NFS roots in *Section 26.3.1, "Importing File Systems with YaST"* and *Section 17.4.1.2.5, "Activating the Network Device"* (https://bugzilla.suse.com/show_bug.cgi?id=938152).
- Fixed misleading statement about `kernel-`*`FLAVOR`*`-extra` in *Section 33.6, "Support of Kernel Modules"* (http://bugzilla.suse.com/show_bug.cgi?id=922976).
- Btrfs/Snapper: Snapshots with new Subvolumes will not be Deleted (https://bugzilla.suse.com/show_bug.cgi?id=910602).
- Btrfs Documentation on Separate Subvolume on /var/lib and Supportability (https://bugzilla.suse.com/show_bug.cgi?id=930424).

A.5 February 2015 (Documentation Maintenance Update)

Chapter 20, Accessing File Systems with FUSE

- Only the ntfs-3g plug-in is shipped with SUSE Linux Enterprise Desktop (Doc Comment #26799).

Chapter 14, The `systemd` *Daemon*

A typo in a command has been fixed (https://bugzilla.suse.com/show_bug.cgi?id=900219).

A.6 October 2014 (Initial Release of SUSE Linux Enterprise Desktop 12)

General

- Removed all KDE documentation and references because KDE is no longer shipped.
- Removed all references to SuSEconfig, which is no longer supported (Fate #100011).

- Move from System V init to systemd (Fate #310421). Updated affected parts of the documentation.
- YaST Runlevel Editor has changed to Services Manager (Fate #312568). Updated affected parts of the documentation.
- Removed all references to ISDN support, as ISDN support has been removed (Fate #314594).
- Removed all references to the YaST DSL module as it is no longer shipped (Fate #316264).
- Removed all references to the YaST Modem module as it is no longer shipped (Fate #316264).
- Btrfs has become the default file system for the root partition (Fate #315901). Updated affected parts of the documentation.
- The **dmesg** now provides human-readable time stamps in `ctime()`-like format (Fate #316056). Updated affected parts of the documentation.
- syslog and syslog-ng have been replaced by rsyslog (Fate #316175). Updated affected parts of the documentation.
- MariaDB is now shipped as the relational database instead of MySQL (Fate #313595). Updated affected parts of the documentation.
- SUSE-related products are no longer available from http://download.novell.com ↗ but from http://download.suse.com ↗. Adjusted links accordingly.
- Novell Customer Center has been replaced with SUSE Customer Center. Updated affected parts of the documentation.
- `/var/run` is mounted as tmpfs (Fate #303793). Updated affected parts of the documentation.
- The following architectures are no longer supported: IA64 and x86. Updated affected parts of the documentation.
- The traditional method for setting up the network with `ifconfig` has been replaced by `wicked`. Updated affected parts of the documentation.
- A lot of networking commands are deprecated and have been replaced by newer commands (usually **ip**). Updated affected parts of the documentation.

`arp`: `ip neighbor`

`ifconfig`: `ip addr`, `ip link`

`iptunnel`: `ip tunnel`

`iwconfig`: `iw`

`nameif`: `ip link`, `ifrename`

`netstat`: `ss`, `ip route`, `ip -s link`, `ip maddr`

`route`: `ip route`

- Numerous small fixes and additions to the documentation, based on technical feedback.

Chapter 3, YaST Online Update

- YaST provides an option to enable or disable the use of delta RPMs (Fate #314867).
- Before installing patches that require a reboot, you are notified by YaST and can choose how to proceed.

Chapter 5, YaST in Text Mode

- Added information on how to filter and select packages in the software installation module.

Chapter 6, Managing Software with Command Line Tools

- Removed documentation about Zypper's rug compatibility mode (Fate #317708).
- Rewrote *Section 6.1.6, "Querying Repositories and Packages with Zypper"*.

Chapter 7, System Recovery and Snapshot Management with Snapper

- Updated the chapter and added new features (Fate #312751, Fate #316238, Fate #316233, Fate #316232, Fate #316222, Fate #316203, Fate #316222).
- Added the section *Section 7.3, "System Rollback by Booting from Snapshots"* (Fate #316231, Fate #316221, Fate #316541, Fate #316522).

Chapter 8, Remote Access with VNC

- The default VNC viewer is now `tigervnc`.
- Added corrections on window manager start-up in persistent VNC sessions.

Chapter 11, Introduction to the Booting Process

- Significantly shortened the chapter, because System V init has been replaced by systemd. systemd is now described in a separate chapter: *Chapter 14, The `systemd` Daemon*.

Chapter 14, The `systemd` Daemon

- Added a new chapter on systemd and the YaST Services Manager (Fate #316631, Fate #312568).
- New section on loading kernel modules (http://bugzilla.suse.com/show_bug.cgi?id=892349 ↗).

Chapter 16, `journalctl`: Query the `systemd` Journal

Added a new chapter (http://bugzilla.suse.com/show_bug.cgi?id=878352 ↗).

Chapter 13, The Boot Loader GRUB 2

- Replaced the GRUB Legacy documentation with a new chapter on GRUB 2.
- Support for LILO has been dropped.
- Added new section *Section 13.4, "Differences in Terminal Usage on z Systems"*.

Chapter 12, UEFI (Unified Extensible Firmware Interface)

- Updated the chapter and added new features (Fate #314510, Fate #316365).
- Added instructions on where to find the SUSE Key certificate (Doc Comment #25080).

Chapter 18, Printer Operation

Updated chapter and section according to new CUPS version and with PDF now being a common printing data format (Fate #314630).

Chapter 19, The X Window System

- Updated the chapter to reflect dynamic configuration during each start-up.
- Updated *Section 19.1, "Installing and Configuring Fonts"*.

Chapter 17, Basic Networking

- NetworkManager is now part of the Workstation Extension: *Section 17.4.1.1, "Configuring Global Networking Options"* (Fate #316888).
- Added section about new `wicked` framework for network configuration: *Section 17.6, "Configuring a Network Connection Manually"* (Fate #316649).
- Mentioned additional options that can be added to `/etc/resolv.conf`: *Section 17.6.2, "Configuration Files"* (Fate #316048).

Chapter 27, Samba

- Added section *Section 27.6, "Advanced Topics"*.
- Added section *Section 27.6.1, "Transparent File Compression on Btrfs"*.
- Added section *Section 27.6.2, "Snapshots"*.

Chapter 26, Sharing File Systems with NFS

- Configuring NFSv4 shares is now mostly similar to NFSv3, especially the previously required bind mount setting is now deprecated (Fate #315589).
- Removed section about NFS server configuration.

Chapter 28, On-Demand Mounting with Autofs

- Added a chapter on `autofs` (Fate #316185).

Chapter 31, Power Management

- Removed obsolete references to the `pm-utils` package.

Chapter 34, Common Problems and Their Solutions

- Added new section *Section 34.3.4, "Root Btrfs Partition Cannot Be Mounted"* (Fate #308679, Fate #315126).
- Removed section about deprecated YaST Repair module (Fate #308679).

Wi-Fi Configuration

- Removed chapter about Wi-Fi configuration with YaST as Wi-Fi configuration can be done with NetworkManager: *Chapter 30, Using NetworkManager*.

Tablet PCs

- Removed deprecated chapter about tablet PCs.

Bugfixes

- Added the section *Section 33.6, "Support of Kernel Modules"* (http://bugzilla.suse.com/show_bug.cgi?id=869159).
- Added a new chapter *Chapter 16, `journalctl`: Query the `systemd` Journal* (http://bugzilla.suse.com/show_bug.cgi?id=878352).

B An Example Network

This example network is used across all network-related chapters of the SUSE® Linux Enterprise Desktop documentation.

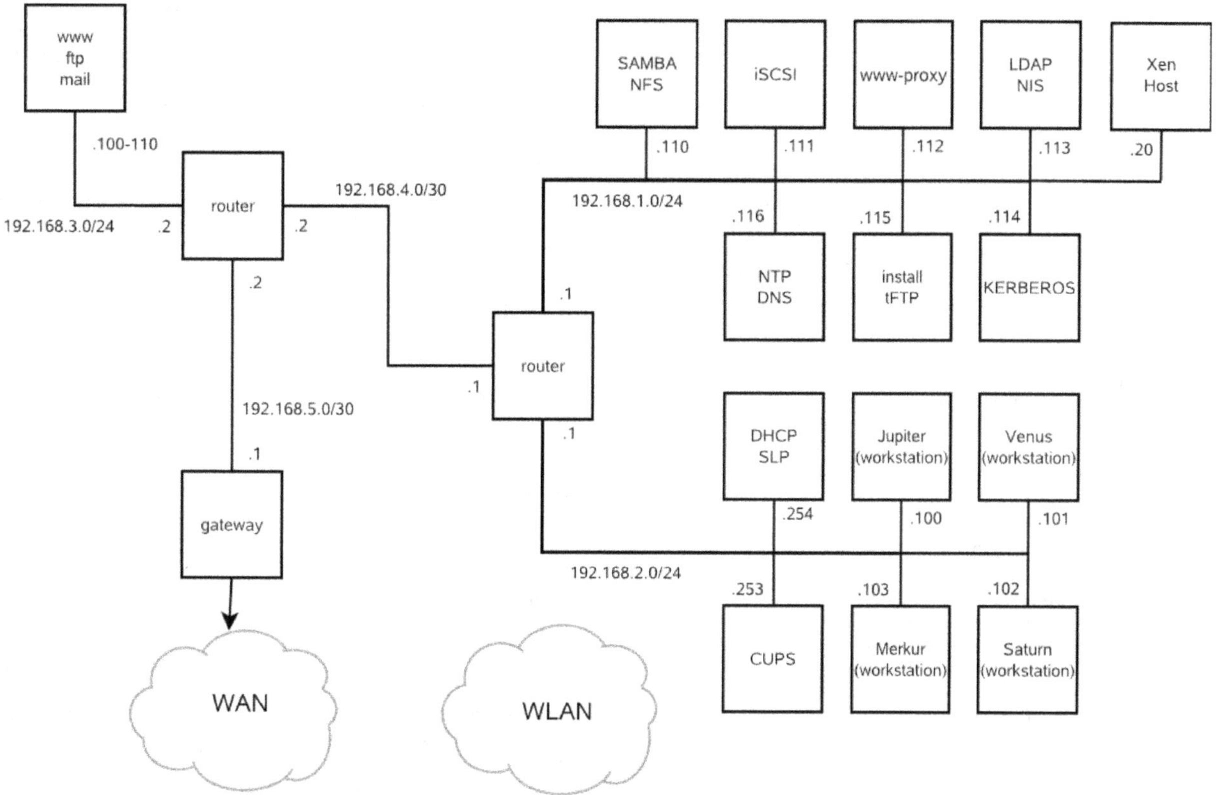

C GNU Licenses

This appendix contains the GNU Free Documentation License version 1.2.

GNU Free Documentation License

0. PREAMBLE

The purpose of this License is to make a manual, textbook, or other functional and useful document "free" in the sense of freedom: to assure everyone the effective freedom to copy and redistribute it, with or without modifying it, either commercially or non-commercially. Secondarily, this License preserves for the author and publisher a way to get credit for their work, while not being considered responsible for modifications made by others.

This License is a kind of "copyleft", which means that derivative works of the document must themselves be free in the same sense. It complements the GNU General Public License, which is a copyleft license designed for free software.

We have designed this License to use it for manuals for free software, because free software needs free documentation: a free program should come with manuals providing the same freedoms that the software does. But this License is not limited to software manuals; it can be used for any textual work, regardless of subject matter or whether it is published as a printed book. We recommend this License principally for works whose purpose is instruction or reference.

1. APPLICABILITY AND DEFINITIONS

This License applies to any manual or other work, in any medium, that contains a notice placed by the copyright holder saying it can be distributed under the terms of this License. Such a notice grants a world-wide, royalty-free license, unlimited in duration, to use that work under the conditions stated herein. The "Document", below, refers to any such manual or work. Any member of the public is a licensee, and is addressed as "you". You accept the license if you copy, modify or distribute the work in a way requiring permission under copyright law.

A "Modified Version" of the Document means any work containing the Document or a portion of it, either copied verbatim, or with modifications and/or translated into another language.

A "Secondary Section" is a named appendix or a front-matter section of the Document that deals exclusively with the relationship of the publishers or authors of the Document to the Document's overall subject (or to related matters) and contains nothing that could fall directly within that overall subject. (Thus, if the Document is in part a textbook of mathematics, a Secondary Section may not explain any mathematics.) The relationship could be a matter of historical connection with the subject or with related matters, or of legal, commercial, philosophical, ethical or political position regarding them.

The "Invariant Sections" are certain Secondary Sections whose titles are designated, as being those of Invariant Sections, in the notice that says that the Document is released under this License. If a section does not fit the above definition of Secondary then it is not allowed to be designated as Invariant. The Document may contain zero Invariant Sections. If the Document does not identify any Invariant Sections then there are none.

The "Cover Texts" are certain short passages of text that are listed, as Front-Cover Texts or Back-Cover Texts, in the notice that says that the Document is released under this License. A Front-Cover Text may be at most 5 words, and a Back-Cover Text may be at most 25 words.

A "Transparent" copy of the Document means a machine-readable copy, represented in a format whose specification is available to the general public, that is suitable for revising the document straightforwardly with generic text editors or (for images composed of pixels) generic paint programs or (for drawings) some widely available drawing editor, and that is suitable for input to text formatters or for automatic translation to a variety of formats suitable for input to text formatters. A copy made in an otherwise Transparent file format whose markup, or absence of markup, has been arranged to thwart or discourage subsequent modification by readers is not Transparent. An image format is not Transparent if used for any substantial amount of text. A copy that is not "Transparent" is called "Opaque".

Examples of suitable formats for Transparent copies include plain ASCII without markup, Texinfo input format, LaTeX input format, SGML or XML using a publicly available DTD, and standard-conforming simple HTML, PostScript or PDF designed for human modification. Examples of transparent image formats include PNG, XCF and JPG. Opaque formats include proprietary formats that can be read and edited only by proprietary word processors, SGML or XML for which the DTD and/or processing tools are not generally available, and the machine-generated HTML, PostScript or PDF produced by some word processors for output purposes only.

The "Title Page" means, for a printed book, the title page itself, plus such following pages as are needed to hold, legibly, the material this License requires to appear in the title page. For works in formats which do not have any title page as such, "Title Page" means the text near the most prominent appearance of the work's title, preceding the beginning of the body of the text.

A section "Entitled XYZ" means a named subunit of the Document whose title either is precisely XYZ or contains XYZ in parentheses following text that translates XYZ in another language. (Here XYZ stands for a specific section name mentioned below, such as "Acknowledgements", "Dedications", "Endorsements", or "History".) To "Preserve the Title" of such a section when you modify the Document means that it remains a section "Entitled XYZ" according to this definition.

The Document may include Warranty Disclaimers next to the notice which states that this License applies to the Document. These Warranty Disclaimers are considered to be included by reference in this License, but only as regards disclaiming warranties: any other implication that these Warranty Disclaimers may have is void and has no effect on the meaning of this License.

2. VERBATIM COPYING

You may copy and distribute the Document in any medium, either commercially or noncommercially, provided that this License, the copyright notices, and the license notice saying this License applies to the Document are reproduced in all copies, and that you add no other conditions whatsoever to those of this License. You may not use technical measures to obstruct or control the reading or further copying of the copies you make or distribute. However, you may accept compensation in exchange for copies. If you distribute a large enough number of copies you must also follow the conditions in section 3.

You may also lend copies, under the same conditions stated above, and you may publicly display copies.

3. COPYING IN QUANTITY

If you publish printed copies (or copies in media that commonly have printed covers) of the Document, numbering more than 100, and the Document's license notice requires Cover Texts, you must enclose the copies in covers that carry, clearly and legibly, all these Cover Texts: Front-Cover Texts on the front cover, and Back-Cover Texts on the back cover. Both covers must also clearly and legibly identify you as the publisher of these copies. The front cover must present the full title with all words of the title equally prominent and visible. You may add other material on the covers in addition. Copying with changes limited to the covers, as long as they preserve the title of the Document and satisfy these conditions, can be treated as verbatim copying in other respects.

If the required texts for either cover are too voluminous to fit legibly, you should put the first ones listed (as many as fit reasonably) on the actual cover, and continue the rest onto adjacent pages.

If you publish or distribute Opaque copies of the Document numbering more than 100, you must either include a machine-readable Transparent copy along with each Opaque copy, or state in or with each Opaque copy a computer-network location from which the general network-using public has access to download using public-standard network protocols a complete Transparent copy of the Document, free of added material. If you use the latter option, you must take reasonably prudent steps, when you begin distribution of Opaque copies in quantity, to ensure that this Transparent copy will remain thus accessible at the stated location until at least one year after the last time you distribute an Opaque copy (directly or through your agents or retailers) of that edition to the public.

It is requested, but not required, that you contact the authors of the Document well before redistributing any large number of copies, to give them a chance to provide you with an updated version of the Document.

4. MODIFICATIONS

You may copy and distribute a Modified Version of the Document under the conditions of sections 2 and 3 above, provided that you release the Modified Version under precisely this License, with the Modified Version filling the role of the Document, thus licensing distribution and modification of the Modified Version to whoever possesses a copy of it. In addition, you must do these things in the Modified Version:

A. Use in the Title Page (and on the covers, if any) a title distinct from that of the Document, and from those of previous versions (which should, if there were any, be listed in the History section of the Document). You may use the same title as a previous version if the original publisher of that version gives permission.

B. List on the Title Page, as authors, one or more persons or entities responsible for authorship of the modifications in the Modified Version, together with at least five of the principal authors of the Document (all of its principal authors, if it has fewer than five), unless they release you from this requirement.

C. State on the Title page the name of the publisher of the Modified Version, as the publisher.

D. Preserve all the copyright notices of the Document.

E. Add an appropriate copyright notice for your modifications adjacent to the other copyright notices.

F. Include, immediately after the copyright notices, a license notice giving the public permission to use the Modified Version under the terms of this License, in the form shown in the Addendum below.

G. Preserve in that license notice the full lists of Invariant Sections and required Cover Texts given in the Document's license notice.

H. Include an unaltered copy of this License.

I. Preserve the section Entitled "History", Preserve its Title, and add to it an item stating at least the title, year, new authors, and publisher of the Modified Version as given on the Title Page. If there is no section Entitled "History" in the Document, create one stating the title, year, authors, and publisher of the Document as given on its Title Page, then add an item describing the Modified Version as stated in the previous sentence.

J. Preserve the network location, if any, given in the Document for public access to a Transparent copy of the Document, and likewise the network locations given in the Document for previous versions it was based on. These may be placed in the "History" section. You may omit a network location for a work that was published at least four years before the Document itself, or if the original publisher of the version it refers to gives permission.

K. For any section Entitled "Acknowledgements" or "Dedications", Preserve the Title of the section, and preserve in the section all the substance and tone of each of the contributor acknowledgements and/or dedications given therein.

L. Preserve all the Invariant Sections of the Document, unaltered in their text and in their titles. Section numbers or the equivalent are not considered part of the section titles.

M. Delete any section Entitled "Endorsements". Such a section may not be included in the Modified Version.

N. Do not retitle any existing section to be Entitled "Endorsements" or to conflict in title with any Invariant Section.

O. Preserve any Warranty Disclaimers.

If the Modified Version includes new front-matter sections or appendices that qualify as Secondary Sections and contain no material copied from the Document, you may at your option designate some or all of these sections as invariant. To do this, add their titles to the list of Invariant Sections in the Modified Version's license notice. These titles must be distinct from any other section titles.

You may add a section Entitled "Endorsements", provided it contains nothing but endorsements of your Modified Version by various parties--for example, statements of peer review or that the text has been approved by an organization as the authoritative definition of a standard.

You may add a passage of up to five words as a Front-Cover Text, and a passage of up to 25 words as a Back-Cover Text, to the end of the list of Cover Texts in the Modified Version. Only one passage of Front-Cover Text and one of Back-Cover Text may be added by (or through arrangements made by) any one entity. If the Document already includes a cover text for the same cover, previously added by you or by arrangement made by the same entity you are acting on behalf of, you may not add another; but you may replace the old one, on explicit permission from the previous publisher that added the old one.

The author(s) and publisher(s) of the Document do not by this License give permission to use their names for publicity for or to assert or imply endorsement of any Modified Version.

5. COMBINING DOCUMENTS

You may combine the Document with other documents released under this License, under the terms defined in section 4 above for modified versions, provided that you include in the combination all of the Invariant Sections of all of the original documents, unmodified, and list them all as Invariant Sections of your combined work in its license notice, and that you preserve all their Warranty Disclaimers.

The combined work need only contain one copy of this License, and multiple identical Invariant Sections may be replaced with a single copy. If there are multiple Invariant Sections with the same name but different contents, make the title of each such section unique by adding at the end of it, in parentheses, the name of the original author or publisher of that section if known, or else a unique number. Make the same adjustment to the section titles in the list of Invariant Sections in the license notice of the combined work.

In the combination, you must combine any sections Entitled "History" in the various original documents, forming one section Entitled "History"; likewise combine any sections Entitled "Acknowledgements", and any sections Entitled "Dedications". You must delete all sections Entitled "Endorsements".

6. COLLECTIONS OF DOCUMENTS

You may make a collection consisting of the Document and other documents released under this License, and replace the individual copies of this License in the various documents with a single copy that is included in the collection, provided that you follow the rules of this License for verbatim copying of each of the documents in all other respects.

You may extract a single document from such a collection, and distribute it individually under this License, provided you insert a copy of this License into the extracted document, and follow this License in all other respects regarding verbatim copying of that document.

7. AGGREGATION WITH INDEPENDENT WORKS

A compilation of the Document or its derivatives with other separate and independent documents or works, in or on a volume of a storage or distribution medium, is called an "aggregate" if the copyright resulting from the compilation is not used to limit the legal rights of the compilation's users beyond what the individual works permit. When the Document is included in an aggregate, this License does not apply to the other works in the aggregate which are not themselves derivative works of the Document.

If the Cover Text requirement of section 3 is applicable to these copies of the Document, then if the Document is less than one half of the entire aggregate, the Document's Cover Texts may be placed on covers that bracket the Document within the aggregate, or the electronic equivalent of covers if the Document is in electronic form. Otherwise they must appear on printed covers that bracket the whole aggregate.

8. TRANSLATION

Translation is considered a kind of modification, so you may distribute translations of the Document under the terms of section 4. Replacing Invariant Sections with translations requires special permission from their copyright holders, but you may include translations of some or all Invariant Sections in addition to the original versions of these Invariant Sections. You may include a translation of this License, and all the license notices in the Document, and any Warranty Disclaimers, provided that you also include the original English version of this License and the original versions of those notices and disclaimers. In case of a disagreement between the translation and the original version of this License or a notice or disclaimer, the original version will prevail.

If a section in the Document is Entitled "Acknowledgements", "Dedications", or "History", the requirement (section 4) to Preserve its Title (section 1) will typically require changing the actual title.

9. TERMINATION

You may not copy, modify, sublicense, or distribute the Document except as expressly provided for under this License. Any other attempt to copy, modify, sublicense or distribute the Document is void, and will automatically terminate your rights under this License. However, parties who have received copies, or rights, from you under this License will not have their licenses terminated so long as such parties remain in full compliance.

10. FUTURE REVISIONS OF THIS LICENSE

The Free Software Foundation may publish new, revised versions of the GNU Free Documentation License from time to time. Such new versions will be similar in spirit to the present version, but may differ in detail to address new problems or concerns. See http://www.gnu.org/copyleft/ ↗.

Each version of the License is given a distinguishing version number. If the Document specifies that a particular numbered version of this License "or any later version" applies to it, you have the option of following the terms and conditions either of that specified version or of any later version that has been published (not as a draft) by the Free Software Foundation. If the Document does not specify a version number of this License, you may choose any version ever published (not as a draft) by the Free Software Foundation.

ADDENDUM: How to use this License for your documents

```
Copyright (c) YEAR YOUR NAME.
Permission is granted to copy, distribute and/or modify this document
under the terms of the GNU Free Documentation License, Version 1.2
or any later version published by the Free Software Foundation;
with no Invariant Sections, no Front-Cover Texts, and no Back-Cover Texts.
A copy of the license is included in the section entitled “GNU
Free Documentation License”.
```

If you have Invariant Sections, Front-Cover Texts and Back-Cover Texts, replace the “with...Texts.” line with this:

```
with the Invariant Sections being LIST THEIR TITLES, with the
Front-Cover Texts being LIST, and with the Back-Cover Texts being LIST.
```

If you have Invariant Sections without Cover Texts, or some other combination of the three, merge those two alternatives to suit the situation.

If your document contains nontrivial examples of program code, we recommend releasing these examples in parallel under your choice of free software license, such as the GNU General Public License, to permit their use in free software.